D0298355

Dumfries and Galloway Libraries, Information and Archives

This item is to be returned on or before the last date shown below.

NEW

2 4 NOV 2009 EW	4/11/11	
1 5 DEC 2009 EW	2 8 SEP 2012 EW	2 3 MAR 201
33i·	0 3 NOV 2012 EW	1 1 APR 2018
	2 3 APR 2013 EW	2 9 JUN 2018
0 4 FEB 2010 SA	1 4 MAY 2013 EW	3 1 JUL 2018
0 4 MAR 2010 EW	1 7 JUN 2013 EW	
- 6 APR 2010 EW	- 1 OCT 2013 EW	- 8 MAR 2019
		- 3 JUL 2019
0 6 MAY 2010 EW	- 6 MAR 2014 EW	
2 5 MAY 2010 EW		1 2 JUL 2019
- 6 SEP 2010 EW	1 2 APR 2014 EW	
2 1 OCT 2010 EW	2 8 APR 2016	
8 Nov 2010	2 9 SEP 2016	
2 9 Nov	2 5 OCT 2016	
1 3 DEC 2010 EW	2 5 FEB 2017	
	1 8 MAR 2017	
1 6 MAR 2011 EW	1 3 APR 2017	
0 2 APR 2011 EW	- 1 DEC 2017	
1 3 OCT 2011 EW	1 8 JAN 2018	

920 CHA

Central Support Unit
Catherine Street Dumfries DG1 1JB
tel: 01387 253820 fax: 01387 260294
e-mail: libs&i@dumgal.gov.uk

Dumfries and Galloway
LIBRARIES
Information and Archives

24 HOUR LOAN RENEWAL ON OUR WEBSITE - WWW.DUMGAL.GOV.UK/LIA

102°

Published by the Royal Geographical Society

MALAYA
Chapman

JUNGLE SOLDIER

JUNGLE SOLDIER

THE TRUE STORY OF FREDDY SPENCER CHAPMAN

BRIAN MOYNAHAN

AS | Dumfries and Galloway LIBRARIES

| 1 | 4 | 2 | 4 | 2 | 3 | Class 920 CHA |

Quercus

First published in Great Britain in 2009 by

Quercus
21 Bloomsbury Square
London
WC1A 2NS

Copyright © 2009 Brian Moynahan

The moral right of Brian Moynahan to be identified
as the author of this work has been asserted in accordance
with the Copyright, Design and Patents Act, 1988.

The picture acknowledgements on page 328 constitute
an extension of this copyright page

All rights reserved. No part of this publication may be reproduced
or transmitted in any form or by any means, electronic or mechanical,
including photocopy, recording, or any information storage
and retrieval system, without permission
in writing from the publisher.

A CIP catalogue record for this book is
available from the British Library

ISBN 978 1 84916 076 6 HB
ISBN 978 1 84916 282 1 TPB

Printed and bound in Great Britain by Clays Ltd, St Ives plc

10 9 8 7 6 5 4 3 2 1

www.quercusbooks.co.uk

for
José and Patch

CONTENTS

LIST OF MAPS

PROLOGUE

BEHIND ENEMY LINES

Freddy Spencer Chapman set off to war from Kuala Lumpur on Christmas Eve 1941 at the wheel of a scarlet V8 Ford coupé. The dickey seat behind him was packed with tommy-guns, grenades and explosives. The Japanese had invaded Malaya two weeks before, and Freddy – he was always Freddy – was driving north to find them. He had two volunteers with him, and a driver to take the car back to KL. Freddy intended to get behind Japanese lines, and report back first-hand on their strengths and weaknesses. In particular, he wanted to see if it was possible for 'left-behind parties' to survive and carry out guerrilla raids in Japanese-occupied territory.

He arrived in Parit, a small town in the rubber country 125 miles from KL, expecting to find British troops. It was a derelict and smoking ruin. The Japanese were the other side of the Perak river. He and the volunteers left the car, plugged the holes in a shot-up ferry-boat and paddled across the river.

As they scrambled ashore, he saw his first Japanese soldiers, cycling three abreast, 'laughing, just as if they were going to a football match', and took cover in the jungle. It was the first time he had been in primary jungle – before the war, he had been a man of cold climes, the Greenland ice cap, arctic Norway, Tibet – but it gave him 'a feeling of great reassurance . . . In one dive, I was completely hidden.'

It poured with rain that evening, flooding the small stream that ran by the road where the three men lay, shivering with cold, observing the Japanese. Freddy 'noticed with delight' that they passed in dense

1

groups of forty or fifty, and had tied their tommy-guns and rifles on the frames of their bicycles, making them vulnerable to ambush. As the water rose higher in the stream, Freddy made a dash for the jungle on the other side of the road. A large party of Japanese swept round a bend and nearly ran him over. They seemed certain to recognise him as a European. 'All I could do,' he said, 'was to put up my arm to hide my face and wave to them.' The Japanese waved back. Freddy's companions, watching from the shadows, marvelled at his presence of mind.

They laid up for the rest of the night. Next day, they moved on through jungle and rubber, within twenty yards of the enemy in places. Freddy confirmed that the Japanese were now on both banks of the upper part of the river, and observed their movements and equipment minutely. They were advancing so rapidly that he had to get thirty or forty miles south before he had any chance of extricating himself from their lines.

That night, in a tiny, flat-bottomed boat, the three Englishmen set out into the swollen river, and were swept downstream. In the dark, they could not see whether they were in the middle of the river, or near the banks, where the Japanese would spot them. 'It was exhilarating to be whirled along at speed, but frightening to be so completely at the mercy of the river . . .' Before dawn, they hid up again in the jungle. The next night, they were back on the river going further downstream. When it grew light, they were told by villagers that the Japanese had not yet arrived, though the British had pulled back. Freddy went on down the river until he reached the British lines.

He reported that the Japanese troops he had seen were 'good second-class material, well-trained but poorly equipped'. They were, he said, 'singularly vulnerable to attack by trained guerrillas'. He was convinced that 'left-behind parties' could inflict real damage, and he pleaded to be given '500 men, or even a hundred'. He was told none could be spared. He would have to rely on the volunteers he had found among the planters and the fervently anti-Japanese among the many Chinese living in Malaya.

On 7 January 1942, with malaria, and running a temperature of 103 degrees, Freddy went back behind Japanese lines, this time for good.

Malaya was overrun, and then Singapore. Churchill called it 'the worst disaster and greatest capitulation in British history'. Other Europeans in Freddy's left-behind parties were soon gone, dead from jungle fevers, or taken prisoner, two of them beheaded by the Japanese. As months and then years passed, he was posted 'missing believed killed'. The Japanese, though, knew he was still alive and they hunted for him as they did for no other.

Field Marshal Wavell, who knew both men, thought Spencer Chapman was the jungle Lawrence. 'He has never received the publicity and fame that were Lawrence's lot,' he wrote of Freddy, 'but for sheer courage and endurance, physical and mental, the two men stand together as examples of what toughness the body will find, if the spirit within it is tough; and as very worthy representatives of our national capacity for individual enterprise.' Perhaps the comparison sells Freddy short: Lord Mountbatten, commander in South-East Asia, thought so, and recommended him for a VC. Unlike Lawrence, he was alone for much of the three-and-a-half years he spent behind Japanese lines, separated by more than a thousand miles from British forces, without supplies or shelter, living on his wits in an environment more brutal by far than Lawrence's. The deserts of Arabia are healthy, but in the Malayan jungle Freddy suffered tick typhus, scabies, blackwater fever, dengue fever, ulcers and sores from leech bites, and was once unconscious for fourteen days with pneumonia and cerebral malaria.

His is one of the greatest tales of endurance and survival in the history of war. It is also a very British story, for the qualities – the genius – that enabled him to survive were, as we shall see, bred in the bone.

CHAPTER 1

A VERY ENGLISH BOYHOOD

The child, more so than with most, was father of the man.

'One good result of my unhappy childhood was that I became both self-reliant and enterprising,' Freddy was to write, 'and I developed an inner fortitude sometimes amounting to austerity.' He was born in Kensington on 10 May 1907. By the time his birth was registered a month later, his mother had died of blood poisoning. At the same time his father, a solicitor with the family firm of Spencer Chapman & Co in the Temple, faced ruin as well as bereavement. His managing clerk had defrauded the firm and a client, and Frank Spencer Chapman became an undischarged bankrupt.

His health undermined, he left on a world tour with a younger unmarried sister to avoid the bailiffs. He was away for two years, whilst Freddy and his elder brother Robert stayed with an aunt. Frank returned briefly to England in 1909. That autumn, he took the two boys by train to Carlisle. Freddy was two-and-a-half and his brother five. From the station, they took a hansom cab for eight miles to the vicarage in the small village of Raughton Head on the northern edge of the Lake District. The vicar, Ernest Dewick, and his wife Sophie, had agreed to bring up the boys. They were fifty-nine and forty-three, with no children of their own. They were only the vaguest of relations – Ernest's brother, also a clergyman, was married to Freddy's aunt – but they were a kindly and affectionate couple. The vicarage is a fine Victorian house of local stone, set in fields and woodland some distance from the church, an ancient building of millstone grit little larger than a chapel. Frank Chapman left his boys after a day or two, to make a new life on a ranch in British Columbia.

Little Freddy soon showed a lasting curiosity and love for all things wild. The vicarage was ideally placed, in woods running down to the River Caldew, swift-flowing through meadowland on a bed of rock and gravel. He collected birds' eggs and butterflies, and tadpoles. Sophie Dewick taught him the names of flowers and birds, and their characteristics. His father had left books on natural history for him. He did not totally abandon his boys, sending them postcards of the animals of western Canada. Raughton Head was a backwater, but the child's mind was open to all its creatures and to the wider world beyond.

When the Rev. Dewick was appointed to a new parish, they moved to Lindale, between Lake Windermere and Morecambe Bay on the coast. The vicarage was larger if not so handsome as Raughton's – it is used for holiday lets now, whilst the Raughton vicarage, also sold off by the Church in this less godly age, sits grandly behind smart new gates with a security camera to vet visitors – and its garden tumbled down to a gloomy church of dark stone. One of Freddy's earliest memories was of tobogganing down the long steep road that runs from the fells down through the village. His main interests, he said, were 'butterflies and wild flowers'. He was an independent-minded little boy, setting off down the valley to the River Winster with a butterfly net, a fishing rod and jam jars. By the water he caught the blue flashes of kingfishers, and the white bib of dippers, with sandpipers, oystercatchers, glimpses of the yellow underparts of wagtail, swallows, mallard, and, in the evenings, bats. The caterpillars he caught became peacock, tortoiseshell and red admiral butterflies.

It was as well he liked exploring, for he had to find his own entertainment. 'As my guardian had little time to spare from his parish duties, my elder brother and I were left much to ourselves . . . Every morning and evening we had long family prayers,' he recollected. 'Each Sunday, as far back as I can remember, my brother and I had to attend Matins and Evensong and listen to interminable and learned sermons.' Those sermons were peppered with quotations in Hebrew and Greek – Ernest Dewick was an Oxford classicist – and were above the heads of the adults in the congregation. It worried Freddy that he understood almost nothing in them. He was sure he was destined for hell. The only way to avoid damnation, he thought, was to learn by heart much of the Gospels. From the age of eight, he also recited long passages from Cicero and Tacitus. 'It seemed to me there was no possible escape from the flames of hell,' he wrote years later, 'and even now I cannot hear church bells without a sinking of the heart.'

His fears did not cow him. They made him more reliant on himself, and mistrustful of emotions, and the long hours passed in the dark church and the 'interminable learned sermons' taught him self-control. There were, also, advantages in being brought up in a parson's household. His elderly 'Unkie' and his wife instilled a decency and moral code that were to serve him well in the extremes to come. He developed, too, respect for knowledge and the ability to apply it to the world immediately about him – the accurate identification of such plants as the primrose, wood stitchwort, meadowsweet, cranesbill, sweet cicely and balsam that grew around the house – that was to make him an explorer-naturalist in the classic sense. So, as a small boy, on his expeditions from an Edwardian vicarage steeped in books, he began to absorb a tradition that goes back to the voyages of the *Endeavour* and the *Beagle*, to Cook and the late eighteenth century, to Joseph Banks and Charles Darwin.

His schooling was assured by a legacy left under his mother's will, which escaped the bailiffs. He had a tutor until he was eight, who took him once on the pillion of his motorcycle to climb Helvellyn by way of Grisedale Tarn. It was a tremendous walk for a small boy and he was moved by the vastness of the Lake fells. 'It gave me an impression of beauty, immensity and physical exhaustion,' he wrote. He had a 'disastrous' term in a kindergarten at Kendal. He was very much his own little boy – the Dewicks sometimes called him 'Frederick the Great' – and he found it difficult to fit in with others.

The First World War began. Frank Chapman volunteered for the Canadian army, though at forty-two he had no need to, and visited the boys briefly in 1915 on leave from France. It was the first time they had seen him for six years. Freddy was now sent over the Pennines to

Yorkshire to board at Clevedon House, a prep school in a large old country house of grey stone. Above it, a cart track leads up to the heathered wastes of Ilkley Moor, and the great rock outcrops called the Calf and Cow, out of bounds to the boys, and thus doubly attractive for them to scramble on. In front of the school, a balustraded terrace stood above a steep shrubbery that gave way to flower beds and lawns and magnificent views over the Wharfe valley. The gardens were large enough for a swimming pool and a nine-hole golf course. Below, down a long hill, was the village of Ben Rhydding, to which the boys were marched to church, and the mill town of Ilkley.

Freddy remembered the headmaster, 'E.W.', Edward W. Stokoe, as a 'man of infinite kindness and understanding'. E.W. was an enthusiastic entomologist, and he encouraged Freddy's wanderings on the moor, his 'happy hunting ground' for oak eggar and emperor moth caterpillars. Glass-fronted cases in the classrooms were filled with local and more exotic butterflies, and E.W.'s love of nature studies was reciprocated by the boys. The headmaster also had great fortitude, never complaining or snapping, despite being in constant pain and near crippled by arthritis. Freddy would reflect that endurance, too, in body and spirit.

In his second term, Freddy wrote to his father – 'Dear Father' he began in sadly formal but affectionate terms to a man he hardly knew, signing himself 'With love from F S Chapman' – about his enthusiasms. 'I am very interested in three main things – astronomy, nature and all about butterflies and caterpillars and moths,' he said. 'I learnt a lot about butterflies and caterpillars from two books from Jennings, who is second top of the second class.' He also begged his father for some of his regimental buttons. 'PLEASE SEND SOME OF YOUR BUTTONS to me. Some of us here collect buttons and badges. I hope you are getting on well.'

The letter was dated 16 March 1916. Six months later, his father was killed at Ypres. Freddy was ten. He had been an orphan, in practice, since he was born, and now he was one, formally. His father had great charm and character, he was still a private when he died, but his commanding general wrote to the boys, speaking of his grief for 'a brave comrade and a loyal friend', which served only to hurt Freddy the more.

He said later that his father 'had lost interest in life', a cruel phrase, and his own sense of duty was magnified by his father's apparent rejection of his responsibility to his sons.

He threw himself into things physical and natural. Another boy told Freddy's first biographer Ralph Barker (1975) that he was 'the most unwashed and independent boy in the school ... His pockets were crammed with birds' nests, caterpillars and any natural specimens he happened to fancy . . .' He loved walking over the Ilkley moors, listening to curlew songs, watching for ring-ouzels and merlins. As a greenkeeper, he kept cows off the golf course with accurate strikes from his catapult. He learnt swimming by being thrown in at the deep end. As a boxer, he did not bother with defence. At night, he sometimes clambered out of his dormitory window and went climbing on the rocks. The boys were allowed out before breakfast to collect poplar leaves for their caterpillars. Freddy, though, would be out at 4 a.m. in summer, alone on the moors, finding the nests of grouse in the heather, and once, to his great joy, a merlin's nest with its purple-brown eggs.

Wherever he was, he liked to have a secret hideout, under the eaves of the Lindale vicarage roof, in the shrubbery below the school. The childhood skills of camouflage and concealment were to serve him well as an adult. He shot his first bird here, a blackbird, with a home-made bamboo bow and arrow, and smoked cigarettes he made of beech leaves rolled in blotting paper. He climbed trees, for conkers and birds' eggs, and was caught by E.W. at the very top of an immense holly tree that sheltered a goldfinch's nest. 'I have always been fascinated by danger,' he admitted. 'It led me into more scrapes than any other boy in the school.' He thought organised games were 'a waste of a fine afternoon', and lessons were to be 'avoided by all means, fair or foul'. His mother's legacy was enough for school fees, but not pocket money, so he became an expert finder of golf balls, and dived for pennies from other boys in the school swimming pool. On visiting days, parents tossed shillings and sixpences into the deep end for him. He was adept at trapping moles and curing their skins with alum and saltpetre before selling them for ninepence a piece. The fear of penury was lasting: worries over money never left him.

Looking back years later, a former schoolfellow thought that the 'future Freddy' was already emerging. He disregarded pain and discomfort, he disliked being part of a crowd, and he was ferociously determined when his interests were aroused, 'anything to do with animals, birds and bugs'. His father's death, the school friend recollected, accentuated another of Freddy's traits: he was developing 'a sort of armour against loneliness and was learning to go it alone regardless of the consequences'. He bred himself to endure. 'I remember boys banging Chapman over the head with cricket bats to see how hard he could take it,' another schoolmate told Barker. 'This was not bullying, he egged them on. He was proud of his toughness.' 'Completely fearless,' a master reported, 'no regard for danger, but careless too of the safety of others, always doing something to place other lives in jeopardy as well as his own.'

He was beaten frequently, as was then the norm for bad behaviour, but to little effect. Mostly, this was for breaking bounds, but his acting ability also got him in trouble. Irritated at being made to field in the deep during an open-day cricket match, he ate acorns to relieve the tedium. A group of parents were worried at this. The food at the school was so bad, he assured them, that it was fill up on acorns, or starve. The master in charge was not amused. Even the end of the war got him in another scrape. When all the factory and mill hooters in Wharfedale sounded when the armistice was declared, Freddy was in the school sick-bay with flu and a high temperature, with strict orders to stay in bed. He rushed to fling open the window when he heard the hooters go. 'Chapman!' E.W. roared as he came in. 'It *would* be you!' And yet this tough and rebellious little boy was made head gardener, responsible for the school's elaborate rock garden, and was thrilled to grow pansies and lobelia from seeds in his own little plot. When he went on to his public school in 1920, at thirteen, he said he left with 'a good knowledge of gardening and a vast enthusiasm for all forms of natural history'.

By now the Dewicks felt themselves too elderly to cope with two teenagers. Freddy and his brother were passed on to another clergyman,

Sam Taylor, the vicar of Flookburgh. This was not far from Lindale, an old fishing village on the Cartmel peninsula. The railway line was close to the vicarage, with the large church and railway cottages next to it, a drab grey Victorian house. But it was close to Morecambe Bay, vast and shallow with prodigious sands and quicksands at low tide. Here he passed the holidays, wild-fowling and bird-watching. His ear picked up all the bird notes as he lay in his hide in the mudflats on summer mornings, 'the soft purring of dunlin, the thin querulous whistle of widgeon, the distant swelling chorus of thousands of curlew, oyster-catcher, lapwing, ringed plover and redshank at the tide's edge'. In the winter, he was in his hide with his gun before light to shoot duck and geese. He thrilled at the sounds of their wings, as distinctive as their cries, the teal beating a muffled throb in the air, the golden-eye a 'sibilant whistle', geese launching themselves with 'clear clarion cries'. The flash of the gun, the splash as the body falls on the mudflat: 'nothing can be greater than the thrill of one's first goose.' As he waited for a flight, he learnt poems by heart: the whole of Omar Khayyam, 'Ode to a Nightingale', Housman's *A Shropshire Lad*, *The Rime of the Ancient Mariner.*

His new school, Sedbergh, dominates the small Cumbrian town of that name, set in a bowl of the Howgill Fells that reach 2,000 feet. It is an old foundation, 1525, and has something monastic in its cloisters and stone towers: in its discipline, too. It was tough, even by the harsh standards of the time, a place where days started with cold baths, and often ended with a beating. Freddy joined his brother in Lupton House, black-and-white gabled, in which fifty boys were crammed. It looks out over the playing fields, in which Freddy had no interest. Behind it, though, is the long mountain slope of Winder, green, then growing in severe and rocky browns as it climbs. This was what Freddy loved – 'it was possible to run for twenty miles there without meeting another human being' – and it was celebrated in the school song:

> 'Tis the hills that are stood behind us,
> Unchanged since our days began,
> That make the Sedbergh man.

His brother, a gentle and simple soul, was nicknamed 'Sheep'. Freddy inevitably became 'the Lamb', a misnomer, since he was always in trouble. 'Poaching, breaking bounds going into the town or slipping out at night, missing call-over, going to cock-fights, keeping ferrets . . .' a school friend said of him. He loathed the 'monotonous bell-regulated routine of school life'. In particular, he could see no point in spending every afternoon 'hitting or kicking a leather-covered ball', though Sedbergh was renowned for its cricketers and rugby players. In his first summer term, he was beaten by his head of house four days running for refusing to play cricket. His housemaster – 'luckily,' Freddy wrote, 'a wise and sympathetic man' – was impressed by his grit. If he really felt so strongly about it, he said, he would be excused cricket, as long as he did not waste his time.

'And,' Freddy said, 'I did not waste my time.' He had three half-days a week. By taking a sandwich with him, or doing without, he was free from lunch time until prep at 7 p.m. He could average six miles an hour on the fells, so those six hours gave him a vast swathe of country to explore. He tested his nerves climbing down to ravens' nests on Coombe Scaur and Cautley Spout. 'Often,' he wrote, 'my life depended on a root of mountain ash or bunch of heather, and the screes I ran, in gym shoes too, were steeper than I would choose to run nowadays even in boots.'

He was always a hunter – and he was already one of the best shots in the school officer training corps – but he was an early conservationist, too. He won the school nature study prize with essays on pairs of birds that he observed over months, with sketches of them in watercolours, and maps of the moors. He described spotting a peregrine falcon's nest on a treacherous crag of rotten rock, tipped off by the bones and feathers of their prey – curlew, grouse and carrier pigeons. He climbed down to the ledge where the nest was protected from falling stones under an overhang. The four eggs were 'rufous and light red, marked with a deeper red', close to the edge of the ledge. He noticed aluminium rings, from the legs of carrier pigeons, which the peregrines had broken off to be able to take the rings, and wondered if peregrines shared the same fascination for bright metal as magpies.

It was difficult to photograph the eggs, since he was trembling, partly from excitement, 'and partly, I confess, by the sight of the screes about a hundred feet vertically below me'. Sometimes he took eggs, but not now. He climbed away before they could get cold, and hid himself to watch the female circling suspiciously before returning to the nest. It was a great pity, he wrote, that little could be done to protect 'such magnificent remnants' of the larger birds of prey. 'Protection laws do, I know, exist; but too little money and effort is spent on enforcing them.'

His hours on the fells gave him self-reliance: 'I could forget myself in the rhythm of tired muscles, in the fascination of following a compass course over the hills in thick mist, in the determination to go just one more mile before turning.' When he was fifteen, he went to stay with a friend in North Wales and learnt the ancient arts of poaching. He found it gave 'more scope for skill and excitement than anything I had known before'. He 'guddled' for trout, feeling for the fish by the bank or under a stone, tickling it until it was in his hands and then throwing it out of the water. He set snares of horse-hair for grouse, and learnt how to recognise game tracks whilst leaving none of his own. He and his friend dug pellets out of their backs with a penknife after an angry gamekeeper fired at them as they fled.

'When I was 16 or 17 I used to disguise myself so as not to look like a schoolboy,' Freddy wrote later, 'and spent enchanted nights ferreting and netting salmon.' He spent an hour hiding beneath the bank of the River Lune, freezing in the water with only his head above the surface, when a beck-watcher spotted him netting for salmon, and methodically searched to and fro with his dog a few feet above him. When another keeper chased him, he swam the river with an egg in his mouth. He had poaching friends in the town. His favourite was the local blacksmith, who had a cockpit in his barn, and Freddy would climb out of the dormitory window and down a drainpipe to watch cock-fights.

His shortage of money meant, a fellow Sedberghian recalled, that he did 'practically anything for half a crown'. Mainly, he was bribed for boyish japes against masters, putting mice in their bags, and so on. He kept ferrets in a hutch in bushes next to a games court and took them up to warrens on the fells where he caught the rabbits in nets as the ferrets drove them out. In the snow, when they could not move fast, he caught them with his hands. He skinned and cleaned them, and sold them to the butcher in the town for a shilling each.

On another summer holiday, he went to Somerset with the Dewicks. His first love was Mary Swainson, 'Bee', the daughter of the vicar of the neighbouring parish. They met when he was fourteen, and she a year younger, and they knew each other until he went up to Cambridge. They rode ponies or walked through woodland and heath. Years later, she recalled to Ralph Barker how they explored together, walking up the shallows of the River Tone towards its source, Freddy climbing trees with a long-handled spoon to collect eggs: 'he always took only one egg'. Her clearest memory was lying with Freddy by the river as the mist began rising from it one evening. He taught her how to 'freeze', remaining completely still, 'inwardly as well as outwardly', scarcely breathing, becoming so much a part of the landscape that rabbits came and nibbled close to them. On rainy days, they laid up in a hay-loft and talked and talked. Her mother was duly suspicious – 'what have you been doing up in the hay-loft all morning?' – but they were both at single-sex boarding schools, and had an innocence that was yet to vanish. There were cats beneath the loft, and she had studied their language as a young child. Bee taught him all the different sounds of cats calling their kittens, milk-time, warnings of danger. Sometimes he would read poetry to her 'until shivers went down my spine with the magic of it'. James Elroy Flecker was his favourite – 'he seemed committed to making "the Golden Journey to Samarkand"' – and when he discovered Omar Khayyam he bought her a copy of the *Rubaiyat*, to the moral outrage of her English mistress at school.

Bee was perceptive. She found that Freddy 'felt his orphanhood very much indeed'. He didn't get on with his brother, whose temperament was very different to his own, and he was alone. He felt 'rootless', despite his homes with the Dewicks and the Taylors. 'I have often wondered to what extent his lifelong craving for exploration was partly a search for a true home,' she said, 'or, to put it the other way round, how far he had to be relatively rootless in order to lead the life he subsequently did.'

His father's death in action made him eligible for a Kitchener scholarship to Cambridge, where Sedbergh had a long connection with St John's College. He gained his award, to read Natural Sciences and Mathematics, and left Sedbergh in July 1926, under a characteristic cloud. He had stayed out all night on the last night of term, drinking rough wine with a night-watchman, and was barred from visiting the school for a year.

He was now ready for Cambridge. His parameters, though, were already fixed: an utterly English childhood – vicarage, moorland, fells, falcons, ferrets – but with an orphan's guilts and fears, reckless risk-taking, love and knowledge of the natural, wild world, fierce independence, and the instinct to wander so characteristic of Defoe's English, that 'ill-bred amphibious mob'. And he was already deeply attractive to women, the looks of a Rupert Brooke blending with an orphan's sadness. A sudden lost look that came on him, when he cocked his head on one side, and stared ahead with 'heartbreaking wistfulness', they found devastating.

Everything about him as a boy pointed to a gift for survival, but at Cambridge, an ill-omen, he had bouts of depression. 'I really am in a very serious condition. I have no principles, scruples or morals whatsoever, I have bad health as a rule, I have no money, I am getting into debt, worst of all I have no brain.' He thought that 'no one realises what an utter rotter and dud I am'. It was a recurrent state. 'I do feel depressed, I hope it will soon pass over,' he wrote. 'I really shall shoot myself soon.' He associated these fits of melancholy with bilious attacks: he could not sleep and he could not eat.

Relief came from risk-taking. He joined the Cambridge Mountaineering Club, bought an old motor-bike and sidecar for £8, and went rock climbing in North Wales and the Lakes and Scotland, with some snow and ice in the Alps. Coming back from climbing in the Dauphiné, he was stung by a hornet whilst riding at speed, fainted and hurtled off the road unconscious. He was more fortunate than Lawrence – killed crashing his motorbike in 1935 – and picked himself up and rode on to catch his cross-Channel ferry in time. He also went night climbing, a rage at between-wars Cambridge. It was, of course, forbidden for undergraduates to clamber over the roofs and pinnacles and towers of colleges and chapels. That added to its natural appeal. The boyhood poacher and rock scrambler had now to avoid the 'Roberts', as bobbies on the beat were called, the college porters, and the roaming proctors and bulldogs, the dons and their enforcers who patrolled the Cambridge streets looking for errant undergraduates.

He learned the tricks of avoiding detection. The best time to start a climb was between midnight and 2 a.m. It gave enough time to complete the climb before the dawn betrayed the climber. Noise had its own rules. A loud, bold noise in the darkness was difficult to locate and often passed unnoticed. It was 'soft, half-stifled sounds', low scratching noises, that were dangerous. He was almost caught when a length of tarry line, falling with a small smacking sound from the roof of King's College Chapel, alerted a policeman, who flashed his torch upwards. Yet two climbers at the top of different pinnacles on the chapel had shouted across to each other, without anyone taking notice.

'We did it partly to keep in climbing trim,' Freddy wrote, 'and also because it provided some excitement in the routine of academic life in the fens.' He hadn't far to go, for his college had some of the best climbs in Cambridge. The Main Gate involved drainpipes, a six-inch ledge and a corner turret. The Bridge of Sighs linking the two halves of the college across the Cam was a delicate traverse for the connoisseur. St John's Chapel was so fearsome that climbers were recommended to 'write their own epitaphs' before attempting it. Freddy was foiled when he tried his first ascent on his last night at Cambridge. 'Unfortunately at about 2.30 a.m. it came on to rain,' he wrote, 'and the overhang was of such severity that it could only be climbed under ideal conditions.'

He was indebted – now, and in extraordinary circumstances, again in 1944 – to a Japanese prince, Hashisuka, for his first expedition after he graduated in 1929. Hashisuka was a fellow-member of the Cambridge Bird Club where Freddy heard a talk the prince gave on how little was known of the birds of Iceland.

15

It intrigued him, and he set off from Leith for Iceland with two medical students on 19 June 1929, planning to spend six weeks away and no more than £30. They were to collect plants for Kew Herbarium and research bird life for the Bird Department at the National History Museum of South Kensington. They sailed steerage on an ancient steamer, all sea sickness, salt cod and sweet sago soup. Then they took a small coastal boat as close as they could get to Cape Horn, its precipitous bird cliffs falling 1,000 feet into the sea at the north-west corner of Iceland. They planned to live off the country, fishing and shooting birds. Even so, Freddy's pack weighed over ninety pounds at times, slung with fishing rod, gun, ropes, ice-axe, blankets, sleeping bag, primus stove, paraffin and a flower-press and bird-skinning tools. A skinned back and exhaustion taught him to travel lighter next time.

The short Arctic night was warm with the colours of sunset in the west merging with the dawn's first bands of pink and gold. They walked through the night, making camp when the sun rose before 3 a.m. Then they cooked and ate, and laid out their sleeping bags in the open, and slept through until noon. Freddy stalked harlequin drakes in the streams with his .410 shotgun. They ate eider and guillemot eggs, boiled if fresh, scrambled if they had been brooded on in the nest for any time. Icelandic farmers fed them great helpings of roast mutton, and *skyr*, made of milk and rennet and eaten with sugar and cream.

Countless thousands of guillemots, razorbills, fulmar petrels and glaucous and Iceland gulls packed the bird ledges of Cape Horn, high enough to escape the spray flung up when storms battered in from the ocean. The nests of ptarmigan, golden plover and purple sandpiper lay in the tussocks and clumps of grasses. It was too wind-blasted for trees. Wild Whooper swans swam on the lakes, and Iceland falcons made ferocious excursions from the crags. Then, on a boat with a cargo of stinking cods' heads, they transferred to Melrakka Sletta, the peninsula in the north-east. He found Great Northern Divers and grey-lag geese nesting, and they walked for scores of miles on winding pony tracks, and across badlands of black lava and sand. He felt that a trip like this was a benefit in itself. It was 'of incalculable value' for any young man to break away for a few months – 'even *one* month' – between 'finishing his school or university days, and being tied down for the rest of his life to the daily round . . .' He thus perfectly anticipated the Gap Year.

In November 1929 he went out to Davos to ski. He thought vaguely that he might then teach, or enter the Sudan civil service, but on the slopes he came across Gino Watkins, a friend from Cambridge who had led a Cambridge expedition to Spitsbergen two years before, and already had a brilliant reputation. He was just back from Labrador. Freddy recalled their conversation:

'Hullo, Gino. How's Labrador?'

'Hullo, Freddy. How's Iceland? What are you doing here? Come with me to Greenland.'

'Right you are. Why?'

CHAPTER 2

JOURNEYS ON THE ICE CAP

A few months later, in July 1930, Freddy was sailing into Angmagssalik, on the east coast of Greenland, watching 'great shoals of kayaks being paddled along furiously by little men in white windproofs and white pilots' hats'. Behind them were larger umiaks full of women. The expedition was sailing aboard the *Quest*, the ship that Ernest Shackleton had used on his last voyage to the Antarctic. It was a big event for the tiny community, and Eskimos – 'Inuit' was not yet used – had come in from remote hunting camps to see them. A dance was held that night on a flat stretch of grass. The British brought their gramophone ashore and the Eskimos danced with them. Freddy found the girls in their pretty clothes delightful – the Danish government had borne this in mind, and Freddy and the others were not allowed ashore before they had been examined for venereal disease – although their dancing was a 'continual jigging'.

Freddy was one of the dozen members of the British Arctic Air Route Expedition. Hard men from the services made up half of them, and the rest Gino Watkins had chosen from among his Cambridge friends. The aim was to find whether the future of transatlantic flying lay in an Arctic route. The pilots of aircraft and airships had found the storms and turbulence of the North Atlantic to be as dangerous to them as to sailors. There was a theory – untested as yet – that the air in the high Arctic was calmer and more predictable. An air route had been sketched out that linked Scotland and Canada via Iceland, Greenland and Baffin Island. It was also the shortest route, and it crossed less water. The great

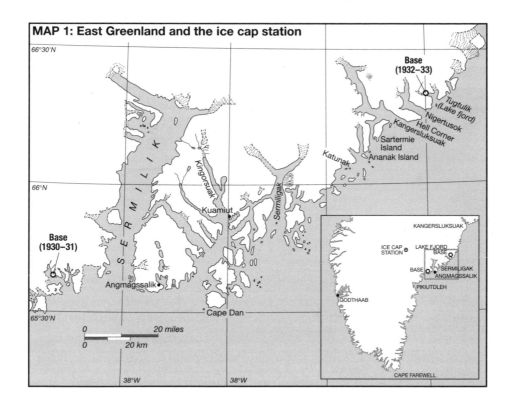

MAP 1: East Greenland and the ice cap station

unknowns were the east coast of Greenland, seen only by a few whaling captains, and the central ice cap. The whole interior of the gigantic island was permanently covered with ice, a deep-frozen uncharted wilderness climbing to over 8,000 feet in the centre. Only a thin coastal strip was ice-free, in summer, and the Eskimos hugged it. There was nothing to sustain them in the interior, a place they abandoned to banshees and wailing spirits.

Angmagssalik was – still is – the only settlement, no more than a dozen or so red and brown wooden houses, roofed with corrugated iron, and dominated by two huge wireless masts. About 700 other Eskimos were scattered along the coast to the north and south of the settlement. There was a Danish storekeeper, with a magistrate's powers, a half-Eskimo missionary and a Danish wireless operator, and their wives and families. Kong Oscars havn, the harbour, was an inlet with a narrow

19

entrance that widened out into a circular basin. The pack ice usually disappeared by the end of August, and returned in December.

Surveys were to be made of the ground and coast, but meteorology was the real justification of the expedition. A weather station was to be set up and maintained at the highest point of the ice cap, so observations of temperature, visibility and wind speed and direction could be made for a year. No British expedition had wintered in the Arctic for fifty years. The expedition had two Moth aircraft, and RAF pilots, to help in mapping and in resupplying the ice cap station. Freddy was signed up by Gino Watkins as ornithologist, ski expert and, after he studied at the Royal Geographical Society, as a surveyor.

The morning after the dance, they sailed on to find a place for a base, close to the ice cap and with an ice-free bay in good hunting country, since they meant to learn Eskimo hunting techniques and get fresh food for themselves and the dogs. A site was found thirty miles south-west of Angmagssalik. On 11 August, a five-man team with twenty-eight dogs set off for the ice cap. They laid a line of flags leading to a point about 150 miles inland where two of them remained to man the ice cap station they set up.

Freddy surveyed the coast to the north, with Augustine Courtauld, of the great chemicals and textiles dynasty, in a whaleboat with an outboard engine. Dense fog was a hazard, cold and clammy, rolling over land exposed to the sea breeze. Angmagssalik had a monthly mean of seven to nine days of fog across the summer months. These conditions developed Freddy's navigation skills. He was also the hunter in the party, and within a few days, his reactions to crisis – and his ability to keep cool and shoot straight – were tested to the limit by the most dangerous of polar animals.

Bears breed far in the north and are then carried south by the polar current when the pack ice breaks up in early summer. Some are swept beyond Cape Farewell, the southern tip of Greenland, and perish on melting floes in the Atlantic. The lucky ones make their way ashore in the south-east, and set out on a 1,500-mile walk back to the north, going across the ice cap and coming down to the sea ice from time to time to hunt for seal. That was what was happening now. 'I put my glasses up. Yes! A bear!' Freddy wrote. 'I took my camera and rifle to the bows.' He made out its head, the yellow tinge to the fur exaggerated by the brilliant white of an iceberg behind it. The bear dived as they closed in on it. Courtauld was running the engine dead slow and it suddenly stopped. Freddy had his Mannlicher at the ready, which was just as well as, with a fierce roar, the bear surfaced at the bow: 'I saw its wicked little piggy eyes and its black snout a mere yard away.' It was too close to miss, but he had to shoot it dead; wounding it would only enrage it further. The boat would capsize if the bear caught its gunwale, and it could maim with a single swipe of its great paws, and kill with two or three. Freddy shot it in the neck, and the great mass of fur and claw sprawled back into the water. It was a monster. When they reached the shore, it was so heavy that they could not haul it up onto the rocks. It took Freddy two hours to skin it and cut it up, standing knee-deep in the ice-cold water.

An hour later, they came across another bear. Freddy had not got any photographs of the first bear, so they followed this one. Freddy was in the bows, looking through the viewfinder of his camera, when the engine stalled again. He glanced up from his camera to find that the bear had climbed onto an ice floe with astonishing speed and dexterity. Snarling, it was about to launch itself into the boat. He dropped his camera and was able to get one shot off with the rifle. 'We were so near,' Freddy recalled, 'that as he fell forward stone-dead he almost upset the boat with the splash of his huge body.' They made camp, and Freddy fried slices of the first bear: it was 'palatable'. Freddy regretted the deaths: he had wanted to shoot the bears on film, not with the Mannlicher. 'I felt distinctly ashamed of myself,' he said. It was 'like going into a field and shooting a cow'. Worse, perhaps, he added, for 'bears are infinitely nicer and more human than cows'.

After they returned to the base, three Eskimo girls came out of curiosity, and to offer to help with cleaning. Freddy took up with Gertrude, the prettiest, with a laughing, oval face and merry knowing eyes. 'Gertrude gave me an embroidered handkerchief and blanket coat . . . Gave silk to Gertrude, she really is a dear . . . Gertrude thought I said girls were beautiful in England. Actually I said I had no girl in England. She wept all afternoon, bless her. I cheered her up but this lingo is hell. She really is a charmer.' Gino Watkins set himself up with Tina, the youngest girl, and the four spent most evenings in the hut's loft. It was not an arrangement that suited the others, as the hut was not built for intimate liaisons. The bunks were in pairs along the walls, one above the other, and the lovers had to climb on them to get up to the loft, where there was scarcely more privacy.

The weather, for the most part, was promising for the air route. During each month of the year, calms accounted for half the observations, and the mean for any month was Beaufort Force 2, balmy, dinghy-sailing weather that barely rippled the sea and the snow banks. In early October, though, it showed how dangerous it could be. In föhn winds, cold air drains off the high ice-covered interior like water streaming down a slope. The violence is worst when a depression is centred off the coast, and there is a steep pressure gradient between the high over the ice cap and the low out to sea. The storms reach hurricane strength. One such

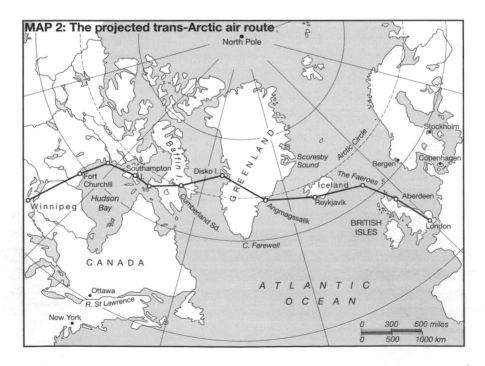

moaned off the ice cap – wind no longer shrieks when it passes 100 mph, but acquires the deep-pitched keening of a lament – on 8 October. The wind in the base camp was north-north-west and the direction remained steady throughout. It started to blow early in the morning and by 10 a.m. the gusts were hitting 129 mph when the head of the anemometer was blown off. The wind went on increasing until about noon and slowly diminished.

Freddy set off for the ice cap station in a five-man team on 26 October. His diary showed some doubts: 'It seems a very hazardous undertaking to take five men who have never driven dogs before, with three scratch teams and heavy loads, up the ice cap in winter, including the shortest day of the year, in bloody awful weather ... I hope to God I shall make it.' Two of them, Augustine Courtauld and Lawrence Wager, another young Cambridge man, were to be left at the station for the winter. It was 150 miles away, and the trip was expected to take three weeks. They ran into a furious storm on the afternoon of 28 October. The canvas of Freddy's tent flapped and bellied wildly. The noise was so great that he had to yell as hard as he could to speak to his tent mate, Peter Lemon, though they were lying in their sleeping bags only a foot or so apart. A glacier below the tent fell away steeply to end in an ice-chute above a frozen waterfall that dropped into a rocky gorge below. Heavy cans were blown off the loads of provisions and skidded down the ice past the tent and over the drop. It was clear that the tent could not withstand the battering for much longer, so the two men dressed and put on their boots.

The end came at about 11 p.m. A gust of 'prodigious force' blew the outer cover off the tent, and sent the boxes used to weight it down clattering into the gorge. Freddy and Lemon were lifted bodily off the ground as they hung onto the poles of the inner tent. They let it go, and crawled into Courtauld's tent. They were packed in so tight that they had to turn over by numbers in their sleeping bags, but even so, 'at every big gust all three of us were lifted right off the ground as the tent swayed ...'

They wore crampons and put canvas boots on the dogs for the last steep slope up onto the ice cap. The sledges were so heavy that they had to hammer spikes into the ice and haul them up with block and tackle. It took four days to get everything to the top. Fine snow added to their woes. 'It gets in everywhere,' Freddy complained, 'fills our pockets, blows down our necks and freezes onto our faces in an icy mass. The snow thaws on one's forehead, runs down and turns to ice on one's eyebrows. My eyes froze up solid.'

Another storm howled in. 'The most fearful night imaginable,' he wrote in his diary on 7 November. 'I really thought no tent could possibly stand against it . . . I wondered how long one could exist in a fur bag before freezing to death. Feet still numb, I wonder if they'll drop off. I wish I knew more about frostbite so as to know what to expect.' It was impossible to breathe outside in a wind he thought was well over 100 mph. 'It must have felt rather like this being under shellfire during the war. If the tent goes we are corpses . . .' He smoked his pipe and read *Tess of the D'Urbervilles* until it was dark. 'Tess is a most suitable book to read in such circumstances,' he noted. 'Elemental strife in both cases.'

Reading at times of stress was a characteristic. Freddy valued books above rations in terms of weight for weight. It became as much a routine for him to pack novels and poetry – usually light classics, like Thomas Hardy, and anthologies of verse – as maps or a knife. They absorbed him; they were a link with home, and England, and he found reassurance in them. 'You want a well-written, exciting story for a sledge trip,' he advised. 'Stevenson is ideal, then Conan Doyle and Dumas. You also want something more solid for lying-up days – Scott, Thackeray or the Brontës.' He read aloud to the others each evening. He found the 'confidence-provoking intimacy' of the battered tent more than offset the frostbite and raw crotch and sopping sleeping bags. 'Nothing like a sledging journey for getting to know a man,' he wrote.

The foul weather went on: '9th November. Another blizzard came in the night and we lay up all day,' he noted. 'Things certainly looking very black – 15 days: 15 miles.' He confided his fear that they might have to turn back. But he was exhilarated – his comrades found him 'in good form running everything' – and realistic. It was already clear that the wind would let them travel one day in two at best: the theory of stable Arctic air was fast being shredded. 'That means that with four weeks original supply of dog food,' he realised, 'we cannot hope to get all the sledges to the Ice Cap Station and back.' Some of them were going to have to turn back.

He went on with Courtauld and Wager. He logged what he wore – three pairs of socks and blanket shoes, fur boots, vest, sweater, blanket trousers and coat, windproof outer trousers and anorak, canvas leggings against the snow, two pairs of wool mittens and wolf-skin outer gloves, wool balaclava and windproof hood – and still he felt the cold. That night he recorded 48 degrees of frost (–27° centigrade). The blizzards pinned the little party down for two or three days at a time. They were making barely a mile a day when they could move, the dogs so unwilling that he found himself behaving 'like an animal . . . hitting them anywhere with any weapon'. Once the dog food was finished, they would have to start killing the weaker dogs to feed to the strong.

He reached bottom on 20 November – 'Worst day I've ever had, several times just couldn't go on' – but over the following few days he found himself and was happy:

21st November. Only a few hours daylight now . . . 23rd November Ears, nose and fingers frost-bitten today. A bitch in Courtauld's team had a puppy. We relentlessly fed it to another team, and the same with three other puppies. Yet the bitch pulled well between each. Poor brute, but what else could we do. 25th November. Sleeping-bags absolutely sodden. Toes and fingertips rotting slowly. I thought a lot about good old Westmorland today and Sedbergh. It's odd to think of life going on just the same there. And us poor shits slaving our silly souls out here – and why? God knows, but it's bloody good fun really.

The wind reached Force 12 on the Beaufort scale that day, and remained at hurricane strength for thirteen hours. Freddy, the orphan in the tempest, had no thoughts of home and family to comfort and cheer him. School took their place.

On the thirty-ninth day of a journey planned to take twenty-one, they arrived at the ice cap station. Freddy had missed the last few flags but he stopped when the sledge wheel recorded the right distance.

Freddy then found the station 100 yards to his left, the navigational sense he had picked up as a boy – 'good old Westmorland' – as sharp as ever. He walked in shouting: 'Evening Standard! Evening Standard!' It was a boyish joke. 'God knows they were glad to see us! We were five weeks overdue.'

That night a new blizzard blew in and lasted for three days. As they lay trapped in the tent, Courtauld asked to be left at the station to winter alone. The two men who were being relieved were against it. They had spent the last eight weeks there. They knew how the weather and the solitude induced strange fears and lassitude – one of them, a naval doctor, had suffered panic attacks. Lawrence Wager felt it humiliating that he should return, when it had been planned for him to stay. But Courtauld insisted it would be 'extremely risky' for two of them to stay. They would have food only to the end of February. The weather they had just gone through showed that it would be dangerous and perhaps impossible for a relief team to get through by then. The only real alternatives were for him to stay alone, with just enough food and fuel on reduced rations to survive, or for the station to be abandoned. It was agreed.

They held a premature Christmas dinner for Courtauld on 5 December, and left him the next day, the weather clear, with the sun just above the horizon casting a pink glow on the snow. He watched the sledges go off down the trail until the specks disappeared. His new home was a circular dome-shaped tent, ten feet in diameter, with double walls. It was enclosed within snow walls, made of blocks like an igloo, with more snow over it. A metal ventilator ran from the tent through the snow covering to give it fresh air. To get into it, Courtauld had to dive down a tunnel and crawl along a twelve-foot passage. He had to read the meteorological instruments every three hours.

Freddy insisted on leaving Courtauld enough food to last him until the end of April, even though a party was due to relieve him by the end of March at the latest. This was to save Courtauld's life, but it left Freddy's returning team desperately short. December was storm-free but fog delayed them. On 13 December, the visibility was no more than twenty yards and they could no longer see the line of flags. Freddy thought they would die if they stopped, so they marched on by compass through the murk. The next day, they burned their last candle. On 18 December, the dogs were given their last feed. Freddy was ruthless. The sledges weighed less now, so they did not need so many dogs. 'I killed Bruno . . . and cut him up,' he wrote, 'a foul job but the dogs ate him with alacrity.' The wind blew all night, but by morning it was clear and they could see coastal mountains. They were home in forty-eight hours. The others were exhausted, but Freddy recorded, 'I was as fit as anything barring toes and fingers.' He found Gertrude 'frightfully glad to see me. 20 days I had told her. Of course, they all thought we were dead . . . So ended that memorable journey, the first one across the ice cap in winter.' They had in fact been away fifty-four days from base to station and back.

He was so content and relaxed that he stopped keeping his diary until March. 'I lived with Gertrude more or less as my mistress and spent my time hunting seals or sledging about.' He was often to think back to those 'three wonderful months at Base . . . I suppose I have never been so happy in my life.'

He left her on 12 March to set off on a long survey trip, inland on the ice cap northwards to the coast at Kangersluksuak. 'Felt very weepy all time so did G.,' he wrote as he started his diary again. 'God knows what the final parting will be like. I shall then become a misogynist again. My temperament can't cope with this sort of thing.' He was better next day: 'God I was miserable yesterday, could still weep if I allowed myself to think. But am getting better, it'll soon pass off I hope.' He had almost reached the stage where 'suicide seems the only option', he wrote, 'but a bit of hard work and one gets dulled again, like a narcotic'.

His depressions bit more for seldom being displayed. His companions, who saw him at the closest range, in hut or tent, noticed little. They all described him as calm – Courtauld found him very pleasant 'but awfully hearty' – but they did notice the extreme love of danger. 'What a likeable chap he was, fresh-faced and with enormous charm,' said Martin Lindsay, later a distinguished army officer. 'No one else came close. He was so obviously capable and competent. But I also detected a streak of fecklessness.'

Risk and intense physical effort were part of his soul. They restored equanimity to a troubled mind: they were the abandoned child's way of declaring his self-worth. Jimmy Scott, a fellow-mountaineer, thought that Freddy was the 'most reckless and idealistic' of them all, 'in search of mental and physical justification by striving against all the difficulties he could find and overcoming them. Then, made worthy by achievement, he could stand upon the summit and admire the glorious views.' Nobody, though, could lead difficult journeys better. 'He had faith and vision,' Scott added. 'He was a tremendous driver – chiefly of himself. He had reserves of imaginative recreation, and he was an unconquerable optimist.'

After a week's sledging and surveying, no longer bilious, he had revived. 'How much one's mental condition depends on one's tummy!' he wrote. The linkage between mind and stomach, and the suicide option, were to break surface again.

Alone on the ice cap, Augustine Courtauld was now entombed in snow. On 18 March 1931, a severe gale blocked the exit from the station. He managed to break through the snow. He should have been relieved by now, but he could see no sledge party on the horizon. Another gale got up, Courtauld wrote, 'and it piled such a weight of snow over the top that I could not move it. This cut off my last exit and from March 21 I was completely snowed up.' He wrote that he was in 'no danger', but he was now trapped in a few square feet of space, unable to take the weather readings, and, for all he knew, so swallowed under the snow that no trace of him remained on the surface.

The relief party under Jimmy Scott had been on the ice cap for forty days. The storms were almost as severe as they were on the coast. They brought no rise in temperature – 'half a gale and 50 degrees of frost often hunted in company' – and the ice cap was swept by low cloud. On 25 March, they were on the latitude of the station and dead reckoning placed them ten miles to its east. A violent storm blew in and lasted for six days, with driving snow that immured Courtauld ever deeper in his tent. By 15 April, the relief party had only three-quarter rations left for four days. They had already killed one dog for food, and they knew they had missed the station.

In their own tent that night, they reflected gloomily that only two options remained. They could trek back and forth over the same ground, still searching, but at the cost of a dog a day for food and the certainty of disaster if they failed. That, or they must turn back at once to pick up food and fresh dogs. 'So we had argued into the night,' Scott wrote, 'but in truth we knew we were beaten . . .' They sledged back at reckless pace, racing past the crevasses and sliding down the last steep slope off the ice cap in darkness. Dark, thick clouds hid the stars and the snow was damp and deep, the air dank and enervating after the cold clarity of the ice cap. The dogs were worn and emaciated, too weak to haul the sledges without help, until they scented the base and ran on barking to their old companions.

Freddy came out of his hut to find the cause of the barks in the darkness. 'Who's there?' he shouted. 'Have you got August?'

They had not. Courtauld had finished his last candle, and lay in darkness except when he ate by the sooty light of burning ski wax. The faintest trace of light came down the ventilator shaft. It gave him some hope that the relief party would find him, but March had slid into April, and he feared that it was itself in difficulties. By now, the ski wax had gone, and he had no light to eat by, getting his meagre ration of pemmican and margarine into his mouth by feeling with his fingers.

At the base, a grey wash of cloudbanks obscured the ice cap, and the filth from the dogs and the refuse from the huts thawed and floated in vile puddles on the melting snow. Gino Watkins outlined the situation in a radio message to the expedition committee in England. He stressed that Courtauld should still have enough food, and that a strong relief party – himself, Freddy and the Australian John Rymill – was setting out at once with provisions for five weeks. He felt he had to add that there was at least a possibility that Courtauld 'is not alive or unwell' and that the station might be covered in snow. He feared that London would think a disaster was brewing, and that an emergency expedition might be mounted from England. He told Lemon, the wireless operator, to 'do his best to discourage them'. Then, at dawn on 21 April, he set off with Freddy and Rymill.

He was right. *The Times* was covering the progress of the expedition and the committee passed on Gino's message. The headline in itself was sober enough – 'Anxiety For Safety of Mr Courtauld' – but the identity of the marooned man made it high drama for the popular papers. The Courtaulds were one of the richest families in Britain. Augustine's parents were on board the *Queen Mary* in mid-Atlantic when news of their missing son reached the liner. His father immediately cabled the committee secretary to mount a rescue operation. Money was no object. The secretary flew to Sweden and chartered a big Junkers aircraft, with a pilot, Captain Ahrenberg, who had Arctic experience, and a mechanic and wireless operator. The aircraft was fitted with skis and floats and extra fuel tanks.

The press lapped it up: 'Arctic Air Quest For An Explorer. Millionaire's Son Alone On Ice ... Father's SOS From Liner – No Expense To Be Spared.' When the *Queen Mary* docked in Southampton, reporters quizzed the parents: 'Mother Says, I Have No Fear.' The papers vied with one another in imparting doom. They interviewed experts who wrote off Courtauld's chances of emerging alive. One embellished a 'further disastrous development' with a final wireless message from the dying man: 'Absolutely without food'. In fact, he had no wireless. A French newspaper assumed that 'Augustine Courtauld' was a woman, and described the desperate efforts of the men to find her as she starved in her icy tomb. The pilot of the search aircraft bought by Courtauld's father was arrested for speeding as he drove to the airfield to take delivery of it. When he appeared before a magistrate next day, he got a reduced fine of £1, and the good wishes of the Bench. Another Arctic expert, Professor Johannesson, was despatched to the limit of the Greenland pack ice aboard a ship supplied by the Danish government. He had a seaplane aboard. He radioed a bizarre message to the men at base: 'What is Courtauld looking for?' They were pondering this Sphinx-like query when another message came in. The Professor had taken off in his seaplane, but had crashed after four minutes.

On the ice, Freddy's relief party made rapid progress. He navigated on the ice cap by compass and sextant, as if on a ship at sea. The course taken by the leading dog team was checked constantly by compass sight. He got an accurate fix of latitude and longitude every two or three days by astronomical observation. After twelve days of sledging, fourteen hours a day, they were close to the station's position. Next day, 4 May, a gale whipped up drifting snow and they could not search or get a position fix. It cleared in the evening and they went out separately on skis. Huge snowdrifts cast black shadows that were visible for a mile, and they mistook several of them for the station, and went racing forward to find a void. Freddy and Gino got back to their tent at about 10 p.m. Rymill was still out, and they got dressed again at midnight and were about to follow his ski tracks when he appeared. He, too, had found no trace of the station.

It dawned clear and bright the next day. They took observations for latitude and longitude. Freddy calculated that they were a mile to the north-west of the station. They positioned themselves a quarter of a mile apart, and began skiing north-west, each with a dog that would show excitement if it scented a man amid the snows. Cresting a rise, they saw a black speck in the distance. It was a flag. They raced towards it. As he got near, Freddy was chilled with misgiving. The place had 'a most extraordinary air of desolation'. The big Union Jack he had left behind in December was reduced to a tattered rag. All that showed above the vast snow heap were the tops of a few meteorological instruments and the handle of a spade. The drift entirely covered the tent and the various snow-houses. Surely no living person could be beneath it. They skied up onto the drift and saw the ventilator tube of the tent a few inches above the snow. Gino knelt and shouted down it. An answering shout came back faintly from the depths: it was 'tremulous, but it was the voice of a normal man'.

They dug away the snow that covered the dome-shaped tent. Through a slit they cut in the double canvas, they looked down at 'a very dirty, wildly bearded monarch, standing in the middle of a squalid, hoarfrost-covered kingdom' just nine feet in diameter.

As they sledged back to the base, a Swedish pilot flew low overhead and dropped them food and papers that spoke of the fears for

Courtauld's life. The little party was irritated by the fuss – 'Damn you, we're all right' – and Courtauld wrote to *The Times* to say he had not been 'rescued' but 'relieved in the ordinary course of the expedition's work by dog sledge'. All the same, it had been touch and go. Gino had packed a prayer book on his sledge in case he had a burial to perform.

Freddy admired Gino for his kayaking skills. Even an explorer as tough and skilful as Nansen had claimed that no European could roll a kayak and harpoon seals from it. 'Watkins said, "Well, if the Eskimos can do it, we can too,"' Freddy quoted with admiration. It was an attitude he acquired himself, and he was to apply it to Tibetan herdsmen, Malayan aborigines and Japanese infantryman as well as Eskimos.

Recovery from a capsize was vital to handling a kayak, and capsize was not always accidental. Faced with a breaking wave, Eskimo kayakers deliberately inverted their little craft, so that the force of the wave was taken on the bottom of the hull, and not by the more fragile deck. Every kayaker could roll his craft with a paddle while a few could do it with the throwing stick they carried to harpoon seals, and an elite could achieve it with a hand. Gino was one of them.

Freddy now had a kayak made for himself. The frame was built of driftwood spliced in the shape of the skeleton of a flat-fish, with long and sharply pointed bows and stern. The cockpit was set slightly behind the middle, the frames running between stem and stern curving so gently outwards that the cockpit was little wider than the hunter's hips. The frame was covered with the half-cured skin of a bearded seal, stretched tightly with thongs and stitched with sinew. Knobs of ivory protected the two ends. A sealskin belt fitted tightly around the wooden ring in which the kayakman sat so that waves could wash right across the deck without any water getting below. Strips of sealskin on the narrow deck held the paddle and the hunting gear. This was the harpoon and its line and float, a white screen for camouflage – Gino had his whole kayak painted white to make it harder for a seal to spot him as he lay in wait in the ice – a gun case and a killing lance. There was no keel, for if thick ice was met, the kayak ran over the ice with the kayakman pushing it along with his hands. The best kayaks were made to measure to fit the individual hunter, shape and buoyancy tailored to his weight and height.

Freddy learned to roll his kayak with his paddle, before his time with the expedition was cut short by a bronchial cyst. Gino asked him to return to England, and to write up the expedition history.

CHAPTER 3

GOODBYE TO A GOLDEN BOY

He was still writing the book – he called it *Northern Lights* – when he set off to return to Greenland the following summer, in July 1932, on a second expedition. 'This is the sort of life I am made for,' he said of the first trip. 'I am sure of it, and I shall be more useful doing this than anything else I could do.' He looked forward to an eventual job at Cambridge or the British Museum – 'I shall never make any money out of it but my ambitions do not lie that way' – on the strength of his Arctic experience, plus books and photography. He had already made the vital discovery, he was to write later, that any hardship can be beaten:

> Mere cold is a friend, not an enemy. The weather always gets better
> if you wait long enough; distance is merely relative; man can exist
> for a very long time on very little food; the human body is capable
> of bearing immense privation; miracles still happen; it is the state
> of mind that is important.

He had adopted, too, a philosophical motto from *Hamlet*: 'there is nothing either good or bad, but thinking makes it so'.

Gino Watkins had returned to England in November 1931. He could not raise the money to go to Antarctica, but was offered £500 by Pan-American Airways to continue with surveys and meteorology work for the Arctic air route. The Royal Geographical Society stumped up £200. *The Times* gave £100 for the press rights.

Gino Watkins was a golden boy of his generation, seen in the London season with his fiancée, an 'exquisitely dressed, rather slight and diffident young man', always with a rolled umbrella – his father was a Guards colonel – but already an international figure as an explorer. It was easy to dismiss him as a feckless toff. His most cherished mementos were the truncheon he had carried as a strikebreaking special constable in the London docks during the General Strike in 1926, and part of the propeller blade of an aircraft he had crashed as the pioneer member of the Cambridge University Air Squadron. Yet he had led his first expediton, to Svalbard Spitsbergen, when he was barely out of his teens. On a whim, he had spent eight days aboard a trawler on the Dogger Bank, sick as a dog but much loved by the crew. 'Gino' sounded too foreign, so they called him 'Our Jim'. He blew his ten-shillings pay in Grimsby, arrived penniless at King's Cross station in the early hours, and walked home to find himself locked out. He went to sleep on the steps. A policeman woke him. This was Onslow Crescent, one of the smartest streets in London, he told him. He couldn't sleep there. 'But officer, surely we can,' he said. 'This is my own doorstep.' The policeman helped him in through a window. The public adored him, and politicians cited him – and Freddy – as evidence that British youth was not decadent.

Mounting an expedition for £800 nonetheless meant cutting corners. No aircraft this time, no pilots, no doctor, no wireless expert. Gino planned to take just four men: himself, Freddy, Quintin Riley and John Rymill. They scrounged instruments from the Air Ministry, and what food they could from manufacturers. They would have to top this up by hunting for fresh food for themselves and their dogs, to Freddy's delight.

He boarded *Gertrude Rask*, the expedition ship, in Copenhagen, and dropped off the final chapter of *Northern Lights* at Elsinore to be airmailed to the publishers in London. Peter Lemon had tried to kill himself after his return from Greenland, and died later, and they discussed the causes of melancholy. Freddy thought that his stomach was as much to blame for his attacks as his head. 'Gino thinks I will shoot myself in a fit of depression after the next expedition!' he wrote, adding, 'What a hope with Jossie about.' Joss Odgers was his new girlfriend, the daughter of a Rugby housemaster. No blues now: 'Jove I am happy. Life is just too good. What a year I shall have. It must be the best of my life.'

His old girlfriend was waiting for him when they reached Angmagssalik on 2 August 1932. They had a 'rapturous' welcome from the Eskimos. Freddy felt 'completely bowled over', though for a different reason. Gertrude told him he had a son. She had called the baby Hansie. After the initial shock, he was glad. 'All is well. Hansie is a fine boy and looks just like me. No one is annoyed apparently.' He added, with evident relief, that Gertrude had no claim on him: 'Hansie's presence doesn't spoil her chances of marriage, thank God.' He was told he would have to give the Danish government £20 towards the baby's support and education. 'Nonsense,' he said. 'He'll go to Sedbergh.'

The old lust was still there. He was sleeping ashore. 'Gertrude is a darling,' he noted in his diary. 'I almost wish I could marry her.' After a week, though, the expedition sailed north. The infant Hansie died in a flu epidemic the following year, so he never had to take up his promise of sending him to his old school. 'Poor Gertrude,' he wrote. 'I adore her still. I shall never find anyone quite like her again.' She married an Eskimo.

They sailed into Lake Fjord in the 'mellow sunshine of an August day . . . full of expectations of joy'. The Eskimos called it Tugtulik, the place where the reindeer live, though there were none. The entrance to the fjord lies between two capes that fall sharply into the sea from 3,000 feet. Islets lie off it. The outermost one is conical and precipitous, reminding them of Ailsa Craig, in the Firth of Clyde, so they named it Ailsa island. The fjord has two arms making a Y-shape from the open sea. The southern arm is narrow and enclosed by steeply rising mountains. At its head, a salmon river flows across a sandbar from a long lake. The waters of the northern arm are abruptly halted by a wall of ice about a hundred feet high, the snout of a glacier fed by tributary glaciers that crawl at frozen pace down from the ice cap. A high rounded promontory separates Lake Fjord from a second fjord, Nigertusok, named for the River Niger, though its cold steel-grey surface is far indeed from the fat and oily waters of its namesake.

Only one European, the Danish botanist Kreuse in 1911, is known to have visited Lake Fjord before the Watkins expedition. The small Eskimo settlement at Nigertusok was abandoned. The last family who had lived there froze to death when a violent north-easterly blew the roof off their house. The winds here are so strong that they have moved stones a cubic foot in size.

At dawn on 10 August, the *Gertrude Rask* bade them farewell with her hooter and set course for Denmark, leaving them only the *Stella Polaris*, a small half-decked boat, no bigger than a launch. They were alone. It was what Freddy had dreamed of as a boy, the 'ideal existence', he thought, like the start of a 'marvellous summer holiday'. He listed the provisions that were to get four men through the winter. Where the manufacturer had sponsored them with stock or money, he was careful to give a name. The chocolate was Cadburys, the self-raising flour McDougall's, the condensed milk from Nestlé, the potted meats from Crosse & Blackwell, the sugar from Tate & Lyle. The Spratts biscuits were intended mainly for the sled dogs, but were 'always a useful standby for ourselves'. No maker was credited with the oats or margarine. The expedition had had to buy them. It was important not to break into these supplies before winter.

Hunting began as the *Gertrude Rask* disappeared. Gino was away in his kayak to harpoon seal. The Greenland harpoon has a wooden shaft about six feet long, with an ivory head on the end to prevent the wood splitting. A thin ivory shaft, like an arrow, a foot long, fits into a slot at the end of the harpoon. At its head is a sharp four-inch metal blade, held in a barbed section of ivory. A strip of sealskin cut to make a line connects it to an inflated sealskin bladder, which sits on the kayak deck behind the hunter. The line is fifty feet long, and it is coiled in a wooden tray in front of the hunter. A throwing stick gives the harpoon more power and range. The hunter manoeuvres to within ten or fifteen feet of his prey. He hurls the harpoon, and paddles hard to move away from the seal so that its struggles do not capsize him. As the line runs out, the hunter reaches behind him and throws the float into the sea. It prevents a dead seal from sinking to the bottom. A wounded seal drags it behind it, the hunter following. A big seal or narwhal can drag the float underwater, and keep it submerged for half an hour. Closing on a stricken seal, the hunter finishes it with a metal-headed lance. He cuts a small hole near its neck, and blows into it with his lips, as if giving the kiss of life, to inflate it. Once the hole is blocked with a wooden peg, the seal rides high in the water, and is ready to tow home.

Eskimos never hunted alone if they could avoid it. It was easier in pairs: easier for one of a pair to distract a seal to the other's advantage, easier to tow seals behind a pair of kayaks, and much, much safer if something went wrong, if a big seal turned on one kayak, if one kayak capsized, if one hunter lost his paddle. Watkins was so sure of his kayaking skills that he hunted alone. The critical factor was the loss of a paddle. A simple capsize was no threat to Gino, even without a paddle. He had practised rolling his kayak with his throwing stick until it became effortless. Then he learnt to do it with just his hand. If a sea was running, though, a hunter could not keep a lone kayak upright without a paddle. He would roll time and again until he became exhausted and he had no way of getting the kayak closer to the shore or a floe. In storms or violent seas, to lose a paddle was 'a death sentence', Freddy said, even hunting in a pair, for the hunter who had kept his paddle could not keep the other upright indefinitely. Lake Fjord was sheltered from the seaway and it had the mirror surface of an August calm on the first day. They needed a good stock of seal-meat to see the dogs through the winter. Rymill and Freddy were busy organising the stores and preparing to fish. Gino with a light heart did what no Eskimo would do without grave hesitation. He went off on his own.

Freddy thought it was 'inevitable': the truth was that Gino preferred hunting alone, 'confidently rejoicing in his own ability and independence'. He did not go as far as saying that Gino was reckless. That was something other people said of Freddy, but they were wrong. He enjoyed danger but he did not run unstudied or ever escalating risks. He had known wild places since he was a small boy, and the romantic in him, the yearning to go beyond the possible, was brought up short by common sense and experience.

Gino came back with nothing, complaining that he had gone rusty on guessing where a seal would surface after it dived. The next day, the wind was up and there were whitecaps on the water, danger signs for the solo kayaker. He brought back a dozen guillemots and a fine seal. The water was too rough for him to inflate the seal for easy towing, so he had battled for hours pulling it back low in the water from the northern branch of the fjord, where he had killed it. He told Freddy that there were plenty of seals, particularly at the head of the fjord where the water splashed at the sheer foot of the glacier wall.

Freddy and Rymill caught eighty salmon that day. In the days that followed they lived on boiled salmon and fried seal liver, and slabs of chocolate. After supper each day, Freddy pressed the flowers he had collected. His eye for flora and fauna was in fine form. He found blue gentian, harebell in clumps, hawkweed, alpine rue, lady's mantle and white arabis on the hills by a lake. Streams flowed down the rocky slopes of scree and dwarf azaleas and rhododendrons grew, with clumps of juicy empetrum berries like the ones he knew from Ilkley moor. His excitement at spotting red-breasted mergansers and long-tailed skuas amused the others, and they invented 'the double-breasted whalecatcher' to rag him.

Fish were so plentiful that Gino was under no pressure to hunt for seal-meat before he had a companion to join him. Several Eskimo hunters were due to come up the coast to winter and hunt seals in Nigertusok fjord close by. He could easily have waited for them.

It dawned cloudy on 20 August. Freddy had planned to go out with Gino to film him stalking and killing a seal. The light was too poor for filming, though, and so he set out with Rymill in the *Stella* for surveying. Gino told them that he was going to hunt in the glacier branch of the fjord, because he was sure to find seals there. The weather soon cleared and the sun came out.

Freddy and Rymill were only a mile from the glacier wall as they began taking bearings on various points for two or three hours. The ability to read a landscape and position himself in it, in mountainous jungle or a vertiginous coastline, was one of Freddy's life-skills. As he mastered the surveyor's tools – theodolite for measuring angles, rangefinder, plane table, sextant for star sights, clinometer for angle of incline – the art of navigation implanted in his boyhood strengthened.

The breaking of the seas on the rocks made a constant soft roar, and from time to time they heard the loud splash of disturbed water as an iceberg 'calved' from the glacier or rolled over. They were used to that and took little notice. At about 11 a.m. both of them heard 'a big crash' coming from across the fjord to the north. They were worried that a big wave was coming that could slam the motorboat onto the rocks. But they spotted no wave and no berg seemed to have rolled.

At 2.45 p.m., they repacked their instruments in the motor boat and started crossing the glacier branch to start surveying on the far side. When they were half-way across, Freddy noticed a sealskin hunting bladder floating among the ice about 200 yards away. It was a good half mile out from the glacier wall. He looked again, and saw that the bladder was on top of a kayak, which was intact but full of water. It settled lower in the water as he watched it. As they steered towards it, they passed the paddle floating 100 yards away from the kayak. The two of them hoisted the kayak on board. Freddy saw that the gun was missing. It might have dropped out of the gunbag if the kayak had rolled. The harpoon was still in its place on the kayak deck secured by a small string of ivory beads.

They stopped the engine and shouted. No sound came back. Freddy climbed the short mast with his field glasses. Nothing. It was possible that Gino had got to the shore and was walking back to the hut. But he had no boots – it was too tight a squeeze in his kayak with them on – and he would have to cross steep rocky hills. Freddy took the motor boat along both shores, and then went very close in along the glacier wall. It had two lines of moraine, debris of crushed rock, and ended in a 'ragged perpendicular wall of blue ice' 100 feet high. The glacier was 'dangerously active'. Each day, he wrote, 'lumps fell off it'. He noted that Watkins knew this, and had 'almost lost his kayak there two days previously'.

And then, in the most hazardous zone only 150 yards or so out from the centre of the glacier wall, they saw something black on the ice. It was Gino's trousers and his kayak belt, the fur apron he wore to stop water splashing into the kayak round his waist. They lay soaking wet in the middle of a small ice floe, about eight feet by six feet. They got onto the floe to recover them. They found that they had sunk an inch or two into the ice as the sun warmed them. It showed beyond doubt that they had been there for some time. Whatever had happened, it had been several hours ago.

They looked for an iceberg large enough to have produced a catastrophic wave as it calved. A block of thousands of tons of ice falling from the glacier face into the sea displaces water in a breaking sea so high and steep that it will overwhelm the most skilful kayaker. Each of the bergs floating in the gentle sun had a distinct watermark where the warm surface of the water had bitten into the ice. None of them seemed to have fallen from the glacier that day, but there was a lot of brash floating about in one spot, and a large berg may have only a small amount of ice showing above the water.

What then? The trousers were 'horribly near' the glacier. Yet the kayak was half a mile off, and the paddle further still. Freddy ran through the scenarios. The most common cause of injuries among Eskimos was an attack by a wounded bladder-nosed seal. Gino's harpoon was not even ready for throwing. So there had been no injured seal to turn on him. He might have capsized whilst shooting – the rifle was missing – and have swum to the ice floe. But the kayak, though waterlogged, was the right way up. It was certain that he could not have lived in the water for long. The sea temperature was a few degrees below freezing. Fresh water would have iced up. They looked for him in the water for a little over an hour. There were many sharks in the fjord, and Freddy knew there was little chance of finding the body. At 4.30 p.m. they steered the motor boat back to the hut. Riley and Enock, an Eskimo hunter who was visiting them, were setting the salmon net in the dinghy. Enock was staggered that Watkins had hunted alone. He himself had hunted from a kayak for twenty-five years, he said, and never once on his own.

The four of them searched the shores along the fjord, in the faint hope that Gino had reached the rocks and collapsed. Freddy and Rymill had ropes and ice-axes, and they set out to cross the glacier at 7.20 p.m. It was 'prickly ice', and little crevassed, but the mountain terrain beyond it was almost impassable to a man without boots. Gino was dead. Freddy was sure of it, though he found it difficult to grasp – he had 'only a sense of unutterable waste'.

It had been bound to happen. 'Only yesterday Quintin and I agreed that any day we expected him not to come home,' he wrote. 'It is too risky, this hunting alone.' Freddy did not mourn him: 'somehow we felt no grief at his loss ... One could never be *really* fond of him,' Freddy wrote. 'He was somehow as cold as ice and quite above the normal bounds of sentiment and emotion.' Freddy said he would follow him anywhere, that he was 'a very great man'. He had his shortcomings, such as being 'too confident ... in the last expedition we were amazingly lucky to get away with it'. He admired him above all because 'he had complete and absolute control over himself and felt it an admission of weakness to show what he felt. So much was this so that one never knew what he was feeling or thinking about anything.' That desire for total self-control, for calmness of mind, was the key to Freddy himself. He had striven for it since he was a child. It meant that for all the wildness in his life – the poaching and night-climbing, the exquisite acuteness of his eye, the deep affection for wild places and their plants and people – there was no lyricism in his descriptions of it. His writing has no edge of passion or fear or emotion.

Freddy was coolly practical. Gino was dead because he had kept taking unnecessary risks. It was his own fault, and it peeved Freddy even as he crossed the glacier: 'I suppose we must go to Tasiusak at once and wire the news home.' He took the opportunity to look for a new high level route back to the base. 'I had an excuse to go on up to the top of a peak,' he wrote, 'as I love to do.' He climbed to the top of a big mountain and watched the stars come out one by one. Away to the west, silhouetted towards the ice cap by the fading orange and crimson sunset, he saw the black outline of needle-shaped mountains beneath purple clouds. It grew dark, a 'heavenly night', a half-moon illuminating the sea. 'The Northern Lights flashed as patches of green light that changed to clear ribbons that waved and quivered, like seaweed caught in a strong tide', he thought. At times, they obscured the sky, but then they faded, and Freddy meticulously ticked off the brilliant stars as they reappeared, the 'great Square of Pegasus', and Arcturus,

Vega, Taurus, Cygna and Aquila. They shone indifferent to the world, and Gino was dead in the fjord.

They made a cross from a couple of beams left over from building the hut. The inscription was simple:

Gino Watkins Aged 25 Drowned August 20 1932 in this fjord RIP

They put it up on the point between the two branches of the fjord. Riley read the burial service. They looked out high over the sea and inland to the steep summit of the highest mountain on this stretch of coast. Gino himself, Freddy allowed, would have chosen that spot to be set apart to his memory. But that, and a line or two of poetry, 'Golden lads and girls all must, / As chimney-sweepers, come to dust,' was the limit of his sentiment.

There was no question of calling off the expedition – 'we found ourselves behaving exactly as before'. That, too, Gino would have wanted. Jimmy Scott wrote Gino's biography. He wrote of the 'one great sorrow of Gino's life' in five words – 'his mother died very suddenly' – without mentioning that she had taken a train from London to Eastbourne, hired a taxi to take her to the great chalk cliffs of Beachy Head, and jumped off. Gino had gone ahead with his expedition anyway: 'I have got the money and the people and it doesn't seem fair to let them down.' These were men who had been taught as boys to keep a stiff upper lip. When Scott was a new schoolboy at Fettes, sent away from his home on Mull to board, suffering from measles, his housemaster had walked into the sanatorium: ''Fraid I've got some bad news, Scott. Cable from Egypt – your father's dead. Don't want you to blub or be silly about it though, you must be a man.' Scott wrote a lyrical farewell for his friend, 'gone in the full pride of his youth and self-sufficiency, gone cleanly out leaving no relics of mortality . . . it was right that none should see him dead'.

Freddy set off with Quintin Riley and John Rymill at once to break the news to the world, going on from Tasiusak to the radio station at Angmagssalik. He also wrote an account for *The Times*, published in a long article as a world exclusive under the heading 'A Greenland Tragedy'.

43

A second nearly engulfed them as they returned to Lake Fjord on the little *Stella*.

A violent wind met them as they entered the open sea from the settlement on 30 August. Gouts of water were flung high as icebergs rolled over 'as if mere brash'. Waves were blown up the smooth side of a fifty-foot berg and streamed downwind off its top 'like a firehose'. In this maelstrom, Freddy was still observant of wild life. The little black guillemots were making little progress as they flew. He saw a party of seven or eight Greenland seals lying comfortably on the ice on the lee side of a berg. When they caught sight of the *Stella*, they raised themselves to peer curiously at the storm-wracked boat, then slithered off the ice and dived into the foam, still as a group.

The wind grew stronger. Black clouds raced by almost on the surging surface of the seas, in which danced 'unearthly' emerald and opal lights. Waves were now breaking over the bow and the *Stella* could no longer make headway. Freddy was steering, and Riley told him to turn back. He managed that, 'somehow', and as they started to run back to shelter at Sermiligak, the seals reappeared fifty yards away with the seas boiling round their long necks.

They were woken next morning at 3 a.m. by the Eskimos who told them it was a good day. The wind had dropped, but there were still gusts and it had snowed during the night above 1,000 feet. They set out in heavy rain, Freddy recorded, and 'soon met trouble'. The wind was blowing strongly against the tide, kicking up steep waves that put the bow under. Freddy was kept dry by his all-sealskin clothes – kayak coat, trousers, gloves and boots – but rain and wave tops swept over the *Stella*. They kept inshore, with some protection from the outlying islands, but they had to round Cape Streenstrup before they could get into the shelter of Ailsa at the head of Lake Fjord.

The engine was spitting badly and they landed on Sartermie island to prepare for the 'final dash' round the looming headland. They took the carburettor to pieces and walked along the shore in pouring rain. Many old graves lay along the shore, and what seemed to be a model house made by children from coloured stones and shells. Waterfalls were flinging up spray in the valleys and the earth was 'sodden like wet moss'. The lingering on the island had an edge of foreboding to it. The weather was foul, the seas dangerously high, the engine coughing and spluttering, and the worst bit of the voyage was still to come. They looked out over the mouth of the Kangersluksuak fjord, which they had to cross. A 'roaring wind' was blowing straight out of it, and there were ten or fifteen very large icebergs like white fangs in its spume-streaked mouth.

Freddy did not discuss his fear: as ever, he was controlled, and silent on his emotions. 'Finally,' he wrote, 'we decided to try the last lap.' The giveaways – the indications of alarm – are in the 'finally' and the 'try'. Freddy did not normally 'try' things. He got on and did them. It was the same with his decisions. They were rarely 'finally' arrived at.

It took the *Stella* an hour to cross the Kangersluksuak fjord, the waves getting bigger, making it difficult to manoeuvre safely through the big bergs lying at the mouth. They decided to head out to the open water beyond the bergs. Freddy watched the seas breaking on a 100-foot-high berg. They smashed onto an ice shelf on the water line and were then caught by the wind and thrown up in a burst of spray higher than the top of the berg. It was a compelling sight: 'fascinated', he noted that the wave explosions were regular, timing them at one every ten seconds. Waves were washing off the bergs at all angles. Riley was steering now, and Freddy watched his 'white set face' as he struggled. The seas got worse. The sun had come out to light the brilliant green sea, smeared with patches of indigo and white breakers. The waves were surging from astern in the following wind and hurling the boat towards the cape. They closed within 300 yards of it, the rock rising vertically in a 1,000-foot wall, whilst seaward of them the huge icebergs were being tossed about like ice-cubes. Lumps fell off them with a deep roar. Freddy estimated the waves at twenty feet, as they were flung off the bergs in a 'filthy maelstrom' of water. They were at the southern extremity of the cape, a point they now christened Hell Corner.

They dared not turn back into the wind since the *Stella* might have broached and capsized as the seas came abeam during the turn. They were running fast with the waves almost breaking over the stern. 'At this point,' Freddy wrote, 'we realised we were playing with our lives.' He was working at the bilge pump, while petrol drums and ration boxes were careering about the boat. Riley cried: 'Cut the kayaks loose!' Freddy watched 'with aching heart' as 'my lovely kayak', with ivory he had been collecting, fell rapidly away astern, standing almost upright on the steep face of the seas. Before he could jettison the other kayak, the *Stella* shipped a big sea and took almost a foot of water in the bilge. She began rolling so badly that her gunwales were going under. The wind then suddenly reversed. A local gale was sweeping down the fjord to the sea, but as they started to round the cape they became exposed to the full force of the north-easterly that was screaming down the coast. Freddy realised that the bergs had been caught in the fjord mouth between the two opposing winds.

The *Stella* shipped another sea. She began to settle in the water, no longer rising buoyant to the waves, the first step on the melancholy path to foundering. Now, 'the worst happened . . .' The engine flywheel was submerged and it was throwing up water from the bilge into the engine itself, which spluttered, and stopped. Rymill tore out the floorboards and began bailing with a bucket. Then the pump stopped working, but as Freddy primed it, Rymill got the sail up. As they clawed away from the berg, a wild gust off the land blew them towards another. At the top of the waves, Freddy looked at the spray dashing 100 feet in the air as the sea hit a berg. In the troughs – 'vertiginous hollows' – he could see nothing but the depths from which he thought they would never emerge.

Riley was a yachtsman, though, and his sail handling kept them a little way off the bergs as he steered back into the Kangersluksuak fjord, seeking shelter from the north-easterly. Rymill gave the engine a turn. Astonished, they heard it start up. The heat of the engine seemed to have evaporated the water on the plugs. Rymill's sleeve was caught in the turning propeller shaft as he bailed, but it ripped off before his arm was mangled, and he was only slightly hurt. A 'lurid yellow light' covered the dark land as they drew into calmer waters. It was a partial eclipse of the sun.

The wind dropped and the sea was calmer in the fjord. Riley curled up and, exhausted, fell asleep. Freddy had been 'quite happy, almost detached, like a spectator' whilst he was working the pump. But when it failed, it was 'like the sudden breaking of a spell', he wrote, 'and I felt we simply didn't have a hope – but the realisation didn't worry me in the least.'

This was very far from fatalism. Freddy would go to any lengths to stay alive: if there was anything to be done, he did it. At the same time, he remained observant and calm and he had trained himself not to fret. Almost any polar problem could be solved if it was 'approached with a willingness to learn from the Eskimos', who had struggled with the same difficulties for thousands of years.

They found an anchorage back behind Sartermie. The compass box was smashed and the tool box had split open, scattering the tools around the bilge. Freddy's photographic cases were full of water. They tidied up and had boiled guillemot and ptarmigan for supper. They pitched a tent ashore, but a high swell was still running, and they kept anchor-watch through the night, two hours on, four hours off. Freddy was awake at 3.30 a.m., as it started to get light, and the sun burned off the morning mist and lined the clouds with crimson. So much loveliness, he thought, so few people to enjoy it.

It was not until 3 September that the swell dropped enough for them to think it safe to leave. The engine got them past Hell Corner and round the cape without incident: though there was no wind, the sea was still heaving and breaking against the cliffs. They were home.

Freddy's knee was still weak from cartilage problems after he had damaged it falling into a crevasse on the last expedition, and he was now laid up for a month to rest it. He contemplated his life. He'd had an 'odd upbringing', he thought, and a 'very severe inferiority complex' was mixed with a feeling that mentally and physically he had something in him that was 'quite alien and superior'. He suffered from big mood swings, a conviction that he was invincible giving way to one that 'I would be mad by the time I was 30'. He tempered himself with self-imposed hardship:

> All the time I was trying to toughen myself by ordeal. I didn't know why but I loved to battle against a gale on the hills and I was happy blinding along on my Norton defying injury, the weather and a thousand other ills. The joy of setting out to do something, and doing it, was strong drink to me . . .

His 'most awful depressions' at being laid up worried Riley so much he feared 'tragedy' might ensue, and felt 'most uncomfortable at leaving him alone'. Freddy wrote in his diary of feeling that 'I will incontinently shoot myself one day . . . an artistic temperature is not good in an Arctic winter.'

As soon as his knee improved, though, the moods passed. 'This is a grand life. Marvellous. Poor shits in offices. God I am a lucky man.' His definition of happiness may seem pure boy scout – 'hearing the evening meal sizzling in the frying pan, while the dogs howl outside or snow patters on the window panes, and then after supper to read until midnight' – but, apart from their intrinsic value, a scout's qualities were a necessity in a far-flung world where self-reliance was more essential to life than it is now. He also concluded that a fit white man could survive extremes of weather or terrain as well as indigenous people. 'I don't think the Eskimos can stand the cold any better than healthy Europeans.' Like hardships in general, it was mental toughness that counted.

The sun left Lake Fjord after the end of September. It still shone on the surrounding mountains, though less and less each day. He had magnificent views of the stars through the window where he lay. He felt he'd become 'friends with them all, the Scorpion, Archer and the Goat, the Fish with the glittering tails'. He shot sea-birds from the *Stella* until the sea froze, standing in the bows with a 12-bore, getting black guillemots and glaucous gulls, and, from mid-October, real delicacies, long-tailed ducks and eider. On a good day, he and the others came back with a score of black guillemots and a brace of ducks and a gull or two. The sea was covered with the larger Brünnich's guillemots when they began their migration, and they shot them until they ran out of cartridges. They gutted the birds and hung them without plucking or skinning them. They soon froze solid, an ample reserve for winter. He worked on his kayak skills, rolling it in water so cold it 'hurts between the eyes', until it froze.

The ice was a foot thick on the lake by the end of October, but the sea still heaved with heavy swells and was not yet freezing. By the end of November, however, when he climbed the hill behind the base, the pack ice stretched as far as he could see. The sea ice in the fjord was now 'bearing': thick enough to move about on. It was now time for sledging. His team had six dogs. The driver needed four commands. *Kar! Kar!* was the Greenland equivalent of the French Canadian *Mush*. It was the order for the dogs to start – *marche!* – and to go faster once they were under way. *Iu! Iu!* told the team to go left, and *Ille! Ille!* to go right. *Ai!* was to stop. Freddy spent hours training his team until exhaustion taught them the virtue of obedience. Great accuracy with the whip was needed to make sure the right dog was punished. At work with their light sealskin whips, the Eskimos reminded him of fishermen casting a fly.

Freddy had seen how Danes and Greenlanders crossed stretches of open water (leads) in pack ice. The driver pulled the dogs closer to the sled as he approached the lead. When they reached the edge of the ice, he freed the traces and the dogs bounded across together to the other side, pulling the sled behind them. 'Sitting well to the back of the sledge,' Freddy recalled of crossing a six-foot lead, 'we did not get wet.'

The orphan boy had no tenderness to spare for his dogs. He was ruthless, and the weak and the unfit-for-purpose went to the wall:

The Alsatians never took kindly to sledging, they would trot jauntily for a bit, and then stop and get bowled over by the traces. Alas! Neither of them survived the winter; they never learnt the art of curling up in the snow. I think perhaps their meagre coats did not prevent the heat of their bodies thawing the snow into pools of water, which, when the temperature fell, would freeze again, together with lumps of their fur.

There was no question of bringing the suffering dogs into the hut, so that they did not lie in the winter darkness in pools of water and ice.

He went on a polar bear hunt with Enock in Nigertusok in January 1933. They saw something that to Freddy looked like a man, following their tracks at a distance. Enock looked through his battered field glasses: '*Nanotiwuckai!*', which Freddy translated as: 'By Jove! A bear!' They dashed towards it at full speed on their sledges. The bear came on towards them, looking from side to side 'as if he had something on his mind'. As soon as the sledges rattled onto hard ice he heard them and began to run up the fjord.

Enock whipped up his dogs until he got onto the tracks of the bear. He let three dogs loose and they harried the bear into the tide crack between ice and land. The bear slipped into it, only his head showing white above the dark water. He lunged at the dogs with his paws when they came too close. He dived from time to time. Enock harpooned him first, for fear he would sink, and then shot him. He pulled the body onto the ice and began to cut it up. There was a strict etiquette in sharing out a bear. Whoever had first spotted it, man, woman or child, was given the bearskin, the head, the ribs and the offal. The first hunter in when the dogs had it at bay took one hindquarter, and the second to arrive the other. The third and fourth were rewarded with a foreleg each.

The six-foot male had little blubber on it – its stomach had some sea cucumber and the remains of a guillemot – but as Enock cut it up they ate some of the still warm kidneys. Freddy found it 'delicious', as good as the raw blubber he ate when Enock shot a seal, which tasted like 'a mixture of cream and nuts'. The liver was immediately pushed under the ice. Men and dogs became violently ill if they ate it. The rest of the carcase was brought back for the women to flense, carefully cutting the skin away from the skull and paws, and storing the joints of bear meat under an upturned umiak that acted as a winter refrigerator.

Whatever Freddy's regrets with bears, though, seals were different: 'I do not love seals.' He had no problem in killing them. He found something sinister in their shiny bullet heads and their 'unblinking watery eyes'. It did not matter what sort they were – ferocious bladder-nose, timid and unapproachable bearded, or inquisitive fjord seal – he looked on them as cunning reptilian enemies rather than the warm-blooded mammals they really were.

Joy was a seal hunt. He was 'never so happy' as lying for hour after hour on the ice at the side of a lead of open water, watching the 'jealous shadow-fingers of approaching night' darken the high snows, and little crystals of new ice form on the water. Then the calm was suddenly disturbed, ripples swirling behind a small dark head that moved rapidly across the lead, sometimes bobbing under the water. He was a natural sniper. His writing leaves no doubt. This is the lone rifleman's dream:

My heart leaps up within me . . . I am so excited I can hardly hold the rifle still; I set the sights and stealthily lie on the ice. Just as I am ready to shoot I give a low wavering whistle. The movement of the snake-like head abruptly stops. Bang! As the echoes reverberate from mountain to mountain, I see with an immense thrill the eddies spreading from the dark object floating low in the water. I think of the mornings I have left my warm sleeping bag while it is still dark; of the long hours I have spent out there in the cold seeing no sign of any living thing, of the seals that dived just as my finger closed on the trigger, of the shots I have missed by miscalculating distance or allowing myself to get excited. As I drag the seal home to the Base, I contemplate boiled ribs for supper and succulent fried liver and kidneys for breakfast.

Out from the shore, Freddy could trace the movement of the waves as they passed under the ice, rippling it up and down. A 'resonant throbbing' hung in the air, the noise of the sea grinding the pack. The seals banged the ice with their heads to make air holes. Bears had a trick for catching seals at these holes that the Eskimos had learned. The bears grouped round a hole, and then all but one would move away, so that the seal thought it was safe to surface again. The remaining bear smashed a paw down with such force that it shattered the seal's skull and the surrounding ice. Enock had seen bears do this twice. A walrus's skull was thick enough to withstand a blow by the paw alone. The Eskimos had seen a bear stalk a walrus with a large chunk of ice in its paws, cracking the walrus's skull with it and killing it.

The sharks had eaten Gino, or so seemed likely, and now Freddy hunted them to feed to the dogs. Enock taught him how. He cut a wide hole in the ice, into which he dropped lumps of blubber weighted by stones. A huge hook, eighteen inches long and weighted with lead, was lowered on a stout wire through the hole to hang just clear of the bottom among the stones and blubber. The line was passed over a stick that shook when the bait was taken. The largest shark he got was a fifteen-foot Greenland shark. These can grow to twenty-three feet, and parts of polar bears and whole reindeer have been found in their stomachs. The meat is poisonous when fresh, but good enough for dog food when left for a time and mixed with seal blubber. The Eskimos hung shark meat until it was almost putrescent, and considered it a delicacy.

His most perilous ice journey was with John Rymill to buy new dogs in Angmagssalik. They left on 6 February.

A 'grim ominous morning' dawned seven days out, 'heavily overcast with a crimson line out to sea'. They were away at 8 a.m., and went out beyond Ananak Island. The ice here was rotten with the dogs sinking in it and the tide sloshing at it from below. Freddy's lead dog Red Fox went right through the ice once, then Freddy put both feet through but held onto the sledge. Only the snow covering was holding the ice together. A mass of slushy ice built up on the dog harnesses. 'Both teams got mutinous,' he wrote, 'and we had to use the whip continuously.' The snow was streaming in the wind out to sea. They hurried to get across the bay to Katunak in case a storm blew in and broke up the ice. It started snowing, and the wind reached them at 3 p.m. The visibility in the driven snow was so poor they failed to find a large stable floe to camp on. A blizzard started just after they got the tent up. They were two miles out from land. 'God, what a night!' Freddy wrote. 'The blizzard got worse and worse.' He read the whole of R. L. Stevenson's novella *The Pavilion on the Links* to John Rymill, stopping from time to time when the shrieking wind and the flapping tent drowned out his voice.

As he finished, he heard 'strange, fearful noises' above the groaning of the storm. A dull concussion shook the tent: 'the pack was breaking up'. Rymill went outside to look, but the air was so saturated with driven snow that he could scarcely breathe or see. The tent had moved and was at a strange angle. 'We looked under the groundsheet and discovered a great crack in the ice diagonally right across the tent,' Freddy recorded. It was soon almost a foot wide and the sea was visible below it. The wind was too strong to try moving the tent. Freddy and Rymill sat on one side of the crack as it widened through the night, expecting the pack to break up at any moment. They hoped when it did that they might be able to get out of the tent onto a floe. At 5 a.m., though, the wind dropped enough to make disaster less likely, and they slept until dawn.

Daylight showed how close death had come. A series of cracks ran under one side of the tent. A wide crack had divided Freddy's dog team, and one of them was hanging by his harness in the water. Huge snow-drifts had built up round the tent. There was open water out to sea, within a mile of the tent, and 'the pack had broken up behind us and alongside . . . A very lucky escape'. They found firm ice and slept that night on an island.

The weather continued dull, but when the sun burst through for a moment on the hilltops, it revealed 'the most austerely beautiful country in the world'. Two days later they came to a patch of thin ice, its fragility masked by a thin covering of fine snow. Freddy was probing with his ice spear when it went straight through. As he shouted a warning, John Rymill fell through over his head. His skis fell off and were stuck under the ice, and he lost his ice spear and a glove. Each time he tried to pull himself out the ice broke under his weight. It took almost two minutes before he got out by spreading his weight on Freddy's skis. Freddy stripped off his warm clothes – 'luckily I always carry a complete change of clothes' – and Rymill put them on and lay in a sleeping bag to restore his body heat. As they struck out for an island, the ice 'sagged visibly beneath our sledges. It would have been fatal to stop.' A huge iceberg rushed by, 'propelled by tide or wind', pushing several acres of high buckled ice in a pressure ridge in front of it, 'a most awe-inspiring sight'.

Then Freddy went through. His sledge floated and he held on to it until they managed to get it out by putting skis under its front runners. Water got into Freddy's sealskin trousers and ran down into his boots.

As darkness fell, they were still five miles from the small settlement at Sermiligak fjord. They pressed on: 'only the stars, and the aurora playing hide-and-seek with the clouds, kept me going'. They heard dogs after three or four hours, and their own teams picked up the scent and raced on. They were welcomed into the settlement, and duly gorged themselves on seal meat and a long-tailed duck. Their hosts were greatly excited to hear of all the bear tracks they had seen on the ice. Then they told them of the tragedies that were so constant a part of the hard Northern life. A bad flu epidemic had carried off several of the old hunters they knew from the last expedition. A boy had fallen through the tide-crack and drowned. A young man had died of exposure in a blizzard that had caught him only a mile from his house. No seals had been caught at Cape Dan and Angmagssalik, and half the dogs were dead, and the people half-starved. A week before, three sledges had gone through the ice near Sermiligak, and all the dogs save one had drowned.

Freddy's diary note for the next day, 17 February, showed his powers of recovery, mental and physical, and his interest and fondness for the native people and wildlife:

Slept like logs. Oh, what a marvellous life! A few hours ago untold misery, and now – all a man can want. Ate all day. Yelmar brought us frozen cod; he told me wonderful tales of bear and narwhal hunts. When he talks slowly I can understand all he says. They have a tremendous respect for the unusual strength and cunning of bears. No one here has ever found a bear embryo; I suppose they only breed away up north.

A north-easterly blew up: he thanked God they were not still out on the ice.

On the final leg into Angmagssalik, they had to climb a long glacier in the dark. At the top, there was a 'desperately steep' traverse to be crossed, with a near vertical fall of several hundred feet into a lake.

A team had fallen down it the year before and all were killed. They could see nothing, which made it more menacing. They got across but now found themselves on a rocky slope, the 'steepest and most formidable place I have ever sledged in'. Freddy lost control of his sledge, despite streaming chain and rope drags. It hurtled down, rolling over and over, throwing him clear to slide down on his back through rocks and big boulders set in six-foot-deep hollows where the wind had blown out the snow. He was amazed that he had no broken bones and the dogs were still intact. They reached the settlement at 9 p.m. on 22 February, with the aurora glowing through the murk.

Freddy bought some dogs, for ten shillings each. He also made an ingenious modification to his sledge, by putting two narrow metal runners on the top. He could then use the normal broad ski runners for deep soft snow. By turning it upside down, and changing the handlebars, it was ready to run on hard sea ice on the new runners. He found it worked wonderfully, sledging at such pace when he left Angmagssalik on 28 February, that he reached Kuamiut before dark.

That evening, an angakok, an old shaman, gave a séance. He sat with his back to the audience, the lamps were blown out and the windows blacked out with skins. A drum and drum stick lay next to the angakok. He spoke in an ancient language, which only the oldest knew, from the days when séances were held for the sick or to end a famine, and it was believed that the angakok visited the moon and the old woman of the sea to plead for help. Freddy heard the sealskins rubbing together to the drum beat, and 'weird voices spoke, coming from all corners of the room'. The audience became ecstatic, the heat stifling, with a 'pandemonium of voices and haunting sounds', and drum beats and rattling sealskins, the atmosphere hypnotic: 'one could have seen spirits with ease'. At last the lights were lit again, and the angakok was helped exhausted to his feet. They all went out into the cool night air: 'I have never before realised the power of mass emotion.'

They were up at 5 o'clock next morning. Freddy and Rymill had ten dogs apiece now, and they kept up a spanking good speed over the ice. They made thirty miles to Sermiligak in seven hours. Next day, they went along the tide crack on the dangerous Sarfax channel. The sledges overturned several times and the dogs became very excited when they picked up the scent of a bear.

They camped on the ice off Hell Corner on 4 March. They were up at 4 a.m. next morning for the final stretch to Lake Fjord. Quintin Riley had been skiing up the hill every day to look out for them and now came down to meet them. They had been gone for a month.

By mid-April, large leads were appearing far out in the pack. The inshore ice was still firm. Freddy found plants were sending up new shoots and turning red to collect the warmth, and dandelions and garden angelica grew, confirming an early thaw. The snow buntings had sung beautifully at dawn, and he heard his first ptarmigan call of the year.

A low fog was hanging over the fjord. He went out onto the ice to see if there were any seals lying out. He was amazed to find cracks in the ice and a swell running below it and making it sway. On the other side of a big berg he found open water: 'How incredible for this time of year!' He had taken the firmness of fjord ice for granted. It was a shock, he said, as brutal as going outside one morning at home and finding a river flowing fast where the flower beds ought to be. He crossed over into the branch fjord at the point where Gino had disappeared. There were some cracks and he could see open water out to Ailsa island when the fog lifted. But an offshore wind was blowing, and he could see no fjord ice that had broken off. 'I thought I was fairly safe if I kept a good watch,' he said.

He skied out to the edge of the ice and waited for seal. The ice was swaying up and down in the swell. He saw a seal and whistled to arouse its curiosity. He got it with his second shot at eighty yards. He was wrapped up in the hunt when he saw a line of black open water suddenly appear behind him and then close up in the swell. 'I knew what this meant,' he wrote, 'and picking up my gun, skis and ice spear I ran like hell.' He had noticed that the sudden release of pressure when a huge surface of ice cracked gave great impetus to each side of the crack, which rapidly parted company. He found the crack was already too wide to jump and was widening at speed.

As he ran along the edge, he found himself on a floe about 100 yards long and 20 wide that was being driven out to sea, where it would rapidly break up. He was in thin summer clothes, with just a rifle and seven rounds of ammunition, and not so much as a box of matches. His reckless streak – hunting alone on unsafe ice – had got him into the crisis. He now showed extraordinary speed of reaction and the ability to read a danger in an instant, as he improvised a way of getting out of it:

> At one end of my piece of ice I found a triangular bit about 5 feet along each side, which was half cracked off from the main floe. I jumped on it vigorously, narrowly avoiding falling into the sea when it broke off. I sat on the bit of ice and paddled back with a ski.

His conclusion? 'One has to watch oneself in this country.' Indeed one has.

Riley and Rymill left him in May and went south in the *Stella*. Freddy had a month alone at Lake Fjord. He had thought he was not cut out for solitude, but he found that a regular routine proved a fine antidote, a discovery that was to serve him well in the jungle.

Apart from tea, he was entirely self-sufficient. He had fried seal-liver or salmon for breakfast. He made meteorological observations at 10 a.m., and went kayaking or collecting insects and plants until another observation at 4 p.m. His main meal was roast eider duck or seal meat, but he varied it with mussels, edible seaweed, cod and trout. Another delicacy he much liked was a mixture of blueberries, rancid seal oil and dried seal blood, eaten with dried seal meat and fresh blubber. Dwarf willow and dandelion leaves, oxyria roots and sedum shoots were also tasty with fresh blubber. He found plants on even the most barren-looking rock: cassiope, saxifrage, salix, empetrum, and dwarf rhodo-dendron, *silene acaulis*, and small ferns. He skinned birds and prepared specimens until the evening observation. Then he read: the Irish poet James Stephens, the naturalist W. H. Hudson, Joseph Conrad, the portrait painter and war artist William Rothenstein. He found their thoughts a stimulating contrast to his own primitive way of life, whose main purpose was to get enough food.

He devised a technique for hunting young seals. He tapped his paddle on the kayak, and, curiosity aroused, the young animal often surfaced near the kayak. Freddy shot it with a shotgun – 'if you use a rifle it will sink at once' – to stun it. As it thrashed in the water, he brought his kayak close enough to harpoon it. He built a stone larder and filled it with fresh ice every day. There were so many fish in the river that he found he could shoot them with a .22 rifle as they came to the surface. He smoked his own salmon, soaking them in brine and then hanging them over a slow fire.

He was proud of being able to feed a whole family of Eskimos when Enock came to Lake Fjord in a big umiak. He heard their laughter and song over the water long before they arrived. 'They are a marvellous people,' he wrote with affection. 'It is fun to be travelling in a country which is still in its glacial period and with people just emerging from the Stone Age.' There were eleven of them, and he prepared a great steaming bowl of seal-meat. After the feast, they danced to the gramo-phone until midnight, the girls hugely enthusiastic, pausing only to change the records and the needle. Enock took his drum and sang for three hours. The Eskimos loved to sing, be it drum contests or petting songs by mothers to their babies. Freddy noted that the 'very word "to sing" is the same as "to breathe"'.

The pack ice was still unbroken to the horizon in June when the *Stella* returned. The temperature never rose above 50 degrees Fahrenheit, and usually it hovered around freezing. It was 8 July before he saw the first open leads, and the end of July before the large icebergs he used to mark the movement of the pack began to drift southwards. It often rained. On clear days banks of fog rolled in along the fjord in the evening, and it was not until midday that the sun burned off the mist. On 6 August 1933 the cloud was down to 1,500 feet and the *Stella* was shipping water in squalls as Freddy completed mapping the fjord. To his amazement, a small seaplane appeared round Cape Wandel, low over the heaving sea, flying over the *Stella* and going on southwards until it disappeared in the clouds. It was Charles Lindbergh, who was also being sponsored by Pan-American to make experimental flights over the Arctic air route. He was flying the Vega seaplane from Clavering Island, heading north-east for Angmagssalik.

Lindbergh was measured about the prospects for the Northern route. Flying over Greenland might be possible in summer, but would have to compete with liners that could cross from Southampton to New York in five days in any weather. A few days later he flew back to Iceland. Freddy thought it was typical of him that he went 100 miles out of his way to fly over Lake Fjord, where he came past the hut low and slow and waved to them.

He left Lake Fjord in mid-August – 'I am sick of the place. Very different from last year!' – to go south by kayak, with Enock and Kidarsi. A large umiak with families went with them, loaded down with skins, tool boxes, cooking pots and clothes, with the meat in the bows, as far as possible from the dogs in the stern. Freddy ate in his kayak, hanging on to the gunwale of the umiak, whilst they fed him water, berries, liver and blubber. He was once in his kayak for twenty-four hours straight. They sheltered under the upturned umiak when it was too rough to stay at sea. He visited a hunting camp, the tents lined with sealskin and curtains of bearded seal gut at the entrance. Bladder-nosed seals, strong and aggressive, were numerous here and half the hunters had been attacked by them, with tooth-marks on their lances to prove it.

On 2 September, he crossed from Kulusuk Island on the final leg to Angmagssalik with two Eskimos. It was sixteen miles across, with no protection from the open sea, and the waves were so big that they washed over him chest high, his kayak hidden beneath the swirling water. He paddled only on the leeward side of the kayak all the way across, and it took all his strength and effort to prevent it coming up into the wind and sea. The Eskimos were so relaxed, though, that one of them killed a Little Auk with his bird dart amid the swells. Freddy joined the schooner *Nordstjern* at her mooring at the head of the fjord at Angmagssalik. She sailed on 20 September.

CHAPTER 4

SCRAMBLES IN SIKKIM

Freddy spent part of the summer of 1934 climbing and touring Europe in a Lagonda he had bought for £200. He lectured, and wrote a well-received book, *Watkins' Last Expedition.* On 17 September 1934, aged twenty-seven, he began teaching at Aysgarth, a preparatory school in the Yorkshire Dales. He taught geography, English and French. He was a favourite with the boys. He rolled his kayak in the school swimming pool, and passed other enthusiasms on, with a bird-feeding table, an aquarium, an aviary and a large display case for bird and butterfly exhibits.

In the spring holidays of 1935 he went with a friend to Lapland, intending to drive a reindeer sledge cross country for 150 miles by compass. He bought a reindeer called Isaac from a Finn for £5. His route ran north-east from Karesuando on the Swedish–Finnish border up to the Arctic Ocean. The aurora was beautiful, waving curtains of light like the grain of walnut wood picked out in phosphorus, green with hints of violet and red, and never still, a 'magic kaleidoscope'. The Lapps, too, were 'delightful gnome-like little people'.

The only darkness in this idyll was cast by Isaac. When the Lapps saw the Englishmen struggling with him, they fell into the snow with mirth. Isaac was only three feet in height, but strong and stubborn. He had to be wrestled to the ground to get him into the shafts of the sledge. A reindeer has a single rein. There is no way of stopping him except by force, and none of getting him started. One of them went ahead, pulling, and the other pushed the sledge, yodelling. Pulling the reindeer as well as the sledge was 'a dead loss' and they began to see Isaac as no more than an emergency meat supply. Before leaving Karasjok, they sold him to a butcher, 'with glad hearts but at considerable financial loss'.

Then they set off on skis on frozen rivers for Kirkenes, Norway's remotest north-eastern outpost. The spring thaw had started, so they had to sleep by day and move at night, when the snow was hard enough to bear them. They had just begun to cross Lake Enare when it started to snow and the temperature began to rise. They could not cross fifty miles of thawing lake, so they went by relays of pony sledges down the still frozen Tana river to the Arctic Ocean. From there they took the mail boat back to Bergen round the North Cape.

Freddy was climbing on Great Gable in the Lakes in the summer holidays when he met Marco Pallis, a climber he had known at Cambridge. Pallis, who had a great interest in Tibet and mysticism, was planning an expedition to the Himalayas. He asked Freddy to join him.

They aimed to climb a peak in the Simvu massif. Three of them then hoped to climb in Tibet, while Freddy and the experienced Alpine climber Jake Cooke continued to climb in northern Sikkim.

The five-man party sailed for India in February 1936. As they sailed through Suez they passed two empty Italian troopships returning from the war in Abyssinia, a portent of what was to come. A dove with lovely lilac-blue wings settled on the ship as they sailed between the bare mountains on the Red Sea: a gesture of peace, perhaps, but it was followed by a kestrel and a flight of kites high overhead going north to the crags of Yemen.

They landed at Vizagapatam, 200 miles south of Madras, four weeks out from Liverpool. As the pilot boat took him ashore for an evening stroll, he saw kingfishers, many bee-eaters, and white parrots and cinnamon Brahminy kites. The smells ashore were overwhelming – heat, bodies, warm dung, a 'sudden heavy breath of flower scent', then a reek of filth and sour milk – to the constant sound of cicadas and murmuring voices. Half a street had more people and happenings than existed in all Greenland. His companions got lost in the welter of streets and wooden shops no larger than cupboards. Freddy navigated as he had on the ice, by the Pole Star, though it was low on the horizon here. By following Canopus he found his way back to the pilot boat. They sailed on to Calcutta. He was not impressed by Bengalis and even less by the whites: 'All the character seemed to be boiled out of them, and I disliked the way they treated the Indians.'

They reached Kalimpong, on the borders of Bengal, Sikkim, Tibet and Bhutan, by train and car. Here, the dark-skinned Hindus seemed out of place as they sat cross-legged in their shops, 'attenuated by malaria . . . the whites of their eyes a sickly yellow'. In the market he saw other peoples, Chinese in long quilted robes, the remnants perhaps of the Chinese army routed outside Lhasa in 1911, 'little hustling Nepalis' in black fezzes, Lepchas, the pale and timid original forest dwellers, short-haired Bhutanese in striped robes ending above the knee, and Tibetan muleteers with pigtails tied round their heads, and whip handles in their belts. Nepali and Lepcha women went past with huge baskets for carrying stones hung from straps on their foreheads.

They selected porters from a crowd assembled by the local secretary of the Himalayan Club. Some were barefoot, others in scarlet and green muleteers' boots, a few in hobnailed climbing boots and puttees, veterans of previous expeditions. They had them run up a hill to see their fitness – 'we would not have behaved like this in Greenland' – and chose twenty of them. The wages were a rupee a day (one shilling and six pence) with a little more for those who went above the snow line.

A note was waiting for them in Gangtok at the Dak bungalow, the rest-house, to invite them to the British Residency. They drove up a tarmac drive – lit by electricity, to their astonishment – to a fine stone building set in lawns and flower beds. The Resident was Basil Gould, a tall and soldierly man, a Tibetan-speaker who was responsible for the Indian government's relations with Sikkim, Bhutan and Tibet. He told them there was little chance of getting permission to climb in Tibet. A British mission to Tibet was being planned, however, and he would need a private secretary. Would Freddy consider it? He would.

They left Gangtok for Lachen on 8 April 1936, to the skirl and the drone of bagpipes and trombones drifting up on the still air from the monastery below. They climbed up through the malarial forests by the

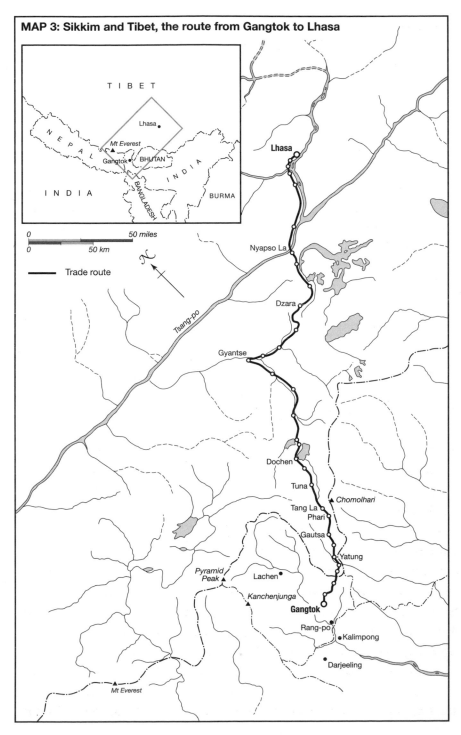

MAP 3: Sikkim and Tibet, the route from Gangtok to Lhasa

Teesta river, brilliant Sikkimese butterflies darting among trees where frogs were croaking. There were butterflies at every damp spot on the road, sucking up moisture, black velvet swallow-tails as big as small birds, and lemon and iridescent green swallow-tails, with others that 'flashed deep purple as they flew'. On the bridges over rivers tumultuous with snowmelt, the porters dropped flowers which they had picked, praying as they crossed.

Freddy collected seeds for the Royal Botanical Gardens at Kew. Botany in Sikkim went back to Sir Joseph Hooker, friend of Darwin, climber, explorer, naturalist and director of Kew. He was in Sikkim in 1848, making his way to Lachen, climbing, and adding twenty-five magnificent new rhododendrons to the fifty then known, so helping create the great rhododendron craze in Victorian gardens. Freddy was in the Hooker tradition. From childhood onwards, both of them adored adventure and the natural world. Neither had money; both were exceptionally good-looking – and both bubbled over with enthusiasm for plants.

Lachen was a pretty mountain village, set in conifer and rhododendron forests. It had wooden houses and shingled roofs above broad eaves, with fine carved woodwork round the windows and doors, and a gold-topped Buddhist monastery to confirm that this was not the Alps. It was dark inside, and smelt of incense and dirt. Grotesque carved faces stared at them from an altar, and the walls were rich with paintings of deities and devils. Before they left, the abbot blessed the whole expedition. He was wearing a yellow silk robe with orange sleeves, like an MCC tie, and red socks and a curious hat, 'somewhere between a boater and a bowler', covered in yellow silk. The porters filed past him, prostrating themselves three times, and he touched each of them on the head. Pallis presented him with a magnificent Chinese painting for the monastery wall. The climbers then went up one by one and knelt in front of him.

They pressed on for the snout of the Zemu glacier, up steep slopes of juniper and rhododendron scrub. Their base camp was set up at 14,500 feet on a mile-wide river of ice fed from the slopes of the high peaks. It was an extraordinary broken place of frozen lakes, vertical ice walls fifty feet high, with patches of earth and sand. Another glacier came down to join it from Kanchenjunga, the mountain itself dramatic as the sun reddened the snows high on it and flung purple shadows into the couloirs that stood out against the translucent blue of the icy slopes.

It snowed at times, and mists blew in, but a burst of sunshine picked out the needle peak of Siniolchu, 'most beautiful and terrifying of mountains', its high slopes and hanging glaciers leading up to the steep flutes of ice couloirs and the summit. Reconnaissance showed it to be beyond their powers. They settled on Simvu, which had never been climbed before. A Bavarian expedition had come close but failed, leaving one of its climbers buried in a rocky outcrop in the Zemu glacier. It was a complicated massif, with several tops, the highest at 22,360 feet, and a variety of possible routes.

They crossed the Zemu and climbed the moraine of the Simvu glacier in early May. The weather was bad with much snow and sleet. On 10 May, they were beginning a reconnaissance when it started snowing hard at 9 a.m. and they had to lay up for the day. Stormbound in their tents, they talked about war, and the differing colonial powers, French, British, Dutch. Freddy pondered his 'job in life': he thought he would go to Tibet and 'think things out' for five years, and then 'organize a new movement in schools'. He had his self-doubts: 'my own character is not high enough I fear'. It was all too easy to put the world to rights from a warm sleeping bag at 17,000 feet, he admitted, but there was an understated and very English idealism to these young men in their tents amid the ice and driving snow. They agreed that education was to blame for most things that were wrong. Schoolmasters should change and 'teach the spirit of Christianity' without 'such deadly emphasis on rituals'. If they did that, and 'implanted an abiding horror of war', the world would be changed in ten years.

These were not idle conversations. The shadows were darkening: they had passed the Italian troopships at Suez, Hitler was in power in Germany, Spain was sliding into civil war, and, beyond Tibet, the Chinese were already exposed to the ferocity of the Japanese militarism that would catch up with Freddy soon enough. If a man is to survive a very long period of extreme and solitary stress, he thought, he needs inner forti-tude of soul. He had no time for doctrine – he had an instinctively English aversion to -isms.

They spent several days probing the massif, always foiled, until they found a very steep nose of ice that led to an arête running up to the summit. If they could climb this ice-wall, the mountain might 'go'. It was 'a most horrible place'. They had to get round a corner, where the ice was near-vertical, and then up twenty feet of steep ice, which fell away below at a greater and greater angle until it dropped sheer to the glacier. It took Pallis a good hour to cut foot and hand holds up the corner. This was technical climbing beyond Freddy's capacity to lead, and he was the last to follow. He found it 'very exposed and airy'. He had to overcome his natural desire to cling close to the ice, and instead stand well away and maintain his control and balance, oblivious to the void below his crampons.

They were exuberant as they arrived on the final arête: 'it seemed that the summit was ours'. They ate sardines and prunes, and calcu-lated that they should be able to reach the summit peak and be back in camp before dark, and that anyway there was a full moon that night. Then, 'horror'. A great gash lay across the ridge, a crevasse twenty feet wide and thirty feet deep running into the void at the end. It was unclimbable. They retreated quickly as snow blew in and clouds formed.

As they went down off the glacier, they met a young Englishman, Jock Harrison, a subaltern in the Punjabis who had set out on a climbing trip with another Indian Army officer, who had fallen ill. Harrison now joined up with Jake Cooke, and Freddy agreed to continue climbing with them.

He had first to confirm his place on the British mission to Tibet. He went down alone to Lachen on his way to see Gould. It had been winter when he came up to the Zemu. Now it was fully spring, and he came down heathered slopes with 'alcoves full of snow' to hillsides covered with azaleas and scarlet tamarisks, and pale yellow rhododendrons, growing four feet high at that altitude. From Lachen the trail on to Gangtok was rough, with many twists and turns, with a fall of 7,000 feet and a climb over the pass of 4,000 feet. Gould held a garden party at the Residency for the Maharajah of Sikkim. Tibetans in scarlet hats did an arm-in-arm dance that Freddy thought the 'very image of the Palais glide'. Gurkha police played bagpipes. After tea and sandwiches on the lawns, they went down to the Maharajah's palace for dinner, and Freddy showed pictures of Greenland.

It took him two days to get back to Lachen, riding a little white pony that left him so saddle-sore that it hurt him to sit down for several days. He helped Pallis pay off the porters who had brought the equipment back from the base camp. He found it melancholy to see how the passage of expeditions had corrupted them. They saw the sahibs as creatures of apparently limitless riches, who casually gave or threw away boots, ropes, packing cases, tents, sleeping bags and other pieces of treasure, simply to avoid the bother of taking them back to Europe. That, in turn, made the porters lose their sense of value. They overcharged, they blackmailed climbers into paying more by staging goslows on the march, and yet, Freddy said, 'they are thoroughly good fellows at heart ... We have only ourselves to blame.'

He now walked 100 miles in forty-eight hours to catch up with Cooke and Harrison, who had set up camp on the Upper Lhonak glacier. This was on the Tibetan border, in the extreme north of Sikkim. A cone of ice and snow, Pyramid Peak, swept elegantly to 23,750 feet above it, with a 22,890-foot summit called the Sphinx on the same ridge. Both peaks were unclimbed. To get up onto the ridge they had first to climb the Langpo La, the curve of steep rock and ice slopes that abutted the glacier below the peaks. The ridge then ran south to the great massif. Ten miles to the east of it was another mountain of great beauty, the Fluted Peak, also unclimbed, which they would attempt if they had time.

It snowed hard on 31 May, and they rested. Harrison, an old Indian Army hand, had brought a sheep with him. They had become rather fond of it, but they butchered it and had excellent kidney and mutton chops for lunch. Freddy spent the afternoon collecting flowers and birdwatching. This was one of the favourite haunts of the 'snow men' – the yetis – whom the locals said lived high on the slopes. They visited a yak-herd whose tent was at 17,000 feet, his yaks and sheep grazing a thousand feet higher at the snow-line. He said he had not seen a snow-man yet this year, but came across their tracks from time to time.

The weather was bad for June. It snowed most days and avalanches were 'continually roaring' from the high slopes. The climbing season in the Himalaya is brief. A window of a month to six weeks of good weather lies between the spring snows and the arrival of the monsoon in mid-June, with another short gap between snow and extreme cold in September.

It was still unsettled on 5 June, clouds swelling in the valleys and the peaks obscured by snowstorms. The three of them set off with the porter Ang Nima. Avalanches had streamed down the steep face up to the Langpo La all night, but they had stopped by daybreak. They were able to kick steps up the firm snow in the couloirs. The 'terrifying roar' of an avalanche broke above them as they were spread out across a snow gully. They were lucky. It roared away down the next couloir a few yards away, and they traced its progress by the white cloud of snow crystals that followed it as it ran far out across the glacier before it stopped.

They resumed, Cooke and Harrison leading on rock, Freddy on ice and snow. The face was at the limit of their ability. They went on only because they were getting perfect belays in the hard packed snow, so that they were anchored well enough to hold the leading climber if he fell. A fine stream of snow poured off the rocks as Freddy cut steps in the last ice couloir. The final pitch onto the La became too steep, and they had to traverse and work their way through tangled seracs at the snout of a hanging glacier. A sloping shelf led on to the La. After eight hours of hard climbing, they had made little more than 800 feet. The gale was screaming over the top of the La 200 feet above them. They had shelter where they were, so they made camp on the shelf, digging out a flat platform for the tent.

They were off at 6 a.m., Freddy leading. Even before he reached the top of the La, he had to crouch and cling to his ice-axe to avoid being blown off. Nothing could survive on the La. They retreated to their camp. Their food was running short, the wind was blowing up again, and Freddy bowed to reality: 'We simply had not the porter-power to lay siege to a peak of such magnitude as the Pyramid.'

The Sphinx looked possible, though. They climbed on two ropes next day to save time, Cooke and Freddy on the first rope, Harrison and their porter Ang Nima on the other. The world was wondrous. Everest, Lhotse and Makalu were above the clouds far to the west, 'like a rim to a flat world', other peaks hid the Tibet highlands, and the Lhonak plateau was a brown and green oasis amid the snow and ice of the glaciers, whose lines of high ice pinnacles were like 'sails in a yacht race'. The ridge sloped down steeply before rising again to the Sphinx. They kept to the crest so as not to be swept off by avalanches. Harrison fell into crevasses twice but the rope held him. At an awkward break in the ridge they had to cut steps up the side of a very steep ice block. They were safely up with only Ang Nima to follow. He fell twice. Three of his friends had been killed on Nanga Parbat in the same way, he said, and he refused to go on. The wind was getting up, so they decided to go back to the tent and try again next day without him.

It was calmer when they got under way at 7 a.m. They made good progress, retracing their route, with the last part of the arête going easily. They reached the summit of the Sphinx at 11 a.m. The descent was difficult for tired men – 'personally I am always more frightened when descending', Freddy said, and the history of climbing accidents since the first conquest of the Matterhorn proves him right. Several times one or other of them fell through the melting snow bridges over the crevasses when they were back on the glacier. The ropes pulled them out safely. Back at base camp, he spent two days collecting plants, finding sixteen species of primula. Most miraculous of the delicate and luminous plants he encountered were the translucent blue petals of mountain poppies, which brought tiny brilliants of colour to the grey of ice and rock.

They set off for the Fluted Peak on 11 June, walking along the meandering bank of the Langpo Chu. Once they were on the mountain, the weather closed in. The rope had soaked up moisture from the snow and now iced up 'like a wire hawser'. They reached a very sharp but horizontal snow ridge. The sun had been on the ridge all morning, and the snow was too rotten to take their weight. The leader sat astride it, pushing off the top two or three feet of snow, so that they could dig their ice-axes into the firmer layer of ice and snow beneath it. They had decided earlier to turn back at 2 p.m. at the latest. Even this supposed that the weather stayed fine. It was now after 2 p.m. and it was beginning to snow.

They were still some distance from the summit, and the going looked difficult. Freddy's was the casting vote. He thought it a 'reasonable risk' to continue, provided the descent was rapid. Cooke went on climbing up the snow arête, the debris of ice and snow he chopped at with his axe spinning into the void down both sides of the ridge. Mist swirled over them. Freddy could no longer see Cooke though a stream of snow and ice crystals fell back on them from where he was working. He had made a tunnel through a rotting cornice. Freddy crawled through this to 'an unpleasant place where the angle of the ridge became vertical'. Cooke had to sweep away the loose surface ice and snow and then cut holds for hands and feet 'for a perilous ten feet'. The final fifty feet brought them at last to the 'blunt, mist-shrouded summit'.

It was a bad place to be. It was 3.30 p.m., for they had taken over ten hours to get there, and it would be dark in three hours. The snow was now falling steadily. Freddy was the last man up. They were only a moment at the top. Cooke lowered Freddy and Harrison down the last vertical pitch on the rope and climbed down himself. As they made their rapid descent, Freddy went through a mental checklist of how to get down a mountain safely: 'lean out on steep slopes . . . keep the rope out of the way . . . hold one's ice-axe so one can stop oneself or hastily throw a loop over it and hold the others . . .'

For all that, he nearly died. He was traversing a rock face to get on to the snow, which was easier and safer. He was feeling his way past 'an enormous flake of rock' when it came away and hurtled downwards: 'I was just able to jump to one side, catch hold of another rock and pull myself on to it until I found footholds. Meanwhile the flake rebounded over the rocks below and an acrid gunpowdery smell reached me.' They unroped when they reached the snow – the rope had frozen and was difficult to coil – and raced down the final slopes of scree, yodelling to alert the porters. They reached camp just as darkness fell at 6.30 p.m., 'deliriously happy', and slept for ten hours.

They thought of trying a last climb, of Korayedu, but monsoon clouds piled up against the wall of mountains between Sikkim and Tibet and rain squalls splashed down on their oilskin capes. A brief rent in the cloud shrouding Korayedu showed two evil-looking hanging glaciers with a brutal rock buttress between them. They went down into a valley and bathed in a warm lake. A willow-warbler nested in a juniper bush. They came on stones built into what seemed a grave with bones inside it. Two big Tibetan mastiffs rushed at them and were called off with wild cries and stones from a yak-hair sling by a smiling and toothless yak-herd. He said that it was a trap for snow leopards.

Next day a postman from Lachen brought letters for them from England. They enlisted him as a porter-guide for the return to Lachen. Next day they rose to the singing of skylarks, and a bathe before breakfast, and set off. Freddy noted a good-looking woman washing wool in the stream, her hair put up in a great semi-circle on a frame studded with coral and turquoise. Dogs slavered to get at them as they passed, held back by yak-herds. In a jade-green lake, with banks of golden sand, yaks stood dewlap-deep in the water, reminding Freddy of paintings of Highland cattle. The high snowfields were covered by cloud, but avalanches streamed down the rocky walls below them.

From Lachen, Freddy had to get to Gangtok to join Basil Gould and the mission. He left the village at 2.30 a.m. A mile or so out, he heard 'something or somebody' following him. Every time he stopped, the footsteps stopped, too, but he could hear breathing from time to time and once a stick snapped loudly. He felt it could not be a man, but a bear or a langur monkey. He went faster, and it did too. He started to run, and he felt it was gaining on him. He flashed the light behind him. He could see nothing, only hear distinct sounds, padding feet and heavy breathing. He became 'more and more panicky', running as fast as he could, shining his torch and shouting. He fell at a sharp corner of the track, falling into bushes. He was unhurt, but he lost his torch. Then, suddenly, he saw the absurdity of his plight, and he began to laugh. He did not look for the torch – he was afraid of leeches – but he was certain that the animal, if that it had been, was gone. He heard it no more. He was told later that bears and langur monkeys did follow people, but more out of curiosity than desire to do them harm.

He reached the Residency at Gangtok at 8 p.m. He had covered the fifty miles of trail, dropping 7,000 feet and then climbing 5,000, in less than eighteen hours. The Alpine Club called it his 'famous marathon run', for the trek normally took four days.

CHAPTER 5

THE MISSION

'BJ', as he called Gould, was going to keep him very busy in Tibet, he wrote back to England. 'I have to take film, and still photos, do bird, plant and bug work, some survey, and personal work for Gould such as ciphering and deciphering telegrams, etc.'

The mission had an imperial purpose. The last Dalai Lama, the senior priest-king of Tibet, had been an Anglophile. He had sent boys to school in England, and encouraged a British school at Gyantse. He had, however, died in 1933. The next incarnation – the present fourteenth Dalai – had not yet been found. The Tashi Lama, the next most holy of the lamas who ruled Tibet, had quarrelled bitterly with the old Dalai and had fled to China. The Tibetans were now imploring him to return, for spiritual life was devastated without either of the two highest lamas present in the country. Tashi said he feared for his safety if he returned, and said he would only do so if he brought an escort of 300 Chinese troops with him. The Tibetans had long experience of Chinese treachery and invasion. They feared the Chinese would use the Tashi to subjugate the country, and refused him permission to return with Chinese soldiers. It was hoped that Gould might broker a compromise, and maintain British influence and prestige. A brigadier, Philip Neame, an Olympic shooting gold medallist who had won a Victoria Cross in 1915, was in the party to advise the Tibetans on military matters. Two young signals lieutenants had a radio to keep in touch with the Government of India.

They left for the Holy City of Lhasa at the end of July 1936. Gorge followed gorge, with 'beetling walls or naked tumbling screes', the noise of mules and muleteers drifting on the night air when they halted. Freddy filmed the mule trains moving along the 'vile track' by a tumbling mountain river. Little sparks of colour stood out against the stones and mud, lavender-coloured campanula, and periwinkle gentian and deep magenta pedicularis. The country changed as he went higher, and he found the 'real Tibet of my imagination': treeless, a waterfall streaming from a rocky cleft, hundreds of yaks on the valley floors, and blue smoke drifting from the dung fires of the herdsmen, who sat naked to the waist eating tea and tsamba, roasted barley meal, from wooden cups. Prayer flags snapped in the wind, and the great dun plateau sloped up to meet the 'Sienna-scarred hills'.

They reached the great fort at Phari. In front of it a lake of cerulean blue lay where none should be – 'it can't be and it isn't'. As he approached it turned into a carpet of forget-me-not and aconite. High above him wheeled lammergeyers and a harrier, while hundreds of mouse-hares watched him from their burrows. Bhutanese traders mingled with the Tibetans, wilder-looking, with robes that went only to the knee, like kilts, and straight swords in silver sheaths. A few years back, they had been attacking mule trains and plundering villages and monasteries. The Phari bungalow shared a cobbled courtyard with a post office, at 15,000 feet, Freddy thought, the world's highest. Tibet was still entirely feudal, and Freddy was amused by the displays of obsequiousness. Servants greeted their superiors with bowed heads, and inhaled their breath sharply, so as not to pollute the air the mighty one was breathing, whilst repeating 'la-les', 'yes sir', with a high-pitched sob.

The village was squalid. Dung lay about in great heaps, the lanes were deep in mud, and skinny curs foraged in the piles of rubbish so high that they blocked some of the ground-floor windows. The women smeared blood on their faces against the sun and the wind, and wore headdresses in the hooped local style, or triangular shapes from Lhasa. Their homespun robes were universally dirty. The bazaar sold bricks of Chinese tea, mirrors, junk jewellery, cooking pots and wooden tea cups. The dzongpön, the fort commander, was as colourful as the village was drab. He invited them to tea, with the 'perfect natural manners' even minor officials displayed, and exquisite dress. He had a long silk robe of violet, with a white silk shirt and the long turquoise and gold earring worn by Tibetans of importance. His hair was in two plaits held by a scarlet ribbon: the British, frustrated at Tibetan bureaucracy, said that even their officials' hair was tied up in red tape. He wore a conical hat of white parchment with red tassels hanging from it like a lampshade.

Freddy was up at 4 a.m., to peer at Chomolhari, a 'forbidding black cone ... incredible', whose height and grandeur gave it a beauty he had only seen before with the Matterhorn. He put on gym shoes and ran up a hill to get a better view, putting up blue hares and a fox. The north and east faces looked unclimbable, but he had a good view of the long southern snow face. It was not too steep, though cut by several ice falls, and before it was lost in the clouds he thought it 'might "go"'.

He rejoined the party to press on for Lhasa. He was saddle-sore, since his pony would only go at a fast trot, and threw him up and down. He practised his Tibetan as he rode. The 'scarified red hills' paled into amethyst in the distance, the landscape washed like a watercolour, with brilliant white snow peaks beyond the bracken and russet of the foothills, and deep violet cloud shadows. They arrived at the government bungalow in Tuna just in time to avoid torrential rain, and to find lunch waiting for them. In the afternoon, he stalked an animal – 'a wolf? a snow leopard?' – but lost it. He ran down scree slopes to talk to an astonished muleteer, his pigtail tied over his tattered felt hat to stop it blowing off in the wind, and quizzed him in fractured Tibetan about the gods of Chomolhari.

Between supper and bed, in a tent since the bungalow was small, Freddy's activities had an agreeably domestic air for a man at 14,950 feet on the Tibetan plateau: 'Pressed flowers; had a Tibetan lesson; listened to a German concert on the wireless.'

Love for the flora and fauna of wild places is an absolute constant in Freddy's life, but he was not a 'twitcher'. He had no list of birds or plants to tick off, no record to beat, no boasts of numbers seen. His knowledge was immense but unassuming. It covered people as well as animals: he wrote anthropological notes on Eskimos, Lapps and now Tibetans, and he was to do the same with the jungle aborigines in

Malaya. The mindset he had been exposed to as a child saw exploring in the fullest sense of the word: enquiring, probing, mapping, noting. The explorer, and the traveller, were expected to observe: the feat of the journey was secondary to the enlightenment gained and passed on. His diary entry for 20 August captures this to perfection. He rode sixteen-and-a-half miles in heavy rain, along the shores of Yamdrok Tso, the 'lake of the upper pastures', fifty miles long and almost as wide. Prayer-walls and rock frescoes abounded by the road, and dzongpöns rode out to greet them with scarves. More than a thousand pack animals passed them going south, half of them yaks, which avoided the track and took to the roughest terrain. He saw a grebe's nest floating on the lake, with many goosanders and an old fish-eagle sitting on a post. A pair of black-necked cranes strutted in a marsh. Exquisite coloured Buddhas were carved into the rocks, which were covered in places by deep blue and violet delphiniums three feet high. A ruined fortress built on a point in a lake, like a Scottish castle, marked the village at Pede Dzong. Here they camped on a flooded field beside the fortress, and then 'spent two hours doing Tibetan, and stayed up until eleven pressing flowers'.

The picture – the hard-as-nails adventurer spending his evenings pressing periwinkles and wine-coloured primula – is vivid, almost comical. But it links him directly to Banks, as his careful skinning of birds connects him to Darwin, if at a lesser level. And his interest in the whole of the habitat about him, evinced here in his learning Tibetan, also improved the odds of his survival amid the Japanese in the jungle.

He did not like all Tibetans, though he 'wished he could'. As they got closer to Lhasa, he went to a monastery with red and ochre walls in a side valley. He found the monks 'hostile, inscrutable', of no use to themselves or others. They had no charity to others, and did nothing to heal or minister to them. They used their status to 'aggravate and exploit' the superstitions of laymen.

The trail went on past ancient ruined forts and houses, some razed by Bhutanese and Tartar invaders, others abandoned during epidemics of smallpox. Six coolies went past carrying a generator, chanting a 'haunting dirge' to keep in step. A little later another coolie came up with a basket with three black-and-white cocker spaniels, on their way to Lhasa as a personal present from the Viceroy of India to the Regent of Tibet. A few willow groves by the streams were the first trees they had seen for a week.

Freddy was enchanted as he rode his pony along the rocky track to see the Holy City unfolding below him, set on a level plain with a winding river and groves of willows and apricot trees. The Potala, the Dalai Lama's monastery-palace, soared above the level Lhasa plain on a ridge of rock, its massive walls adding in tier after tier to the sense of height, topped by the golden pagodas over the tombs of the dead religious rulers which gleamed in the early morning light through the haze of smoke from yak-dung fires and incense burners. There was colour and decoration on every surface. Each pony in the Dalai Lama's stables had its own fresco in its loose box. By contrast, he saw 'men and women just squatting in the streets like dogs, in indescribable filth . . . floods cover the waste ground beside the road, the water dark and slimy'.

He went to official luncheons with thirty courses, sliced yak tongues, fish abdomens, sharks' fins, sea slugs, washed down with draughts of chang, barley beer, served by girls he found 'remarkably pretty', in ankle-length dresses of purple brocade, and with triangular crowns of seed pearls and corals on their lustrous black hair.

After a little, he became restless in Lhasa, and found himself a journey. It became a characteristic, even in the jungle. Exhaustion and extreme discomfort gave him much 'vicarious pleasure', he admitted. The reason, he thought, was clear: 'Our sensibilities and characters were made to be sharpened against the hard faces of Nature.' Few people now had the chance to test their endurance to the breaking point, to 'feel cold fear gnawing at their hearts', or to make decisions on which life depended. That was why men 'flocked so easily to war', to 'test a manhood that is perverted by the present state of civilisation'. Dangerous sports – climbing, skiing, motor-racing – were 'but makeshifts for this vanished birthright, narcotics to alleviate the monotony of existence that has become too safe and easy'.

The trip he now made, in mid-winter, was to accompany one of the mission's army officers part of the way on his return journey to India, and to meet up with another arriving to take his place. They set off in a December sandstorm. The wind whipped up a river they had to cross, and they had to wait until it calmed a little. The ferry was half full of ice and it was tricky getting the ponies on and off it. Freddy's eyes were badly inflamed from the driven sand. The cold and violent winds continued, whisking sand devils 1,500 feet into the air. Post runners jogged past, the bells tied on their spears jingling to their motion. He had a grand farewell dinner with the officer in the guest-house at Nangartse. The room was warm and snug with smouldering sheep-dung fires, and a glass window looked out over the darkening plain 500 feet below. They had tomato soup, chicken with fried potatoes and carrots, cherries and custard, and whisky.

On 20 December he went along the track to meet the new arrival, Major Finch. A huge black yak passed him with a wild-looking driver in a sheepskin hanging loose off one shoulder despite the cold, with coral and turquoise and a charm box hanging from his untidy pigtail, and a black beard. He was turning a prayer wheel as he rode, and carried an old prong gun across his back, with prayer flags tied to the prongs fluttering in the wind. He looked, Freddy thought, 'like John the Baptist'.

A pair of horsemen appeared. Freddy advanced 'with a "Dr Livingstone I presume?" feeling'. He saw that one rider was wearing Wellington boots, and rightly concluded it must be Finch. He found him 'just the man for the job ... tremendously interested in everything, already a great admirer of the Tibetans'. Freddy had found a soul-mate. They rode together towards Tremlung, nattering happily 'about everything under the sun, from polo to politics'.

Freddy and Finch sent their ponies on ahead and stalked three snow-cock, big grey birds with striped flanks and orange-red beaks and tails like black-cock. They ran off clucking when Freddy closed within twenty yards to photograph them. A vicious gale and dust-storm whipped up before they reached Chaksam. They stayed in a lovely old house, in a dark and ancient altar-room with a rack of sacred books, and a collection of prayer wheels, charm boxes and chang pots. Freddy found one of the girls of the house to be 'extremely beautiful'. Her skin was filthy, and her cheeks coated with black pigment to protect them against sun and wind. Her hair was full of dust and straw, and her homespun robe was engrained with grease and filth. Freddy was smitten, though: 'she has perfect features and eyes like a gazelle,' he noted in his diary. He went for a walk, thinking of her, through groves of willows, poplars and walnuts, and watched a family of laughing-thrushes and a hoopoe.

He was back in Lhasa for the celebrations of the Tibetan New Year, which fell on 12 February. Freddy doubted that more than one or two living Europeans had ever seen it. Its high points were the Great Lama Dance and the Devil Dance, which was held in the great eastern court-yard of the Potala. Freddy photographed the high officials as they turned a sharp corner on their ponies on the zigzag ride up to the northern gate of the Potala. The Regent was dressed in yellow and vermilion silk, with a large yellow hood so that the camera caught the merest glimpse of his face and his dark glasses. The great courtyard was full of soldiers in old armour, in plumed headdresses or hats with black-tail feathers streaming from them like Italian bersagliere. They broke into war dances, firing their ancient muskets and flintlocks, the courtyard misty with smoke and acrid with gunpowder. Bursts of sound came from the great trumpets, and gongs and cymbals, pierced by the more strident notes of small trumpets. The 'Laughing Buddha' walked across the courtyard, pausing every step with a foot raised, in a vermilion gown and a monstrous grinning mask, a rosary round his neck. It was medieval, like some fantastic Hollywood production.

The mission returned to India the same month, February 1937: the Tashi Lama died on his way back to Tibet. The present Dalai Lama, the fourteenth, was found the same year. He was only two, and the Regent continued to rule until 1950.

Freddy had 500 plant specimens for the herbarium at Kew, seeds, and many observations on birds. On his way back, he rode for several days within sight of the 24,000-foot Chomolhari. The name means the 'Divine Queen of Mountains'. It is a sentinel peak, soaring 10,000 feet from a dusty and wind-scoured plateau to mesmerise with its height and remoteness. It was ten miles as the raven flew from the summit to

Phari, the bleak village at its foot. Looking at it from there on the way to Lhasa, he had thought that the southern ridge might 'go'.

Whilst he was in Calcutta, contemplating his return to England, Freddy thought longingly of the mountain. He doubted he would be allowed to climb it since it was one of the holiest places in Buddhism, but he went to Kalimpong in April to ask permission from the Maharajah of Bhutan. To his surprise, it was granted. He had met Charles Crawford in Calcutta, who had taught at Sedbergh and was now working for Imperial Chemicals in Calcutta. He had no serious mountaineering experience, only some scrambling in Skye and the Pyrenees, but he was very fit, Freddy liked him, and there was no one else. He persuaded him to come, though he had to be back in Calcutta by 23 May.

Crawford got to Kalimpong on 6 May. Freddy had managed to borrow or buy most of the climbing gear they needed. The cost worked out at £19 12s 6d each. That included the small amount of equipment they had to buy, all the food, pay and cigarettes for porters and three Sherpas, transport and the hire of mules to Phari and back, photographic film, and 'bungalow expenses', the rest-houses and meals en route. The Everest expedition that was taking place at the same time, for which he had been rejected as inexperienced, reached only 23,000 feet at a cost of thousands of pounds. He was particularly amused by a pressure cooker left behind at Kalimpong by Eric Shipton, who had been on the 1933 Everest expedition. Shipton had said that he would rather be without his sleeping bag than this elaborate machine, which looked like 'a diving helmet with a steering wheel and valves attached'. Freddy noted that it had cost more than his whole expedition.

They left Kalimpong on 7 May, climbing over the Natu La Pass to reach Kargyu monastery. Freddy knew the abbot from the year before. They chatted away – 'my Tibetan was quite good in those days' – and the abbot first laughed and then became sad and serious when Freddy said he wanted to climb Chomolhari. He asked why, and when Freddy said it was to see the goddess who lived there, shook his head and warned that she would throw him off. Messages were waiting for them at the telegraph office in Yatung, from Lhasa and the Maharajah of Bhutan, confirming permission for the climb. An ad hoc little climbing party would normally never be allowed onto a most sacred peak. Freddy's charm had delighted the Tibetan government and the Maharajah's advisers alike. It was 14 May before they got to Phari, leaving desperately little time before Charles Crawford had to be back in Calcutta.

As they scrambled up the outer foothills to find the best approach, the mountain was hidden by clouds. They heard an 'intermittent roaring' coming from its flanks, as violent winds battered the higher slopes. In the afternoon, the sky suddenly cleared and they saw Chomolhari towering above them. Giant crevasses and ice-falls gave way to almost perpendicular final ice slopes in the 3,000 feet below the summit. It was a vision of impossible beauty: the mountain could not be climbed on this face.

They skirted round to the southern ridge of the mountain next morning. The local porters had returned to Phari, and so they were carrying loads of eighty pounds each. The path led so steeply down that they had to lower themselves with handholds on the birch and rhododendron bushes. They came out in grassy fields with patches of deep purple *Primula royalii*. Three yak-herds gaped at them by an old barn but said nothing. A trout stream meandered along the valley bottom with grassy fields and willows with yellow catkins. Freddy watched a buzzard mewing and then an eagle whirled down on it with a 'tremendous whizzing noise', its wings tucked back for speed. The two birds flew acrobatics across the brilliant sky as they chased one another, in earnest or in play. They climbed out onto a ridge. Four hours of very exhausting climbing brought them to 17,500 feet, just below the snow line, where they set up camp.

It dawned calm and fine next day. Freddy could see down to the dark valleys of Bhutan, and a finger of light caught the summit of Chomolhari, making it glow 'like the crater of an active volcano'. They roped up for the first time and climbed a sharp snow ridge with belts of crevasses on either side. It led to a dome marking the southern end of a long snow and ice ridge. Cloud came down at 11 a.m., and they were forced to camp. The sunlight was so diffused by the cloud that they had no depth of vision despite their snow goggles.

They had three Sherpas. Two of them, Nima Thundup and Kikuli, had been on Everest and Kanchenjunga, and a third, Pasang Dawa, who was younger. They left Nima alone at the camp with the two larger tents. He was a chain-smoker, and the oldest of them, and too unfit to go higher. Freddy and the others set off as the sun was rising at 4 a.m. They climbed to a point where the ridge narrowed and was cut by large crevasses. To their relief, the narrow snow bridges between the ice walls and crevasses were holding firm. A fluted, knife-edged ridge of hard blue ice led upwards with huge drops below it. It was too severe technically, and the exposure too tremendous, for an inexperienced party.

On its left a couloir with huge flakes of fallen ice like tumbled séracs offered a way up. In places they had to cut hand- and footholds up the steep edge of the flakes. The snow was knee-deep and the air thinning with the height. They panted three breaths to a step. The glare of the sun produced an inertia Freddy called 'glacier lassitude'. Kikuli spat blood whenever they stopped and huddled in the snow. It was worrying that the better of the two remaining porters was ill, but Pasang was going 'like a warhorse', though Freddy had to teach him how to use his ice-axe and the rope. They went up several ice-ridges to a ledge about 800 feet up the couloir, where a vertical ice-wall blocked the route. A sérac had fallen away from the wall, and they were able to climb its side, scooping fresh snow off it as they progressed. Another steep ice-field lay ahead for another 800 feet, with a broken ice-fall below the final arête.

They were exhausted, with Kikuli on the verge of collapse, but it was unsafe to camp for fear of avalanches. Freddy led for another hour up a steep snow slope where they sank almost to their waists. They worked they way to the eastern side of the south face, to a saddle 100 feet from a sheer drop off the mountain to the valleys below. It was the only place safe from avalanche, unless the whole face came down. They camped at 3 p.m. at about 20,000 feet.

Freddy was awake at 3 a.m. next day, 19 May, and out of the tent at 5 a.m. Only Pasang responded when he called. Kikuli stuck an arm out of his tent and poured a cupful of blood into the snow. He refused to leave his sleeping bag. Freddy examined him and found it was nothing internal but his gums that were bleeding. He went on with the other two, leaving Kikuli in his tent, and they climbed towards a short but almost vertical ice-wall. The glare off the new snow stripped the skin from their nostrils and lower nose, and left their faces and lips raw and bleeding. They worked their way up the eastern side of the slope, sometimes cutting steps as it grew steeper. It became clear that they could not get up the ice-wall from here. Crawford was 'completely used up' and Pasang was down to a crawl. They went back down to the tents.

It started to snow again as they reached camp. They were lucky the new snow did not avalanche, for the slopes were steep and it had not compacted and was lying loose. Crawford had to return to Calcutta and Kikuli would go no further. It dawned fine on 20 May. The conditions were good enough for Crawford and Kikuli to go down alone whilst Freddy sorted out his gear for summiting with Pasang. They took a bivouac tent, a 100-foot rope, two pitons – he was always very precise, knowing the calamity the lack of a single piece of kit could bring – double-eiderdown sleeping bags, primus and paraffin, pot and mugs and spoons, a tin-opener. Their rations were three tins of sardines, one of herrings and one of tongue, two pounds of pemmican, four half-pound slabs of chocolate, oatmeal, butter, a brick of tea and sugar.

Freddy and Pasang retraced their steps up and then worked their way further east on the face, to see if they could find a way to force the ice-wall where it met the rock. They found a fallen flake of ice leaning against the ice-wall, which was a vertical twenty feet high at this point, with a gaping bergschrund below where the ice was split from the rock. Freddy cut foot- and handholds up the edge of this ice for two hours. He managed to get onto the slope above it, where the ice was easier. Clouds started forming around them as they cut steps up the steepening slope with their axes.

The blizzard came on them from the west, in one moment wrapping them in snow, lashed by a 'maniac wind', as they curled up over the ice-axes for protection. They could not move. Freddy's nose and cheeks began to get frostbite, but he dared not take his hand out of his glove to rub them. It thundered, though they saw no lightning. After two hours, he knew they would freeze to death where they stood if they did not get shelter. It was impossible to retreat down the ice-flake in this tempest. He made out the dark shadow of a sérac just above them. Though it was a steep climb up, he thought they could dig out a platform at its base for the tent, and the sérac would protect them from avalanches.

They were at a height of about 21,500 feet. The tent had a faulty zip fastener and whenever it swelled in the wind, the entrance was torn open and snow blew in. Freddy secured it with safety pins and they crawled into their sleeping bags in all but their boots. They fell asleep, grateful to 'be alive at all', until they were woken by the cold dampness as the snow on the tent melted with their body heat and soaked their sleeping bags. The sérac kept the avalanches off, as Freddy intended, and snow slithered down it onto the tent, half-burying it and insulating it against the blizzard.

It was a beautiful morning, windless and sunny, when they got under way at 4.30 a.m. They worked their way across to a red outcrop of rock that separated the snow slope from a 'tremendous rock precipice'. Then they kept to the edge of the slope, going up between rock outcrops. The going was good. They had a perfect climbing rhythm – 'kick, pause, step; kick, pause, step' – and they moved steadily up the 2,000-foot slope, pausing to belay one another on the rope only where it was particularly steep or icy. They reached the top of the slope just before midday, after seven 'most exhilarating and enjoyable' hours of climbing. Chomolhari's isolation allowed them to see vast distances in all directions. To the south, they made out the valleys of Bhutan, steep and wooded. Unconquered Everest and Makalu, made yellow by distance, stood out above the snows to the west.

They were, though, on the false summit of the mountain. The actual summit was another 500 feet above them and to the north. A sharp, snaking ridge separated them from it. It was very exposed. On one side it fell almost vertically to a frozen lake thousands of feet below, and on the other a drop almost as severe down walls of ice and snow. The wind was getting up from the west, with the tatters of cloud that presaged a blizzard. It was 'questionable' whether it was wise to go on – and Freddy's body had no desire to do so – but they did. It was quickly done. The last 300 feet were up a snow slope that was steep only at the very top. A triple ridge of snow marked the top. They shook hands, and Freddy took Pasang's picture. They stayed five minutes. Clouds were drifting in from the west 'with icy breath' now. He hurried to leave, and get down the knife-edge summit ridge.

As they got off the ridge onto the slope, Pasang fell and slid past Freddy, pulling him off on the rope. They fell very fast, 'occasionally bouncing on outcrops of ice', face first at times, at others on their backs. Freddy failed twice to get the point of his ice-axe into the snow to check their fall. He knew that the slope soon became so steep that he would not be able to stop, and would hurtle off the edge of the rock band at the bottom and fall 3,000 feet down the face into Tibet. Then he managed to dig his axe in, and they came to a stop: 'I lay still for several minutes, choking, gasping, fighting for breath.' Pasang lay still a few yards from the rock band at the edge of the precipice. They had fallen four or five hundred feet, but both were unhurt.

They were back in the camp at 3 p.m. They made some tea, but spilt it and were too tired to make more. The little platform they had cut out for the tent was precarious. Freddy thought it safer to go on down and camp below the ice-fall. A blizzard struck when they had climbed down about 300 feet and were immediately above the ice-fall. The route down it was too perilous in white-out conditions. They waited an hour, ever colder and more miserable, and then began to climb back up to the ice platform. 'I had no strength left at all,' Freddy wrote. 'That climb of 300 feet back to our ledge is one of the most dreadful memories I have.' When they got there, they fell asleep and had to rouse themselves to put up the tent in driving snow. Pasang had broken his goggles in the fall, and his eyes were watering. He groaned and sobbed all night. His boots were frozen solid in the morning – he had slept with them under his head – and they had to use the stove to thaw them out.

It took them several hours to get down the ice-fall. Pasang kept falling. Freddy had to cut steps down, and then climb back up to belay the Sherpa on the rope as he went down. Even so, Pasang's rucksack burst open during one fall, and their only cooking pot and much of the food hurtled away on the long drop to the glacier. They came to a belt of crevasses and the snow came on before they could cross them.

They were forced to camp, though it was only 11 a.m. The situation was grave. Pasang, splendid on the ascent, was 'now only a passenger'. Freddy was still fit, but his face was badly burnt and his lips had lost all their skin. When he slept they stuck together and bled badly when he opened them. Their matches were now finished – bad planning – and they could not use the primus.

The nights, he said, 'were awful'. They would fall asleep at once after camping early. The cold would wake them, and they would think it the next morning, then find it was only midday. This repeated itself in the afternoon, and by the time darkness fell, he would no longer be tired and could not sleep. Instead he shivered as if he had 'the ague'. He was a connoisseur of uncomfortable nights, he thought, and had had his fair share in blizzards on the Greenland ice cap and on splintering pack ice at sea. For 'sheer, interminable, shivering misery', though, 'I have never known anything like those six nights in our bivouac tent on the slopes of Chomolhari'.

They made little progress on 23 May in snow that they sunk in up to their thighs, and they had difficulties climbing down the gully. They were too wet and miserable to worry much about food. Freddy found he could melt snow on his boots for drinking water, because their black surface heated in the sun. The night was 'mere shivering misery'. It took them time to get going on 24 May. They came to a belt of crevasses, so heavily covered in snow that only the widest were visible. Freddy probed carefully with his ice-axe at the narrowest point on the first one they came to. He found that it was about five feet across. It was bridged by snow but Freddy doubted that it would bear his weight, and decided to jump it. He spoke carefully to Pasang in Tibetan, though neither of them was fluent in it, and explained what he was going to do. He told the Sherpa to be sure to give him enough rope to get across. He was in mid-air half-way across the crevasse when there was a violent jerk as the rope came tight, and he fell thirty feet into the crevasse. Pasang was pulled towards the crevasse, but the deep snow slowed him like a dragging anchor, and the rope cut into the snow. After slithering further down, Freddy came to a halt. He was hanging in the void, with no bottom to the crevasse in sight, snow in his nose and mouth, and the rope crushing his chest. In the article he wrote for *The Times* he said that 'I cut a ledge on which I could stand if I pressed myself against the opposite wall.' In his book, *Memoirs of a Mountaineer*, he expanded on that:

> I tried to swing far enough to one side to get a footing on a ledge which protruded from one wall of the crevasse, After several attempts I managed, as I swung by, to grapple the ledge with my ice-axe and then to hold myself there by jamming the fingers of one hand into a crack in the ice, while I cut away the top of the ledge to make a place large enough for me to stand.

He was able to unrope and Pasang pulled his rucksack to the top. He roped up again, and realised 'with horror' that the crevasse was not narrow enough to climb out by cutting steps on both sides and strad-dling it. He remembered that he had read that it was impossible to get out of a crevasse by cutting steps up one wall, but had no alternative. He began to climb, cutting feet and hand holds in the hard blue ice of one side of the crevasse. It was 'desperately hard work . . . a task which I suppose is the most difficult I have ever attempted'. It took him an hour for each ten feet he climbed, for he had to descend to his ledge several times for each step he cut, and the ones he shaped for his fingers got broken by his boots and had to be recut. After three and a half hours, 'I at last put my head over the lip of the crevasse'. He found Pasang was sitting in the middle of the snow bridge, less than six feet from the hole through which he had disappeared.

They got through the crevasse belt into the amphitheatre. It began to snow heavily, and they had to make a camp. Freddy had strange dreams in a troubled sleep, finding himself at a ceremonial feast in a large Tibetan monastery, and putting cones of rice into the folds of his robe before slipping out to give it to two miserable men, 'half dead from exposure and starvation', on the glacier outside. He was woken by fits of uncontrollable shuddering, the wet tent wall clinging to him.

They were away early next day, and went rapidly down to the lake. They slept there until they were woken by two women who were singing as they called their yaks back to their farm. They took them in – a lama was sitting on the floor chanting Buddhist scriptures, and a handsome Bhutanese girl was weaving a bamboo basket – and gave them yak curd and cheese and Tibetan tea. They slept twelve hours that night, to the tinkle of bells from the yaks tethered in the fields.

It rained hard on the twenty-mile trek on to Phari. It was dark with driving mist and snow when they woke the watchman at the rest-house. He took them for ghosts, thinking they were dead. Crawford feared so, too, and had organised a search party. They hired two mules and rode on next day for Yatung. A dinner party was held for him when they arrived. The Viceroy had sent a telegram of congratulation. The *Daily Mail* had somehow heard of his triumph, and wired him with an offer for exclusive rights to the story. 'Lone Briton conquers Queen of the Snows,' it splashed. Freddy was more circumspect when he wrote for *The Times* on 26 July 1937: 'A Himalayan Conquest: 24,000 Feet for £20'.

An after-dinner speaker at a climbing club in England called Freddy's safe return from the mountain the 'Eighth Wonder of the World'. There were soon doubts and sarcasms, however. It has to be said that his account of his fall into the crevasse was almost certainly one of what his friends called his 'divide by two and call it nearly' moments. If the crevasse wall was vertical, as he said it was, it would not have been possible for him to have climbed it by cutting steps. A modern ice climber, wearing the latest 'Rambo' crampons with front as well as vertical points, and with hand ascenders, 'Deadman' holding plate, 'Turbo-Express' ice screws and ice flutes, harness and a light, short-shaft ice-pick in each hand, would be hard pressed. Freddy makes no mention of wearing crampons. He had one unwieldy ice-axe, a single rope and just two pitons. Had Pasang sent him down another rope, and he had made rope stirrups, with one boot in each, he might have made some progress, by lifting one boot, tightening the rope on it, then lifting the other, and so on. No mention of that, either. The likelihood is that the crevasse wall sloped, at a fearsome angle for an exhausted man, no doubt, but it was not vertical.

Had he got to the summit at all? Crawford and the two experienced

Sherpas had given up. Pasang was young, inexperienced and very shaken: he told a Nepali-speaking friend of Freddy's that 'I lost all love for my body, but the sahib brought it back safely.' Several of the photographs he took on his Contax camera were spoiled in the fall, including the picture of Pasang on the summit.

It was thirty years before the whispered doubts surfaced in print. Two articles claimed he had lied: one by August Gansser in *The Mountain World* and the other in *Les Alpes* by Rudolf Hanny. Two mountaineering writers of repute, D. F. O. Dangar and T. S. Blakeney, looked into the evidence. They published their findings in the *Alpine Journal* of November 1967. They concluded that Gansser and Hanny had simply disbelieved Freddy: they had no other grounds for dismissing his claim to have reached the top. A crucial factor was Freddy's diary entry on seeing the summit:

> There was this long ridge of snow falling sharply on each side, then a final hour's plod up steep snow to the summit. The latter is a three-pointed ice ridge, one pointing towards Campa Donga and the third towards Tuna, whose rose-coloured hills appeared now and then between fleeting cloud.

This was an accurate description, and Freddy could only have written it if he had got that far. Dangar and Blakeney also arranged for Pasang to be interviewed. 'He promptly volunteered his recollection,' they reported, 'of how they reached a false summit (at first hoped to be the real one) and had had to go along the ridge to the true top – which is just what Spencer Chapman says.' Pasang was by then one of the 'Tiger' Sherpas, a most respected man who had climbed with Sir Edmund Hillary, the conqueror of Everest, in the 1950s. Dangar and Blakeney concluded that 'Spencer Chapman's diary and the printed accounts based upon it, must be regarded as fully authentic records of a mountain adventure.' They added that Gansser and Hanny might reasonably now be required to explain their suggestions. Instead, there was silence. The *Alpine Journal's* vindication was never challenged.

He sailed back from India on 12 June 1937. He got little done on the voyage – 'I met a woman on the boat,' he told Crawford, 'a married one unfortunately, husband in India' – though he was contracted to write a book on the Lhasa mission by the end of September. His publishers wanted another book, on Chomolhari, in the New Year as well.

That winter, he was invited by the Courtaulds for a cruise in the Dutch East Indies. He set off to join them, sailing third class on a French ship. He was the only Englishman aboard, with 'half-caste Dutch Javanese who can think of nothing but women ... a woman from Martinique, another from Tahiti not up to romantic standards, and several French prostitutes'. He detested snobbery – 'the way the 1st and 2nd class passengers look at one' – and when he was invited up to the New Year's Eve ball on the first-class deck, he in grey flannel suit and they in dinner jackets, the women 'even refused to dance with me'. They docked in Singapore on 14 January 1938. He flew next day to Surabaya towards the eastern extremity of Java to join the *Virginia*, the Courtauld's graceful yacht, with only five guests aboard. It was his first glimpse of the jungles, mountains, paddy fields and rubber estates of South-East Asia. He sailed back from Penang to England, writing his book on Lhasa during the voyage.

He bought an MG on his return, and crashed it. He tried for a job teaching at Eton, but they turned him down as they could only have a geography man if he also taught Latin: 'I *ask* you!' He had better luck at Gordonstoun, a revolutionary new school in Scotland founded by Kurt Hahn. His Cambridge friend Bobby Chew was a master and Freddy was invited up to lecture. Hahn convinced him that 'the only useful outcome of my life so far is to harness it to teaching ... Expeditions are narcotics'. He offered him a housemastership, and to put him in charge of expeditions, as well as teaching geography, history and English. Hahn had put the school near the sea – 'they sail their own boats to the Shetlands and Norway, etc' Freddy wrote excitedly – and close to mountains.

In the Easter holidays in 1939 he led a school expedition to Lapland. Talk of war had reached the Arctic. 'Annoying to think that Bicker and I, and some of the boys too, may be cannon fodder in six months time,' he wrote. His timing was accurate. The war was close, and 'Bicker', his fellow-master Robert Bickersteth, would be killed in it.

CHAPTER 6

TO WAR

Back at Gordonstoun, Freddy joined the Seaforth Highlanders as a Territorial. He was sure that war was coming. At the end of the summer term, he sailed for Canada to see his brother Robert before it broke out. Ever short of funds, he got himself taken on as second steward on a wheatboat for pay of one dollar. He cut short his trip as the crisis unfurled. He sailed back on the first transatlantic convoy of the war, and reported to his regiment. He must, he said, be 'the most ignorant lieutenant in the army'.

The army, though, recognised his talents. His Arctic experience fitted him for a secret ski battalion being formed to fight with the Finns, whom the Soviets attacked at the end of November 1939. The unit assembled at Aldershot under the cover name of the 5th Scots Guards and was sent to Chamonix for intensive training with the elite Chasseurs Alpins in the French Alps. It was brought back to Glasgow and was to sail for Finland when the Finns capitulated.

Freddy returned to the Seaforths. He was then sent back to Chamonix, this time to find a training area for a mountain division that was to be formed to fight in Norway. He was on Mont Blanc on 10 May 1940, his thirty-third birthday. At 4 a.m. that day, Adolf Hitler arrived at the Felsennest, the Nest in the Rocks, his field headquarters hidden in the forests of the Eifel. The assault on the West started an hour or so later. The blitzkrieg had begun to overwhelm France as Freddy made his way back across it.

He did not fancy rejoining the Seaforths for a second time with his tail between his legs. He managed to get a posting to a Special Training Centre that was being formed on the west coast of Scotland. Bill Stirling, his brother David and a few others had been cooling their heels waiting further orders after the Germans overran Norway. None came. Forgotten by the army, they lived as guests of the Stirling family in a large country house outside Stirling. They shot and hunted, blew up trees for practice, rock climbed and trekked with full packs across the rugged country. Eventually, their existence was recognised, and they were merged with SOE, the Special Operations Executive, a covert organisation set up by Churchill in July 1940 to wage irregular warfare. Their new role was to set up a school to train staff for other schools that would prepare men for guerrilla operations in enemy-occupied countries. They set themselves up in a fine old country house on an estate overlooking Loch Ailort. Jim Gavin, a climber in the Royal Engineers whom Freddy knew, was in charge of demolitions. Major the Lord Lovat, a cousin of Stirling, was the fieldcraft instructor. Freddy was also a fieldcraft expert.

A mission was sent to set up a training school in Australia. A regular officer, 'Mad' Mike Calvert, was in charge of demolition, with Freddy for fieldcraft. They sailed in October 1940 via the Panama Canal. The two became close friends. Calvert found Freddy a strange mixture. He 'talked like a liberal and acted like an anarchist', and Calvert was amused at how quickly he switched between the two. 'One minute he'd be talking about snow buntings in the Arctic, the next how to strangle your adversary in unarmed combat.' He even taught his pupils how to distract an enemy's attention by making a bird call, and then killing him. Calvert, as a professional soldier, was impressed by the amateur's speed of thought and his toughness. Ashore in Colon, at the entrance to the canal, they saw a group of Panamanian policemen beating up an American sailor. Freddy piled straight into the police, catching them off balance, and the American got away.

The training area was on Wilson's Promontory, which runs out from the southernmost point of Victoria into the Bass Strait. It was ideal for teaching fieldcraft, with every sort of ground, dense forests of eucalyptus, bush, sand dunes and swamp, and grassland and rock, sweeping up almost 2,500 feet to the top of Mount Latrobe. Freddy, with his

Seaforths kilt, his good looks and his public-school accent, was a red rag to the Pommie-mocking Australian trainees. They were further outraged when he chose the distinctive call of the British tawny owl as their rallying cry. He was, though, tougher than any of them. He outran them, outclimbed them, and outshot them. He set a record of two-and-three-quarter hours for climbing Mount Latrobe. An Australian beat this by thirty minutes to general delight. Freddy at once set out for the top and completed the climb in one-and-three-quarter hours – a time that was never beaten – and came down at a canter. He was, too, a master of his art. He taught how to live in the wild, how to make shelters, how to make traps and find food, how to navigate by the night sky, how to read tracks and avoid capture. He was 'the best man at all forms of fieldcraft' that Calvert ever knew, and Calvert, who went on to command a Chindit brigade in Burma, knew many.

Whilst he was there, Jim Gavin was posted to Singapore to start a new Special Training School, No 101 STS. He arrived in May 1941. Here he met Colonel Alan Warren, a tall Royal Marines officer. Warren knew the East – he had served his first tour in Shanghai in the 1920s – and he had experience of special operations, having run secret courses for British businessmen working in foreign cities and ports where military intelligence could be gathered. Gavin found a site for the school at Tanjong Balai, a headland at the mouth of the Juron river on Singapore Island. It had a vast and luxurious bungalow with ornate Chinese pavilions on lawns that swept through palm groves to the sea. He requisitioned it from an Armenian millionaire who had made his fortune in wildcat tin mining.

Gavin asked for Freddy to be sent from Australia to be his Number Two. He arrived in Singapore on 8 September 1941. It was at peace, relaxed and laissez-faire – 'anything also can' in the 'Singlish' spoken by Singapore Chinese – in a world at war. The white flannels of cricketers stood out against the luscious green grass of the Padang in the heart of the city. Officers and their wives went to the 1,300-seat cinema in the art deco Cathay Building – *How Green Was My Valley*, filmed in a Hollywood replica of a Welsh mining village, was the great hit of 1941 – and danced in the ballroom at Raffles Hotel, or drank stengahs, whiskies and soda, round the mighty pool of the Swimming Club. The soldiers' quarters were light and airy, and the officers' mess in the Tanglin barracks looked out onto a golf course and the orchids and bougainvillea of the Singapore botanic gardens. In Kuala Lumpur, always 'KL', planters up from their estates dined in the 'Spotted Dog', the Selangor Club, built in black and white 'tropical Tudor' style.

The Japanese were fighting in China – they had seized Peking in 1937, with the notorious massacres at Nanking following a few months later – and by now they held much of coastal China and Vietnam. They were also looking south, to British-ruled Malaya, rich in rubber and tin, to Singapore with its great harbour and dockyards, and to the oilfields of the Dutch East Indies. Their intelligence was brilliant. Almost half the fish landed at Singapore came from Japanese boats, whose skippers surveyed the coast and took soundings off the beaches. The photographic studios in many Malay towns were run by Japanese, who took pictures of roads and railways and military camps as well as the usual family portraits. Japanese ran chemists and hotels and taxidermists. Other Japanese owned barber shops. At the well-known Yamashita Hairdressing in Bishop Street in Penang, they cut the hair of British and Australian troops, listened to the gossip, and appeared in Japanese uniform after the invasion. An army colonel, Tsugonori Kadomatsu, worked as a waiter in the British officers' clubs for six years, listening to the chatter and gleaning valuable tidbits. Japanese companies mined iron ore, bauxite and manganese on a large scale.

The British were alarmed enough to set up a Japanese unit of the Singapore Special Branch in the mid-1930s. There were warning signs. The manager of a Japanese rubber estate next to the new big gun emplacement at Pengarang Point protecting the dockyard was a 'former' Japanese naval officer. The press attaché at the Japanese consulate was discovered taking the planning chief of the Imperial Army HQ in Tokyo on a tour of strategic locations.

On its idyllic little headland, 101 STS trained men in small arms, explosives, wireless, ambush tactics and small-boat handling. Freddy handled the fieldcraft. The explosives instructor at the school was John Sartin, a sapper sergeant, who had joined the army as a boy bugler when he was fourteen. Sartin was one of the first men to serve under Freddy in his new guise as a military man. He lumped officers into two camps, ex-public schoolboys and those who had worked their way up from the ranks. Freddy should have fitted into the first slot, but Sartin found that he did not. He was, he told Ralph Barker, entirely different from any other officer he had known. He treated him as an equal. Almost as soon as he met him, Sartin said, Freddy was 'round in the barrack room, sitting on the bed, talking to us. He was a man you could talk to. Whatever the problem, he'd sit there and talk it out with you.' He found Freddy 'unpredictable and slightly disjointed', but 'when he was actually working, the job was all he thought of. He became a professional.'

They were well supplied with weapons and lightweight explosives. They had tommy-guns, whose bursts of firepower made for an effective jungle weapon, and they made their own special timers for the explosives. Wireless was the great weakness. The few Mark I sets they had were designed for short ranges in Europe, not for the greater distances in Asia. The sets were lightweight, but designed for mains electricity. Heavy generators and petrol had to be carried, not ideal loads in steep jungle.

Gavin and Freddy worked out a detailed plan to raise 'left-behind parties' of men to be sited throughout the Malayan peninsula. The planners were confident that a Japanese invasion of northern Malaya would be held by regular troops, with the aircraft based on the large up-country airfields. If the British were forced to give up ground, they could fall back on the impregnable fortress of Singapore, before counter-attacking within six months when reinforcements arrived. This scenario envisaged a period when left-behind parties of men trained at the STS could attack the roads and railways used by the Japanese. Men, though, were in short supply. The STS had ten officers and forty other ranks, some of them specialists in explosives and wireless. Gavin and Freddy wanted each party to be led by an army officer trained in irregular warfare, with European civilians who knew the country and the languages, and carefully selected Chinese, Malays and Indians. The Chinese were in a slight majority over Malays within Malaya at the time, with Indians making up about ten per cent of the population. The Malayan

Communist Party (MCP), almost entirely Chinese, was eager to help. It was well organised, and its members were highly motivated.

The plan was turned down flat. The authorities had no intention of enlisting the help of Chinese 'subversives'. British planters and tin miners were needed at work, not playing war games in the jungle. The very word 'left-behind' was thought to be defeatist and bad for morale. Freddy trained parties for Hong Kong, French Indochina, Burma and southern Thailand, but none for Malaya. The best he could do was train some local planters and police. He found them excellent material, a far cry from the 'whisky-swilling whites' of legend.

Rumours of war swirled ever fiercer. A cartoon in the *Malaya Tribune* on 3 December showed a Japanese soldier in nappies learning his ABC. The paper spoke of 'short-sighted, buck-toothed little men' who 'neither by land nor sea nor in the air have even a glimmer of victory'. But it was the British who were blind. Japanese bomber pilots flying from Saigon were over the dark jungles of Johore in the pre-dawn darkness of 8 December, two hours before the attack on Pearl Harbor, when they picked up the glowing lights of Singapore. Dockers were already at work unloading a brilliantly lit freighter. Freddy was fast asleep in the partitioned main bedroom of the millionaire's bungalow. He shared it with Gavin, who was awakened by what he thought was distant thunder. When he realised it was bombing, he roused Freddy and they stood at the window watching the raiders. The street lights remained switched on and no sirens were sounded. At 6 a.m. Radio Malaya announced that Singapore had been bombed and that Britain was at war with Japan.

Far to the north, on both sides of the borders of Malaya with Thailand, the Japanese 25th Army was pouring ashore from its invasion fleet. Two British Indian divisions advanced to meet them. They took heavy casualties and retreated. At dusk, the battleships *Prince of Wales* and *Repulse* and four destroyer escorts left Singapore to intercept the landings. The squadron, Force Z, had no air support. The Japanese had tanks ashore the following day. They helped capture Kota Bahru not long after noon. General Tomoyuki Yamashita, the Japanese commander, began a powerful drive to seize the vital road and rail junction at Jitra.

The British expected the Japanese to be vulnerable to air strikes as they advanced, but the RAF's Brewster Buffalo fighters were obsolescent and easy meat for the Japanese, while at the big RAF base at Butterworth, all but one of the Blenheim bombers were destroyed on the ground as they manoeuvred for take-off. On the third day, *Prince of Wales* and *Repulse* were both sunk by Japanese bombers. 'In all the war,' Winston Churchill wrote, 'I never received a more direct shock.'

British forces on the ground well outnumbered Yamashita's 25th Army. But the Japanese now had total air and sea supremacy, and their battle-hardened troops had tanks – and better tactics. British planners thought that Malaya's mountain spine, its rivers and the 'almost impenetrable jungle' would make 'well nigh insuperable barriers'. Instead, by 12 December they had thrown the British out of Jitra. On the east coast, they followed the railway down through the jungle. To the west, they used the excellent, well-surfaced main roads and the network of gravel and earth roads on the estates and to the tin mines.

One- or two-man patrols with submachine-guns led the advance. They were followed by groups of sixty to seventy men on bicycles, making a steady eight to ten mph, each man with seventy to eighty pounds of equipment on his cross-bar. If the 'stalker scouts' drew fire, the men behind them infiltrated the enemy positions and attacked their flanks and rear. When the British counter-attacked, the lead Japanese units allowed them through and fell on them after they passed. They used makeshift rafts to infiltrate beyond the front on the fast-flowing rivers. On the coast, they leapfrogged British positions by landing parties of troops from launches and fishing boats they had seized. They made clever use of noise, one or two men letting off firecrackers and shouting and howling to simulate an attack whilst the real one came in quietly from another direction.

The accelerating disaster led the High Command to reverse its ban on recruiting Chinese for 101 STS. Japanese atrocities in China had long inspired the overseas Chinese to support resistance with blood and treasure. Huge sums of money were sent home. Japanese imports were boycotted, and fish from Japanese trawlers was ruined with kerosene. Money was collected door to door. Chinese prostitutes sold red flowers for the cause in the streets, a campaign known as the 'fragrance of the chrysanthemum sisters'. The communists put aside the struggle against capitalism and British colonialism, under the slogan 'All for anti-Japanese'. They were eager to be trained at 101 STS, and Freddy was keen to have them. Special Branch officers in Singapore had kept close surveillance on communists whom they suspected of subversion and fomenting strikes. Some had been arrested. It was now suggested that they were released and trained at the school. A meeting between Freddy and the Secretary General of the MCP was arranged by Special Branch for 18 December.

By then the front in Malaya was collapsing. The Japanese had taken the large airfield at Alor Star early on 14 December. They found porridge, still warm and ready to serve, amid the glowing silver on the table in the RAF officers' mess. They flew in aircraft later in the day, fuelled them with British aviation spirit and armed them with the British bombs they found neatly stored on the airfield. By evening, they were dropping them on the retreating enemy. Next day, Yamashita set up his headquarters in Alor Star and invited his staff officers to dine in the abandoned officers' mess. The remnants of the British Indian 11th Division were dying or seeking to surrender in the rubber plantations.

Penang, the 'pearl of the Orient', was the place where the British adventure in South-East Asia had begun in 1786. It was a magical island, home to every race and influence in the East: Arab, Malay, Chinese, Tamil, Bengali, Siamese, British. The air was rich with the scents of their spices and cooking and, in places, with the sweet smell of opium. It was freighted with temples, mosques, churches, with the Eastern & Oriental, the 'E & O' with its hundreds of yards of sea frontage and domes and balconies, the 'Premier Hotel East of Suez', with rickety wooden shophouses and rattan weavers, joss-stick makers, woodcarvers and fortune tellers.

The island was all but defenceless, the troops transferred to the mainland. Japanese aircraft came in waves and attacked at will, so low the pilots could be seen as they machine-gunned the streets and markets. Five thousand were killed and wounded. Fourteen operating tables in the general hospital were working at once. Anaesthetic ran out. The firemen trying to control the blazing city thought that Japanese pilots were targeting them. Sixty of the 200 on duty were killed. Japanese radio broadcasts taunted the British. 'You English gentlemen. How do you like our bombing? Isn't it a better tonic than your whisky soda?'

The order to evacuate Europeans came in the night of 16 December. They gathered at the E & O, though many were ashamed and angry at abandoning staff and servants. The main quay was cordoned off by armed volunteers. Only Europeans were allowed through. Survivors from the *Prince of Wales* manned the ferries evacuating the women. There was no British officer left to surrender the island. Instead, it was the Indian editor of the *Straits Echo* who lowered the Union flag at Fort Cornwallis. News of the surrender of the town was delivered by a Eurasian racehorse trainer who cycled twenty-one miles to Sungei Patani on the mainland to tell the Japanese and to ask for the bombing to cease.

That day, Freddy went to a meeting in 'a small upstairs room in a back-street of Singapore'. Also there, he wrote in *The Jungle is Neutral*, his book on his time in Malaya, were a Chinese-speaking police officer from Special Branch and two Chinese, 'one of whom was secretary general of the MCP ... To complete the air of conspiracy, both Chinese wore dark glasses.' It was agreed, he said, that the MCP would provide as many young Chinese communists as 101 STS could cope with, and that after training they could be used against the Japanese 'in any way we thought fit'.

The room was, in fact, above a charcoal shop, a communist safe house, in the shabby Geylang section of Singapore. What Freddy did not mention was that the Secretary General was called Lai Te, and that he was a double agent who had been turned by the British. Lai Te was the only communist present. The other Chinese was a Special Branch officer, Wong Ching Yok. The Chinese-speaking police officer Freddy referred to was Innes Tremlett. He and another officer, G. E. Devonshire, were Lai Te's handlers. There was, as we shall see, good reason why Freddy gave no names, even writing after the war. SOE's successors did not want Lai Te's treachery revealed. For the moment, though, Freddy was delighted to welcome the Chinese to the school. They were, he found, 'young, fit and probably the best material we had to work with'. It was too late to train up mixed parties of British and Chinese. The communists were trained as independent stay-behind parties.

Freddy thought that six was the ideal number for a party, setting up ambushes at night in teams of three, since they could 'move very fast and with practice can almost think and operate as one man'. To pass as Tamil coolies, the British carried dhotis and white shirts with them. They learned to darken their faces and hands and feet with a mixture of lamp black, coffee grounds, iodine and potassium permanganate. The Chinese volunteers who passed through 101 STS had no need of such camouflage, of course. They were guerrillas in the classic sense, part of the local community and indistinguishable from it.

At best, volunteers had a week at the school. John Wilson, a locally based irrigation engineer, had only a day. In the morning, he had a 'short course in tommy-gun, hand-grenade and revolver training, and in the afternoon, a course on explosives, their uses and the various types'. In the evening, after some form-filling, he was issued with uniform and clothes, and arranged for food and arms, ammunition and explosives. Rations were meant to last for three months. Each five- or six-man party was issued with a dozen bottles of whisky and two dozen bottles of rum – Singapore, as a large naval base, was liberally supplied with potent naval rum – and cans of food that were dipped in candle wax to preserve them in the moist jungle. They had bully beef, sardines, condensed milk, sugar, tea, and packets of biscuits and porridge. Fishing lines were issued, and most parties had shotguns and hunting rifles to help them live off the land.

The day after the meeting with Lai Te, Freddy was ordered to hand over control of the school and go to Kuala Lumpur. He and Warren were charged with organising and leading reconnaissance parties behind enemy lines. He asked if he could greet the first batch of thirty Chinese communists nominated by Lai Te. He welcomed them at one of the school's pavilions on 22 December, whilst Sartin drove Freddy's scarlet Ford V8 coupé to the stores and loaded the dickey seat with fuses, explosives, tommy-guns and rations.

Then they drove to Kuala Lumpur. 'It was an ideal way of going to war,' he wrote. 'I felt so like a crusader that when we passed a wayside Chinese temple, I almost suggested that we should go in and have our tommy-guns blessed.' A new training school had been set up in the grounds of a Chinese school in the heart of the city. Police in Ipoh who had been arresting young communists a month before were now releasing them from prison and organising lorries to take them to Kuala Lumpur. The first twenty-strong batch completed the course a fortnight later, and set themselves up in Perak as the first detachment of the MPAJA, the Malayan Peoples' Anti-Japanese Army, on 10 January 1942.

Freddy was briefed at 3rd Corps headquarters on the deepening calamity. The Japanese were advancing on Grik, threatening to cut off the 11th Division in Kedah. A company of the Argylls had fought a gallant delaying action down the Grik road. But the division had had to fall back, and it was now defending a line along the Perak river. It was not expected to hold the river for long. An Australian raiding party, guided by two rubber planters, Frank Vanrenan and Bill Harvey, was planning to make a night landing behind the Japanese lines at the mouth of the Trong river. Freddy said there was no reliable intelligence on Japanese transport and armour and the flow rate of reinforcements. He suggested that he and Sartin cross the Perak river and make their way to the landing beach to meet and brief the Australian raiders. Opinion at advance headquarters, he said, was 'that I was absolutely crazy and ought to be forcibly detained'.

In the end, as we have seen in the Prologue, he had his way. He set off with Sartin in the Ford, crossed the Perak and had first sight of Japanese troops as well as his introduction to the jungle – its tree trunks 'like the pillars of a dark and limitless cathedral', black as Purbeck marble, the vines and lianas looped like the 'crazy rigging of a thousand wrecked ships', and a place so easy to hide in that his confidence soared. He had to abandon the Trong meeting place, and regained British lines by going down the Perak river.

He met up with Vanrenan and Harvey back in Kuala Lumpur, and they spent the night of 30 December swapping stories. He enlisted them, together with two other planters, Richard Graham and Boris Hembry. Freddy worked on a plan for stay-behind parties, basing it on the fact that the main road and rail links from northern Malaya down south to Singapore pass through an area fifty miles wide between Kuala Lipis to the east of the Main Range, the mountainous jungle spine that runs down the Malayan peninsula, and the Slim river to the west of the range. He proposed setting up bases on both sides of the mountains to harass Japanese troops and convoys as they moved south.

Freddy set off on New Year's Day 1942 with Harvey and Sartin to find a site for a stores dump on the far, eastern side of the Main Range. He was going to look at the country round Tras – 'Teras' today, a little town of dusty forecourts selling small tractors and mechanical hoes, and food stalls and repair shops. Japanese bomber pilots were flying constant low-level missions looking for targets, and several of them picked up the red Ford as it sped northwards along Route One, the north–south trunk road that runs clear down the west side of the Main Range. Freddy was lucky that there were rubber estates along the highway in the sections where the bombers attacked, and he was able to drive the car off the road into the trees.

At Kuala Kubu, he turned right on to the small road that rises dramatically up the Main Range. It swirls through virgin forest in great S-bends, clinging to the side of the slopes, so steep in places that the car is at tree-root level on one side of the road, and almost above the tree-tops on the other. Short bridges and culverts cross streams and water-falls – the road is little changed – and families of monkeys play chattering by the tarmac. At the top is the Gap, at 2,793 feet, the pass that marks the border between Selangor and Pahang. A road goes north from here, in another elegant sweep of bends, rising another 1,500 feet to Fraser's Hill, a resort of half-timbered hotels and tea-rooms, and English lawns and gardens, cool and cloudy with a softer humidity than the sticky heat of the plain. It is single-track, and in peacetime, when people came up from Singapore and Kuala Lumpur for a weekend of golf and drinks and chatter, the cars drove up and down at alternate hours.

The bungalow next to the Gap rest-house belonged to E. O. Shebbeare, the chief game warden of Malaya. Freddy drove up the short drive and found him in. They had met in the Himalayas, and Shebbeare had just been surveying jungle routes into Thailand with SOE. Freddy thought his jungle expertise would help to offset his own ignorance of the tropics. Shebbeare volunteered to join the group later and mentioned an Australian gold mine near Raub as a possible place for a camp.

Freddy drove on down the east side of the Gap, the jungle of Pahang stretching away to the east and the South China Sea in ever deeper purple until it seems at last to become part of the sky. After Tras he took a small side road that ran for five miles to a hydro-electricity plant by the Sungei Sempan (*sungei* is 'river' in Malay) which supplied power for the gold mine at Raub. The pipeline that carried the water for the turbines ran steeply up into the jungle on the flanks of the Main Range. Small paths led up to Fraser's Hill and down to Raub. The power station was run by a Eurasian Tamil, Alves, whom Freddy found 'immediately helpful'. It was characteristic for people to help Freddy, not just now, when a European with a scarlet car full of weapons still retained his prestige, but later, when he was a fugitive, and a member of a defeated race whose acquaintance spelt death if uncovered. Alves promised to lend Freddy his Sikh foreman and fifteen coolies to carry stores up the pipeline into the jungle. Freddy found the place so perfect a hideout he decided on the spot to make a self-contained operational camp here: 'If things got too much for us on the other side,' he said, 'we could simply walk or bicycle over the Gap road and start work again.'

He left Harvey and Sartin to oversee the stores dump. He was machine-gunned from the air twice on the drive back to Kuala Lumpur. The Japanese pilots were close enough to killing him for him to stop at Kuala Kubu and smear mud all over the V8's sparkling scarlet paint.

Next day, Freddy drove up Route One with Vanrenen to sniff out a site for the camp on the western side of the Main Range. He drew blanks round Kuala Kubu and Kerling. The towns sprawled out from the main road and the railway stations, with lanes and houses mixed with vegetable gardens running up to the rubber estates. He was luckier four miles from Tanjong Malim. A side road led to a derelict tin mine. Plank bridges had been dismantled to stop the Japanese from using them. The planks had been left lying, though, and Freddy found that it was just drive-able when he replaced them. This was old tin-mining country, called tin-tailings, where the soil and subsoil had been stripped off to the red laterite below by the tin miners' high-pressure water pumps. Freddy said it was like 'a landscape in the moon', and it remains a barren place, more Martian than lunar, with the laterite scars showing red and ochre through a thin scrub of bracken and grass, and the surface scoured into gullies and rivulets of mud the colour of burnt sienna. The softer hues of Straits rhododendrons and ground orchids are all but swallowed up, but Freddy noticed them.

The Sungei Salak, the Barking river, lies two miles up the track. A few Chinese houses stood among patches of bananas and tobacco and vegetable gardens. Freddy noted that there were 'only Chinese here, which augured well for the security of our camp'. There is a touch of hindsight in that remark. Freddy did not yet know that the Japanese would try to gain the allegiance of Malays and Indians, if half-heartedly and fitfully, whilst consigning the Chinese to torture and massacre.

Isolated little settlements like this were common, a few houses with tin roofs and vegetable gardens next to a stream, reached by a dirt track on the edge of an estate or in the valleys that drift slowly up into the Main Range. Two of the Chinese here were *towkays*, the word for merchants that also covered those with a few acres of rubber or palm-oil, and small-scale tin mining. Freddy warmed at once to Leu Kim, 'small, shrewd, humorous', a businessman and rubber-estate owner who had fled to the jungle when Tanjong Malim was bombed. The other, Leu Fee, was an illicit tin miner. Both were friendly, and offered to use their coolies to move stores from the end of the motor track into the deep jungle.

From the derelict mine, a bicycle path led across more tin-tailings to the foot of a pipeline that ran up for several miles in steep jungle to the headwaters of the Sungei Bernam. Freddy sited the camp a short distance up the pipeline. From the head of the pipeline, it was only ten miles east to a footpath that Freddy's map showed running to the Sungei Sempan gold mine dump. As the crow flies, the two camps were only fifteen miles apart. Men, though, would have to climb 4,000 feet of steep jungle to get across the Main Range. Freddy wanted to open up a jungle track to connect the two camps, so that one could shuttle between them without touching a road. 'In our innocent enthusiasm,' he admitted, 'we even planned to have a private hill station half-way across.' Here, if without the whisky stengahs and thé dansants of the real thing, they could still have a vegetable garden and come for sanctuary if the Japanese were closing in on the main camps, or they needed some rest.

Freddy drove back to Kuala Lumpur that night, leaving Vanrenan to make ready for the arrival of men and stores. He spent the next two days getting stores, weapons and explosives together. They could not drive by day because the Japanese had total air superiority, and they were cruising above the main roads, barrelling in to strafe and bomb anything they saw moving.

On 3 January, the British abandoned Kuantan on the east coast. The Japanese sprang a trap on the withdrawal route inland to Jerantut, falling on the 2/12th Frontier Force Regiment with such ferocity that only forty men survived. The Jerantut road ran on westwards past Raub and the Sungei Sempan base. The enemy were closing in. Freddy ordered Graham and Hembry to join Vanrenan at the Sungei Bernam tin mine camp. On their way, they met two old planter friends, Bob Chrystal and Bill Robinson, and told them what they were up to. Both of them at once volunteered to join a stay-behind party, though they were middle-aged First World War veterans. The Medical Officer who examined them doubted their sanity, but passed them A1 physically.

By the end of the day, two more volunteers had joined them: a New Zealander, Frank Quayle, an ex-miner from Thailand, and Clarke Haywood, a Royal Navy Reserve officer, who was working with a big electricals company in Kuala Lumpur. Another group was formed under Captain Stubbington RE, another STS-trained ex-Thailand miner, who had been in an abortive SOE mission to seize positions there, but had managed to get out. He had been in Malaya since the 1920s and knew the area round the Raub-to-Benta road well, and this is where he sited his camp. A further recruit was Pat Garden, 101 STS-trained and a Local Defence Force (LDF) officer. His party got Chrystal, Robinson, Quayle and Haywood.

Gavin acquired all the stores he wanted: food, uniforms, arms, equipment, medical supplies, and some large rubber bags to bury them in the jungle. It was a race to stock the hideaways before the Japanese arrived.

The trucks were constantly strafed and three were lost, though the drivers survived. Both the Garden and Stubbington groups left Kuala Lumpur on 4 January. They ran into the exhausted troops of 22 Brigade, packed nose-to-tail in trucks on the Bentong-to-Kuala Lumpur road. They had fought their way out of Kuantan on the east coast, but the Japanese had now made a seaborne landing on the west coast near Telok Anson, and the brigade was being hauled off to try to contain it. Garden found Bentong crammed with troops, in tents among the rubber trees, or sleeping in trucks and abandoned bungalows. The hospital was full of wounded. The police station was empty and there were no local civilians. Small groups of fleeing European civilians arrived from the east coast, mixed in with the tail of the retreat. They made their way to the rest-house but it was already full with brigade officers and Garden's men.

Garden headed south on Route 9 to Karak, where he set up a hideout in the jungle west of the road. Stubbington's party went north towards Dong, beyond Raub. Stubbington had three tin miners, Rand, Pearson and Darby, and a Malay volunteer, Shuka Bin Uda. They were later joined by another volunteer, Lieutenant Elkin. They left on 6 January in a car crammed with supplies and a wireless receiver. But eleven miles from Raub, Stubbington found the bridge destroyed by retreating troops and had to take to a bicycle.

Gavin drove to Vanrenan's tin mine with stores on 5 January. Tanjong Malim was full of field guns hitched behind trucks and troops moving up to a new defence line at Slim river. Most of the townspeople had fled or were behind locked doors. The planters were all in the Volunteers and the Club was empty. The military hospital was being evacuated. The railway station had been bombed, and the wounded were carried on stretchers along the track to a waiting Red Cross train. He found his way to the turn off the main road and drove as far as he could. A gang of coolies was waiting to carry the stores into the jungle. Gavin told Vanrenan that Freddy hoped to join him within a day or two, and certainly no later than 16 January.

When Gavin got back to Kuala Lumpur, the first group of trained Chinese under a senior communist, Tan Chen King, was ready. Their SOE liaison officer was Richard Broome, a former district officer in Ipoh, and he was joined by his friend John Davis, who had been a senior officer in the Malay Police.

On the moonlit night of 6/7 January, Japanese tanks drove down the bright tarmac of Route One on the Argylls' positions north of the Slim river at Trolak (now Terolak). The Scots held them for two hours, without armour or air support, but their losses forced them back. The rear defences did not know of the Japanese thrust. The Slim river road bridge fell intact to Japanese tanks and infantry. A terrible slaughter now began among the rubber trees and oil palms. Two brigades were annihilated. The Japanese took 3,200 prisoners, and acquired a treasure-chest of what they called 'Churchill supplies', hundreds of British trucks, heavy and anti-aircraft guns, ammunition, food and medicines.

A bout of fever had prostrated Freddy on 6 January: 'I had a terrible pain behind the eyes, ached in all my joints, felt alternately boiling hot and freezing cold, and ran a high temperature.' A blood test showed he was suffering from 'benign tertiary', a virulent form of malaria, but, as he would find, by no means the worst. News of the collapse on the Slim river swept Kuala Lumpur next morning. Freddy sent a message up Route One by despatch rider to Vanrenan saying that they should meet at the Escot Estate bungalow if the bridge at Tanjong Malim was blown. The rider came back to say that the bridge was already down, and that he had been unable to get through.

Freddy had no way of joining or getting in contact with Vanrenan. All he could do was to get back to the gold mine camp at Sungei Sempan, and then, when the fever had left him, walk with Harvey and Sartin over the Main Range to Vanrenan. Before he left Kuala Lumpur, he met Shebbeare, furious because all his books and diaries were still in his bungalow at the Gap. Freddy told him exactly where the gold mine camp was, and Shebbeare said he would join him later. He never saw him again.

He persuaded Gavin to drive him to the gold mine camp to join Harvey and Sartin. They loaded the dickey with explosives, food and whisky. The Ford picked its way through the heavily cratered streets, past wrecked cars and blasted houses, and out through rubber plantations with tented army camps. As they got nearer to the front, the road blocks were heavily manned. Finally, a Sapper officer told them that they had run out of road. His men were about to blow the bridge – they had driven through the British front line, and he expected the Japanese at any time. Finally, the Sapper let them pass, though he said Gavin must be back within two hours, when he would blow the bridge, unless the Japanese appeared first. The trip on to Tras was eerie, with no traffic, no civilians, no troops, a heavy emptiness. When he reached Sungei Sempan, Freddy's temperature was 103. Gavin dumped him and the supplies, and raced back to Kuala Lumpur.

When he got back, he found bumper-to-bumper traffic as people began to flee south – fire-engines, staff cars, wood-burning civilian lorries, motor-cycles weaving in and out. The new supreme commander, General Wavell, had arrived in Kuala Lumpur. He realised that the remnants of 3 Corps would disintegrate if it tried a fighting retreat. He ordered the Australians to form a defence line across Johore from Mersing to Malacca. He gave General Heath, the commander of 3 Corps, seventy-two hours to abandon Kuala Lumpur and fall back behind the new Australian line.

Black clouds rolled across the city from burning fuel dumps, oily particles raining down beneath them. Half-burnt papers drifted on the wind as records and files were heaped on bonfires. Wheels were blown off railway wagons and rail lines and points destroyed. Looters had yet to move through the trim bungalows and fine gardens in the European suburbs. Gavin and his SOE party were probably the last to leave Kuala Lumpur. They strewed the buildings at the RAF airfield with booby traps and mines, laid tripwires connected to grenades, and opened the fuel tanks. As they left, they drove past Pudu prison. It was empty, though soon enough it would hold men from the stay-behind parties. The railway station was on fire. Looters were sifting through the shops. The road south had many cars and trucks, abandoned undamaged when they ran out of petrol. Gavin and his men blew them up until they ran out of explosives.

The Japanese entered the city in the evening of 11 January 1942. Two Chinese with discarded British rifles ambushed and killed a three-man patrol. The Japanese caught and decapitated them.

Freddy was deep behind enemy lines now, and he would remain so for longer than anyone could imagine.

CHAPTER 7

ACROSS THE MAIN RANGE

Japanese convoys had started streaming through Raub, only four or five miles to the south-east, almost as soon as Gavin had left him. None turned up the track, but Freddy had cut it very fine. He lay in the front room of the Alves' bungalow, the fever slowly leaving him, whilst Harvey and Sartin carried stores with Malay coolies up to an atap hut beside the pipeline. They had grenades, tommy-guns, revolvers, explosives, ammunition, a case of whisky, money, canned food, a case of books – Freddy would never be without that – and tents and bivouac equipment. They planned to carry them on up a small stream to a hiding place in a bamboo grove. There were still no Japanese in their valley.

Freddy was woken at dawn on 13 January by the sound of explosions and gunfire in the jungle above the bungalow. He grabbed his tommy-gun and rushed up to the atap hut. It had been plundered. The looters had tried out the grenades and guns after drinking a bottle of whisky. The outside of the hut was riddled with bullet and shrapnel holes, which had failed to set off the 1,500 pounds of high explosive that was still inside it. Most of the materiel was found abandoned close by, but the thieves had made off with the bulk of the hand-grenades, the whisky and almost all the funds, $2,000 in small notes. Freddy found out later that they were members of a well-known Chinese robber gang. They had tossed some of the grenades around in Raub, to intimidate people. Freddy was delighted to hear later that the Japanese had caught them and displayed their heads on poles in the town.

The rest of the stores were moved up the stream, and a camp was

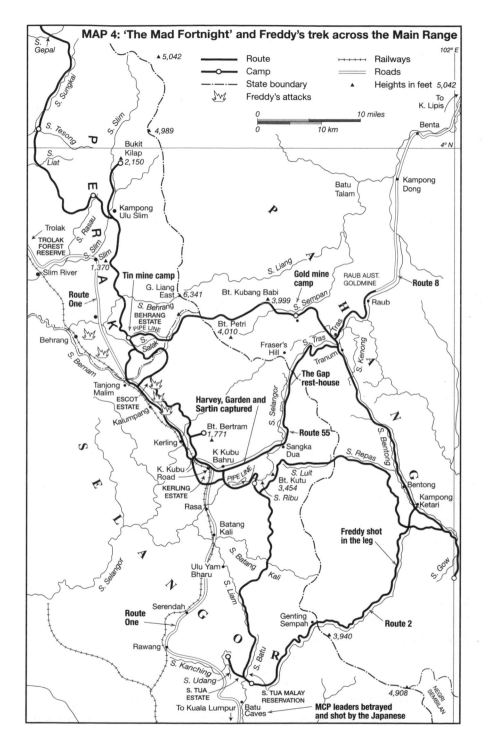

MAP 4: 'The Mad Fortnight' and Freddy's trek across the Main Range

made with well-camouflaged tents. They heard on Alves' wireless that the Japanese had already reached Johore. They needed to link up with Vanrenan and his party at the tin mine camp, and start operations with them as soon as possible. They could not risk going by the Gap road, which the Japanese were using round the clock, so they would have to climb through the jungle.

It was barely fifteen miles in a straight line, but it involved crossing the Main Range in virgin jungle that reaches a height of 6,431 feet in this section. Freddy thought they could do it in five days – 'call it a week, to be on the safe side' – and he was sure they could shoot pig and deer and find nuts, berries and fruit on the way. 'Alas!' he was to admit. 'How little I knew in those days about the Malayan jungle.'

Each of them carried twenty-five pounds. They had two tommy-guns with eight full magazines, six grenades, a pistol each, food for a week, medical supplies, field glasses, maps, a compass, and *parangs*, sharp Malay knives. They carried a groundsheet each, but no blankets. No concentrated army rations had reached Malaya, so they had tins of corned beef and vegetables, and oatmeal, sugar and biscuit. Freddy wore soft leather boots with the tops laced lightly over khaki drill trousers to keep out leeches. Harvey had a theory that it was best to be in shorts and gym shoes, so that he could intercept the leeches as they crawled up his legs, and pull them off before they sank their teeth into his flesh. Neither of them was right. Nothing stopped leeches.

They set lethal booby traps round their tents, and enough Scotch was left to ensure a 'magnificent farewell party' with Alves. They left at dawn, on a 'nightmare journey', Freddy recollected, 'the most unpleasant journey I have ever done'. The bed of the Sungei Sempan was too deep and uneven to follow, so they had to climb along the sides of the steep river valley, choked with bamboo, thorns, atap and 'thickets of every kind'. They tore their hands clutching at branches to steady themselves when they lost their footing on wet ground. The tommy-guns were heavy and the handles, catches, trigger guards and knobs caught on creepers and scraped and bruised their hips and ribs.

They were still beside the stream when they camped on a sandbank above it on the first night. When they stripped to bathe, their bodies were covered with bloated leeches. It had started raining in the afternoon, and that brought out the two-inch browny-green wisps, like strands of noodle, with head and teeth and the power of smell. Their heads wave around in the undergrowth as they sniff for blood. A human is a feast beyond measure, and they move fast in their curious manner. The head grips the ground, or the flesh once it is on the body, and pulls the foot after it, the foot then attaching itself as the head moves on, in an endless ballet. When they reach the boot, they climb for the blood they smell further up, in the leg. As it feeds, the head burrows into the skin, whilst the foot keeps it anchored.

The leeches were unable to get through to Freddy's legs, so they crawled higher until they found openings, and bit him round his waist and neck. He pulled off scores of them during the day. He knew that some had got through when he felt blood running down his chest. Harvey had been badly bitten on the ankles and hands. He had used a stick to part the undergrowth, and the leeches climbed up it until they got to the web-like flesh at the base of the fingers, finding it the choicest part of the human body. The leech injects an anti-coagulant as it bites, to make sure of a good blood flow as it feeds. If it is ripped off, it tears the victim's skin with its teeth, leaving a wound that takes half an hour or more to stop bleeding, and that often festers. It was best, if there was no glowing cigarette end or salt to make it release its grip, to let it continue to gorge itself until it released its teeth and dropped off naturally. But Freddy thought that all the theories on how to get rid of leeches were nonsense. 'My experience,' he said, 'is that the wounds bleed just as much and are just as likely to become infected however they are removed.'

They cut piles of branches to sleep on and made a lean-to out of their groundsheets as a shelter. Freddy had revived a ritual from Greenland and Tibet. Before they went to sleep, they took it in turns to read aloud from C. E. Montague's *The Right Place*, the only book they had brought with them. Montague was a pacifist who had dyed his white hair black to enlist as a soldier in his late forties in 1914, and survived the trenches to renew his onslaughts on war and English society which he held to be redeemed only by the 'ineradicable decency of the plain man'. He was a thinking man, but this affront to Freddy's resolutely non-thinking ideal was offset by Montague's love of climbing and of the Alps and the Lakes. Freddy said that *The Right Place* was 'my particular vade mecum'. It had a wonderful sense of wild places and travel, and in their sopping lean-to in the darkening jungle the three read each other passages full of the intimacy of the English landscape and its lakes and fells.

It rained hard all that night, and they learned how quickly a jungle stream can rise. Their sandbank became an island and they had to cross a fast-moving torrent to the bank, where they sat 'shivering disconsolately' until daylight. They climbed out of the river valley next day, and set a course due west. It was hot, and for the first and only time in the jungle, Freddy had a burning thirst. That night, it began raining again, and they collected water with groundsheets. It was so cold that, though they huddled together for warmth, it was almost impossible to sleep.

The air next day was sodden and the damp found its way inside their packs and dissolved the adhesive tape from the tin that held their matches. The sugar got soaked, too, so that it ran away as a liquid as their packs worked on their backs, and their biscuits and oatmeal became a wet pulp. They finished the tinned beef and peas. Just one bag of raw oatmeal survived intact and this was now their only food. The jungle teemed with wildlife, with hundreds of species of birds and mammals, and less welcome creatures, snakes and scorpions and parasites. But the only living things they had seen were the leeches, and they, far from providing them with a meal, were feasting off them. They mixed a little water with the oatmeal each morning and evening, until it ran out.

The going got worse, on hills so steep they had to pull themselves up with their hands, and then gingerly lower themselves down from branch to branch, their feet sliding on wet roots and leaf mould. The valleys had huge granite boulders covered with layers of moss and roots, treacherous, threatening a fall into the spuming stream below if there was a moment's lack of balance. Their tommy-guns 'nearly drove us demented', bruising them, catching on branches, causing them to lose balance. It was dry in the mornings, but the rain returned at midday and stayed with them until well into the night. They were always wet, and their sodden clothes 'rubbed away the skin in the most tender parts of our bodies' so that it was a torture to start moving again each dawn.

These miseries lifted briefly as they reached the top of a ridge and came out of the tree cover into the sunlight. Only small parts of the range had been explored, but here a surveyor had cut a large clearing. It opened up a vast panorama and had enabled him to sight his theodolites and range-finders on distant landmarks. Since then, the clearing had filled with rhododendron scrub so thick that Freddy's feet did not touch the ground, but the view remained and he gazed at it in awe. 'For the first time,' he said, 'I realised the terrifying vastness of the Malayan jungle.' Tree-clad mountains ran in every direction, ridge after ridge, 'purple at first, then violet and blue, fading at last into the paler blue of the distance'. In 1905, the surveyor J. A. Sheffield had recorded at least sixteen peaks above 6,000 feet. Six miles to the south a cluster of red-roofed bungalows on top of Fraser's Hill, still abandoned but soon to fill with convalescing Japanese troops, was the sole sign of man. Otherwise, the wilderness stretched beyond the horizons to north and south, primeval, untouched. No noise broke the stillness as they gazed. Only at night did the forest creatures cry out. As for the rain in the monsoon downpours, they heard it first in the treetops, rustling them like a breeze, and then swelling into a throbbing, drumming noise, with a dimming of the light and crashes of thunder. Branches and leaves hurtled to the ground. But the rain itself did not penetrate. It exhausted itself in the canopy, eighty to a hundred feet up, registering below as clouds of moisture. Where there was a clearing, and the ground was unprotected, it fell in sheets so solid that they cut back the visibility, bouncing back off the soil almost to waist height, and filling the streams with torrents of liquid earth.

On the lower parts of the range, the temperature seldom fell below 15 degrees centigrade and often went above 30 degrees centigrade. It cooled quickly when it rained, and then soared back as soon as it stopped. At altitudes over 3,000 feet, in the cloud forest where Freddy now was, fog and mist often clung to the foliage. The trees stripped moisture from the clouds, which condensed and dripped from the canopy or ran down the trunks. It was cold enough to drop to freezing at night. The cloud and damp were almost constant above 5,000 feet and the mosses thick. There were no seasons, so close to the equator, and night and day were of equal length.

The deep forest around him had five layers of vegetation. Monster trees pierced the canopy to rise in solitary splendour, no more than one or two to the acre. The great hardwoods on Freddy's route were the dipterocarps, so called for their two-winged fruits. These were the first trees to catch the attention of loggers, and were felled for the riches of their timber, and their aromatic essential oils, balsam and dammar resin. The grandest of them, a Shorea, was recorded at 289 feet from its buttressed base to the top of its crown, where raptors nested. The canopy below them was a ceiling made of the crowns of the lesser trees. From above it was a carpet of green, but the lower canopy had darker green-blue leaves, and reds and whites where a tree was flowering. The tree crowns were close but not interlocking so that canopy dwellers had to negotiate the gaps by climbing, leaping, gliding or flying. More than four-fifths of the life that teemed in the rain-forest lived above the ground, returning to the earth, if at all, only to nest or breed.

High above Freddy's little party were arboreal crabs and anteaters and porcupines, and 'flying' squirrels, lemurs, geckoes, lizards and snakes that glided more than flew. The *Draco splendens*, the flying dragon, covers a hundred yards and more in a single flight in its hunt for tree ants. The twin-banded tree snake and the paradise tree snake invert their ventral surfaces to gain lift when they launch themselves from a branch. They can glide at least 65 feet forward through the forest.

Freddy was able to find their position by taking back bearings on Fraser's Hill and other mountains on his map. It was the first time he could do so. Navigating in the jungle was made immeasurably difficult by the lack of landmarks, and visibility was limited to twenty-five yards or so. They were a little further north than he had intended. It was a remark-ably small error, and a compliment to the dead reckoning skills he had learned in Greenland. He made a new course along a ridge to the south-west. They blazed a trail as they marched, because they intended to make this a permanent route between the two hideouts. The lead man, relieved of his tommy-gun, cut a path with his parang that he could just elbow through. The second man widened it and marked the route with bent saplings and blazes on tree trunks. The third man followed, carefully checking the course with a compass. Unless watched like a hawk, the lead man could turn a half circle within a few minutes – Freddy, alone and ill, was later to spend two days stumbling round and round in immense circles – without being in the least aware of it, for he had no horizon and no landmarks on which to march, and no sun, either, for that and the sky were above the treetops and invisible in the green void at which he slashed. Every thirty minutes, they changed places. Their wet hands blistered terribly, rubbed by the handles of their parangs. Their clothes were ripped by thorns and their faces lacerated.

They were up each day as soon as it was light enough to move, about 6 a.m., and though their sores hurt as they moved, they were glad to get some warmth into their bones. They stopped at 3 p.m., partly through exhaustion, and also to get some rest before it was too cold to sleep. Freddy cursed himself for not bringing blankets and sweaters. But Bill Harvey was an old Malaya hand, a planter, and he too had not realised how bitter the cold was in the high jungle, above all in the two hours before dawn.

They were getting skilled at making a leaf shelter each day. As soon as they stopped, they de-leeched themselves, then made a framework of saplings lashed with vines, with the outline of a sloping roof. The roof was thatched by intertwining the largest leaves they could find in the framework of the roof. A thick pile of branches and leaves served as a mattress. They put on all their clothes and covered themselves with groundsheets. Freddy then spent twenty minutes working out their position by dead reckoning from the compass direction they had tried to keep during the day and the rough distance covered. He also tried to compare the valleys and ridges they had crossed during the day with the maze of ridges and valleys on the map. He was never successful in getting a good match. 'I tried to preserve my optimism,' he said, 'but in reality I had absolutely no idea where we were.'

They ate a ration of oatmeal and water. Then they read – 'the only happy hour of the day' – and tried to sleep. As night fell, the jungle became alive with noise, the grasshoppers, cicadas and tree frogs sounding like 'bicycle bells, cymbals, hunting horns, road drills, fishing reels, the infuriating clicker with which a lecturer asks for his next lantern slide'. The loud and mournful voice of the hornbill reminded Freddy of a heron. He occasionally spotted one during the day, a huge black ungainly body, with a fantastic white bony hornbill on its head, hurtling past the treetops to the loud rhythmic beat of its wing pinions.

Insects plagued them after dark. Mosquitoes were less menacing in daylight than in rubber plantations and the plains, but they bit savagely at night. Worse, far worse, were the midges. They made no noise, unlike the shrill mosquito, but they gave a real bite that itched like a nettle sting. They were worst in the early hours, and often woke them before dawn. The night's bites became so puffed up that at first light their faces were almost unrecognisable, their cheeks sometimes so swollen that their eyes were closed and they could not see until they had bathed them in cool stream water.

One ridge was so steep and long that it took them a day to climb it. They stumbled over roots that became ever more fantastic as they gained height, helping the trees survive the gales that blew at altitude. As they neared the top, they met stunted scrub and thick mosses, a sure sign that they were well above 4,000 feet. There was no view at the top. They did not know where they were. By now – it was the ninth or tenth day, Freddy wasn't sure – their strength was beginning to give out. Harvey and Freddy were worried about Sartin. He rarely spoke and was behaving 'strangely'. Harvey had lost so much weight he had taken in six holes in his belt. Freddy was still weak after his malaria and 'not going really well'. Harvey wanted to go back before it was too late. Freddy felt he had a week's travel still in him. He had faith in his navigation – the confidence built up on the Greenland ice cap – and was sure they must be near the western edge of the mountains. Sartin thought he couldn't go on. Freddy was dismissive: 'there's nothing good or bad but thinking makes it so' – and Sartin was doing too much thinking. He quoted *Macbeth* to himself:

Freddy (above left) with his brother Robert. Endurance was bred in him as a boy. He was tough, and proud of it, egging on other boys to bang him on the head with cricket bats, to 'to see how hard he could take it'. Danger already fascinated him, he confessed, 'leading me into more scrapes than any other boy at school'. He built up his stamina on the fells and moors round Sedbergh, and on the school's exhausting Ten-Mile Run (above right).

Freddy was fiercely independent, but he was a leader (centre left, as a school prefect). An orphan, he earned his own pocket money with his fieldcraft, selling moles and rabbits he caught and skinned. His guardian was an elderly Lake District vicar. Though Freddy recalled his 'interminable and learned sermons' with a shudder, a moral code was instilled that was to serve him well in the extremes to come. So did the childhood skills of camouflage and concealment: he built himself a secret hideout under the eaves of the Lindale vicarage (below left), and evaded gamekeepers and water bailiffs.

On the wind-battered coast and ice cap of east Greenland, Freddy learnt the life-saving arts of navigation. The dozen members of the British Arctic Air Route are seen in 1930 with Eskimo friends at their base hut (above). Freddy is with his girlfriend Gertrude (middle row, third and fourth from right). The leader was Gino Watkins (fifth from right). Gertrude – 'she really is a charmer' – posed for Freddy with a pair of sled dogs (left). He learned all he could from the Eskimos: their language, their customs, how they hunted, how they survived.

Freddy made a desperate journey by sled in April 1931 (above) to relieve Augustine Courtauld, alone and starving in a tent on the ice cap. Wind speeds of hurricane strength had all but obliterated any trace of him. The tent was deep under snow, but they found it (left). Courtauld (below, second from right) posed between Freddy (right) and Watkins on their return.

Freddy returned to Greenland with Watkins in 1932. Watkins was a brilliant kayaker (top), but ran huge risks by hunting alone. The ice wall of a glacier towered high above the fjord where he went out for seal. When it 'calved', huge breaking waves were thrown up as ice crashed into the sea. When Watkins failed to return, Freddy found his waterlogged kayak, but no trace of his body. Freddy made a simple cross for him (left). He then made a hair-raising trip in a small boat (below) to a wireless station to break the news to the world.

A GREENLAND TRAGEDY

WATKINS'S LAST DAY

SEARCH PARTY'S FINDS

The following article, by a member of the Greenland Air Survey Expedition, is the first detailed account of what happened on August 20, when the leader of the expedition, Mr. H. G. Watkins, lost his life while hunting seals in Lake Fjord. A second article will describe how the party is carrying on.

By F. Spencer Chapman
World Copyright Reserved

ANGMAGSSALIK

Having mastered the art of rolling his kayak, Watkins felt he was safe in any ordinary emergency. On the boat journey to Julianehaab last year he hunted alone all the time, often being away from the others for eight hours on end.

Freddy reported on Watkins's disappearance in an article for *The Times* (left). The coast of east Greenland (below) was as wild and forbidding as the interior, its seas dwarfing the open boat, and the ice dangerous after it froze. The summer sea was choked with icebergs. Violent winds produced waves that Freddy saw sweep up the side of 100-foot high icebergs and break in a welter of foam at the top. He was caught two miles offshore whilst sledging on the ice in winter. The ice beneath his tent began to crack and open.

Freddy poses, arms akimbo, by a lake on his journey in Tibet in 1936 (above left), and relaxes with members of the British Mission (above right). He was photographer as well as secretary to the mission, filming (below) scenes of 'feudal splendour' that reminded him of a Hollywood blockbuster.

The mission was led by Basil Gould (opposite, top, in striped trousers; Freddy is in the back row, dapper in a suit for once). Freddy caught the ethereal beauty of Chomolhari (opposite, bottom), with a supply train, the drivers with old flintlocks and turquoise earrings. He collected seeds and took bird notes each day: in the evenings, the hard-as-nails adventurer pressed periwinkles and learnt Tibetan.

THE ASCENT OF CHOMOLHARI

A HIMALAYAN CONQUEST

24,000 FEET FOR £20

We publish below an account by Mr. F. Spencer Chapman of his ascent of Chomolhari (23,930ft.), the "Divine Queen of Mountains," which he accomplished alone with one porter at the end of May.

By F. Spencer Chapman
Copyright

In August, 1936, on my way to Lhasa, and again in February this year on my return, I rode for several days within sight of the imposing sentinel peak of Chomolhari, rising straight from the level plateau to a height of 24,000ft. and giving an extraordinary impression of sheer height and inaccessibility. It is one of the most beautiful mountains in the world.

Freddy took a classic picture of the Potala Palace looming over the plain at Lhasa (above). On his journey, he had been captivated by Chomolhari, an unclimbed sentinel peak that soared above the wind-scoured plateau. He made the first ascent, with a solitary Sherpa as companion, almost losing his life in a crevasse. He wrote an exclusive for *The Times* (left), proudly pointing out that he got to the 24,000-foot summit for less money than the last Everest expedition had spent on one newfangled pressure cooker. He returned to England with 500 plant specimens for the herbarium at Kew, and many observations of birds. Freddy's adventures always had a purpose.

> I am in blood
> Stepp'd in so far that, should I wade no more
> Returning were as tedious as go o'er.

They went on.

That night, they finished the oatmeal. To lighten their loads, Freddy suggested dumping a tommy-gun. Sartin's whole ethos as a regular soldier rebelled. Freddy, 'rather ashamed of myself', apologised for suggesting it.

Next day, 28 January, the eleventh day of the journey, they came across a beer bottle on the top of a high ridge. It was the first sign of man. They saw blazed trees and the faint outline of a path running down a spur to the south-west. They followed it until it became a definite path, then camped in lighter spirits. They carried on down the spur the next morning, and found a wide stream. A bowl in the stream had been dammed with rocks to create a deep pool, and a pipeline ran down from it into the jungle. Freddy saw from the map that this was the Sungei Bernam, and that the long spur had led them between this stream and its tributary the Sungei Lempong. He thought it a miracle that they had found the path and the spur after such a journey. The mountains on both sides of the spur ran much further west, and had they gone there, Freddy thought, 'we should probably not have had strength to get through'.

An excellent track ran down next to the pipeline. It had naked footprints of recent date. No booted Japanese had passed this way. The pipeline ran steadily down, traversing ravines on crazy bamboo scaffolding. They came out of the jungle into an open patch of ground. They took off their clothes and bathed in the sunshine. The weight loss over twelve days was astonishing. Their bones stuck out of skin that was a sickly yellow, except for the scores of purple spots marking the site of leech bites. Their hands, knees and faces were criss-crossed with cuts and thorn scratches. As they lay, they watched a gibbon – a *wah-wah* to the Malays – swinging itself from branch to branch round the clearing. Hornbills apart, it was the only animal they had seen on the whole journey.

They saw a party of men moving up the pipeline. The one in front was dressed in khaki and was carrying a double-barrelled shotgun. Freddy mistook them for Japanese for a moment, but they were Malays, and very friendly. They took them to their kampong close to the river. It seemed like paradise – thatched houses raised on stilts, with wooden ladders leading to shaded verandas, and fruit trees, coconut palms, flowering hibiscus and the vivid green of paddy fields – and they lay on soft grass in the sun, eating bananas and pineapples, looking up at slender and attentive bee-eaters, their plumage green and yellow, hunting for flies with lustrous black bulbuls.

The Malays told them that many British soldiers had passed along the edge of the jungle, the detritus of the battles at Slim river and further north, often close to collapse. They brought them a fine curry, with chicken, eggs, fish and vegetables, but Freddy found his stomach had shrunk, and he could not do it full justice. Their generous hosts gave them Malay cheroots, and warm sweet coffee, and saw them onto a steep descent that led along old tin-tailing ground to Leu Kim's kongsi-house.

To their bitter disappointment, there was no sign of Vanrenan and his party. Leu Kim was out, and his womenfolk gave them more coffee and sweetcakes, nervous with the three desperadoes, faces swollen and scratched, and scuffed by twelve-day growths of beard, their emaciated bodies festooned with hand-grenades. When Leu Kim returned he did not at first recognise Freddy. He explained that after the stores arrived on 5 January, Vanrenan, Hembry and Graham had begun moving them into the jungle with a large gang of coolies supplied by Leu Kim and Lee Fee. They had half the stores hidden by next afternoon, when a Chinese dashed up, shouting that the Japanese were already in Tanjong Malim, and were behind him on the little side road: 'They are coming!' It was not true, but they were not to know that. The coolies fled, and Vanrenan's party grabbed their tommy-guns and hid in the jungle, spending the night in an atap hut near the pipeline. They returned at dawn next day to find every packing case had disappeared. Not a coolie – or a Japanese – was in sight. Leu Kim told Vanrenan that Lee Fee's coolies had come in the night, unknown to him, and carried off all the stores into the jungle. The Chinese helped Vanrenan search, but they did not recover a single case. There was no sign, either, of the radio set and the bicycles, which had been stored under cover in a deserted atap hut. Vanrenan had no stores and no radio, and there was no sign of Freddy. He felt he had no choice but to follow the retreating British forces. He and his party had left and made their way towards the coast.

Freddy pondered this body-blow. His raiding party was now not six, but the three of them, exhausted and so weak that they felt dizzy if they moved too abruptly. Leu Kim's women made it clear that they were not welcome to stay in the kongsi-house. If the Japanese got wind of it, they would have their heads cut off. Leu Kim led them instead to a shelter he had prepared to use in air-raids. It was a perfect hide-out. They reached it through a desolate wasteland of scrubby red laterite broken into cliffs and ravines by the rain. They passed on over dry stony ground that left no footprints, through a grove of bamboo and along a deep trench to a chamber hollowed out of a steep bank of red clay. It was surrounded by a belt of tangled bamboos fifty feet high and thick enough to hide the smoke of a dry wood fire. The cave had a sleeping bench of lashed bamboo. Leu Kim brought them a grass mat to throw over it and three scarlet blankets. Food, too: an earthenware pot of fragrant boiled rice, with fried salt fish and aubergines flavoured with soy sauce and ginger, and a bottle of strong sweet coffee.

The Chinese opened up now that he was away from his family. Freddy was reconciling himself to fleeing to Sumatra, since the two tommy-guns and eight magazines he had with him were not going to do the Imperial Japanese Army great harm. But Leu Kim told him now that he had recovered some of Vanrenan's stores and had hidden them in a cave. He also said that the Japanese had repaired the blown bridges at Tanjong Malim. Day and night, convoys of men and equipment were pouring south on Route One towards the front in Johore. The railway was also being used round the clock. Freddy would have targets in plenty.

Next morning, restored by food and sleep, the three men decided that – provided explosives were among the stores Leu Kim had saved – they must justify themselves as a stay-behind party by attacking

Japanese trains and road convoys. The British might still win the campaign, 'for in those days', Freddy recollected, 'we still believed in the impregnability of Singapore'. In the event, they found that the looters' main interest had been the food and tobacco. They had left the heavier boxes, with explosives, grenades, ammunition, medical supplies, maps, bundles of clothing and gymshoes. Sartin found fuses and timers in plenty, but no detonators.

That night, they went to Lee Fee's house in the jungle, a huge kongsi-house, and called him out from the darkness. He appeared, shaking with fear at the tommy-guns, at the head of fifty men, women and children. He claimed that it was Leu Kim's coolies who were the thieves, not his. He presented them with chickens, eggs and a British army case of raisins, but no detonators. Sartin found more grenades, and said he could make detonators from the primers supplied with the grenades.

They recovered for two or three days. They took Leu Kim into their confidence – telling him that if they attacked the road and railway it would diminish the Japanese attack in Johore – and found him loyal to China, with deep hatred of the Japanese. He would do all he could to help. They shaved, bathed in the stream, put on fresh uniforms, slept round the clock and ate vastly of Leu Kim's feasts of curried chicken and cucumber soup. Freddy also prepared a three-inch-to-the-mile map of the area round Route One and the railway for six or seven miles north and south of Tanjong Malim. This was to be their area of operations.

CHAPTER 8

THE MAD FORTNIGHT

Freddy made reconnaissance trips to fill in details of paths and game trails and areas of dead ground where they could not be detected. On one, he was walking along a pipeline when a tiger bounded over it some distance ahead. It gave him a fleeting impression of 'infinite grace and strength' before it disappeared without a sound. He had no fear of it. Only diseased and toothless tigers became man-eaters, and this one was in his prime.

Police tracker dogs were a different matter. They planned to walk along stream beds for part of every sortie, to make sure they broke the trail of their scent. Height was another problem. They were too tall to pass for Chinese or Malays – Freddy was a whisker under six foot – but the Tamils who worked as rubber tappers on the estates had a similar build. They were dark-skinned, almost black. Freddy concocted a dye by mixing lamp-black, the soot from kerosene lamps, with iodine, coffee and purple crystals of potassium permanganate, used as disinfectant. Once blacked up, they completed the disguise with a white shirt, a dhoti or sarong round the middle, and a dirty white cloth tied round the head with the tail left hanging down. It helped that Tamils were a 'notoriously timid folk' and kept to themselves. Harvey was a fluent Tamil speaker, too. They came within sight of patrols of Japanese on bicycles, looking for them. Once they were so close that Harvey 'whined to them in abject Tamil'. Freddy covered his face and bowed low to them, in the gesture of submission the Japanese demanded of all passers-by, though, as he said, if you were tall, and your face was running with sweat that might be washing the Tamil colour from your English features, 'you were only too glad to bow down before anybody'.

Each was to carry a tommy-gun, a pistol and two hand-grenades, and an army pack filled with explosives and fuses, and British battle-dress. They planned to change into uniform as they approached a target, so that they would not be executed as spies if they were captured. They were to operate at night, leaving the camp as the tropical darkness began to fall after 5 p.m. It was pitch dark before moonrise. Leu Kim gave them a torch, and they slipped a green leaf in front of the bulb to give a ghostly green light that preserved their night vision. Freddy found that putting a few fireflies or luminous centipedes in the torch reflector gave enough glow to read a map or lay a charge if the battery failed. If still out at daybreak, they planned to rest up in the jungle, wading up a stream bed in case the German shepherd dogs from Tanjong Malim were sent after them, to track them. Towards nightfall, they would change into their Tamil outfits, keeping a pistol and a grenade tucked away in their sarongs, and slip quietly back to camp.

A single click made with the side of the tongue and the teeth meant 'stop' or 'danger'. Two clicks was 'OK' or 'go on'. Freddy taught the others a rallying call to use if they were lost or scattered. He again chose the hunting cry of the British tawny owl, denizen of ancient woodland and churchyards. Country boys called up owls by blowing into cupped hands through their thumbs, making an eerie, shrill *kew-wick*, to which the owl made answer. Wordsworth captured it in his poem, 'About a Boy':

> And there, with fingers interwoven, both hands
> Pressed closely palm to palm and to his mouth
> Uplifted, he, as through an instrument,
> Blew mimic hootings to the silent owls,
> That they might answer him. – And they would shout
> Across the watery vale, and shout again,
> Responsive to his call, – with quivering peals,
> And long halloos, and screams, and echoes loud . . .

Freddy, of course, had been such a boy in Wordsworth's Lake District.

The piercing cry carried a great distance in the thickest woodland. It could not be confused with any other jungle cry, he said, yet 'to the uninitiated, and we included the Japs in this class, it passes without notice in the variety of weird nocturnal noises'.

They wrapped their tommy-guns in tape so that they did not gleam in the moonlight. They brushed their battledress with mud to break up its outline, and ran past one another to make sure nothing caught the light or rattled. They went through cramp-inducing practice to walk heel first on hard ground, and toe first on soft, to minimise the sound of each step. Faces blackened, bodies camouflaged, they found they could pass within ten yards or so of villagers without being spotted. When a Tamil or Malay looked directly at them, and spotted their ghostly figures, he sometimes took them for spirits and rushed off with a scream.

The ambush sites were at least five miles from the kongsi-house. They approached them from the Escot Estate, a large rubber plantation on the edge of the main road and the railway near Tanjong Malim. This was a rubber town, mainly Chinese, but with enough Indians for an elaborate Hindu temple. Its shop-houses, cluttered with merchandise at street level, with the shopkeeper's family living above, were crammed under tin roofs in narrow lanes. The purple line of mountains they had crossed from Raub loomed over the low rounded hills to the east of the town. The high hills came much closer to the road south of the town towards Kalumpang.

By 3 February, they were ready. The first targets were bridges on the railway line half a mile south of Tanjong Malim railway station. The station itself was on the main road half a mile or so from the town. It would take the Japanese about twenty minutes to react with troops from the town garrison, although there was always the danger that they might run into a patrol that was already out and active.

The bridge was a three-hour walk from the camp. They crossed the Bernam river into the Escot Estate as soon as it was dark, then followed the edge of the wide estate road towards the railway, detouring deep into the rubber when they passed the coolie lines, the long wood and brick hutments where the tappers were housed. When they reached the bridge, they made out the dull gleam of the rails running north, and the white dust of the road alongside it.

The dynamiters' dream, Freddy said, was 'to cause the head-on collision of two trains, both full of troops, in a tunnel'. There were no tunnels here. The bridge he chose carried the line over a river. It was one of the heavier types of Malay Railways' suspended girder bridges, set in stone abutments. They could carry no more than 100 pounds of plastic high explosives, plus their weapons and grenades, between the three of them, and that was not enough to bring the bridge down. The best Freddy could do was to put thirty pounds of explosives in the middle of the track on the north side of the bridge, while Sartin connected the charge to a pressure switch under the rail. The weight of a locomotive would set it off. Freddy hoped that the engine would crash into the side of the bridge and topple the structure into the river.

They walked on to a second bridge of solid masonry that carried the line over the main road. They set a series of five-pound charges along the line to be detonated by time pencils. When they squeezed the copper pencil, a phial of acid inside it broke open and began to eat through a fine wire. When the wire snapped, it freed a spring which struck a percussion cap, setting off the fuse. The delay varied from thirty minutes to twenty-four hours, dictated by the thickness of the wire, with the time indicated by a coloured band on the pencil. After laying the first night's ration of explosives, Freddy climbed a telegraph pole along the track, and cut the lines with a pair of pliers.

As they left the track and regained the rubber, they heard a train leave Tanjong Malim station. 'Our excitement was so great that we could scarcely breathe,' Freddy recalled. Yard by yard, with agonising slowness, its 'clanking and chugging and wheezing' drew closer. He had convinced himself that the pressure switch was a dud when a sudden blinding light and crash split the night and echoed off the hills. Bits of metal hissed into the air and fell with thuds hundreds of yards from the explosion. Shouting mingled with the hiss of escaping steam. The three men resisted the urge to slip back and look at their handiwork. The moon was brilliant by now, and they sped back through the dark plantation to their camp. They heard two more explosions as they went.

Leu Kim told them next day that the train had run off the line, but had not overturned or done much damage to the bridge, though the locomotive was wrecked. The Japanese had sent patrols out through the kampongs south of the town to look for them, arresting Chinese as they went. Freddy and the stay-behind parties were not the only resistance to the Japanese in mainland Malaya. The Chinese trained at 101 STS, and their guerrilla bands, both Kuomintang (nationalist) and communist, were still at large. They had the huge advantage of anonymity. The Chinese were everywhere in Malaya, and a majority in a good part of it, and they could come and go in the towns and along the roads without exciting much interest from Japanese sentries. Japanese atrocities fanned resistance. Informers abounded, but most Chinese were sympathetic to the guerrillas. Many risked torture and hanging by the Kempeitai (Japanese military police) to help them.

Freddy had asked Leu Kim to put them in touch with the guerrillas. Two young communists – smartly dressed, on bicycles – duly came to the kongsi-house. They agreed that they both had the same aim, of ultimately defeating the Japanese. If the worst happened, and Singapore fell, Freddy suggested that the guerrillas might help the British reach the coast to get out to Malaya. If they did, they could keep whatever arms and explosives remained as a reward. The Chinese said they would have to consult their Party leader about cooperation, but they agreed they would help with moving stores. They promised to send a party of twelve Chinese cyclists to Sungei Salak not later than 3 p.m. on 15 February.

Freddy decided to strike the line north of Tanjong Malim on their next raid on 5 February. A group of iron bridges crossed streams just to the south of the station at Kampong Behrang, seven miles up the line from their last raid. A bridge now carries traffic over the line and the rebuilt station to the new west coast expressway. A sizeable village has grown up round the station, with a Chinese Methodist church and stores, lorry repair shops and builders' merchants. When Freddy and his little party came calling, though, there was no high point from which a Japanese machine-gun could command the line.

The three set off at dusk and made good progress to the Behrang rubber estate. Two miles of rough ground lay between them and the railway. It was a swill of hillocks, streams, and patches of jungle and rubber seedlings, difficult to distinguish in the darkness. When they reached the line, they heard men approaching. Freddy took them for a Japanese patrol. The moon was behind him, and he hid with the others in the long grass beside the track. Some of the men were wearing broad-brimmed hats, they were noisy and seemed very tired, and they trailed a scent of sour sweat and tobacco behind them. Freddy found the odour 'strangely familiar'. He realised that they were British soldiers still on the loose. He decided not to go after them. He might be wrong, he rationalised, and anyway there were more of them than Leu Kim could cope with. Better to let them go.

Freddy helped Sartin put a charge on the line at a curve above an embankment, ideal for a derailment. Harvey kept watch. Suddenly, Sartin gasped: 'Christmas!' The former boy soldier could not bring himself to swear in front of an officer. Then he said: 'You're lucky men!' Indeed they were: by rights, their body parts should have been sprayed across the embankment. Sartin had put ten pounds of explosives under the outer rail on the bend, and connected the detonating fuse to the pressure switch. He had to pack this up with stones so that it just reached the bottom of the rail, where the weight of a passing train would trigger it. But he shoved it too hard and activated the switch. The percussion cap, 'by the grace of God', was a dud.

Dawn was getting close. They put the rest of the explosive on a little girder bridge just south of the Behrang station. It took half an hour to put separate charges against the rails and girders, and to connect each one so that they would go off simultaneously as the train tripped the pressure switch. They were still tying the charges in position to stop them being dislodged by vibrations when Freddy thought he heard a train well away to the north. They listened. Nothing. Then a definite whistle. A train was approaching fast. But they mislaid the pliers and Sartin had no time to set the switch. He connected the main fuse to a simple detonator on top of the rail.

The train got so close that they could see its 'dark mass' as they raced along the track, gaining on them until they slid down the embankment and fell waist deep into a foul-smelling swamp. A blinding white flash exposed them for a moment, mouths open with shock, holding their tommy-guns above them to keep them out of the water. The explosion battered their eardrums a moment later, shaking the mud under their feet, and lapsing into a ferocious shriek and grinding of tortured metal. Missiles roared over their heads and crashed into the jungle and swamp, lumps of coal or metal or bits of body, they could not tell. The train did not stop, but 'dragged itself slowly over the bridge', clanking with distress. The cab of the locomotive went slowly past them, less than ten yards away, crowded with Japanese troops. It came to a halt a little further up.

The two terrified Tamil drivers came back down the line with an escort of Japanese with submachine-guns, who flashed their torches at the goods wagons as they passed. Freddy covered them with his tommy-gun but they did not see him. They came back a little later with three more Japanese from the brake van. They satisfied themselves that the locomotive was out of action, and set off south down the line for Tanjong Malim.

Freddy climbed out of the swamp as the Japanese left. Water and steam were gushing out of the engine onto the line. Harvey threw a grenade into the firebox, and they took cover as it exploded. The brick abutments were damaged, and the foot-thick girders of the bridge were cut in two. It was getting light, and they sped away through the rubber, slackening their pace when they regained thick jungle. They heard the time pencil charges exploding for hours afterwards.

Leu Kim brought them reports later of the two wrecked trains still lying on their sides. Freddy still feared that they were not hurting the enemy as hard as they should. Blown road bridges had barely made the Japanese pause during their advance, and their emergency rail gangs soon had damaged track up and running again. He feared that locomotives could jump a six-foot gap in a rail – he thought cutting both rails for at least ten feet was the minimum needed to derail a train – and he was worried that they were running out of explosives. Leu Kim brought them fresh detonators, fuses and several hundred pounds of gelignite from a friend in tin-mining. But they were using a hundred pounds of explosives a night, and risking capture by the stepped-up Japanese patrolling of the railway, whilst their arsenal of tommy-gun ammunition and hand-grenades went untouched. Freddy decided to look for targets on the main road instead.

Route One ran from Singapore through Kuala Lumpur and on up to the Thai border. It skirted the Main Range, which rolled to its east in an unbroken line, first black against the rising sun, then purple with heat and bruised with rain clouds as the day wore on. The foothills broke on the plains in a welter of green and the yellow of tumbling streams. It was a sturdy, well-built road, with neat culverts and cuttings and black-and-white mileposts, and every so often a pile of gravel and an atap shelter against the rain for the road-mending crews. Rubber estates bordered it for much of its length from Tanjong Malim to Ipoh. In places it passed the red scars and derelict moon landscapes of old tin-tailings.

Most of the daylight traffic was made up of Japanese lorries, staff cars, motorcycles, and large numbers of cycle troops moving south. The few civilian pedestrians and cyclists disappeared at night. Large convoys of trucks and staff cars moved south through the small hours. They drove very fast with full headlights and little interval between them, 'just asking to be ambushed', Freddy thought. They came across their first target by chance, as they were returning from setting time charges on the railway. Six 20-hundredweight trucks were parked in the grass beside the road. Their sidelights were switched off, and there were no signs of sentries. Harvey heard snoring coming from them. They worked carefully from truck to truck, pushing a couple of pounds of explosives between the crankcases and clutch. It took them an hour, working in absolute silence. They connected the charges with four feet of safety fuse, giving them two minutes to get well clear. Freddy was bitterly disappointed that none of the trucks caught fire in the explosions, but he noted that neither the trucks nor the drivers were 'much further use to the Japanese war effort'.

They invented a new bomb to use on the road. Several hundred pounds of gelignite had deteriorated in the heat and humidity so badly that the nitro-glycerine was seeping out of it. It was highly unstable but they were reluctant to dump it. Sartin was storing it in lengths of bamboo. It struck them that a length of bamboo lying on the road would not be noticed. The explosive inside it could be detonated by a pull-switch, set off by a length of wire pulled by the bomber lying at a safe distance. If there was no cover for him, the bomb could be set off automatically by a trip wire. Sartin prepared a five-pound bomb in an eighteen-inch section of bamboo with a pull switch. They found a good position for an ambush by the 50th milestone from Kuala Lumpur. This lies south of Tanjong Malim, close to the little railway station at Kalumpang. The road runs parallel and close by the railway here. The rubber trees grew up to the roadside and a bank gave shelter against the bomb blast. The railway line would allow a speedy getaway.

They started the night's work on 8 February along the rail line. Fifty separate charges operated by time pencils were set on the sleepers at the junction of lengths of rail, so that both rails would be damaged. Then they took up ambush positions on the road. A bamboo charge was put in the middle of the road. Sartin held the wire. He was to pull it when Freddy tapped him on the back. Freddy and Harvey would then throw two grenades apiece, and empty their tommy-guns into the target, before making off up the railway line for the Escot Estate.

As they waited, 'in intense excitement', the first of their railway charges exploded. They heard a train coming down from the north, but it stopped at Tanjong Malim. Suddenly they heard lorry engines on the road and Freddy counted six sets of headlights coming towards them. He waited until the lead vehicle was almost on them and tapped Sartin's shoulder. The bomb exploded beneath the truck's fuel tank and set it on fire, a brilliant blaze illuminating the ambush site like a stage set. A second large truck crashed into the wreckage, and a third slewed sideways under violent braking. Harvey emptied his tommy-gun in a single protracted burst. Freddy threw his grenades and fired, and 'found myself racing down the path, floodlit by the funeral pyre of the Jap lorries'.

The Japanese did not have their weapons ready – they had been caught by surprise – and the three reached the railway line before the enemy opened fire. But a frightening sight came into view. In the 'clear moonlight', Freddy said, 'we saw a party of men with lanterns a hundred yards up the track'. It was a Japanese patrol sent down from Tanjong Malim to investigate the earlier explosion, and they opened fire. The fleeing trio plunged through the rubber, the night 'hideous with the noise of rifle, machine-gun and even mortar fire'. They were in real peril as visible targets for less than a minute, but the Japanese kept on firing for over an hour. Once they were safely past the coolie lines on the Escot Estate, the three rested and got their breath back, congratu- lating themselves on a highly successful – 'though very terrifying' – ambush.

Freddy fretted over ambush techniques. The Japanese were fully alerted by now – they thought that several hundred British and Australians were on the loose – and surprise would count for less. But in several places the road passed through cuttings, which gave the ambushers the advantage of height. They could fire down onto the road from the top of the cutting. This protected them from exploding vehicles and the blast of their own grenades. It also left the Japanese very vulnerable if they tried to climb the slope towards them. Their natural reaction would be to go to ground behind their trucks whilst the trio made off.

Several short cuttings lay on the road north of Tanjong Malim before the turning off to Behrang station. To increase the size of the killing ground, the trio took positions thirty yards apart from each other. They beefed up their hand-grenades with their own hand-made bombs, made by putting a stick of gelignite with a fuse inside a tin or a length of bamboo. They timed the explosions to continue after they had fled. And flee they must. They were three men, living rough, unsupported. The convoys they were attacking could contain a company of Japanese cavalry, 170 men, outnumbering them by more than fifty to one.

At dusk, for four or five nights, they left the camp, and made their way to an ambush site, avoiding the coolie lines on the rubber estates. They chose a rendezvous spot to meet after the action, in case they were split up. Then they waited for a convoy. They stopped the first vehicle with a tug on a wire-controlled bomb. As the other trucks squealed to a stop, they fired tommy-gun magazines in short bursts, and threw fused bombs and then hand-grenades. All the while, Freddy said, 'we shouted and yodelled at the tops of our voices', to keep up their spirits, and to convince the Japanese that a large force was attacking them. As the fused bombs began to explode, they ran off to the rendezvous point. Sartin failed to appear after the second road ambush. The cutting was a shallow one, and his grenade bounced off the canvas cover of a truck and stunned him when it exploded. He recovered consciousness, and saw at least thirty wounded or dead Japanese before crawling off. Freddy had given him up for lost when he limped back covered in earth.

Some of the convoys only carried stores and there was little fighting. Others had trucks packed with troops, and the firing went on long after they had fled out of range. In the end, though, the Japanese worked out how to defend themselves. They stopped using the road at night.

By now, Freddy said, 'our muscles and nerves could stand no more'. They felt exhilarated and alive – Sartin spoke of his 'thorough enjoyment' – and that was the danger. The greatest risk in living dangerously, Freddy wrote, be it 'rock-climbing, driving a motor-car fast, or shooting tiger or Japs', came when vigilance became prey to over-confidence and exhaustion. 'We had begun to forget the taste of fear,' he said. Each raid took twelve hours or so, and they had to cover as many miles in careful silence, carrying fifty-pound packs. They were short of explosives and fuses, and would have to go to the Sungei Sempan dump to get more. The Japanese had massacred Chinese in several kampongs close to Tanjong Malim in retaliation for their casualties. Leu Kim told Freddy that they had held back 2,000 men – two regiments – at Tanjong Malim and Kuala Kubu specifically to hunt him. They had posted sentries on all the rail bridges, and their patrols were getting closer and closer to the kongsi-house. Leu Kim could not sleep for worry of what would happen to him and his family if they so much as suspected him.

Freddy couldn't be sure what he had achieved, in darkness illuminated only by explosions and burning fuel. His best guess was seven or eight trains derailed, fifteen bridges severely damaged, rail track cut in about sixty places, and forty trucks and cars damaged or destroyed. They had used a thousand pounds of explosives and more than one hundred grenades and home-made bombs. He put the casualties inflicted at between 500 and 1,500 Japanese troops.

He decided to leave the area on 15 February, if the Chinese communist guerrillas did not show up as promised, and return to the Sungei Sempan gold mine camp. At the least, he felt he had proved that his 'mad fortnight' had fully justified the idea of stay-behind parties. Had he been given a large number of British officers, backed by hundreds of Chinese volunteers, and Malays and Indians, he was sure that they would have slowed down the Japanese enough to have allowed the British 18th Division and the Australian 9th Division to have gone into action. As it was, the British arrived in Singapore just in time to be taken prisoner, and the Australians got no further than Java.

By dusk on 15 February, there was no sign of the Chinese guerrillas. To stay any longer would put Leu Kim in ever greater danger, and it was unsafe to try to get past the Japanese garrison at Kuala Kubu near dawn. They did not know it, but Chin Peng, a young rising star in the Perak Communist Party, was frantically cycling to catch them before they left. He had been instructed to liaise with the 'stay-behind' parties by Lai Te, the turncoat Party leader, as well as running the guerrilla forces in Perak. His bicycle broke down several times on the way. He came across groups of Japanese troops at the roadside. They yelled 'Banzai!' to him and he wondered why. He was two hours too late. The three Englishmen had set off to return to the gold mine camp. Each was carrying a tommy-gun, a twenty-pound pack and thirty pounds of explosives, with which to bid farewell to the Japanese.

They put a thirty-five-pound charge on the railway line as they crossed it after emerging from the Escot Estate. Sartin dug it in a foot below a sleeper and connected it to pressure switches on both rails. They had only got half a mile, to the bridge carrying the main road over the track, when they heard a train coming towards them from the south. It passed them as they hid below the parapet – Freddy almost succumbing to the boyish temptation of dropping a grenade down its funnel, 'a thing I always wanted to do' – and chugged smokily on. They had a 'magnificent grandstand view' from the parapet of the great flash and explosion as lumps of metal whizzed through the air. The train came off the track, but it did not overturn, and Freddy thought it was probably an empty goods train.

The rubber trees come right up to the roadside towards Kalumpang, and they were able to duck into them when they saw headlights approaching from the south half an hour later. They counted seven lorries going past flat out, full of Japanese in helmets with their weapons at the ready. They presumed that the garrison at Tanjong Malim, still convinced they were up against 'hundreds' of Australians and British, felt they needed reinforcements from Kuala Kubu to deal with the saboteurs. After a bend, Route One runs dead straight through the little town of Kerling, with the usual rows of shop-houses and a Chinese temple. Though there was no moon or streetlights, lightning was playing over the mountains a few miles to the east, and they were terribly exposed as they tiptoed along the pavement past padlocked stalls and shop-houses. Wooden verandas hung over the pavement from the first floor of the buildings, and they heard the 'heavy breathing and snoring' of sleepers as they passed beneath them. A red glow revealed where someone was smoking a cigarette on the other side of the street.

They were safely through the town when fresh headlights showed on the road behind them. There was only seedling rubber at the roadside here, but it offered some camouflage and they ran into it. They did not see the barbed wire fence protecting it. 'For God's sake, keep still,' Freddy cried, as they became entangled in it. 'Don't move a muscle.' Headlights 'floodlit' them as several trucks passed, possibly returning from the wrecked train site. The three men hung on the wire in strange poses. A barb entered Freddy's forehead, giving him a lasting scar. They had blackened their faces, and their uniforms were dark with mud, but they thought that their tommy-guns and square packs must catch the eye. The trucks did not stop, however.

A temporary wooden bridge carried the railway over Route One a little further on, where the retreating British had blown up the original stone structure. Freddy intended using the last of the explosives on it. They approached along a deep cutting that took the road under the railway. The Chinese had warned them that the Japanese now guarded many bridges at night. They were very close when a flash of lightning illuminated two sentries, who were leaning against the wooden piles of the bridge on both sides of the road. They took to the rubber and worked their way round the bridge, leaving the explosive on a long time-fuse in a culvert a mile further on.

The road passes a few stilted houses at Kampung Gumut, the more prosperous ones built above concrete blocks, with the village a few hundred yards off up a lane. Route One begins to pass through a series of deep cuttings in hillier country as it runs south. They knew the danger of being caught by headlights in one of them. Gutters on both sides of the road offered a little protection. They carried their packs in their hands to keep their profiles low, and camouflaged them with fronds and branches. The longest cutting is more than a quarter of a mile long. They were half-way through it when they saw more headlights behind them. It was a large convoy of trucks. The lights lit up the cutting and they were thoroughly frightened, but truck after truck rolled past a few feet from them without spotting them.

At the turn-off for Kuala Kubu, they smelt the 'pungent fragrance' of Japanese tobacco and saw a cigarette glowing. There was a sentry box facing the main road. They stole round it in the shadows. Freddy was willing to pass through towns at night as he lost his fear of Japanese sentries. 'The Japs do not like the dark,' he found, and their sentries normally came in pairs. They gave their position away by chatting in loud voices, or doing arms drill to keep warm. On a still night, he said, he could hear them a quarter of a mile away. If the sentry was on his own, he 'invariably seemed to be a chain smoker', and the end of his cigarette was visible from 400 or 500 yards. If the worst came to the worst, and he heard something, he would flash his torch around. 'Then if he saw us he had to drop the torch before he could shoot,' Freddy said, 'and then of course he couldn't see anything as his night vision was spoiled.' Not only that, he added, 'Jap sentries were the world's worst shots.'

They reached the town of Kuala Kubu at four in the morning. The Japanese had taken over the European bungalows on the outskirts. The lights were still burning, and they could see uniformed figures moving about through the windows. They heard singing and shouting, probably to celebrate the victory in Singapore, though it was two days before the fugitives learnt that the island had fallen. The bungalows were set back from the road in gardens, and there was little chance of them being spotted from there, but they had to take care to steer clear of the drunken soldiers who were reeling about.

Beyond the town, they found a woodcutter's path leading steeply up off the road into jungle. A stream flowed down next to it, and they found open ground to spread out their groundsheets and sleep. Sartin fixed up a booby trap with a creeper as a trip-wire and a pull-switch and instantaneous fuse. They slept all next day, 16 February, and set off for the Gap once it was dark. The last time Freddy had been on the road, at the beginning of January, he had swept up in the powerful Ford V8. They had seventeen miles to cover now, and 2,500 feet to climb, and they tried to rest their legs by stealing on to the back of a bullock cart that a Tamil was driving up the road. All went well until he turned, and saw three tall white men in filthy rags nursing tommy-guns on the back. He let off a great scream and fled wildly away into the dark. Freddy had fondly imagined that 'any fool could drive a pair of bullocks'. He found that the three of them could not get the beasts to budge an inch.

The road steepens as it climbs and winds. Its great beauties – glimpses of a lake through the mighty trees, and the tumbling waters of the Sungei Selangor, steep enough for white-water rafting today – were hidden in the darkness. They grew exhausted, 'our packs seemed filled with lead', and they could not stay awake when they paused for a rest. They found a road mender's hut by the road. All a hut needs is atap palm for roofing, and bamboo and rattan for the framework, materials that were free and often close to hand, and the frequent downpours provided a motive, so that there were – still are – many such shelters by the roadside. They went inside and slept for a little.

The final stage up to the pass is gruelling, the S-bends following each other tightly. They moved carefully when the road abruptly levelled off. They reached the Gap, and they thought there might be sentries about, but they could smell no tobacco, the surest sign of Japanese soldiers. They went cautiously through the bungalows on the slope above the road. Shebbeare's bungalow had been looted, and was a mess, but Freddy rescued some copies of the *Himalayan Journal* and one of Shebbeare's Everest diaries. They had meant to sleep in the jungle, but it dawned with a cold mist that turned to rain. The Gap had – still has – a rest-house, without the chintz and cocktail chic of the hotels along the watershed at Fraser's Hill, but a solid and dependable place, painted black and white to give it a half-timbered air, with verandas and big stone fireplaces and a games room and a bar with sporting prints, like an inn or a shooting lodge in the Scottish Highlands. It is built high above the road on a bank faced with granite blocks.

It was the last place, so Freddy hoped, that the Japanese would think to look for them. Only the small furniture had been looted. He noted that the best bedroom had 'some excellent spring bedspreads' – it has a huge bathroom, too – and its windows look directly down over the road. So they set themselves up in this comforting place, barricaded the door and manhandled a wardrobe so that they could clamber through a trap-door to the roof, and fell deeply asleep. Japanese cars and lorries passed immediately below their window. In the afternoon, they found kidney beans and English potatoes in the garden above the rest-house and cooked them in the kitchen. Some Chinese were living close by and they bought chickens from them. The Chinese said that the Japanese had broadcast that Singapore had fallen. 'We refused to believe it,' Freddy said.

As night fell, they left for the twenty-mile journey to Sungei Sempan. It was all downhill, and the road was more precipitous on this side of the Main Range than coming up from the west. They bought three bicycles at some Tamil coolie lines along the road, and raced down, getting to Sungei Sempan before dawn. They were shocked to find that the power-station was 'ablaze with light' and that a large Rising Sun flag was nailed to the wall of Alves' bungalow. They hid their bicycles and climbed directly up the pipeline to their camp. Sartin remembered the booby traps they had left behind them just in time to prevent them being blown up. They called on Alves later in the morning, after watching the bungalow carefully to make sure no Japanese were about.

He was a changed man. The Japanese had visited him, left him the flag, and terrified him. He feared they might reappear at any minute, and said that the valley was full of Chinese and Malay informers. All his Malay coolies had fled. His wireless was working, and they listened to a Japanese broadcast from Singapore in English. It confirmed the catastrophe: Singapore was lost. They were utterly alone. They went back to their camp, and ate their fill of porridge with milk and sugar, a treat they had been looking forward to for days. Then they slept.

CHAPTER 9

DISASTERS AND DECAPITATIONS

Next day, they thrashed out what to do now Singapore was gone. There was no possibility of resupply. Only Catalina flying boats had the range to get to Malaya, and they were too slow and vulnerable to be considered, while the west coast of Malaya shelved so slowly that it was dangerous to approach it by submarine. White men were instantly recognisable for what they were. They were too tall to pass for Chinese, and dyeing themselves to look like Tamils passed muster only at a distance. Soon enough, Freddy was posted 'Missing, believed killed'. A friend or two who knew his resourcefulness doubted it, but it was the only fate reasonable to presume.

It was, he said, 'obviously no good continuing to stick pins into the Japs'. All it would achieve was to 'bring down their wrath on our heads', and torture and death on all who helped them. The first objective must be to get out of Malaya, so that they could train a much larger force for when the time was ripe to return. Freddy never had the slightest doubt, now or later, that the British would eventually return. We, of course, are blessed with hindsight and we know that he was right. His certainty seemed half-crazed – blimpish, or quixotic at best – at the time. That same day, 19 February 1942, the Japanese 1st Air Fleet was bombing the port at Darwin in northern Australia. In the Dutch East Indies, seventy-five Allied fighters were shot down over Java in the course of the day. That night, after Japanese troops had landed on Bali, four Japanese destroyers drove off a much larger force of Allied cruisers and destroyers. The Japanese 15th Army was ripping through British and Indian troops in Burma. The 14th Army had trapped American troops in the Philippines at Bataan. Fierce fighting continued, but the end was not in much doubt in any of these three theatres.

Freddy had seen the Japanese at very close quarters, though, and his confidence was based on first-hand observation. They were brave, and energetic: but he noted how recklessly they allowed their arrogance and brutality to turn the occupied peoples against them, and he found them very poor jungle soldiers. This was ironic, for, unknown to Freddy of course, it was often said how brilliant they were in the jungle. It was a convenient way of explaining their lightning successes. He found they had little jungle discipline. They were reluctant to patrol deep into the jungle. When they did, they followed a compass course, blundering along in as straight a line as they could manage, instead of adapting sinuously to the lie of the land. They left a trail of crushed foliage and waste behind them, scraps of paper, rations wrappers, cigarette butts. He had already noted their fear of the dark, and the way the smell of tobacco gave away their positions. He was to owe his life to their failure to steal up quietly on the camps he was in, or to set ambushes on the escape routes. They were seen or heard long before they had got close.

For the minute, though, his thoughts were on getting out to India. He planned that they should return to Tanjong Malim and contact the guerrillas. They would hand them the spare arms and explosives, and train them in their use as time allowed. They would then make for the coast – where Harvey had already earmarked a boat – and set sail for India with the north-east monsoon. He hoped to take a few Chinese with him to train as officers for their eventual return.

The north-east monsoon blows until early April, and the south-west monsoon does not pick up until late May. This timetable gave them the luxury of a full week's rest at Sungei Sempan. It was, he said, 'one of the most pleasant holidays I have ever had'. It was not bragging to talk of a 'holiday' – though it seems so, with angry Japanese swarming about – and it was certainly not fatalism. The temperament that Freddy inherited from the Victorians had a seafaring streak to it from the days of sail. The random violence of the elements at sea bred patience, and preparation: a man made himself shipshape and snug, and this Freddy now did.

He took every precaution. To get to the hideout, the enemy had to climb a riverbed for half a mile, and cross two fallen trees and a side stream. The final obstacle was a bamboo thicket, which, like the riverbed, retained no footprints. He and Sartin fixed up trip-wires with lengths of instantaneous fuse. Anything that made a noise – chopping wood, listening to the wireless set – was done after dark. They spoke softly among themselves. Once secure, they set about their creature comforts. They levelled a platform outside the tent and used packing cases to build a table and three armchairs. A roof kept off the daily showers. They found some roses and a camellia bush in an old garden, made a vase out of bamboo for the table, and filled it with flowers.

Then they were ready to holiday. They swam in the river, and fished by dropping gelignite into the pools. The birdlife was magnificent. Fraser's Hill, which towers a few miles to the west, is renowned for its 260-odd species. It now attracts scores of birdspotters each June, who compete in teams in an International Bird Race to spot the greatest number. Freddy had its wonders – the Malayan whistling thrush, the Kinabalu friendly warbler, the green magpie, the sky-blue, long-tailed broadbill – almost to himself in 1942.

Singapore had already been renamed Syonan, 'Light of the South', by the Japanese. Its main newspaper, now the *Syonan Times*, carried a declaration by Tomoyuki Yamashita on 21 February. He said that his men had 'taken the sword of evil-breaking' and overwhelmed Malaya in two months. British power had 'collapsed in a moment' and was now 'a fan without a rivet or an umbrella without a handle'. He urged people to co-operate with the Nippon army to establish the 'New Order and Co-Prosperity Sphere'. If they did not – if they 'still pursue delusions . . . indulge in private interests and wants . . . disturb the public order' – then the 'Nippon army will drastically expel and punish them'.

To make the message clear, severed Chinese heads were put high on the bridges crossing the Singapore river, on poles in the central Penang market, and in other unmissable places. In Taiping, the heads of forty-three Hainanese canteen workers were given special prominence. *Sook ching*, 'purification by elimination', was a mass investigation of the whole Chinese population. In Singapore, it was carried out by 2 Field Kempeitai Group, a Japanese military police unit, under Major Satoru Onishi, a man who was to devote much time to catching Freddy.

All Chinese men between eighteen and fifty were ordered to report to assembly camps bringing a week's rations with them. They were paraded past hooded spies and informers. These were pre-war Japanese residents – the barbers and photographers who had passed information to Japanese intelligence before the invasion – and captured communists who had turned under torture, or secret society members trying to save their own lives. A crook of the finger by a hooded man was a death sentence. As a rule, teachers, lawyers, Hainanese, Chinese-born men who had come to Malaya after 1937, the year Japan invaded China, and men with tattoos were most at risk. The tattoos indicated members of secret societies, and the Hainanese were suspected of communism. Spectacles-wearers were killed in some places, as intellectuals, together with anyone connected with anti-Japanese organisations like the China Relief Fund. Those let go were given a one-inch square piece of paper, which said 'Examined' in Chinese. 'In the days to come,' a survivor wrote, 'that slip was worth its weight in radium.' Thousands of others were led away.

Cheng Kuan Yew was one of a batch of 400 or so Chinese loaded into trucks, twenty or so to a truck, and driven off. They thought they were being taken to Changi prison, but the trucks drove past it and on to the Changi beach. They were told to step down. Their hands were tied with telephone wire in groups of eight or ten. A pillbox stood on the sea-wall of a demolished bungalow. Cheng could see machine-guns through the pillbox slit. The machine-guns opened fire once they had lined up by the water's edge. Cheng was at the end of his group. As his companions were hit, they fell and 'pulled the rest of us down. As I fell, I was shot in the face . . . The machine-gunning stopped. The soldiers came round to bayonet us. I shut my eyes. A soldier stood on me to bayonet my neighbour. He did not turn the bayonet on me. I shut my eyes and kept them shut. I heard the sound of trucks driving off. I opened my eyes. Night had fallen. There was moonlight . . .'

Day after day, bodies washed ashore, some well-dressed, many tied together in threes and fours.

From Singapore, the masked informers and the *sook ching* crossed to mainland Malaya. In Johore Bahru, hundreds of Chinese were shot after digging their own graves in the grounds of the Civil Service Club, or were machine-gunned on the sea front. The Eurasian community was massacred en masse in a house in a kampong outside the city. In Ipoh, suspects were kept in an amusement park before being shot. In Negri Sembilan, the Kempeitai massacred whole villages. 'The prisoners were taken one by one to the spot where they were to die, and made to kneel with a bandage over their eyes,' a survivor said. The Kempeitai 'stepped out of the ranks one by one as his turn came to behead the victims with a sword or stab him through the breast with a bayonet ... The babies were thrown up into mid-air, and as they came down the soldiers pierced them with bayonet and sword.' A group of children who stood at attention when the Japanese approached them, raising their hands to their foreheads and shouting '*Tabek! Tabek!*' ('Salute!' in Malay), were 'whisked away to be killed'. The Overseas Chinese Association was coerced into making a 'voluntary' contribution of $50 million to expiate the Chinese community from its 'hostility' to Japan.

On the surface, the Chinese appeared quiescent, though the Japanese had no illusions over the reason. 'They cooperate outwardly with us,' an early report said, 'since they valued their lives and wanted to gain profits.' Inwardly, though, the atrocities consolidated the loathing for the invaders, and deepened admiration and support for the guerrillas – and for Freddy and the stay-behind parties. He would not have lasted a day without it.

As it was, Freddy and the others were three days into their idyll when they thought the Japanese had them. They were splashing about naked in the river, catching fish they had half-stunned with a gelignite blast, when two bearded faces emerged from the trees on the bank. They dashed for their pistols, thinking a Japanese patrol had surrounded them. The newcomers were in fact Pat Garden and Clarke Haywood, from another stay-behind party, whom Freddy had briefly met in Kuala

Lumpur. Garden was a mining engineer working in Pahang who had trained at 101 STS and had plenty of local knowledge. Haywood was an electrical engineer, and another experienced Malaya hand. They had set up supply dumps and hideouts at Sungei Gow, off Route 9 road in hilly jungle between Bentong and Menchis, near the little town of Karak. When they heard of the fall of Singapore, they set out to find Freddy's party. Freddy agreed to return with them to Sungei Gow to collect the other members of their party before they all set off for the coast to try to get to India. Haywood was a keen yachtsman and would be invaluable on the long voyage across the Bay of Bengal to Ceylon.

The three of them set out for Sungei Gow on about 26 February, with Harvey and Sartin staying behind to bury the stores. They wore uniforms with rank badges, and carried their military identity cards. They memorised cover stories as officers accidentally left behind in the retreat. Harvey took the role of a Japanese interrogator, cross-questioning them until they were word perfect. They went by bicycle, on the main road south from Tranum, Route 9, covering the thirty-odd miles in a single exhilarating night. The road drops steeply and they freewheeled in the dark at speed. They reached Bentong at 2 a.m., riding for over half a mile down the wide main street. The police station and the hospital were lit up, and there were other cyclists about, some of them smartly dressed with suitcases on their carriers. A curfew was in force, and the cyclists looked straight ahead and ignored each other. Freddy hoped that they were Chinese, and that they would pretend they had not seen three British officers in uniform pedalling furiously through the sleeping town.

Their luck held at Kampong Ketari, just south of the town, where they branched off Route 9 onto the Karak road, Route 8. There was a sentry box on the road, but they freewheeled past without being challenged. They turned off the road before reaching Karak. A timber track ran steeply uphill for three miles to Garden's camp by the headwaters of the Sungei Gow. Here Freddy met Chrystal and Robinson for the first time. The two were Perak rubber planters who knew the area well. The last member of Garden's party was Frank Quayle, who had been at sea as a ship's engineer before running a tin mine in Thailand.

The camp was 2,000 feet up, a good height that brought cooler days and nights during which they tucked themselves up in blankets. Garden had befriended a Chinese timber towkay – merchant – and they had hired one of his woodmen who lived with his wife down the valley. He had built them a comfortable atap hut, with a sleeping bench and a loft.

Chrystal thought that Freddy's plan to get to India involved mad risks: 'it probably allowed us a bare one per cent chance of getting through'. They had to get to Lumut on the coast, avoiding Japanese patrols, and there 'beg, borrow or steal' a Chinese junk. Freddy was to navigate, using a pocket compass and a sextant Haywood had made from the lid of a tin of Quaker Oats. He hoped the monsoon would take them to Calcutta in about a month. Quayle thought the prevailing winds were more likely to blow them to South Africa. But they fell in with the scheme nonetheless. Freddy, Chrystal found, was 'a most forceful personality, with an enthusiasm that aroused all one's boy scout instincts'.

They needed five more bicycles, as eight of them would be in the party for the coast. The towkay got the machines for them, though it took him until the beginning of March. They haggled with him, settling on $150 and leaving him with all the stores they could not carry. They celebrated the deal with a bottle of whisky. The towkay passed out drunk and they put him up for the night in the camp.

The journey back to pick up Harvey and Sartin was fraught and difficult. The bicycles were ancient and infirm, and heavily laden, and they had to wheel two of them. The route from Bentong was uphill this time, and they became strung out over five or six miles of road. A compact party could sweep past a sentry before he was fully aware of them, and clatter over the planks of repaired bridges in one go, but stragglers would find themselves in a hornet's nest. Chrystal remembered two cars coming on them with headlights blazing, passing by a few feet away as they flung themselves in a ditch. Then a Japanese bicycle patrol, in shorts and white singlets, 'shot past' them without giving them time to get off the road, apparently without noticing them. 'It must have been our night,' Chrystal said, shaken. Freddy made no mention of these incidents in his book. The bicycles broke down from time to time, and they had to stop for punctures before Raub. To get through to the camp before dawn, they left Garden and Haywood to lie up in the jungle to repair them. They reached the Sungei Sempan camp the following night.

At Sungei Sempan, they prepared for the trip to the coast and the voyage to India. Freddy reckoned it would take six weeks. Each bicycle was allotted a load of 100 pounds, of arms, ammunition, clothes, and rations, biscuits, butter, sardines and herring, raisins and sugar. Most of this was slung in army packs on both sides of the back wheel. A haversack of essentials, medicines, maps, and a little food, was tied to the handlebars to grab in an emergency. They buried the rest of the stores in the jungle. Haywood and Quayle, both engineers, spent three days getting the bicycles in working order. Experience showed that a group of eight cyclists would get too spread out, so Freddy divided the party in two. He and Haywood left with Chrystal and Robinson on 8 March. Harvey, Garden, Quayle and Sartin were to follow two nights later.

The journey was a disaster. The first party set out on Friday 13 March, Chrystal said, after a 'bumper dinner, a bottle of whisky and some boisterous horseplay. To choose a Friday the thirteenth for starting a perilous journey was, I think, stretching our luck a bit too far.' The first stage was to the old tin mine hideout at Sungei Salak. It was sixty miles by road, and they hoped to do it in two nights, but the first leg included the 2,000-foot climb up to the Gap. There was no moon until after midnight and they crashed the bicycles, which were badly balanced with so much weight on the rear wheel. A party of Malays flashed torches in their faces and ran off into the rubber. Headlights appeared and in the scramble to hide two of the bicycles plunged into the river beside the road. They had to be unloaded to get them out. Chrystal and Robinson fell behind as they toiled up the hairpin bends to the Gap. Haywood and Freddy stopped to let them catch up, but fell asleep: that, at least, was Freddy's recollection, though Chrystal was to tell the writer Dennis Holman that it was Freddy and himself who stopped, and that the whisky had made them sleepy. In the pitch dark, the others did not see the white towel Freddy had left in the road, but cycled on.

They had not found each other when dawn broke – they narrowly missed being seen by some Tamil coolies walking to work – and they had to lie up. The emergency rendezvous was the wooden seat at Walsh's Corner, a bend of the road below the Gap that looks over the mountains rippling away past Fraser's Hill, and eastward across the plain towards the South China Sea. Freddy and Haywood waited there the next night, and were relieved to hear the others whistling 'The Lambeth Walk', which they were using in place of the tawny owl cry. They found they had been within a hundred yards of each other when they had camped at dawn.

They passed the rest-house at the Gap during the night and crossed the watershed. It was too dark to freewheel down, the bends too tight and the road too narrow. So they walked, and they were still eleven miles short of Kuala Kubu when dawn broke. They lay up for the day. Freddy was sitting on his bicycle the next night, waiting to set off, when the back wheel buckled under the load. He changed bicycles and left Chrystal and Robinson in the jungle to wait for the second party. He said he would send a Chinese back from the tin mine camp with a spare wheel. He then set off with Haywood, but within a mile his front forks collapsed. Haywood managed to repair them, but Freddy had to dump his two packs under a bridge to lighten the load.

As Kuala Kubu came into view below them, they saw a bright arc light shining over the road. Freddy looked through his field glasses, but could not see any troops or sentries. If they went full tilt, Freddy was confident that they could be past the lighted area before anyone had time to react. He hoped there were no troops in the darkness beyond. As they pedalled furiously down they passed a truck with men dozing on the running board. A voice yelled at them, but they hurtled on towards the junction with the main road. They knew a sentry box was there from their previous trip, and it was on them sooner than they expected. Instead of quietly walking their bicycles round it in the shadows, they clattered up to it.

The sentry flashed a light at them, and opened fire, shouting all the while. Haywood's chain broke but they freewheeled on as the shots went by, and swerved off to the road leading to the Kuala Kubu railway station. They cut the telephone wires and Haywood fixed his chain before they joined Route One to pass through Kerling. Freddy feared the little town would be a death-trap, but they were through it safely before his front forks collapsed again. They were dumping the bicycle in the rubber trees when two trucks full of troops roared past. The Japanese were obviously thoroughly aroused, and they decided to lie up as soon as they were out of the rubber trees, which were too open to offer good cover. Haywood rode the surviving bicycle whilst Freddy loped beside him carrying his tommy-gun. They found some overgrown tin-tailings before Kalumpang where they lay up in the tangled scrub for the day, taking turns to keep watch, fearing that the soldiers who had passed in the trucks would return in a sweep looking for them.

They tiptoed through Kalumpang that night in the dust, pushing the remaining bicycle. They were startled by a loud cough, which sounded 'just beside us', and lay flat when someone lit a cigarette ahead of them. A party of six armed men went past. They could not make out who they were, but at length reached the Escot Estate, hid the remaining bicycle, and made their way to the Sungei Salak hideout before dawn.

They found Leu Kim's kongsi-house had been burnt to the ground. The old man and his coolies had vanished. They met a Chinese who said that Lee Fee had informed on Leu Kim. He was lucky that the Japanese had only burned his house. Elsewhere, they had rounded up all the people in a kampong who might have helped with the attacks on the railway and the road. They lectured them on their duty to help Nippon, and, at their whim, let some go and bayoneted and machine-gunned the others. A little to the north, they had collected over a hundred Chinese, the old, women, children, and burned them to death in an atap hut.

Despite this terror, the Chinese offered to put them in touch with the guerrillas, whom he said were stronger than before. He took them to a hut where he and a score of other Chinese were lying low from the Japanese. They were given a good meal, and taken to a hideout further into the jungle. It was 'absolutely typical' of the Chinese, Freddy said in admiration, that they were willing to help him in every possible way, even though he had brought the Japanese and their atrocities down on their heads. He wrote a letter to the head of the Perak guerrillas, explaining that he had trained their original parties at 101 STS, and asking for one of their leaders to meet him as soon as possible. In due course two guerrillas came to Freddy from the headquarters of the Perak Anti-Japanese forces, who were in a camp about thirty miles north at Ulu Slim. They said that their leaders would come to meet him soon, and that they were to help him in the meantime.

Freddy sent one of them – he had to teach him to whistle 'The Lambeth Walk' – to take a letter to Chrystal and Robinson. They were still where Freddy had left them, in a camp they had made on the hill above Kuala Kubu, waiting for the second group. On the third night, Garden and Harvey had shot past them before Chrystal had time to whistle 'The Lambeth Walk', but he managed to stop Sartin and Quayle who were a little distance behind. Quayle's bicycle was in poor shape, and he stayed with the campers. Sartin went on to catch up with the other two.

The guerrilla messenger found Chrystal, Robinson and Quayle. Freddy's letter warned them that it was too dangerous to move along the roads and that he was arranging for guerrillas to pick them up and guide them through the jungle to the big camp at Ulu Slim. In the meantime, they should sit tight. When he got back, the messenger gave Freddy a letter from Chrystal. It said they were safe for the moment, though some Malays had spotted them. It added that they had no news of Harvey, Garden and Sartin, who had sped on. Worryingly, the messenger told Freddy that three Europeans had been seen tied up with some Chinese in the back of a Japanese truck. They were being driven to Kuala Kubu.

Pat Garden and Sartin survived the war, as prisoners, to recount the dreadful fate that awaited Harvey. They had reached the point above Kuala Kubu where the arc light gleamed over the road. They were wheeling their bicycles past it when they ran into a Japanese infantry patrol. Each waited for the other to start shooting, and they were taken prisoner. Freddy thought this meekness was 'very unlike Harvey', who was the leader of the little band, and put it down to physical exhaustion. They were taken by car to Kuala Lumpur next day, and put in Pudu jail. There Harvey was to recover his initiative, and pay for it with his life.

The prison held other stay-behinds, including Vanrenan and Graham. They had got to the coast and sailed a sampan across the straits to Sumatra after the failed rendezvous with Freddy. They crossed back to Port Selangor to search for him. They also sabotaged arms dumps and ambushed a train. The Japanese took several villagers hostage and said every man, woman and child would be shot unless Vanrenan surrendered. He and Graham did so on about 25 March. Hembry, the third man, had been too ill to follow them. He had got himself to Java, and then on to Australia on a tramp steamer. He survived the war.

Two survivors of Stubbington's stay-behind party were also in Pudu prison, betrayed by local Malays. The Japanese had attacked the camp and they fled with their weapons into the jungle, following tracks to get to Jeruntut on the Pahang river. Having stolen a boat they were moving fast down the swollen river when they struck a rock in darkness and capsized. They lost their kit and tommy-guns and had only their revolvers. They set out again to follow the river to the coast. On 17 March, local Malays again betrayed them, and they were ambushed by the Japanese. Stubbington, Rand and Darby were killed in the firefight. Elkin and Pearson were seized, beaten and made to dig their own graves. When these were thought deep enough, they were bound and made to stand next to them. Then a Japanese suggested that they should be questioned before being killed. They were thrown in the back of a captured British army lorry and driven to Pudu prison. Here they were joined by the others. The Japanese now had half the left-behind parties in Pudu, though they did not realise it.

Vanrenan decided to escape, with eight others including Harvey and Graham. Several of them could speak Malay or Tamil, and they got hold of sarongs and Malay shirts, hoping to pass themselves off as natives. They forced a gate and walked off into the night. At midday next day, the main gates of the prison were opened, and the badly beaten and shackled men were prodded back through with bayonets. Local people had betrayed them. They were kept chained for two days, and refused food and water and visits to the latrines. They were taken in trucks to Kuala Lumpur cemetery and forced to dig their own graves. Later that day, covered in cemetery soil and filth from their cells,

Vanrenan, Harvey, Graham and five others were executed. The ninth man was in Bentong hospital with a broken leg. When it was healed, he was beheaded also.

Shortly after the messenger returned with Chrystal's note, the three leaders of the Perak guerrillas arrived in the camp. Freddy described Chin Peng as 'a young and attractive Hokkien' who became 'Britain's most trusted guerrilla representative'. He might have added that during the communist insurgency after the war, the remarkable Chin Peng, who had been awarded an OBE, became Malaya's most wanted man. The others were Commander Itu, the military head of the Perak patrols, and Lee Far, a highly thought-of English-speaker. Freddy called their meeting a 'conference'. In name it was grand indeed – the representative of Britain's Special Operations Executive parleying with the Malayan People's Anti-Japanese Army – but in reality a stained and weary English fugitive squatted in a clearing outside the hut with three meek-looking Chinese, the youngest of them, Chin Peng, still a teenager. At this meeting, however, the alliance with the guerrillas was confirmed. To Chin Peng, it was a marriage of convenience. 'The British were desperate and found us useful,' he wrote. 'Conveniently, we both wanted to defeat the Japanese.' Once the common enemy was defeated, he added, it was the British aim as colonialists to remain in Malaya – and it remained his aim as a communist to remove them. Freddy, though, remembered the atmosphere as 'cordial'.

It was agreed that Freddy and Haywood would go to Chin Peng's camp at Ulu Slim. The guerrillas had picked up rifles, Bren guns and pistols, and ammunition and grenades abandoned by the British in the fighting at the river. Freddy would train them in using them, and guides would be sent to bring Chrystal and the others to the camp.

Ulu Slim was only twenty miles north on the main road, but it took them a week to get there. They travelled with Lee Far, elegant in the jungle, in lavender trousers and immaculate white shirt, with patent leather shoes and a white topee. They had new guides every few miles, who carried his spare clothes. The Japanese were suspicious of ragged Chinese. It was safer to be well turned-out. They crossed ten rivers, torrents racing between granite slabs, and across deeply scoured tracks where water buffaloes had dragged out hardwoods for the timber mills. They slept in deserted woodcutters' huts and villages abandoned by Sakai, the aborigines of Malaya, who had moved further into the mountains for fear of the Japanese.

They were welcomed to the camp by Chin Peng and a guard of honour with a motley of weapons. It included two girls with bobbed hair, and no make-up, but Freddy judged their black Chinese blouses and trousers to be 'severe but attractive'. He began weapons training and lectures on fieldcraft and demolition. He gave them PT in the morning and thirty minutes of games in the evenings. Chrystal, Robinson and Quayle arrived on 6 April. Freddy said they were 'indifferent travellers' and arrived exhausted. This was unfair – Chrystal was to make spectacular jungle journeys – but Freddy brooked no rivals in fitness and endurance.

The five men discussed their future. Freddy thought that it was now too late to ride the north-east monsoon to India. Instead, he wanted to get the guerrillas to find a boat for them to sail to Sumatra, where he hoped that local Chinese communists would find them another boat to sail to Australia or India, depending on the time of year. Chrystal said that he was all for pressing straight on for the coast. Freddy explained that the guerrillas were against them leaving yet – they wanted help with their training – and that it would be futile to try to get to the coast and find a boat without them.

Next night, Freddy was woken by an excited Chinese. The man pulled down his blanket, looked at a large scar Freddy had on the back of his right knee, and vigorously shook his hand. Freddy thought he was mad, but then remembered he had told his Chinese students at 101 STS that they could always be sure of his identity if they checked his scar. He recognised the man as Tan Chen King, the leader and interpreter of the first course of students at the school. He was twenty-two, a former worker at the Ford plant in Singapore and now leader of the guerrillas in Selangor, with headquarters near the Batu Caves outside Kuala Lumpur. The MCP Secretary General, he said, wanted to meet Freddy at the Batu Caves camp. It was agreed that Freddy would go there with Haywood, leaving Chrystal and the others to continue the training at Ulu Slim.

They split all the money they had with them, $200, and Freddy and Haywood left to go south. They had alarms on the way. Their guides often got lost, and crashed into cattle pens on an estate at night, and they were chased by a large party of estate workers, Sikhs and Tamils, who thought they were cattle thieves. They ran from a patrol of Malay police who spotted them as they worked their way round a tin dredge at Kalumpang. When they reached Kuala Kubu, Freddy lay up in a small patch of jungle that overlooked the town. He spent the day looking through his field glasses. He did not spot any prisoners – Sartin, Garden and Harvey had already been transferred to Kuala Lumpur – though he was interested to watch the Japanese drilling and at mortar practice.

It took three days of hard jungle slog to skirt Rasa and Batang Kali, the two towns to the south. The Chinese houses in the Sungei Liam valley were all flying Japanese flags. The guerrillas were well-liked, though, and they travelled openly by day, with Freddy fussed over and well fed when they stopped. They made contact with guides from the Batu Caves camp who had bicycles with them. Malay villages were ahead and they sped through them at midnight, to reach the camp before dawn. It was a little over fifty miles by road, and Tan Chen King had done it in a day on his bicycle, but it had taken them a fortnight.

CHAPTER 10

BIRDS AND BULLETS

The Batu Caves camp had a cookhouse by a stream, a long, low atap hut with sleeping platforms along each side, and a parade ground. It was safe enough from the air, lost deep in a valley, but it was only half a mile from a rubber plantation, and Freddy fretted at its vulnerability. There were five girls among the seventy Chinese in the camp. They were fairly well armed, with two machine-guns, four tommy-guns and a score of rifles and pistols. Four men had been at the Training School in Singapore, and they had a good amount of explosives and detonators supplied by 101 STS.

There were also six British soldiers. Four were privates, two of them gunners, and two very young Argylls. The other two were sergeants, a mortar sergeant and a tin-mining engineer from Thailand called Regan, who had trained as a wireless operator at 101 STS. Freddy said he was 'the best' of them. That was to sell Regan short. He had been left behind on the River Krai to gather intelligence, and had trekked almost 150 miles through the jungle before being found by the communists.

All of them were suffering from beriberi. Freddy got some groundnuts and rice bran, which restored vitamin B to their diet, and soon reduced the swelling for five of them. They brought out the ruthless unsentimentality in him, as surely as the sick Alsatians in the Arctic. More than vitamin deficiency, he said, it was 'their mental attitude, which was slowly but surely killing them'. 'In my experience,' he said with brutal frankness, the life expectancy of the British private who found himself a straggler in the jungle was 'only a few months'.

The 'average NCO', he said, 'being more intelligent, might last a year or even longer'. They thought of the jungle as hostile, riddled with fevers, poisonous snakes, scorpions and man-eating tigers, and peopled by natives with poisoned darts. It unnerved them. They could not adapt to it, nor to a diet of rice and vegetables. In the 'green hell' they had imagined for themselves, they expected to be dead within weeks – 'and as a rule', he added, 'they were'. The opposing school of thought – of the jungle as tropical paradise, teeming with tasty birds and fish, lush with 'paw-paw, yams, breadfruit and that' – was equally misleading. The truth, he said,

> . . . is that the jungle is neutral. It provides any amount of fresh water, and unlimited cover for friend as well as foe – an armed neutrality, if you like, but neutrality nevertheless. It is the attitude of mind that determines whether you go under or survive. 'There is nothing either good or bad, but thinking makes it so.' The jungle itself is neutral.

This was the Greenland philosophy, complete with *Hamlet* quote. It had worked in snow and ice, and it worked now in the moist green wastelands. Freddy's instinct to survive demanded the suppression of personal feeling. Thought was dangerous, be it good or bad, and the most positive-seeming of emotions, hope, was in practice the most dangerous of all, for it slides seamlessly into despair at the slightest rebuff. He abandoned the past – it had gone, utterly, snuffed out by the Japanese for a thousand miles around – and fretted little over a future he could do little to change, other than struggling to make sure he remained physically a part of it. His life had become a narrative. He wrote of what he did, almost never of what he felt. And that, we may assume, was because he indeed felt and thought as little as possible: living – not to die – was all. Some like their heroes hot-blooded, but Freddy had to an extraordinary degree the quality of coolness the French call sangfroid.

He had immunised himself against emotional distress and physical discomfort as an orphan child. The mores of Edwardian England were stamped in him the deeper for never having been mothered. The upper lip did not quiver. The heart was never worn on the sleeve. These were practical qualities – the imperial virtues of a race that had crewed the world's ships, and explored its every inhospitable nook and cranny, and that still ruled a quarter of humanity – and he needed them now. His situation was in every respect more desperate than that, say, of Lawrence of Arabia. Freddy was a remnant of a defeated army, not in the vanguard of a victorious one. But he was not a prisoner, where imagination consoles the caged body, and thoughts of home inspire the will to endure. He was free, and feelings were an encumbrance to a man who each day had to earn his existence among the living.

The camp was filthy. The latrine was upwind, a pit full of a 'stinking mass of seething maggots', so disgusting that most of the men used the stream immediately below the camp. The refuse from the kitchen was thrown into pits by the stream, which were black with flies. The mortar sergeant was the first to die. His limbs were horribly swollen with beriberi, and he was dead two days after Freddy arrived. Sergeant Regan was still cheerful, despite swollen legs. The other four, Freddy said baldly, 'had given up hope and could not last long', though the Chinese did all they could to help them.

One of the gunners had a persecution mania – he thought the others were stealing his food and plotting to kill him – and he had tried to escape from the camp several times. Tan Chen King wanted him shot. Freddy refused to do so, but gave the Chinese permission to kill him if he threatened the security of the camp.

After a few days, the sentry at the edge of the rubber opened fire on two Malays who were prowling about, clearly looking for the camp. He missed them, and it was almost certain that they would tell the Japanese. An attack was likely next morning. Tan Chen King prepared to move everyone to a new camp. Freddy found it a 'heaven-sent opportunity' to study the Japanese in action. He persuaded King to leave a Chinese with him to guide him to the new camp site after he had observed the attack. The others left, with Haywood looking after the sick British, whilst Freddy spent the evening making a hideout on the thickly wooded slope overlooking the camp. He and the Chinese kept guard in turns through the night.

At the first pink of dawn, at about 5.45 a.m., two or more mortars began firing from the rubber. Freddy soon found himself alone. His companion had not been under fire before, and he took off. Every hut was hit by mortar fire. The Japanese then machine-gunned the camp for about ten minutes. Even if the guerrillas had been in the camp, Freddy noted, they could have disappeared into the jungle after the first mortar landed, and only equipment too heavy to grab would have been lost. The shooting stopped. Freddy watched as about 100 Japanese troops, and the same number of Malays and Indians, charged into the camp with battle cries and fixed bayonets. When they reached the parade ground, they stopped and stood in a huddle, 'gazing round them like a party of tourists . . . I only wished I had a machine-gun with me.' They jabbered to each other with wild gesticulations for a little, and then set fire to the huts and left.

Freddy learned later that these over-excited troops had already been involved in a massacre that morning. At 4 a.m., they had surrounded a Chinese kampong a mile from the camp. They had loaded the 160 inhabitants, men, women and children, into trucks and drove them to a desolate area of tin-tailings on the road to Kuala Lumpur. The Japanese made the men dig a trench. They stood everybody in a line next to it, and killed them with gunfire and bayonets. Anyone suspected of helping the British or the guerrillas faced a terrible end: shot or decapitated, after torture by the Kempeitai, often accompanied by his family or whole community. There was every incentive for Malays and Indians to betray the Chinese guerrillas and their white man. The Japanese made no bones about their racial contempt for Chinese, and the massacres they had inflicted in China since 1937 gave the Chinese in Malaya added reason to detest them. The Malays and Indians had less reason for loathing – the Japanese made fitful and half-hearted attempts to win them over – but equal reason for fear. Being spotted by anyone was dangerous, of course, but the risk was highest with Malays.

Freddy's Chinese guide reappeared after the troops had gone. They walked through vegetable gardens and rubber estates, across a high ridge and along a jungle track that led north. They heard the others from a good distance before they caught up with them. The cook was carrying his biggest rice-pot with a loose ladle inside it, which sounded like 'the beating of tom-toms in the night'. The guides had lost the way and the party had split in two. One of the British gunners had a temperature of 104 degrees and had to be carried. They got to a small Chinese kampong by the Sungei Udang river, at the end of a woodcutter's path, and rested in a large atap shed. Next morning, they scouted a site for a new camp. Haywood stayed with the sick gunner, as he 'still hopes to save his life', Freddy said: he himself had written the man off, and he left at first light with a small party of guerrillas. They needed a place that would not be stumbled on by Malays, but which was not too remote from Chinese kampongs for food supplies. The approach needed to be easily overlooked, to give warning of Japanese patrols, with good escape routes. There had to be a stream, and plenty of rattan creepers and atap palms for building the huts. Freddy found a suitable stretch of ground beside the Sungei Kanching. It was two miles from the road between Rawang and the Batu Caves, a favourite spot for picnickers before the war.

The gunner died as they were building the new camp. Freddy skimmed through the event in two sentences:

We buried him – as we had buried the mortar sergeant – in a grave near the edge of the jungle. I could not procure a Prayer Book in order to read the Burial Service, so we had to be content with saying the Lord's Prayer and Fidele's Dirge from *Cymbeline*, after which the guerrillas sang 'The Red Flag'.

Then he was straight back to his narrative: 'Altogether Haywood and I spent almost a fortnight with this patrol ...' The burial could have breathed pathos and drama had he allowed it to. The jungle here is softly rolling, with orchid bursts high under the green canopy, and rushing streams and shallow waterfalls. Scents drift from citronella trees, tall and slender ghosts with white trunks. The brilliant white flowers of coral rhododendrons are textured in intricate patterns. Wild raspberries and bananas grow. Carnivorous pitcher plants tempt the insects they eat with water in their whitish-yellow flowers. The grave was a yellow scrape amidst all this, and the men at the little service desperate and hunted, an eye always on the forest for fear of what might spring from it, the British in rags of uniforms, the two Argylls boys themselves near death, the young Chinese dog-tired and dirty, singing 'The Red Flag' as a gesture of respect, not as an ideological claim. Freddy's recital from *Cymbeline* was wonderfully well chosen, the Japanese defied by Shakespeare:

> Fear no more the heat of the Sun,
> Nor the furious winter's rages;
> Thou thy worldly task hast done,
> Home art gone, and taken thy wages:
> Golden lads and girls all must,
> As chimney-sweepers, come to dust.

But Freddy gave no more than a place, 'near the edge of the jungle': he set no scene, and gave the dead man no name or age.

The camp was swiftly finished. The frames of the huts were made of poles of green timber five or six inches thick. Standing trees were strongest, and they used them to support the main roof beams. Rattan was used to lash the joints. It is a climbing palm with a thin stem that snakes for hundreds of feet along the ground before climbing a tree to explode into a palm top of leaves when it reaches the light. They hauled a length of stem down from a tree and stripped off the shell that protects the thin green bamboo within it. This was split with a sharp knife into thin strips to use as ties. The fronds of the atap palms were pulled down and the stalks cut off, leaving lengths of fifteen feet to intertwine for roofs and walls.

Freddy spent the next two weeks cramming the guerrilla commanders with some grasp of tactics and strategy. The English acquired a military sense through a sort of social osmosis: if they had not been cadets at school, they had fathers or uncles who had been soldiers, they had watched troops drilling, and they had seen war films and read war comics. Most of these young Chinese had been students or shopkeepers or clerks a few weeks before. The only soldiers they had seen were white or Indian, and they had no military background. Freddy worked late into the night writing simple manuals on the weapons they had – British service rifles, pistols and Bren guns, light machine-guns, and tommy-guns from 101 STS – and on explosives and basic tactics.

He missed accurate news of the war. He still hoped that the tide would soon turn, and that British troops would be rolling back into Malaya. He had heard nothing reliable since the fall of Singapore. Stories picked up from Japanese-controlled stations were uniformly grim: the Japanese had overrun Burma, they were landing in Ceylon, Australia was in danger.

The Nipponisation of Malaya itself was now beginning in earnest. Clocks had moved forward two hours to Tokyo time. The year 1942 became 2606. Any promotion in government service depended on knowing 'Nippon-go', the Japanese language. English schools were reopened as Japanese schools. Most private Chinese schools closed, and for a time the Chinese language could not be taught. In Penang, book-shops had to hand in Chinese books for censorship. More than 200,000 volumes were burned. In Singapore, Raffles Hotel reopened as Syonan Ryokan, a Japanese officers' club where newly arrived German and Italian officers also dined. The press was controlled by the Japanese Domei News Agency. The Ee Hoe Hean, the famous Chinese millionaires' club, was transformed into a high-class restaurant and bordello. John Little's renowned department store became Daimaru, with the best goods marked 'For Nippon-gin Only' ('for Japanese only').

Some form of normality was returning by now. Race meetings were being held again in Kuala Lumpur. In Syonan, the Worlds, the huge amusement parks with their arcades and restaurants and Chinese operas, reopened, though the censors finally caught up with the big box-office hits, and banned all British and American films. It took them another four months to turn on British and American music, with the banning of 1,000 proscribed songs, including 'Colonel Bogey' and 'Kisses in the Dark'.

Despite this, Freddy never lost faith that the British would return. Whether that would be in months or years he could not judge without one of the army wireless sets with the power to pick up broadcasts from

India. He had left a set at Sungei Sempan, and Garden had left another one with the timber towkay at Sungei Gow. It made sense for him and Haywood to collect a set, and also to bring back the large amounts of ammunition and explosives that were hidden in the same dumps. There was food there, too, sugar, biscuits and army ration tins, which he thought might save the lives of the Argylls and the surviving gunner. Tan Cheng King agreed with this plan. He suggested that he should go with them, and also Ah Loy, the leader of the guerrillas in Pahang, who was staying in a kampong near the Batu Caves. When they returned, they hoped that the Secretary General, whom they had been waiting to meet, would at last have appeared.

They left the camp for the Sungei Gow dump at the beginning of May 1942. It was fifty miles away by road. Freddy was leery of cycling after the disaster on Kuala Jubu road. Ah Loy assured him that the Japanese never used the back roads at night. Freddy insisted on roadworthy bicycles and a set of spanners in case of trouble. Ah Loy gave them a splendid meal before they set off: fresh rice, chicken, pork and curried aubergines, and pineapple, bananas and coffee. Most communist leaders were dour. Ah Loy was an exception, an earthy Cantonese, the son of a rich pawnbroker in Bentong who had run away from home and joined Mao's famous 8th Route Army guerrilla school in northern China. He loved his food – so did Freddy, who savoured the few fine feasts he had – and was excellent company, though Freddy found him too rash and mettlesome to be a good leader.

The first part of their route took them through rubber plantations to avoid the main road. The paths had narrow plank bridges across ditches and streams. Freddy and Haywood crashed off them several times in the dark. Soaked and muddy, they reached the quiet Route 68 road that runs steeply uphill past Genting Sempah to cross the Main Range. Graceful coconut palms met overhead in brilliant moonlight as they pedalled through sleeping Malay kampongs. Exhilaration gave way to exhaustion as they struggled to keep up with the Chinese when the road began to climb. They were weakened by the poor camp diet, wet rice and scraps of fish and vegetable, and Haywood's puffy hands and feet were the first signs of beriberi. They climbed 1,000 feet in the last seven miles of the night's ride, and at last reached the 20th Mile, where stores had been hidden in a derelict charcoal-burner's furnace. Despite the moon, they could not find the track that led up to it through thick jungle. They waited until dawn in a coffee-house by the road, kept by two aged Chinese who behaved as if it was quite normal to serve a pair of English desperadoes with *samsu* (rice spirit) and coffee in the early hours.

With light, they found the dump. Bears had broken into it, smashing the big containers of rice and sugar. The explosives, grenades and rations tins were intact, though, and a party of guerrillas packed them into suitcases and took them off on the carriers of their bicycles. They could risk being seen on the road in daylight. Freddy and Haywood, who could not, lay in a clearing high above the road. It toiled upwards in dramatic S-bends to cross the pass below the summit of Genting Sempah. The mist that often shrouds the jungle on its upper slopes is pierced now by the colossal gaily coloured walls and watch towers and templed roofs of fun palaces, slot machine arcades, gambling halls, and two-thousand-bedroom hotels, like a lurid Potala on a plinth of jungle so steep that the cable cars carrying visitors almost brush its foliage and chattering birds. There was not a brick on it as Freddy gazed up in 1942: but the birds were there, and Freddy spent the day 'sleeping in the sun or making notes on the innumerable varieties of birds, most of which were new to me'.

They did not set off again until midnight. Freddy knew that there was a sentry post at Kampong Ketari, where the Karak road turns off Route 68 a little short of Bentong. He hoped the sentry would be comatose, and he did not want to pass him before 2 a.m. They ate in the coffee-shop again, a good meal of rice and curried fish, chatting with the two old Chinese, who told them of the 'innumerable cold-blooded massacres' carried out by the Japanese, particularly in places where guerrillas were thought to be. Freddy was astonished that these old men were delighted to help him, though they faced certain death if they were caught. Later, he found Chinese help was 'so universal that I ceased to wonder at it': he attributed it to their 'most bitter hatred' of the Japanese, yet they often betrayed one another, and there must have been a personal quality, of warmth, or sympathy, that protected him, as well, of course, of his use to the guerrilla cause as a trained instructor.

Even late at night, there were Chinese cyclists and some Tamil bullock carts about as they sweated slowly up to the pass. It was at over 2,000 feet, and from there it was twenty miles of free-wheeling down to the crossroads at Ketari, then largely downhill for ten miles on to the Sungei Gow, a little short of Karak. Freddy flew down the curves in brilliant moonlight, the tall trees flashing past at the roadside, the air cool with night and altitude. Ah Loy had the only puncture mending kit, and they lost time when Tan Chen King's tyre burst, and one of the guerrillas had to pedal frantically to catch up with Ah Loy and bring him back.

The curves become more gentle lower down. The road runs along by a river with steep banks and some run-down rubber trees before a bend leads to a bridge. It had been blown during the retreat, but it was repaired with planks. Freddy stopped for a moment after he had rattled across to wait for a guerrilla who had lagged behind. Three cyclists came suddenly round the bend and drew up by him. One was a Malay policeman with a double-barrelled shotgun laid across his handlebars. He saw that Freddy was a white man, let out a surprised grunt, and lunged for his bicycle. Freddy had his .38 revolver in his belt. 'At that time I did not feel I was at war with Malays,' he said, 'and the idea of shooting him never even entered my head.' Instead he hit the policeman's arm as hard as he could, fended off another Malay, and yelled to Haywood to 'Go like hell!' The Malay shot four times at Freddy as he pedalled madly away, and the third shot burst his back tyre and tore the muscle of his left calf. The leg was useless now, but he managed to cling on to the back of Haywood's bicycle, and they met up with Tan Chen King and Ah Loy, who had turned back when they heard the firing.

The valley opens out at this point, with rubber trees at the top of a steep bank to the left of the road, river and jungle to the right. Freddy stopped the others, and they clambered up the bank and drew their pistols. They opened fire as the Malays rode up, dropping the leader ten yards in front of them. Freddy paid him tribute as 'a very brave man'. As he lay on the road, the policeman fired both barrels of his shotgun at them, and then crawled across to the other side of the road, dragging himself into a dense patch of jungle bananas. The two other Malays disappeared.

It was already 3 a.m. They cut the telephone wires, but feared that the Japanese garrison in Bentong had been alerted by the gunfire, and would be waiting for them six miles ahead at Kampong Ketari. Freddy's wound prevented them from taking to the safety of the forest. His calf was streaming blood and he could hardly walk. The bone seemed untouched, but the torn muscle made his ankle useless and he was in severe pain. It was too dark to dig out the shot, so he tied a field dressing on it, and gritted his teeth. His own bicycle was useless, the rear wheel and tyre ruined by shot, and he took the policeman's machine from the road, and had himself towed along by Ah Loy. The strange little bicycle convoy, a bloodstained white man holding on to the pistol belt of a Chinese, weary, their machines weighed down by boxes of hand-grenades and explosives, rolled through Ketari without incident – the sentry was asleep or absent and they reached the path off to Sungei Gow before dawn.

As it got light, they washed the blood from Freddy's leg and found that the wound was a single gaping hole. Tan Chen King fashioned a probe and a pair of forceps from bamboo. He began excavating the wound deep inside the calf. 'Fortunately,' Freddy noted, 'I fainted and was thus spared the pain.' When he recovered consciousness, Tan Chen King presented him with a half-inch motorcar nut. The policeman had made up his own, highly lethal cartridges: 'I was extremely grateful that none of his shots at close range had found their mark.' The wound was syringed with stream water and Freddy added some iodine from his medical kit. He was lucky. He could not move his ankle without severe pain for several days, but the wound healed well with no infection, and the swelling slowly went down.

There were still two miles to cover to the house of John, who worked for the Chinese towkay, and had helped Haywood and his party. Bamboo had been newly cut along the track, and it was treacherous and slimy underfoot in the morning dew. Freddy could remember 'few more unpleasant three hours in my whole life'. They reached the house at midday on 2 May. Freddy at once collapsed with high fever.

He had the classic symptoms of acute pneumonia. Chest pains and fevers wracked him and he breathed in desperate gasps and groans. He suffered abdominal pains and an attack of dysentery. He fainted when he went to the emergency latrine made for him at the side of the path, and rolled down the slope to the stream below. He was confused and unsteady, flitting in and out of consciousness, with no appetite and severe weight loss. On 5 May, he said, 'I felt so ill that I thought I was going to die, so I started to write my will.' He was too confused and weak to finish it, and he dictated it to Haywood.

The Japanese were searching the jungle edge along the Bentong to Karak road looking for him. It was no longer safe to stay in John's house, and Freddy was carried on a stretcher up the conical hill behind the house to Haywood's old hut. Haywood now collapsed. They were both desperately ill, running dangerously high temperatures, shaking violently at times and at others lying unconscious. Their temperatures went up and down by as much as ten degrees in a day, as they alternately shivered under blankets and groaned and sweated with the heat of fierce fevers. Freddy's most critical period was between 5 May and 23 May. He always kept a diary, and on the 23rd he thought he had failed to write it up 'today and yesterday'. Haywood gave him the diary, and he realised he had written nothing for seventeen days. Haywood told him that he had been semiconscious at best, and that he had often had to check that he was still alive.

From then on, as Freddy began to mend, Haywood deteriorated. Freddy nursed him, and saw what he had gone through himself. In the mornings, Haywood's temperature was several degrees below normal, and he complained of the cold despite being covered in blankets. The shivering and breathlessness that wracked him were so fierce that his teeth rattled and the hut's sleeping bench shook. The colour drained from his face and his lips faded 'to a bluish-grey'. This was the classic sign of cyanosis due to poor blood oxygenation in the lungs, and the textbooks warn that it indicates the onset of death, and requires 'immediate attention'. In the afternoons, Haywood's temperature began to soar, and he fell into fevered and sweat-sodden sleep, awaking in a 'state of delirium'. Freddy could do no more than feed him a little tinned fruit that the towkay had brought for them.

A small clearing ran round the hut. Freddy found it a grand spot for bird-watching as he recuperated and nursed Haywood. The camp was set in increasingly steep jungle to the west of the Karak road. The rubber estates and banana plantations that gave the little town its modest prosperity – a motor repair shop and petrol station, a large mosque, Chinese temples and a church – were on the flatter land to the east of the road.

The jungle here has great beauty and Freddy still had his Zeiss field-glasses with him to observe the teeming wildlife. Malaya has over 500 breeding species of birds, and thirty types of cuckoos alone, including the plaintive, Asian emerald, green-billed, and chestnut-breasted. It is no surprise that Freddy's rendezvous call of the British barn owl passed unnoticed. There were seventeen species of owl in the forests around him, joined at night by frogmouths, with hooked bills and a frog-like gape, and nightjars, their soft plumage mimicking bark and leaves. The many larks and warblers competed with other songbirds like the bulbul, with its yellow and orange vents and cheeks. The rat-tat-tat of woodpeckers – crimson-winged, laced, flamebacks – mingled with the sharp shrill cry of the blue crown hanging parrot. Along the streams were kingfishers and swifts. Bee-eaters vied in brilliance of colour with broadbills and bright green-and-yellow leafbirds, and the bulbuls, parakeets, parrots, the magnificently plumed peacock pheasant, and the no less splendidly named lesser adjutant, the grey-breasted babbler and the black-naped monarch.

When his eye became accustomed to the semi-darkness, it made out brilliants of colour in the forest gloom, purples, soft yellows, lipstick reds, of orchids and berries, and the occasional harlequin glimpse of a multi-coloured bird. The flowers pollinated by birds had bright, cup-shaped flowers, and those on which bats drank were white nocturnal blooms with much nectar. Butterflies have good colour vision, a rarity among insects, and they were attracted by reds and oranges and mild scents. Bees recognise colour, odour and shape, and they enjoyed extravagant flowers, white, yellow or blue.

167

It was not in Freddy to idle a day away: he must always be doing. And it was a part of him, too, that he did not think of survival as an achievement in itself. He was faithful to the ethos of the old botanist-explorers, for whom a true expedition needed a purpose beyond mere sensation and miles put behind one. So this emaciated man, his normal weight of 170 pounds now shrunk to 100 to 110 pounds, barely able to flex his wounded leg, still suffering from a hacking dry cough that kept him awake each night, and subject to continuing bouts of dysentery, spent much of his time identifying new species of birds and writing up copious notes on their appearance. 'I now had the most wonderful opportunity,' he rejoiced, 'to study the natural history of the jungle.'

His one concern – 'it worried me very much' – was not that the Japanese might appear, but that he knew nothing about the flora and fauna of Malaya. 'For all I could tell,' he admitted, 'the vivid blue flycatcher or scarlet minivet I was observing might be the commonest species in the country or entirely new to science.' He had to invent his own names for the birds, and give them numbers. So many birds passed through this clearing that he had reached No. 107 within a month. He also began making a collection of pressed flowers for Kew Herbarium. 'I had always made a point of doing this in any country I ever visited for any length of time,' he wrote, 'and I saw no reason why the presence of the Japs should prevent me now.' The Japanese would doubtless have been perplexed had they shot him, and found neatly pressed violets and valerian on his corpse, not realising that they were as important to him as his pistol or tommy-gun. They were the armour of his mind: they sustained his spirit and kept him from brooding.

He also kept up his intelligence duties. He knew that if he did get out of the country, the British in India would be agog for any information on what was happening in Japanese-occupied territories. Before they had left to return to their camps, Tan Chen King and Ah Loy introduced him to a young towkay from Karak. Ah Kow was highly educated and spoke perfect English. He was allowed to drive to Kuala Lumpur and other towns. Freddy used him to build up intelligence reports on the location of prisoner-of-war and internee camps, on garrisons and airfields, and on the atrocities that had turned even wealthy Chinese from cooperation to hostility to the Japanese. Ah Kow also sent one of his coolies with fruit, eggs, tinned milk, oatmeal and other luxuries for the sick men. He came himself every week or so, though the Japanese were still searching the jungle.

Freddy was astonished that it was possible 'to lose so much flesh and yet remain alive', but he was walking again and exercising his leg. Haywood was still sickly, and could not move unaided. Freddy was afraid he would die if they remained in the hut, and he was anxious to get back to the Batu Caves camp to see the Secretary General. Ah Kow suggested taking them round by road hidden on one his banana lorries that plied the route from Karak to Kuala Lumpur. The Japanese were searching the traffic, though, and they had redoubled their sweeps in the jungle. Freddy was resigned to remaining in the hut, and rigged up a tommy-gun to the framework so that he could welcome the Japanese with a burst of fire straight down the track by pulling a cord above the sleeping bench.

At the end of June, they were back in touch with the Pahang guerrillas. Lah Leo, the political leader at Ah Loy's new camp in Menchis, visited them with Ah Ching, a helper who spoke some English. They were worried for the Englishmen's safety, and suggested that they should move to their camp. Menchis is the next town about twenty-five miles south of Karak on Route 8. They had a Chinese doctor in their camp and said they had plenty of good food. They wanted Freddy and Haywood to help them set up a training course for their men whilst they recuperated. Once they were fit, they would help them over the Main Range to return to Selangor, or wherever they wanted to go.

Freddy and Haywood were happy to move. They gave the guerrillas the rest of the stores that were cached near their hut – a couple of tommy-guns, ten rifles, 100 grenades, 3,000 rounds of ammunition, and 1,500 pounds of explosives with detonators – and the precious wireless set, which they had recovered although they had no batteries for it. Lah Leo wanted them to bicycle to the Menchis camp. Haywood was too weak even to walk any distance, though, so Lah Leo said they would carry him by stretcher to the road and take him on by car. He said Route 8 was never used by the Japanese at night. He arranged for a car to pick up Haywood and Freddy at a factory on the Sabai rubber estate, the long sheds with furnaces and drying rooms where latex was prepared.

CHAPTER 11

'JAPUN! JAPUN!'

They left the hut on 9 July 1942. It took two days to get to the estate. They had to take to the jungle to avoid the houses scattered in the vegetable gardens and banana and coconut groves round Karak. The going was easier through the plantations to the south. Freddy coped easily with walking at the slow speed taken by the relays of Chinese porters who were carrying Haywood. The towkay at the Sabai Estate was a generous host and agreed to lend them his Morris 8 saloon, with his brother to drive it. It lacked the glamour of the scarlet V8, and the Japanese had removed the wiring and headlight bulbs of all civilian cars, but the guerrillas had replaced them and it was a good runner. Ah Loy was there with a group of a dozen guerrillas who were going to carry the arms and explosives to the Menchis camp by bicycle.

Freddy was worried that the Japanese would still be out and about when they left the estate factory at 9 p.m. on the night of 11 July. Ah Loy was sure they would have no problems, and was anxious to be off. They crammed the little Morris chock full. The towkay's brother and two other Chinese squeezed into the front seats, with Haywood, Freddy and a third man behind them. Ah Loy and another guerrilla stood on the running boards, holding Freddy and Haywood's tommy-guns. Their packs were lashed on the back of the car. They tied planks of wood on the roof to get them over damaged bridges. Haywood and Freddy had a pistol and a grenade apiece. Freddy also had a pair of field glasses and a first-aid kit. The other weapons and explosives had gone on ahead with the party of cyclists.

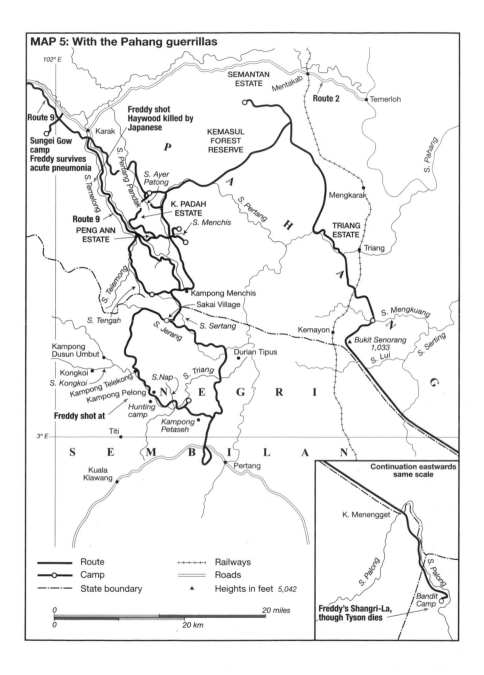

MAP 5: With the Pahang guerrillas

102° E

SEMANTAN ESTATE

Mentakab

Route 2   Temerloh

Route 9

Freddy shot Haywood killed by Japanese

Karak

KEMASUL FOREST RESERVE

Mengkarak

Sungei Gow camp Freddy survives acute pneumonia

S. Pahang

P

A

H

A

N

G

S. Pertang Pandak

S. Temelong

S. Ayer Patong

K. PADAH ESTATE

S. Pertang

S. Menchis

Route 9 PENG ANN ESTATE

TRIANG ESTATE

Triang

S. Telemong

S. Mengkuang

S. Tengah

Kampong Menchis

Sakai Village

S. Jerang   S. Sertang

Kemayon

Bukit Senorang 1,033

S. Serting

S. Lui

Kampong Dusun Umbut

Durian Tipus

Kongkoi

S. Kongkoi   Kampong Telekong

S. Nap   S. Triang

N   E   G   R   I

Kampong Pelong

Freddy shot at

Hunting camp

Kampong Peteseh

3° E

Titi

S   E   M   B   I   L   A   N

Pertang

Kuala Klawang

Continuation eastwards same scale

K. Menengget

S. Palong

S. Palong

Bandit Camp

Freddy's Shangri-La, though Tyson dies

Route

Camp

State boundary

Railways

Roads

Heights in feet   5,042

0   20 miles
0   20 km

The estate road to the main road was badly overgrown. With the planks and seven of them to manhandle the car, the driver was able to get through. The main road, Route 9 to Menchis and on to Malacca, was in excellent condition. Freddy found it thrilling to barrel along with the headlights boring a brilliant tunnel of light past the elephant grass, jungle and rubber. Between the 90th and 91st Mile, the road goes through a series of bends that are gentle enough to drive but which cut the forward view to a hundred yards or so. They suddenly came on approaching headlights. Ah Loy leaned in from the running board and shouted: 'Japun! Japun!' Freddy knew that Haywood was too weak to run: 'I said to myself, "This is the end!" and to Haywood, "Give me your grenade. Get out the moment we stop and lie in the ditch. I'll try to create a diversion. Then get away as fast as you can."'

Whilst Freddy held a grenade in each hand, Haywood pulled the pins out. They were caught in the headlights of a truck. The Morris slewed to stop a few yards away from it. The truck was full of Japanese troops, shouting 'triumphantly' as they jumped out onto the road. Haywood and the Chinese got out of the car and made for the left side of the road. Freddy lobbed the two grenades into the truck and crawled under the Morris for cover. The Japanese moved to the left of the road and exchanged fire with the Chinese. Freddy decided to make a break for the rubber trees on the right of the road. He had to run across the truck's headlight beams and he was caught in the crossfire. He was hit twice before he could get into cover. One bullet passed through his left arm. Another cut the cartilage where his left ear joined his head and grazed his cheekbone. This was a superficial wound – the damage to his arm was much worse – but he thought he had been shot through the head. He slid down behind a rubber tree, expecting to pass out at any moment, and hastily scraped out earth to bury his incriminating diaries.

The din of battle was frantic. The Japanese were firing at least one mortar, whose thuds were stitched by continuous machine-gun and tommy-gun fire. The road separated Freddy from Haywood and the Chinese. He ran through the rubber parallel to the road until he was beyond the glare of the truck headlights. A mortar bomb burst next to him and flung him hard against a tree. He was surprised that he was still alive, despite a 'terrible buzzing' in his head. He ran across the road. A tommy-gun opened fire in front of him. He hoped it was Ah Loy. He slithered over fallen tree trunks, his left arm hanging useless at his side, shouting 'Ah Loy, Ah Loy! Don't shoot! Don't shoot!' The end of Ah Loy's thumb had been shot off, but he was otherwise unharmed. The hooting of the tawny owl mixed with the gunfire as Freddy gave his rallying call for Haywood. Ah Loy said that he had seen Haywood fall to the ground just after they got out of the car. There was no sign of him or the others. The Japanese were still firing continuously. Freddy found a stream just behind him, and he and Ah Loy sank down into it.

Freddy never realised it in the darkness, but retracing his route shows that the presence of the stream-bed that saved him was a near-miracle. The Karak-to-Menchis road has not so much as a ditch running beside it until the corner where they met the Japanese truck. At that point, the rubber still grows on the west side of the road. On the east, or left side, stands of bamboo and shrubs give way almost at once to a deep stream bed, with jungle beyond. The stream runs close to the road for no more than thirty yards, before bending away into hills. Freddy and Ah Loy slid into it at that exact spot, now marked by piles of worn-out tyres, left by truck drivers who find it the only natural dumping ground on that stretch of Route 9.

The machine-gun fire and shrapnel whizzed harmlessly over their heads. Freddy was violently sick, and he was wracked by bouts of dysentery for the rest of the night. His left side was caked with blood. He thought his arm was broken. Ah Loy helped him put a field dressing on it, and he tucked it into his webbing. After quarter of an hour, they set off along the stream, aiming to get back to the road again further south. Ah Loy said that they had to get through the next village at Telemung and on beyond Menchis before dawn. As soon as it was light enough, the Japanese would start searching through the rubber and jungle.

It was fourteen miles to Menchis. Freddy said that he had a theory, from Greenland days, that the time never comes when it is impossible to take a further step on level ground or going downhill. 'As long as a man is reasonably fit,' he said, 'the capabilities of the human body are almost unlimited.' His problem was remaining conscious. He had lost a lot of blood and he was further weakened with dysentery. They regained the road, and on the flat he was able to keep going.

A bamboo barrier was stretched across the road by the Chinese temple that still guards the entrance to the village at Telemung. Torches flashed, and Freddy made out men in blue uniforms carrying shotguns. He took cover and was about to open fire with his revolver when Ah Loy shouted at him not to. The men were Chinese police in Japanese service – they wore Rising Sun armbands – but they had come to a live-and-let-live arrangement with the guerrillas. They noisily refused them permission to pass through the village, in case their officer was within earshot, but they let Freddy and Ah Loy by-pass it. The police station was at the far end, and they gave it a wide berth.

It was not easy going and they got lost, stumbling through tapioca plantations and thorn thickets, with 'all the dogs in Asia barking at us'. With daylight coming, and the Japanese alert and angry, they were in deepening peril until Freddy caught a glimpse of Antares, the red star of Scorpius, through a gap in the clouds. He knew it was in the south-east at that stage of night, and provided a rough guide to regain the road. They marched on it, and soon came to the concrete bridge that carries Route 9 over the Sungei Padak. Experience from the distant Greenland ice cap saved him once more.

He had to stop frequently for his bouts of dysentery, but, as the terrain suddenly broadened out past banana plantations, they reached Menchis a few minutes before dawn. It is called Mancis now, but the police station still stands on Route 9 at the entrance to the town. They walked past it, and the concrete row of shops and the school beyond it. Neat houses with tin roofs and gardens stood in the rubber outside the town. Ah Loy led the way to a kongsi-house a good mile into the rubber on the edge of jungle. Freddy washed and changed his blood-soaked clothes for a Chinese coolie's jacket and trousers, leaving the dressing on his numb and swollen arm. He was fed, and climbed up to a bed in a loft under the atap roof.

An hour later, Ah Loy shook him awake. A truck full of Japanese had already rolled into Menchis. They were searching the town house by house. Freddy had to leave for the camp at once. It was only three miles on the map. He had to climb about 450 feet through jungle, though, and his legs no longer responded mechanically as they had on the flat road. They baulked at the slightest rise. He could get along, step by step, if he kept close behind Ah Loy and let his mind wander far away. If Ah Loy forged ahead, he went at only half speed. He supposed that Ah Loy was subconsciously drawing him along: 'an interesting sidelight on the psychology of travel', he mused. It took him nine hours to cover the three miles.

He and Ah Loy were the first of the party to get to the camp. Others straggled in over the next week. They reported that Haywood had been shot through the chest only a few yards from the car. The Chinese who buried him said he seemed to have died at once. The car driver was also killed. Two other Chinese were wounded. At some stage during the night – 'I could never discover exactly when or where,' Freddy complained – the party of cyclists with the wireless set and weapons and stores had run into a group of Japanese. They had abandoned their bicycles and loads, but kept their rifles.

As to the Japanese, Freddy discovered later that there had been forty-two of them on the one truck. It was with 'great satisfaction', he said, that he heard that 'my grenades had accounted for eight of them and wounded many more'.

He reached the Menchis camp with his revolver, field glasses, wrist watch, a borrowed coolie's jacket, the bloodstained rags of his uniform. Haywood was dead. Freddy's heart was walled up deep within him. He said no more than that 'I had lost my congenial companion' – noting with brutal lack of sentiment that Haywood 'had been carrying our last few dollars, so I had no money' – but there was a wistful sense of loss that hints at a deeper mourning. He added that from now 'I saw no white men'. The fellow countrymen he had entered this adventure with were distant, dead, decapitated, or prisoners. All the comforts of life he had gathered at Sungei Gow – 'blankets, clothes, books, food and medicines' – were gone, too, abandoned by the bicycle porters. His bird notes, butterflies and pressed plants, even his compass and maps, were lost in the rucksack in the back of the Morris. He had buried his diaries in the rubber at the side of Route 9.

His hosts were the West Pahang guerrillas, or, as their grand and formal title had it, the No. 6 Independent Anti-Japanese Regiment. He arrived with them on 13 July 1942, and he was to stay with them for more than a year. This was the only group that had grown up on its own – the others were formed round a nucleus of men and weapons inserted by 101 STS – although it was in touch with the communist headquarters, and the shadowy Secretary General Freddy wanted to meet.

The group had started in a camp in an old tin mine back up Route 9 in the hills near Bentong, not far from Freddy's gold mine camp. It was betrayed in March 1942, and attacked by the Japanese. The survivors fled under the command of Lah Leo to the solitary and still heavily jungled mountain that rises from the flatter land south-west of Mentakab, on the road from Bentong through to the coast at Kuantan. They were again betrayed and attacked, in May. Despite these setbacks, they had enough men for two patrols. One moved south of Mentakab, to a camp near the railway depot at Triang, now Teriang. The other patrol was based in Menchis camp, seven miles south-west of the town.

Freddy said it took a fit man three hours to walk to Menchis. Fit indeed. It would be a good time even today, when the land beside Route 9 has been cleared to a depth of a mile or so for a palm oil plantation, and a track meanders through the jungle for a further two miles as far as a small forest clearing with tapioca and bananas. Here two *orang asli* (aboriginal) families now live in atap huts, and fish in the Sungei Sertang where they have created a large pool with a low dam of piled rocks. The camp was further upstream on the steepening upper reaches of the river. It could be found only through treachery.

For his first few weeks, Freddy was very ill. His leg muscles, still weak from his gunshot wound, had suffered more in his rushed march to get past Menchis before dawn. They were so stiff that he could not take a step without being supported by two men. His dysentery was so bad that he had to have a special latrine with armrests like an armchair built for him, and he was passing blood. Sometimes, he said, 'I fainted with the pain.'

Neither the promised doctor nor the wonderful food that Ah Ching had promised materialised. Ah Ching had been a shopkeeper in Menchis – Lah Leo had also had a shop, in Mentakab, but where he had rejected his petit bourgeois background in his devotion to the Party, Ah Ching was never a convinced communist – and had been able to collect food whenever he wished. The guerrillas had been able to eat dry rice, vegetables, fish, meat, chicken and eggs. There was even milk for the sick. They tormented Freddy with their recollections of it. Menchis was full of informers now, and Ah Ching no longer dared go near it. The morning meal was watery rice with boiled tapioca and sweet potato leaves, with more rice with a little pumpkin or beans in the evening. There was no meat or fish, no doctor, either, and a scant supply of Chinese medicines.

He was luckier with the people. Lah Leo was a slender, hushed Cantonese with 'a whimsical expression and great charm of manner', but when roused, he was 'very excited and eloquent'. He was missing half an ear, sliced off with a parang when he had fought off some Malays trying to stop him making off with a stack of arms abandoned by the British. 'I liked Lah Leo very much,' Freddy said, 'and he invariably treated me with absolute fairness and honesty.' He was fond of Ah Ching, too, who became 'my greatest friend among the guerrillas'. Ah Ching was an athletic twenty-five-year-old, whose great ambition had been to win the silver challenge cup for badminton. He liked the British, and had often hunted with them for pig and deer before the war. Freddy admired his initiative. Between the British retreat and the arrival of the Japanese, he had held a meeting for local Malay and Chinese leaders, and they had jointly prevented the looting and inter-racial violence that had swept many country towns. He also liked the way Ah Ching made no bones about his fear of being caught and tortured.

In these early days, the guerrillas wore what they could get, shirts or high-necked Chinese jackets, patched with rubber latex, long trousers or shorts, though some who still spent time in the outside world were spotless in white shirts, knife-creases in their trousers, slicked back hair and smart felt hats. Later, they had uniforms of khaki shorts, shirts and caps with one or three red stars sewn on them. Freddy found the Chinese girls invariably attractive. Their hair was cut in bobs, and 'their slim figures showed to advantage in wide black trousers and long-sleeved, high-necked smocks of gay colour and pattern . . .' He often saw them plucking each other's eyebrows.

The routine was more or less the same in every communist camp in Malaya. A whistle blew at 5.30 a.m. The guerrillas slept fully dressed with weapons and spare clothes packed in canvas bags or rattan cases next to them. They were on parade, fully armed and turned out, five minutes after the whistle. The roll call was taken. PT was held on the parade ground for half an hour from 5.45 a.m. Freddy sometimes took it himself, or a guerrilla who had been a professional teacher of Chinese shadow-boxing. Freddy thought the exercises too strenuous for people on a poor diet, and he despaired of the habit of shouting out in unison from one to ten in time with their paces as they ran. In the eerie still of the jungle dawn, sound carries a long way.

Ablutions filled fifteen minutes from 6.15 a.m. They went to the stream below the camp to wash and clean teeth. Each Chinese had a face flannel, with 'Good Morning' printed in English and Chinese in red across the bottom. Freddy made his own toothbrush out of pig-bristle. They dressed for the day, keeping their modesty with cotton underpants only removed in the atap bathing hut. The Chinese, Freddy noted, 'as a race are extremely modest in such matters'.

A formal parade was held at 6.30 a.m. They fell in in front of the flagstaff on the parade ground. The Chinese saluted with the communist clenched fist as the flag was run up the pole. Freddy alone saluted in British style with extended fingers. At first, they used a big Soviet flag with the hammer and sickle. Later, this was replaced by three yellow stars, for the Chinese, Malays and Indians. Then they sang 'The Red Flag'. Freddy sang along with them, and thought it a fine song when sung fast and furiously as a marching song. The Chinese, he thought, spoilt it by dragging it out as a hymn. A propaganda pep talk followed.

It could last as long as half an hour. Military training took up ninety minutes from 7 a.m. They marched, did arms drill and grenade throwing, and Freddy took training exercises. After the precision of British parade grounds, he found the Chinese almost comical. He had 'unlimited respect for their fighting spirit', he said, but he found them 'surely the most unmilitary nation in the world'. He had thought it impossible for men to drill so badly.

After a short break for cleaning weapons, a whistle sounded for breakfast at 9 a.m. They marched down a steep path to the cookhouse, filling their mugs with 'watery rice' from the big kerosene drum it was boiled in. They squatted in circles round a big bowl of boiled tapioca and another of sweet potato or vegetable leaves. A whistle sounded and they helped themselves with chopsticks and spoons. No talking was allowed. Another whistle sounded after fifteen minutes – they had to bolt the food – and they had a drink of hot water and washed their mug and spoon in the stream. Tea and coffee were reserved for special days.

They had a few minutes to themselves in their huts, whilst the girls tended the sick. Many had terribly ulcerated legs and the girls bathed them in hot water with a drop or two of disinfectant. A single bottle of Lysol had to last the camp for several months.

An open discussion was held at 9.30 a.m. Each section went through its tasks for the day and how best to achieve them. It was a serious offence to question a section leader's conduct in private. In public, though, anyone could say what he liked. Freddy found this undermined the leaders' prestige and control, for 'the men tended to go into committee about every decision instead of getting on with the job'. This could be disastrous when a section was out on patrol, and was unsure what route to take. They 'went into a huddle' and wasted critical time discussing every alternative in loud voices.

Mandarin lessons followed for the next hour. Some of the guerrillas were illiterate old woodcutters and squatters, and it amused Freddy to watch a fourteen- or fifteen-year-old boy or girl teaching them. The senior classes read aloud from broadsheets printed in the camps, and from propaganda books on Soviet Russia. Freddy set himself to learn

Mandarin. He was good at languages – his Eskimo had been fluent, his Tibetan workmanlike – and he was astonished at his lack of progress. The political leader at the camp was Ah Chong, a lean, large-nosed man who thought Freddy was a British spy, and went through his papers behind his back. He was one of the very few Chinese whom Freddy cordially disliked. Ah Ching tipped Freddy off that Ah Chong did not want him to understand Mandarin, and was having him taught a different dialect each week.

Two hours of manual work followed. They built huts, cut trees and split logs for firewood. They also winnowed stocks of rice left behind by the British. These were infested with weevils and with lime used as a preservative.

One of the officers gave a lecture for an hour at 1 p.m. Russia, and Mao's China, were the normal fare. Another hour of oratory followed. Everyone in the camp was taught to get up and make a speech. Freddy was impressed with their range of gestures and emotion, though he understood hardly a word. Personal time from 3 p.m. to 4 p.m., for washing and mending clothes, studying and writing, was followed by bathing. He found them far cleaner than British troops. They washed from head to toe, behind little atap screens for modesty, scooping the cold waters from the mountain stream over them. When they ran out of little bars of Girl in the Moon soap, they made a substitute by mixing the ash from burnt coconut shells with palm oil and lime, and pounding into it a mixture of leaves, flowers and cinnamon bark. Salt or finely ground charcoal was used in place of toothpaste.

Supper was at 4.30 p.m. It was the main meal of the day: dry rice mixed with sweet potato or tapioca and a little dried or salt fish. The ration was a pint a day at best, where a coolie was used to three pints at a sitting, and they were malnourished. Soy sauce vanished. A substitute – made from coconut milk, peanuts, potatoes and starch – was sold in the towns but they could rarely afford it. Freddy was penniless. He was surprised to be given $10 to buy himself a gift when he finished his first training course. Like the widow's cruse, the note never ran out, because though he asked for cheroots and coffee on the strength of it, they never allowed him to pay for them.

They sang after supper, mostly dreary, wooden propaganda songs, but also old Chinese folk songs. A choir led by a tenor with a lovely voice sang these, and Freddy found them a joy. At 6 p.m., the flag was lowered, and they sang 'The Red Flag' again. A silent hour for reading followed. Freddy had lost his English books, and he scrabbled through some communist encyclopaedias, wondering how one page had pictures of the Victorian politician Joseph Chamberlain, Catherine the Great, Nietzsche and the poet Longfellow, linked by a quotation from Marx he could not understand. A debate then ran until 9 p.m. They discussed many things: whether they should give up smoking, whether captured Japanese should be killed or converted to communism. Some patrols voted to stop smoking. Freddy was glad his did not. He had a pipe made from a gnarled bamboo root, one of the sweetest he ever had.

A whistle blew for lights out at 9 p.m. They slept alone. Freddy noted that the best attended lecture was on Love. They were told that love was a good thing – 'after all, you have to keep up the supply of little guerrillas and communists' – but that it had to be excluded from the camps, as it interfered with fighting the Japanese. They lived up to it, perhaps because they took themselves so seriously. Ah Chong had been engaged since before the war to one of the girls in the camp. A 'most attractive girl she was', Freddy said, and though he shared a hut with her and Ah Chong, he never once saw anything that hinted at their deep attachment. If a man and a girl fell in love, everyone in the camp met to decide whether it was in the interests of the cause for them to marry. The moral tone was very high. Freddy did not come across a single case of theft in all the time he was in the communist camps.

The rituals, the lack of humour, the earnestness, and the Marxism so repulsed Robert Chrystal that he left his communist patrol and sought out an easy-going, semi-bandit group of Kuomintang guerrillas, nationalists who owed allegiance to Chiang Kai-shek in China.

Freddy refused point-blank to discuss politics. He was willing to make life-sized portraits of Marx and Maxim Gorky to hang in the camp lecture hall, and insisted on doing Churchill and Roosevelt, too. He asked if he could write a news-sheet for English speakers. It took months to get permission through the Party bureaucracy. He called it 'Truth' and wrote it in longhand. A hundred copies were cyclostyled in blue and red ink. It was all they had paper for. Since anyone caught with it could expect to be decapitated, Freddy presumed it was read with great interest. He wrote an editorial on British India for the second number. It was too imperialist for the Party censor. They were too polite to tell him this: it was printed and then the copies were quietly burned – 'and that', Freddy said, 'was the end of Truth'.

Their Marxism he could ignore, but he found his guerrillas maddening to instruct. They had an extraordinary appetite for useless detail – they wanted to know the number of turns of rifling in a barrel, the exact muzzle-velocity of a tommy-gun – and no interest whatever in learning to shoot straight or to use cover. They did not look through vegetation when laying an ambush, but over it. They tied their tin mugs on the outside of their packs so that they rattled against every twig. They would strip a weapon with great precision, and totally ignore the safety catch. They carried primed grenades by hanging them from the ring attached to the split pin. 'Every few days they would take them to pieces for cleaning,' he added, 'a process which I always watched with fascinated horror.' The final straw was that they were the 'worst shots imaginable, except for the Japanese'. From practice with water-pistol, cap gun, air-gun and sporting gun, the Englishman had been used to closing an eye and aiming since childhood. Freddy found that one Chinese in three was 'constitutionally incapable of closing his left eye only'. Others who could only close the right eye shot from the right shoulder and aimed with the left eye. He resigned himself to the depressing fact that this contortion, added to the heavy British service rifles they were using, which were too long in the stock for them, meant they rarely hit the target.

He liked them, though, and admired them, despite the 'bedlam' of living with them. They practised songs in his hut, and read aloud to themselves, and smoked their cheroots next to comrades lying seriously sick with malaria. He found it uncanny that the victim joined in the laughter when anyone hurt themselves, even with a bad slash from a parang or a hornet sting. He did not know what they made of him. Most had never been at close quarters to an Englishman before, and they gazed at him as if he was a strange and exotic animal. They admired knowledge, and the fact that he had been at Cambridge impressed them much more than his rank as a British officer.

Camp concerts were held to celebrate Soviet and Chinese festivals. The nearby kampongs provided a pig, and a few ducks and chickens, great luxuries that were eaten with rice and chicken soup with ginger and groundnuts. Blankets were hung on a part of the parade ground to create a stage. Freddy dreaded the long opening speech from Ah Chong, but that gave way to folk songs and Chinese shadow-boxing. Freddy introduced them to wrestling, holding his own against the younger but slender Chinese. 'Chepmin-tongtse' – Comrade Chapman – was also called on to sing, and he gave them a yodelling solo, and an Eskimo song from Greenland. A morality play followed. Freddy saw lots of them, and they were all basically the same. In the first act, a Chinese family discuss the war. The son asks if he can join the guerrillas. The father refuses him. The Japanese arrive in the second act, brutal little men in black moustaches with huge round spectacles. The son escapes as they ravish the daughter and tie up the parents before getting drunk on a bottle of samsu. The son returns with a band of guerrillas to slaughter the Japanese. At the end, deep into the tropical night, they sang the 'Internationale'.

The concerts amused him, and he had enough to keep him busy, but he felt frustrated and impotent. His hopes of getting out to India had all but gone: the south-west monsoon was blowing now, pinning boats to the coast. He knew the Japanese were vulnerable to ambush – 'a sitting target', he said, and he had attacked them repeatedly without casualties – but there was little he could do to hurt them now. They were still looking for him. Strong Japanese patrols, accompanied by Indians and Malays, were penetrating further and further in from the Menchis–Karak road.

Aircraft circled about for several days, the Japanese reconnaissance pilots searching for the camp. The patrol abandoned it, and moved to the east of the road. It was only six miles in a straight line, but it took them three days. Freddy dashed across the road at dusk, but had to spend a miserable two hours crouching in a cloud of mosquitoes in pouring rain waiting for the tail-enders. They went through a patch of jungle burned off so recently that the still-incandescent tree trunks reminded him of the pillars of flame that had guided the wandering Israelites. One of the girls was swept away in the flooded Sungei Pertang, and was lucky not to drown.

The new camp was at the headwaters of the Sungei Menchis. It was sited in the path of 'Sumatras', squall lines of extraordinary violence that are formed from the south-west monsoon over Sumatra in the night and pre-dawn. They sweep across the straits to Malaya as a thick band of cumulonimbus cloud towering to great heights, and smash into the Main Range. Thunderstorm cells are embedded in the squall lines, with downbursts savage enough to destroy aircraft and buildings.

One roared into the camp a few days after they arrived. The noise increased in volume and terror as it came nearer, finally reaching such intensity that Freddy mistook it for an air raid, with a squadron of aircraft 'zooming just overhead'. The guerrillas rushed out of the huts. The ferocious wind-bursts kept to a narrow path, hurling huge trees to the ground and filling the air with their sheared-off limbs. A big hard-wood was uprooted and hurled across the headquarters hut. A sick man had been left there in the rush. He was decapitated.

Freddy was almost done for himself a day or two later. He was out hunting alone, following a timber track beside the Sungei Pertang, when he was ambushed with a shotgun. A pellet lacerated his right thumb, and others went into his right buttock and thigh. As soon as he heard the explosion, he turned and ran before the shotgunner could get off the second barrel or reload. The wounds gave him great pain for several hours, but the pellets had only lodged in the muscle. He did not get a glimpse of the would-be assassin, but it was obviously someone trying to collect the reward money the Japanese had put on his head, dead or alive. Ah Ching and Ah Loy dug the pellets out with a pocket knife.

A little later, three Chinese informers were brought in. Freddy described their end: 'Two, after being burned with brands and beaten almost to death with rattans, were finished off with a bayonet in the grave that had already been prepared for them.' He did not embellish: no cries, no screams, no blood, no moralising. He described it as a common-or-garden incident, and that, in terms of its frequency and the indifference of the executioners, is what it was. Freddy was amazed at how easily the Chinese betrayed one another. It overcame their normal courage, and hatred of the Japanese: he found the urge to inform strange and compulsive.

CHAPTER 12

THE BETRAYER

Had the Party's crème de la crème known, in the moments before their deaths, who had betrayed them, they would have suffered a special torture. The Secretary General, the shadowy figure spoken of with such awe, the man Freddy wished to meet but who was too grand and elusive, the absolute master of the Malayan Communist Party (MCP), Lai Te, was the traitor of all traitors.

Lai Te had a long career in double-dealing. Freddy knew that the British had turned him, from the meeting with him above the charcoal shop in Singapore in December 1941, and the Special Branch officers who were with him then may have filled him in on Lai Te's exotic background. He was born Nguyen Van Long – Lai Te was one of many aliases – in Saigon in 1903, of a Vietnamese father and Chinese mother. He was at high school and technical college in Saigon, and joined the Vietnamese Communist Party under Ho Chi Minh. He was arrested by the French Sûreté Générale Indochinoise in 1925 in Saigon. They released him after he agreed to become a double agent for them. He was allowed to go to study in France. From there he went to Moscow, where he worked with the Third Communist International, Comintern. He was sent to China in 1929, where he ran foul of a warlord, Zhang Zuolin, and was sent back to Moscow. He was back in Shanghai in 1932.

In August 1935, Lai Te went to a grocery shop in Hong Kong which was a front for a cell liaising between the Chinese and Malayan Communist Parties. After a coded conversation with Wu Si Li, the 'grocer' – 'I am selling sea food' . . . 'we don't deal in sea food' . . . 'I mean lake products' – he was accepted as being sent by the Comintern in Moscow. Wu Si Li bought him a first-class passage on a ship to Singapore. He was less likely to be grilled by British officials if he arrived first class. In fact, the French Sûreté had passed him on to British Special Branch in Hong Kong, and he had become a mole for the British within the communist movement.

He was welcomed at the kongsi-house of the Vegetable Growers' Association, another front, by Chen Liang, then the MCP leader. Lai Te introduced himself as the senior Comintern liaison official in Hong Kong, a veteran crisis-solver sent to Malaya to sort out a split within the MCP. His credentials – his time in Moscow, the Mecca, his Comintern connection – were dazzling for the trusting provincials. But the Singapore Special Branch ran him from the moment of his arrival. His case officer was Innes Tremlett, the Special Branch assistant superintendent who was at the December 1941 meeting with Freddy. Lai Te led a spectacular coal miners' strike in March 1937, in which the miners set up their own Soviet. It was short-lived – Lai Te was, after all, in British pay – but it confirmed him as the Party giant. Also following his arrival, several senior MCP figures were assassinated. One central committee member was murdered with a parang whilst cycling in Malacca, others were betrayed to the British, who expelled them to China. In 1938, Lai Te took over the Party, and the killings stopped. He launched a six-month 'offensive against the opportunists' that resolved the internal wrangling, carrying out a purge, and wiping out the 'last remnants of incorrect inclinations'. Having restored 'ideological unity', Lai Te emerged as the 'beloved leader' of the Party. He was elected the Secretary General of the MCP in April 1938.

He was picked up by the Japanese in March 1942, probably betrayed by former Chinese detectives of the Singapore Special Branch. He was taken to Kempeitai headquarters in the art deco former YMCA building on Stamford Road in Singapore, and interrogated by Major Satoru Onishi. He confessed that he directed all communist activities in Malaya and Singapore. Onishi treated him well, with food, cigarettes and a comfortable cell. He was released after ten days. By then, Lai Te had agreed to work with the Kempeitai in return for his life. Onishi was his new case officer: Innes Tremlett, his old British handler, had got out to Ceylon.

Onishi and Lai Te struck a bargain. Lai Te would gather all the MCP leadership into one place where the Japanese could liquidate them. In return, his life would be spared and he would be given a large amount of cash. He walked out of the Kempeitai building a free man at some time in April 1942. It was agreed that contact with Onishi would be made either at a café in Orchard Road or at the home of Lee Yem Kong, a photographer from Johore who had mingled with Japanese photographers before the war, and who was now working as a Kempeitai interpreter. It was a closely kept secret that Lai Te had been arrested – only four Kempeitai officers knew of it – and although he had been seen to be arrested after the *sook chings*, the Japanese purges of the Chinese in Malaya in February, MCP members accepted that he was released soon after. He had built up a formidable personality cult – banners had been draped across the MCP headquarters, 'Lai Te the most loyal disciple of Stalin', 'Support our able leader Lai Te' – and this blinded them to his treachery.

Clever and ruthless, Lai Te betrayed most of those who might have queried him. They were then shot or imprisoned by the Japanese. A Singapore Central Committee member called Li Ying Kang discovered the link with the Kempeitai whilst in prison, and got word out. When Lai Te heard of this, he arranged with the Japanese to have Li released. He then confronted Li, convinced the Party that Li was lying, and had him buried alive. Another released communist, Ah Ling, later warned Party officials of Lai Te, but was himself executed in Johore Bahru as a traitor.

Lai Te's betrayals began in May 1942. He revealed the identities of the Singapore Town Committee members who had survived the *sook chings*. They were arrested or murdered. The Johore State Committee was exposed and arrested in July. Lai Te then moved to Negri Sembilan, Malacca and Selangor. He passed details of the MCP committees to the Kempeitai, who liquidated them. The plot to liquidate the Central Executive Committee (CEC) began in August 1942. Lai Te arranged a full meeting of the CEC, state Party officials, and group leaders of the Malayan Peoples' Anti-Japanese Army (MPAJA) to take place at the Batu Caves, about ten miles from Kuala Lumpur. Lai Te passed the details of the rendezvous to Major Onishi, who took personal charge of the operation. The Batu Caves was and is a popular place for picnics at weekends. For two Sundays before the meeting, Japanese soldiers frolicked and picnicked with cabaret girls. They were in fact Kempeitai officers surveying the area for Onishi.

The meeting was to be held in a small village near the caves. The CEC members and other leaders and their bodyguards arrived in the village late on 31 August. At daybreak next morning, a large Japanese force surrounded and attacked the village. A fierce gun battle took place. Twenty-nine MCP officials and MPAJA political commissars and their bodyguards were killed. Fifteen were arrested. Freddy wrote that a girl guerrilla was the heroine, enabling a handful to escape by giving them 'covering fire with a tommy-gun until she herself was shot'. Machine-guns, rifles, grenades and several printing presses were seized. Japanese casualties were light, one NCO killed and three wounded. As they fled, the survivors gave thanks for one thing. Their beloved leader had not yet arrived. Lai Te was safe.

In fact, he had never left Singapore. As the communists furiously debated the identity of the traitor, the Kempeitai in Kuala Lumpur threw a celebratory party for Major Onishi. He toasted the true instigator of the Batu Caves slaughter, the leader of the MCP, Lai Te. 'It is an interesting but dirty story,' the major wrote in the Kempeitai magazine of running counter-spies. 'Distrust, double-cross, selling your friends, covering up for yourself.'

The date of 1 September became a 'martyrs' day' which the MCP commemorated each year. Its most enthusiastic participant was Lai Te, of course, who claimed that he would have died too but for his car breaking down before he could get from Singapore to the meeting. He had not, yet, betrayed Freddy because he felt he might have use for a British officer at some future date. He could have had him dead with a click of the fingers – the communists had specialist camps whose sole purpose was selective killing – but for the moment he restrained himself.

Freddy did not know that, of course. He had accepted the 'executions' of the two Chinese informers at the camp as routine, however odious, and now even found reason to be grateful to the third suspect. His guilt was less obvious or they wanted a more elaborate confession – Freddy was not sure – but he was kept alive with his hands tied behind him for a further 'trial' the next day. He escaped in the night. Since he knew all about who and where they were, the guerrillas had to move again, and Freddy was delighted to find that they migrated to a 'much more pleasant' site.

The new camp was six miles north-west at the end of a low spur. To get there, they crossed the Peng Ann and Kampong Kadah rubber estates at night. It then took only a few hours to get the framework of the huts ready. Elephant palm was the best material for thatching, though nipa and sugar palm were also long-lasting and sturdy, and kept the deluging rain at bay. Below the roof, the living and sleeping areas were raised above ground level, to be dry and to keep creepy-crawlies at bay. The floors were made of poles covered with palm leaves or ferns. A fire platform was made of a thick layer of dried mud on the floor, which had two levels. The higher one was to sleep on, the lower one to store kit and dry wood. In swampy and flood areas, the sleeping levels were raised high on poles, with a ladder to climb up to them.

Freddy went out hunting whenever he could. It lifted his spirits and varied the monotony of camp food. Pig were his main quarry. In a herd, they lost some of their caution, and he could get close to them. The jungle pig usually foraged alone, though, and it was wary, lifting its snout to scent the air, listening hard. Several times, Freddy was following a pig's tracks when he heard it stop, and blow its nostrils to clear them, and sniff. Once alarmed, a pig did not give a second chance. The mud-turtles in the swamps of the Ayer Palong were easier. They betrayed themselves by a slight cloudiness in the even colour of the mud, and he scooped them up with his hand. Their meat was tender and made a fine soup. Monitor lizards grew to six or seven feet, and their eggs were as tasty as their meat. He ate snakes, too, finding their meat excellent, a 'mixture of chicken and lobster'. The Semelai, the aboriginal peoples of the wetlands and swamps, suspended nets in the water currents to catch reticular pythons and freshwater snakes. They caught giant frogs, too, and the false gharial, the slender-snouted crocodiles valued for their meat, eggs and skin.

His hunt for pigs, barking deer and monkey took him several hours away from the camp. Once he had a brush with a bear. He was hunting monkey with an ancient single-barrelled shotgun, made in Connecticut, an awkward weapon that came in two to reload. The cartridges swelled in the damp, and it took time to change them. He had just four of them, a lethal round with a single large ball, a buckshot charge, and two No. 4s whose shot was useless for anything larger than a monkey. He was walking down a steep track when a 'large greyish animal' ran off with a curious rolling gait. Its footprints – as large as a man's but with toes the same length – showed it to be a bear. Freddy changed the No. 4 shot for the lethal ball and gave chase.

A great roaring noise came from down the slope, the sound of more than one animal, and he moved gingerly. The Malay bear is the smallest but most aggressive of all bears, with long sickle-shaped claws, strong paws and sharp canines. An old bear came at him steadily, his 'wicked black head' swinging, his white muzzle stained red by the clay he had been digging. Freddy dropped to one knee, and let him come to ten yards, aiming between the angry eyes. The ball blazed a white streak in the dark fur of the bear's forehead but it failed to penetrate the skull. The bear kept coming, now with a howl of fury. Freddy fled back up the hill, and heard the bear routing in the shrubs as he loaded his large buckshot cartridge. He found a spattering of blood leading into a thicket in a little ravine, guarded by fallen trees. Freddy decided that he had not survived the long months in the jungle to die at the claws of a bear – 'a Jap would have been a different matter' – and he dashed back to the camp to get a rifle. Heavy rain had wiped out the bear's track by the time he came back and penetrated the thicket. He heard a dull thud above the splash of the rain, and found fresh blood on the leaves at the point the thud had come from. He never found the bear.

They moved camp again in November, going twelve miles north-east. They traversed the Kemasul Forest Reserve, flat and swampy land, jungle and reed beds and peat islands, criss-crossing the Sungei Pertang as it coiled its way east. It was slow-flowing, but the guerrillas were frightened of its many crocodiles. A Sakai was reported to have been taken by one a month earlier. There was a regular track in places, cut by the forest wardens before the war, with small huts built high in the trees out of range of wild elephants. The new camp was built almost on the summit of an isolated hill that rises 820 feet out of the swampy jungle.

It was only four miles south of the main east–west road at Mentakab – it is clearly visible from the modern Eastern Expressway – but any Japanese patrol would be spotted from its slopes long before they reached the hill. The camp itself was in the mouth of a little valley shut in by thick rattan and thorn jungle. Here they had as much fresh fish as they could eat. The Sakai prepared a poison that stunned the fish over a stretch of water. It came from tuba, the fine roots of a vine, which they pounded with wooden clubs on flat rocks, like washerwomen. This produced gallons of a milky liquid which they poured into the river. The small fry were affected at once. It took longer for the bigger fish to float belly up. In the deeper pools, the liquid was too diluted to work fully, and Freddy plunged in with the others to take the half-comatose fish in his hands.

He became extremely fit at the Mentakab camp. He met the guerrillas bringing heavy sacks of rice and sweet potatoes back from the kampongs, and carried them up the steep climb to the camp. He prided himself that he could carry a load as large and as swiftly as any coolie. He felt utterly secure, and profoundly bored in this sheltered valley. He went out, and deliberately lost himself, lancing his ennui by drawing on every ounce of his resource and energy to get himself home. It is more difficult to navigate in jungle than anywhere else on earth. The lack of light restricts vision to fifty yards at best. It is easy to become severely disorientated. A man can lose his sense of position almost as rapidly as a pilot trying to fly in cloud without instruments, for tree trunks are indistinguishable one from another. A man alone cannot verify his course with a compass as he can if he has another in front of him. Freddy tested himself to the limit by going alone and without a compass.

Several times he failed to get back before dusk, and slept out in the jungle. As the light faded, he trained himself not to panic. Instinct told him that he was an intruder in a hostile world full of predators: tiger, elephant, snakes, scorpions, red centipedes as thick as a finger with venomous fangs. A rustle of leaves set off his nerves, and his terror rose, until he slowed his pace and breathing with deliberate effort. He built up his self-confidence, and calmed his fears, learning to gauge his position by the flow of streams and rivers. Before long, he was happy to be out with no more than a parang, a rifle, a box of matches and a piece of rubber as tinder to start a fire.

He was sure he could last at least a week alone in the most barren stretch of jungle. Water was abundant. Even in rare spots where no streams ran, water-bearing vines and palms produce a clear liquid when cut, though those with a milky sap must be avoided. The pithy core of the wild banana gives off an evil-tasting but thirst-quenching liquid when it is twisted. Nipa palms have a pleasant sugary fluid that can be milked every twelve hours, by bending a flowering stalk downwards, and cutting a thin slice off the stalk.

Mouse deer, wild pig, barking deer (muntjac) and monkeys were most common on the jungle edge, from where they raided plantations. Rats, squirrels, porcupines and tapirs were found in deep jungle, and there were fish and freshwater crabs in the streams. In many places, chewing bamboo shoots and nipa and sago palms would keep a man alive for a long period. Fruit trees were thinly scattered through the forest. The fruit was often too high to reach – like the wild figs in the high canopy – and hornbills and fruit bats, birds and monkeys stripped a tree as soon as it was ripe. But there were yams and coconuts, too, and wild rice and jungle bananas, and various nuts.

The many abandoned *ladangs*, clearings made by the Sakai, had tapioca and sweet potatoes and pineapples and survivors of other crops the aborigines had cultivated before moving on. The tender pinkish flesh of the ciku fruit, and the vile-smelling but sweet-tasting durians, were delicacies. The hulking, yellow-green nangka or jackfruit weighed up to twenty kilos, bursting with segments of bright yellow flesh. He knew to avoid the deadly fruits, the clusters of pear-shaped brownish fruits on pangi trees, with their heart-shaped leaves and spiky green flowers, the flowers and nuts of the rengas tree, and the fleshy, orange-red berries of the evergreen strychnine tree.

JUNGLE SOLDIER

He was moving more fluidly through the jungle now, scanning for natural breaks in the foliage beyond the trees and vegetation immediately to his front, his body bending and his feet changing rhythm with the undergrowth. From time to time, he stopped and bent low to pick up any game trails he might use. The going was easier along them, and they often led to water. He listened, too, for sound carries a long way in jungle, a reason why he cut vines and branches with an upward swing of his machete when he had to. It reduced the noise. He carried a stick, parting vegetation with it and giving warning of his approach to snakes and spiders and biting ants.

At dusk, he made shelters from atap and wild banana leaves. In the Mentakab swamps, he cut four bamboo poles and drove them into the ground to make a rectangle, then four poles were cut and lashed to form the sides of the rectangle, before more poles were laid across the rectangle, with palm leaves and foliage on top of this crude bed frame to form a soft surface for sleeping on and to keep him and his pack above the wet. He put clay and mud on a corner of the bed to dry out and use as a fire pad. Other sleeping places were in caves, at the foot of large rocks and in fallen trees with thick boughs. He avoided low ground, ravines, narrow valleys and stream beds, for they collected cold air at night.

He never had the least fear of the Japanese, though he knew very well that torture and decapitation were his likely lot if they found him. He found their racism ridiculous – 'for all the much-vaunted brotherhood of New East Asia, if you met a Japanese,' he noted, 'whether you were a Chinese, Malay or Tamil, you had to cover your face with both hands and bow down low before him' – and he was quite sure that he was more than equal to them in combat.

Snakes, though, frightened him at first. It took him three months to get used to going barefoot in the jungle. He looked constantly for snakes, or scorpions – he had seen them 'as big as dinner plates' with shining black claws. Snakes were indeed present throughout the forest and swamps and plantations. The danger did not lie with the giant constrictors – pythons, variously carpet, reticulated, black-blooded – but with those that bit. Seventeen of Malaya's 105 species of land snakes are venomous. The fierce equatorial spitting cobra, *Naja suma-trana*, almost perfectly oil-black in colour, yields 110 milligrams of venom, enough to kill a hundred people. The soft green and brown king cobra – *Ophiophagus hannah* – is a colossus among poisonous snakes, growing up to 18 feet or 585 centimetres in length, able to rear its hooded head as high as a man. It is found in forests and plantations, from the low levels up to 2,000 metres, patrolling forest streams, an excellent swimmer and tree-climber, the female strikingly aggressive in guarding her young. A single bite may be fatal. The blue Malayan coral snake is a creature of great beauty, dark blue with a light blue stripe on each side, with bright red head and tail, front-fanged and highly venomous. The Malayan krait, another highly toxic mankiller, a metre long, slender-bodied and boldly banded in black and yellow, more active and dangerous at night, gives no warning hiss before it strikes. Triangular-headed pit vipers, so called for the heat-sensing pits on their cheeks that locate their prey, pass the day lying coiled in trees, and sheltering under logs and in piles of leaves, before hunting at night for birds, rats, small mammals and other snakes.

Nonetheless, most of the Chinese and all the Sakai went barefoot in the jungle. Freddy never met one who had trod on anything worse than thorns. The cases of snakebite he heard of happened whilst people were frog-hunting at night, and harvesting rice and tapioca roots, and they were rare enough for him to lose his reluctance to go barefoot. The soles of his feet never became infected, and the worst that happened to them was not meeting snakes or scorpions, but sharp stones and tree stumps hidden in thick mud.

He retained, though, a healthy respect for other animals. He recollected returning to camp alone at dusk after a day's hunting. 'I was padding homeward, barefooted, along a muddy track,' he wrote, 'when suddenly I heard something following me ...' Whenever he stopped, it stopped, too, and when he set off again, it followed, silent and invisible: 'It was all I could do not to scream and run wildly down the track.' The same feeling had once overwhelmed him in Tibet. He got a party of Chinese together as soon as he was back in camp, and they went back along the trail. They found the paw prints of an 'enormous' tiger, but no sign of the beast itself.

Elephant had something 'terrifying' to them, he found, and he stalked them 'just for the sake of experiencing the thrill of danger'. They were uncanny, merging perfectly into the jungle, their great grey-black bulk disappearing into the soft greens and browns and yellows, even though his every nerve and sinew and his sense of smell screamed at him that one of them was very close. He marvelled at their power to remain entirely silent when they in turn sensed him, while the noise they made when they thought themselves unobserved was 'incredible . . . the deep sinister roaring, the shrill trumpeting, the crashing of bamboo stalks, the pounding of the ground with their trunks, and a strange hissing noise like escaping steam'. Young male elephants, and mothers with their young, can be aggressive and highly dangerous. The head is held high, the trunk curled between the tusks to uncoil at the moment of attack, the ears cocked, the whole immense figure enlarging to the bursting point with each piston movement of the massive forelegs. The attack is silent, apart from a first shriek of purpose. The pace does not change from a walk – the elephant cannot canter or gallop – but the forward shuffle reaches fifteen miles an hour, just negotiable for a sprinter on a running track, but inescapable in the rough of the wild. The male pins the victim with its tusks. The female smashes with its forelegs, and stamps the victim to death. It was exhilarating to use the skills he had learned as a boy to track the dangerous leviathans. Frightening, too. Only having to sleep in a haunted house, he admitted, in his 1953 book *Living Dangerously*, would 'really terrify me even more than an elephant'.

The seladang, the wild ox or bison, is the most dangerous of all. It is liable to attack on sight, bringing up to 1,200 kilos of flesh and horn to bear when it charges. When wounded it is cunning and brave, vengeful and enduring. Freddy saw them often enough, but only once had a shot at one, in the great swamp spreading south of the Mentakab camp. He was out for porcupine with his old single-barrelled shotgun. Among its other eccentricities, it jammed unless the safety catch was eased back after it was released. He was cutting a hunting track through a part of the swamp where the reed beds and waterlogged bushes are interspersed with firm going. He saw a 'huge brown animal' browsing on bushes, and moved quietly round it to a spot facing it as it grazed its way towards him. He loaded a buckshot cartridge and dropped to one knee. The seladang caught a scent and made off at a fast walk. Freddy was close enough, eight or ten yards, he thought, to catch a 'strong sweet smell of cattle'. He aimed just behind the shoulder – the bull was so huge that he seemed to be firing at it upwards – but he had forgotten the foible of the safety catch. He pulled the trigger, but there was only a click, and soon the noise of the beast lunging through the jungle died away.

CHAPTER 13

JOURNEY TO SHANGRI-LA

It became oppressive at Mentakab, always with the same patrol to teach. He felt trapped without a 'kindred spirit' – another white man – with whom to dream of getting to the coast and sailing for India early in 1943 on the next north-east monsoon. He had a letter from Chrystal in October. It had been censored by the guerrillas, but it said that Robinson and Quayle had been very ill. Chrystal said that he had met Pat Noone, a young anthropologist who was an expert on the Sakai, and who had taken to the jungle with them after the invasion; he and Noone were moving further north. He also had letters forwarded by the patrol at Triang, a camp not far away, from two Englishmen who signed themselves Cotterrill and Tyson. Ah Loy told him that they were living with 'bandits' – the word the communists used for all groups but their own – near Segamat to the south of the state border with Johore.

He pined to meet them. In November 1942, he was asked to go to train two guerrilla patrols at Triang, which took him further south, towards Johore, and he welcomed the move. The camp was on the Sungei Mengkuang six miles south of Triang, a small plantation town of warehouses, stores and machinery shops on the railway down to Johore. It was only twenty-five miles on the map, double that over the ground. He set off at a cracking pace with Ah Ching and a runner along the boundary path that skirted the swamps and jungle of the Kemasul Forest Reserve. It had not been used since the invasion and the jungle was already reclaiming it.

They came to the Triang river at dusk, deep and wide and fast, and regularly patrolled by the Japanese in motor-boats. The runner had a sampan hidden under the bank, and they pushed off into the middle of the current. Freddy spotted a line of crouching men on the far bank. He heard rifle bolts working to put rounds into the chambers. He jumped into the river, keeping a hand on the side of the sampan. Bullets snapped well above the boat, and then stopped. They were the Triang guerrillas Freddy had come to train, who were lying in ambush for an informer, and had realised their mistake. Ah Ching ribbed Freddy for going into the water, and told him the river was stiff with crocodiles. The sampan was unholed and Freddy observed that he would have to teach these guerrillas, too, how to shoot straight.

That night they slept in a Chinese kampong. They were on their way before dawn, crossing and recrossing the river, with six of the men who had shot at them. They walked south all day, skirting along the railway, and edging through a corner of the Triang rubber estate. They hid close to the little railway halt at Mengkuang until dark, before scampering across the track. They went to a hut on the edge of a kampong that night. The camp was only four miles away to the south, and they planned to reach it next morning.

All the dogs in the kampong began barking furiously at about 2 a.m. They slipped out of the hut and moved on through the jungle. They were very lucky. They heard next day that Japanese troops had come down the railway line and searched the village looking for them. As they sped on in the early hours, they came to a huge clearing, and Freddy was thrilled to see the heavens full of stars. It was his first glimpse of a night sky in all its glory after four months beneath the trees. At dawn, they walked on through a big tapioca plantation. Jungle cocks were crowing around them, the call identical to the domestic cock but for its sudden ending. Freddy was highly alert. He spotted a sentry's white shirt from half a mile, without his field glasses. The Triang guerrillas had no more idea of fieldcraft and camouflage, he reflected, than of aiming a rifle.

The sentry post looked out from the edge of the jungle over tapioca and oil-palm plantations. The camp was further back in the forest. A hundred men were in the patrol there, with sixty more in a small camp a little to the north. Freddy met 'many old friends' here from Menchis. The tapioca plantation was owned by a rich Chinese who supported the guerrillas. Freddy was 'most warmly welcomed', well fed, and given personal supplies of coffee, sugar, cheroots and bottles of samsu, the fiery rice spirit.

Ulcers were a fresh problem. His legs had been badly cut and scratched by swamp grasses and thorns on the long trip from Mentakab, and they became infected. He counted twenty sores on his shins and ankles, 'stinking and suppurating', half an inch across and deep almost to the bone. Pus 'poured' from them, and the infection inflamed the lymph glands in his groin. A Chinese herbal paste called *kow-yok* was often used to draw out the poison. It was spread on a piece of cloth and put over the wound, protecting it from leeches and from rubbing against plants and shoots. Any contact with an ulcer brought excruciating pain. But *kow-yok* did not work for Freddy, and the Japanese tightly controlled the sale of Western antiseptics. He could get Epsom salts, however. He got some relief by soaking a concentrated solution of salts into kapok pods – he had no cotton wool – and placing them on the sores, kept in place with palm leaves. The wounds went on festering until, for no reason he could see, they began to heal. It was six weeks before he could walk normally.

The camp was less than 200 feet above sea level. The jungle surrounding it was – it still is – 'swampy and miasmal'. The country here is undulating, and the patches of remaining wilderness between the estate roads are low-lying and remain damp and sickly-looking. The water was fouled almost black by the discharge from a tapioca factory in Triang. The guerrillas suffered from malaria and 'other strange fevers'. The leader of the patrol died and others fell so sick they had to return to their homes, with all the risks of informers. One fever was marked, Freddy said, by curious white hairs with forked roots that grew on the chest. They were treated by rubbing with fowls' feathers soaked in hot water until they came away. If this failed, the Chinese believed the patient would die, and, Freddy said, 'he usually did'.

Through November and December, it rained as he had never seen it. The camp became an island as the streams around it rose by twenty feet. It needed a sampan to get to the kampongs for food. The water quality improved, though, as the tapioca waste was flushed out, and he was able to sit with his legs in clean running water. As he became more mobile, he asked again about going down to meet his fellow-Englishmen in Johore.

He was more than paying for his keep with his training courses. He had to lecture twice a day. The officers would not lose face by being seen to learn with the men, so he saw them privately in the evenings. He feared that he was too valuable to be let go. These Pahang communists, though, were very keen to convert the 'bandits' in Johore to the cause and Freddy was their only means of doing so. The problem was the route. The distance was only thirty-odd miles in a straight line, but the only route the guerrillas knew involved two to three weeks' travel, much of it through kampongs where informers would alert the Kempeitai to the passage of a tall stranger, even if in Tamil disguise. Freddy came up with a different and almost direct route. He noticed that the boundary between the states of Pahang and Negri Sembilan ran almost the whole way between the camps. British surveyors had cut paths along the state boundaries as they mapped them. If this one still existed, it would cover twenty-five of the thirty miles.

Approval was given. Freddy was an ally, and not formally subject to Party orders, but in practical terms the guerrillas could vet his movements. This was immensely dangerous, for Lai Te was continuing to betray his fellow Party leaders. A new act of treachery unfolded on 18 December. The Kempeitai raided a meeting of the commanders of a new secret Party organisation, the Self-Defence Corps. Twenty-three more officials were arrested in a series of Kempeitai swoops in early 1943, each following Lai Te tip-offs. By April 1943, he was the only pre-war Central Committee member to have survived.

Freddy knew nothing of this, and he had the luxury of getting the two best jungle men in the camp to cut a path to the state boundary. The summit of Bukit Senorang to the south-west of the camp stands out vividly in the flatness of this part of Pahang. It took them three days to cut a track a yard wide. Freddy walked behind the men with a compass to keep them straight, returning to the camp each night. Then, at Christmas 1942, he set off with Ah Ching and three of the Triang guerrillas. A good path had indeed been cut from the state boundary atop Bukit Senorang along the ridge that ran south to the Lui river.

The Sakai here had made great whirligigs from wood, and tied them in the tops of tall trees, so high that Freddy felt a kinship with them as the boy who had swarmed over the Cow and Calf in Ilkley. As the wind whirled the blades, they span off a roaring wind noise that carried a great distance. The purpose, so the Sakai said, was to ward off devils. The path tailed off after a little while. Freddy's fitness was back. He pounced on and held a mouse-deer, the size of a hare, and as tasty. They made a lean-to for the night.

Next morning, they looked for the *batu*, the surveyors' stones that marked the boundary. They met some Sakai, who took them to a concrete block on the forest floor with a piece of piping coming from it. Freddy could see the outline of the surveyors' track progressing southwards. It was marked now by secondary jungle where new growth had swallowed the path in thickets of bamboo, and long stretches of *mengkuang*, a coarse grass with pointed fronds twenty inches long, with rows of curved thorns on each edge, and another down the central spine. The batus were a furlong apart – the old measurement for English racecourses, 220 yards – and every eighth one was a much larger mile marker. He paced out the distance, keeping to a compass course, and then they looked to left and right for the stone.

They expected to be six days getting to the Sungei Palong. They ran out of rice after two. He feared the others would abandon the journey if they were not fed, so he set out to hunt for pig after they had made an atap lean-to for the night. He found the deep track made by a heavy pig and followed it eagerly for half an hour, stopping when he heard a 'strange gurgling noise' in front of him. He went down on his hands and knees and crawled under thick atap and rattans. Ten yards in front, towering above him, he saw a 'hideous pinkish-coloured animal'. It was staring at him, a great pig on its haunches wallowing in red laterite, which stained its flanks. He was so astonished – 'evil wrinkled snout dripping with mud ... diabolical pointed ears' – that he froze. It was turning to bolt when he got off a hasty shot with his rifle. It gave a loud bark, 'like a dog', and was gone.

It left a trail of blood behind it. It was soon dusk and he had to give up his pursuit and follow his own track back to the shelter. They were finishing their last grains of rice an hour later when they heard a gasping nearby. Freddy lit a large bamboo torch, 'for courage', and began the search. He found the pig 'breathing its last'. It was a grizzled old boar, and very large, three feet tall and weighing perhaps two hundredweight. Its six-inch tusks were knife-sharp. They cut off enough meat for a week, grilling some at once in the ashes of the fire.

After two days finding their way from furlong post to post, they reached the Sungei Serting. It was in spate, its brown waters roiling with currents. They found a Sakai dug-out under a bank. One of the guerrillas got in it, but it was swept away. He could not swim, and he was not seen again. The boat gone, they walked the bank until they found a fallen tree that bridged the river. They crept carefully across and picked up the batu line once more. They made slow progress towards the Palong river for the next four days, slashing their way with parangs. The pork was finished. Freddy shot another big pig, and two monkeys, which they ate with the boiled heart of a cabbage palm.

A track as broad and easy as Freddy had hoped for now opened up along the state boundary. They found some little atap huts next to it, with sleeping platforms made of saplings. The ground was carpeted with monkey skulls, the shells of mud-turtles, fish-bones and the peel of durian fruit. The Sakai had feasted here, and they had the luxury of a hut each, but they were alive with cockroaches and mosquitoes, and the sleeping platforms sagged more each time they turned over.

Footprints and a pocket handkerchief were on the track next morning. The feet were shod and the handkerchief was machine sewn. Freddy did not say that his heart chilled, or that fear pierced him, simply that 'we were rather alarmed . . . but met neither Jap nor Malay'. They crossed the Palong soon after, and recrossed it again after five more miles of jungle, and then – 'we were in Johore'. On New Year's Day, 1 January 1943, Freddy was shaking hands with Cotterrill and Tyson. He had found his kindred spirits.

*

Their camp was in a green valley of paddy fields and coffee bushes, edged by hibiscus, and gardens with banana, papaya, pomelo and champada. The Palong was unlike any other river Freddy had seen. It reminded him of the Yorkshire Dales, flowing 'merrily over shingle beds and ledges of grey rock'.

The Englishmen were lucky to have found their Shangri-La. They had been left in the north to report on the Japanese advance with a transmitter and a Chinese radio operator supplied by 101 STS. In mid-January 1942, they had been on their way south to Segamat when the radio operator, who carried all their money, was murdered and robbed by another Chinese. They worked their way south, mostly by raft, until they reached the Keratong river. Here they were told that the Japanese were already in Johore. They had hidden with an old Chinese couple for a month, before being put in touch with the band of armed Chinese in the Palong camp.

Tyson had what Freddy thought was a bad chill. He had never really recovered from bad leech bites in the small of his back some months before. He continued to sink. They did not realise how ill he was, until on 8 January, 'much to our surprise and sorrow', he died. How they buried him, with what ceremony, Freddy did not say, but at least poor Tyson had the consolation of dying among friends.

The Chinese in the camp were bandits. Freddy made no bones about it. They dressed the part, in Australian slouch hats they had found, and draped themselves with holsters and bandoleers. He found them 'cheerful and likeable rogues', mercifully free of all the politics and propaganda of the communists. Some of them had been moonshiners before the war, distilling potent samsu and selling it in Segamat. The invasion put paid to that, so they had made a forty-strong band which preyed on the richer Chinese towkays. They used patriotism as a smoke-screen – they claimed their victims were collaborators – but in truth they were running a protection racket.

They had asked Cotterrill to drive the getaway car in their latest raid on towkay houses. He refused, thinking it best for a white man to lie low, but it had gone ahead, netting suitcases heavy with all manner of loot – tinned food, clothes, silk, jewellery – and $7,000 in cash. They had sound business sense. They were careful not to kill their golden geese, sparing the towkays' lives, and allowing them to keep half their possessions, so that they would recover, to be tapped again. The bandits were heavy samsu drinkers and half were opium addicts. Freddy complained that the opium pipes made them so talkative he could scarcely sleep. He longed to smoke himself, but he resisted it, not through fear of becoming an addict, but 'so as not to lose face with the guerrillas, who were bound to hear of it'.

Discipline was 'non-existent'. For all that, Freddy thought the bandits were first-class material, 'thirsting to have a crack at the Jap'. It is easy enough to mock that phrase now, like a speech bubble from a boy's comic. This was no fantasy, though. The fresh grave of the leech-infested Tyson, the bandits living with their women in squalid shacks along the jungle edge, or with the Englishmen in a tin-roofed hut in the middle of a jungle clearing – these were real, and so were 'the Jap' and the attendant horrors.

The bandits were much better armed than the guerrillas. Freddy noted four machine-guns, ten tommy-guns and thirty rifles, and so much ammunition that they amused themselves by blazing away at trees, well pleased if they managed to hit one. They happily admitted to complete ignorance of military matters, and were so eager to learn that he found them 'the best pupils I ever had'. The Triang guerrillas tried to win them over, urging them to speak educated Mandarin Chinese and teaching them to sing 'The Red Flag', none of which was to their taste. The guerrillas, appalled by the womanising and opium-smoking, and recognising that they would never make Marxist converts, returned to Triang with lurid tales of the *orang samun*, the robbers.

Freddy, though, was at his happiest. He found it 'a joy to be with my own countrymen again' – the plural was a slip, for poor Tyson was soon dead – and for the first few nights he and Cotterrill nattered into the small hours. It was especially good, he found, to laugh again. He went hunting, and shot a pig every time. They came out of the jungle at dusk to forage for tapioca and nuts, and they were still in the ladangs at dawn, when Freddy came for them. He was out for deer when he saw some bandits coming back to camp with sacks of rice. As he came out of the elephant grass to greet them, they opened fire at him with tommy-guns and rifles. 'Fortunately,' he wrote with his usual brevity, 'they were full of *samsu* and shot high.' He was back in camp before they swaggered in, saying they had just annihilated a group of Japanese.

His new bandit friends wanted him to stay with them, to train them and lead them against the Japanese. He was sorely tempted, but a new intake of 200 recruits was due at Mentakab. He had promised Lah Leo that he would come back and instruct them. He also felt that, as a British officer, it was his responsibility not to work with *orang samun*, 'however charming they might be', but with the guerrillas. While Cotterrill stayed on, he left Palong with Ah Ching on 9 January. It took them only four days to get back to Triang along the track they had cut before, but the journey brought him a fresh attack of ulcerated legs. He was laid up for most of February in the Triang camp.

The Japanese celebrated the anniversary of the British surrender with a minute's silence on 15 February. Traffic stopped. All were ordered to pray for Japan's 'glorious dead'. Then bells, drums and sirens sounded from mosques, churches, temples and fire stations, to give thanks for Shinsei Mala, New-born Malaya. Crowds were assembled to bow to the Japanese governor in each state. They shouted 'Banzai!' three times, and then sang the Kimigayo, the Nipponese national anthem:

> The master's reign
> shall last 1,000 and 8,000 generations
> til the pebbles
> becoming rocks
> shall be covered with moss

The *Syonan Times* revelled in describing how it had been a year before:

Whisky and rum flooding the drains, millions of dollars in notes going up in smoke ... Asiatic women looking for their fleeing British husbands, widows and orphans baying at the closed doors of banks to withdraw funds . . . praying all over Singapore was the desperate Tommy who fled the last ditch – it was through this hell that the 800,000 people of Singapore lived to greet the sunny Monday morning which saw the birth of Syonan, 'Light of the South', a year ago.

Reality was rather different. Brutality was everywhere: 'in the streets,' a Chinese said, 'at the hands of the ordinary soldier and the inside of the Kempeitai HQ . . . Every Japanese sentry swaggered, enveloped in his own importance. The lowest ranking were the worst of the lot.' Anyone who hesitated a second before bowing to any Japanese soldier was slapped. 'They slapped and slapped, and never got tired of slapping,' N. I. Low wrote, 'and nearly all the faces slapped happened to be Chinese. One marvelled at the assiduity and enthusiasm with which the Japanese slapped . . . A variation was to induce two Chinamen to slap each other.'

All Japanese forces were on the look-out for Freddy, of course. But the Kempeitai was also using more specialised and exotic formations, turncoat Indian Army soldiers, Malay volunteers, Chinese in Japanese pay. The Kempeitai, a blend of Gestapo and military police, were a law unto themselves. Literally so, for an individual could only be arrested or disciplined by his superior Kempeitai officer. Their brief was broad and bloody. They enforced security, and 'discipline', and carried out 'special warfare' against enemies like Freddy and his guerrilla friends. They controlled civilians, registering them, issuing travel passes, and making great use of paid spies and informers to rout out dissidents. The Malay police were under them, with standing orders to report anti-Japanese activity to them immediately. The police were armed with shotguns, the Japanese not issuing them with rifles or revolvers: had the policeman who shot him been better armed, Freddy might well have been killed.

The Kempeitai also ran the Jikeidan, an auxiliary police force they launched in September 1942. It recruited men who displayed 'fikiran sempurna', or 'suitable thinking', meaning subservience to the Japanese and a willingness to inform on neighbours. The Jikeidan had branches in every town and district. It was propagandised as a sort of neigh-bourhood watch, catching thieves and petty crooks. But it made regis-ters of all local families and their occupations, and its primary task was to look out for anything anti-Japanese, and to report strangers and odd happenings. Members of the Jikeidan were liable to be punished if any hostile activity – communist leaflets scattered, telephone wires cut, slogans painted – took place on their patch.

There was a Malay volunteer army, too, Giyugun, and a volunteer corps, Giyuta. Collectively, they were known as the Giyu-hei, the Malayan Protection Army. The Giyugun men wore army uniforms and were armed with rifles and machine-guns taken from the British. This was a proper military force, living alongside Japanese troops. The Giyuta was less martial. Its 5,000 men were trained by Japanese officers, though, and filled in for the police at night, manning police stations and road blocks between 6 p.m. and 6 a.m., the hours when Freddy was about.

The Tetsudo Aigo Kumiai was a voluntary corps for railway protec-tion. This, and a similar one for road protection, were flowers in Freddy's cap. They were formed because of the damage he had wrought. The volunteers were responsible for sections of road and rail near their homes.

Many, many people had a lively interest in Freddy's whereabouts.

He returned to Mentakab and the waiting recruits in early March 1943. A little later, he was visited by the leader of the guerrillas in Negri Sembilan, a pale, intense young Chinese who spoke English and called himself Martin. Freddy had heard many tales of hundreds of white men – usually Australians – who were supposed to be hiding out with the guerrillas in the Negri jungles. Martin said there was only one, an Argyll sergeant called Andy Young, who was ill and wanted Freddy to visit him. Martin was himself keen for Freddy to go. The Japanese had taken ferocious reprisals for the few attacks made on them – a huge massacre had taken place in the Chinese mining area, around Titi – and he wanted Freddy to train them to defend themselves.

Freddy did not know it but a column of 3,000 British troops had crossed the Chindwin river to get behind Japanese lines on 13 February

1943. These 'Chindits' were under the charismatic but ill-starred Orde Wingate, and one column was led by Freddy's friend, 'Mad' Mike Calvert. They suffered terribly. A third of them had been killed or taken prisoner when the remnants struggled back across the Chindwin at the end of April. Six hundred of the survivors were too badly wounded or sick to return to the fighting. The Japanese railways they had been sent to disrupt were back running again in a week. The Chindits got plenty of publicity, unlike Freddy, of course, though he had raised real havoc with just three men in his 'mad fortnight'.

Permission to move from Party headquarters did not come through until mid-June. Two runners came from Negri to take Freddy back with them. They stayed at night in Sakai villages, mostly of about a dozen huts made of bamboo and bark, with a family to each, growing hill rice, maize and tapioca, with tobacco patches and huge sweet bananas. They passed a string of empty kampongs, one after another, the pretty thatched houses perfectly intact, set among groves of coconuts and hibiscus and vegetable gardens, still with chickens and goats and herds of water buffalo, but without a living soul. The men had been shot and the families removed as punishment for the guerrilla attacks. Freddy was eating fallen durians when a patrol of Japanese, Sikhs and Malays cycled by thirty yards away, heavily armed and 'obviously looking for trouble'.

The guides got him to the Negri camp at midnight on the fourth day. They lit the way with bamboo torches as they approached and shouted their names out to warn the sentries they were coming. They held a torch close to Freddy to show he was not a Japanese, but a sentry still shot at him from twenty yards. He might have been killed, but a girl on duty recognised the guides' voices, and knocked away the rifle as the sentry fired. Freddy was wearing a wide-brimmed Gurkha hat, and the sentry had taken him for a Sikh.

Andy Young had become separated from his battalion of Argylls in the fighting in January 1941. Some Chinese found him roaming along the jungle edge, weak and barefoot, and looked after him. He had been in the camp for a year. Between bad bouts of illness – beriberi, malaria, tick typhus – he had led several firefights with the Japanese, personally shooting a high-ranking officer. He had trained the patrol, and taught them bayonet drill, before giving way to illness, sleeping twenty hours a day, and getting up only to eat. A morose sickness like this was seen as the prelude to desertion in the camps, and the guerrillas were talking of shooting him. Freddy thought Young's problems were in the mind, too, and indeed his malaise lifted with Freddy to talk to, and he was soon recovered enough to help him give a week's intensive training to the guerrilla section commanders. An attack was expected at any time.

They moved camp, and Freddy rigged explosives and trip wires on the approaches. He joined a hunting party in the deserted kampongs. He found it a relief to be in the open paddy fields and coconut groves. They waited until the Japanese patrols had gone before shooting water-buffalo and pig. They butchered the carcases by the light of bamboo torches, and carried the meat down to the river stark naked, to avoid ruining their clothes with gore. The materials to build a house, a canoe or a raft were always at hand in the jungle. They made a raft about thirty feet long, and four wide, with bamboos lashed together with vines, and a crosswise deck of shorter bamboo poles in the middle for the cargo of meat. They poled the raft downriver, the current taking it once they were away from the bank. They lay on it, steering with poles, and jumping overboard when it snagged a tree trunk to free it, passing the ashes of two old camps that the Japanese had burned down.

In early July 1943 Hideki Tojo himself, the Japanese prime minister, was to visit Singapore. Fifty thousand Chinese, 10,000 Indians and 5,000 Malays were ordered to assemble on the Padang. They feared another *sook ching* until they were given Rising Sun flags, and were told to wave them, and shout 'Banzai!' three times. Tojo came out in front of them at the Municipal Building, and then was gone: 'a Godiva's ride . . . like a dream he came, like a dream he passed'. At his side was Subhas Chandras Bose, Japan's ally in his effort to raise an anti-British Indian National Army (INA). It was a vassal army, created at the initiative of a Japanese officer, Major Fujiwara Iwaichi. Indian troops had been recruited into the INA since the surrender. At a mass rally at Farrer Park in Singapore, they were given the choice of enlisting, or rotting in detention camps. It is probable that half of the 45,000 Indian troops in Singapore at the rally volunteered. Others came forward after Subhas Chandra Bose arrived, wearing uniform and top boots, haranguing a rally to the chant of 'Chalo Delhi!', 'To Delhi!', the cry of the mutineers of 1857. The Gurkhas refused to join the INA and did menial work in Singapore instead. Most volunteers were Sikhs.

At dawn one morning, Freddy was lying on a mound of meat when the raft swept round a bend in the river, and he saw two Sikhs and a Japanese soldier sitting on a fallen tree trunk further downstream. It was misty, and Freddy and the others on the raft were able to swim the raft under foliage on the bank without being seen. They waited until the enemy moved on. He found it exhilarating to watch the jungle float past from the raft, to be free of it, and to gaze up at the vast steep wall of trees that soared up the valley slopes to the brilliant blue sky a thousand feet above him, and then to bring his eye down to the intricate mass of nasturtium-coloured creepers that overhung the banks.

A severe bout of malaria hit him whilst he was collecting food, and based at a hut in a deserted kampong. He began vomiting as he was picking up durian. He left a guerrilla to gather the last fruits, and went back to the hut to wrap himself in blankets. The others were winnowing rice. A shot and a tommy-gun burst came from the sentry post 100 yards away. Within ten seconds, Freddy claimed, he had grabbed his gear and was concealed in the jungle, putting on his clothes. The man he left with the durian was not seen again. It was thought that the Japanese had got him. A few days later, when Freddy was back at the main camp, news came that two guerrillas had been picked up while buying food. The guerrillas at the camp hoped that they had twelve hours to move out before the two succumbed to torture and revealed the camp's location.

They had less than that. Freddy was still sick with malaria, and he was trying to get the camp nurse to give him a little quinine when the booby traps he had rigged on the approach to the camp exploded with 'a tremendous detonation', followed by tommy-gun and rifle fire. Andy Young called to him that he had taken his kit into the trees with him. Freddy joined him to act as a rearguard for the other sick men. A section of Sikhs, part of the Japanese raiding party, closed on him. They were armed with tommy-guns. Freddy had only a .38 pistol. The lucidity that the malaria-weakened fugitive now brought to bear was born on the Yorkshire fells, nourished on the Greenland ice cap, fine-tuned in Tibet: which is no more than to say that it was his life-skill, personal to him, but wholly English, for no other people knew the earth quite as they did. He calculated – 'I knew' – that the Sikhs had itchy fingers. They would empty their tommy-guns the instant they had a target. That would give him a window – quite a good window, ten seconds or a little more – to get away while they changed magazines. He drew their fire by putting his head round the left-hand side of the tree he was hiding behind. They blazed away. As they paused to reload, he appeared round the right-hand side of the tree, and shot the two Sikhs nearest to him. The range was ten to fifteen yards. He dashed off one way. The surviving Sikhs, their nerve gone, retreated 'in disorder' in the other.

He lay hidden in a brake of bamboo above the camp. After an hour, he heard a voice shouting in Mandarin: 'Comrades! Comrades! Come back, come back, the enemy have all gone away!' This was a favourite Japanese trick. It was only in the evening, when he recognised the voices of the men calling, that he returned. The Japanese had pulled down the huts and used them as fuel for a gigantic funeral pyre for those who had been shot or killed by the booby traps. The 'stink of burning flesh was revolting', Freddy said, but it did not stop the less squeamish from raking the ashes to count the skulls. The score was eight. It appeared that Freddy had killed the two Sikhs. The guerrillas had suffered no casualties. Freddy's great loss was a pouch Andy Young had missed when he had rescued the rest of Freddy's kit. It had contained his precious Zeiss field glasses and a Rolex watch he had had for thirteen years.

They were hunted for the next week by three mixed groups of Japanese and Sikhs, each a force of about 200 men, as they fled on rafts along the river, and slept in abandoned huts. Freddy was lying in one with a violent fever when a party of Japanese and Sikhs was spotted by a sentry. He fled with the others up a steep hillside in teeming rain.

As they lay hidden, they heard the Japanese closing on them. 'Unfortunately,' Freddy related, 'I chose this moment to have a most violent rigor.' He had to be gagged to prevent the chattering of his teeth betraying them to their hunters.

Early in September 1943, a message came for him to go immediately to the main camp of the Perak guerrillas, where someone urgently awaited him. He had been trying to meet the senior Party leaders for more than a year, and he hoped the summons was for that. He was also told that the Perak group had a new lightweight type of tommygun. That thrilled him: it suggested contact had been made with the British in India.

Ah Chong and Martin gave him a farewell feast and a concert, and presented him with a five-pointed star in red enamel as a hat badge. It was a mark of real affection and respect, and Freddy reciprocated. 'It was with great sadness that I left this patrol,' he wrote, 'who had looked after me so well for more than a year.' He found out later that many of his friends in the camp had died. Andy Young was carried off by fever early in 1944.

Freddy himself was still weak from fever during the long trek north into Perak. He had six guerrillas with him, and it was as well he had. He managed the flat and downhill on his own, but his leg muscles gave out on the slightest uphill gradient, and he had to be pushed or pulled on a rattan line. The guerrillas were poor guides. They were often lost, and instead of sheltering with friendly Chinese, they slept in the jungle, soaked by rainstorms, and eating a little rice cooked in tin mugs. The route took him north close to Bentong, and then west past Kuala Kubu, before turning north again to Tanjong Malim and on to Slim river. He was too ill to move for three days near Bentong, and the journey on to a new camp on the Sungei Ribu two miles east-north-east of Kuala Kubu camp took a week. The march on to a camp at Kerling should have taken no more than a night and a morning. The guides got lost, despite the moonlight. He knew they were going in a circle – the railway line kept appearing from a different direction – and it was an area he knew from the 'mad fortnight', but since he had no idea of the destination, he could do no more than wait for dawn. They did not reach the camp until the next night. It was on the heavily jungled slopes of Bukit Bertram, which rises almost two thousand feet a mile or two east of Kerling, on Freddy's old stamping ground of Route One and the west coast railway.

He did not know that 101 STS was now a part of a new organisation called Force 136. Australian and British commandos of the force were brought by fishing boat from Australia to an island 125 miles from Singapore. They paddled in canoes from there to Singapore harbour, where they laid charges that sank seven Japanese ships on 26 September 1943. The Japanese suspected that civilian internees and prisoners in Changi gaol had passed information. The Kempeitai lashed out with the 'Double Tenth' interrogations, named for the date they began, 10 October. Internees who had held high rank in the pre-war administration were brutally tortured by the Kempeitai, fifty-seven of them, including the bishop of Singapore and three women. The acting colonial secretary, Hugh Fraser, was one of the fourteen who died under extreme torture. On the wall of the YMCA where the detainees were kept was a notice in English: 'No preaching, membling [sic], groaning'.

Also being tortured now was P. G. Pamadasa, a teacher on the staff of St Francis's Institution in Malacca. Only medium-wave radios were allowed: their limited range restricted them to Japanese-controlled propaganda stations. The penalty for having a short-wave radio capable of picking up foreign broadcasts was death. Pamadasa, who had a short-wave set, was betrayed, tortured and sentenced to hang. The day before he died, he wrote a final testament for his old boys:

> I am writing this in my cell with manacled hands on the eve of my execution. I am no felon but a patriot condemned to death for listening to the BBC News and telling it to pro-British friends. I did this for 2 years till I was betrayed. The Kempeitai tortured me and finally sentenced me to be hanged ... I have no regrets ... I have always cherished British sportsmanship, justice and the Civil Service as the finest things in an imperfect world. I die for these. My enemies fail to conquer my souls. I forgive them for

Freddy ended the war a much-decorated lieutenant colonel (left), but he started it as a humble territorial with the Seaforth Highlanders. After training with a secret ski battalion in the Alps, he joined SOE, the Special Operations Executive, and was posted to Singapore to teach fieldcraft and irregular warfare. When Japanese troops entered Kuala Lumpur on the evening of 11 January 1942 (below), Freddy was behind their lines organising 'left-behind parties' to harass them. He found they were not as formidable in the jungle (bottom) as people thought. He tracked them by their noise, the smell of their tobacco, and the trail of litter they left behind them.

Freddy and two others – John Sartin (left), who was later taken prisoner but survived, and Bill Harvey, who was captured and decapitated by the Japanese – blew up seven trains and fifteen bridges, and killed or wounded up to 1,500 Japanese during their 'mad fortnight' in early February 1942.

On 15 February 1942, the Japanese took Singapore (below). Freddy was now utterly isolated, but his nerve held. He stayed at the Gap rest-house (opposite, left) under the noses of the Japanese, and became expert at building shelters (opposite, right). He was lucky. Though wounded, he was able to shelter in a stream-bed (opposite, below) after the Japanese killed his British companion Clarke Haywood.

Pat Noone (above left) was a young anthropologist who had married Anjang (above right), a beautiful girl from a tribe of Sakai, the aboriginal people of Malaya. Noone had gone missing, and Freddy set out from the camp where he was training guerrillas to find him. He stayed with Sakai families (below) and noted how they made poison for their blow-pipes from the sap of trees (bottom). Freddy was not to know it, but Noone had been murdered by blow-pipe by a jealous lover of his wife.

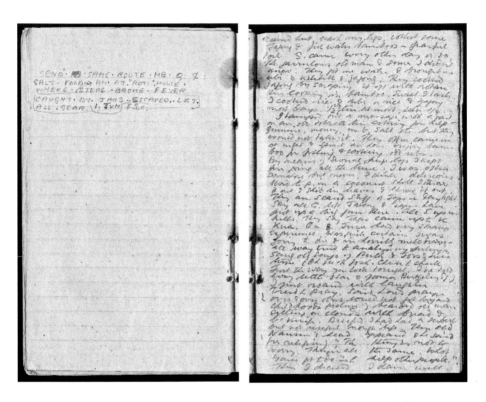

Freddy himself was held by bandits, and captured by a Japanese patrol. He escaped, but he was near death when he wrote these diary pages. One (above left) records the desperate note he sent to the camp: SEND MB (sulfadiazine) Q (quinine) $ (money) SALT . . . FEVER . . . CAUGHT BY JAPS ESCAPED LOST ALL GEAR. The other tells of lying alone with fever and singing the love songs of distant England, 'Cheek to Cheek', 'Just the Way You Look Tonight . . .'

John Davis, infiltrated to Malaya from Ceylon by submarine at the end of 1943, was the first to find that Freddy was still alive. No word was got out, however, because they had no working radio. The network of agents they tried to build up was compromised when the courageous Lim Bo Seng (right, with Davis) was caught and murdered by the brutal Kempeitai, Japanese field intelligence.

Chin Peng, the young communist guerrilla whom Freddy much admired, was given campaign medals by Lord Mountbatten (below left) and later an OBE for his wartime services. Chin Peng did not realise, though, that his own boss, Lai Te (below right), the Secretary General of the Malayan Communist Party, had betrayed his comrades and was working secretly for the Kempeitai. Lai Te could have snuffed out Freddy's life in an instant. He did not, because before the war he had worked for British Special Branch in Singapore, and he was hedging his bets on who would win. Lai Te's status as a British *and* Japanese agent was so sensitive that Freddy was never to mention it.

Major Satoru Onishi of the Kempeitai was Lai Te's Japanese spymaster. He arranged the murder of senior communists at the Batu Caves – ensuring that Lai Te 'miraculously' escaped – and led the hunt for Freddy and the guerrillas. He is seen here (opposite, top) wearing No. 6 at the trial in Singapore in 1947 that dealt with the perpetrators of the *sook ching*, the massacre of thousands of Chinese at the start of the Japanese occupation. Onishi was sentenced to life imprisonment.

Japanese troops in Malaya were reluctant to surrender when Japan capitulated. Freddy returned by parachute, and had several tense moments before personally taking the Japanese surrender at Kuantan on the east cost (above). Freddy proudly wore the kilt (right) at his wedding in India a few months later.

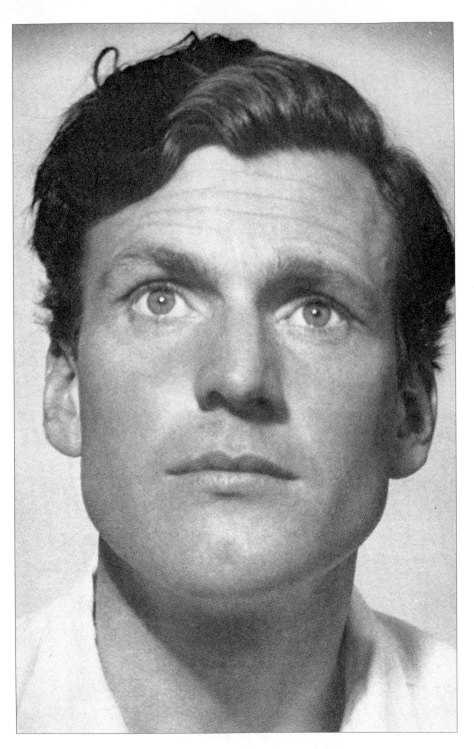

Freddy had the 'looks of a Rupert Brooke blended with an orphan's sadness', with a sudden lost look that came on him, when he cocked his head on one side, and stared ahead with 'heartbreaking wistfulness', that women found devastating.

what they did to my poor frail body . . . To my dear Old Boys, tell
them their teacher died with a smile on his lips . . .

Those qualities of sportsmanship and justice – and, beyond the red tape,
the essential decency of British administration – were bred in Freddy's
bone, as schoolboy and schoolmaster. As Pamadasa was hanged, Freddy
was keeping them alive in the jungle, in expiation of British failure to
preserve Malaya, perhaps, but also as proof that the surrender had not
been total. A fellow-inmate, a Muslim, recorded that the evening before
he was hanged, Pamadasa 'sang hymns beautifully from the condemned
cell and all those who heard him cried'.

Freddy waited a week in the Bukit Bertram camp. The guides who were
to take him on were collecting gelignite – damp and unstable, and liable
to explode at any moment – to take to the Slim camp to exchange for
rifles. He busied himself giving a concentrated course to the patrol
leaders. He also met some men who had escaped from prison in Kuala
Lumpur. They showed him the scars where the Japanese had pushed
needles under their fingernails, and the burns on their faces and chests
made by cigarette ends and hot irons.

It took another three days and nights to skirt Tanjong Malim and
reach a small kampong just to the north. The guides again got lost,
doubly maddening for Freddy since he knew the country so well from
his raiding days. He slept round the clock in the kampong, waking only
to eat big meals of rice and fried beans and aubergines. He needed to
build up his strength for the next fifteen-odd miles to the Slim river.
It had taken him twelve minutes along Route One in the Ford coupé,
but on foot, skirting the mountains six or seven miles to the east of
the road, it was against the lie of the land. Spur after spur comes off
the Main Range, tailing down to the plain, with rivers flowing fast
between them. The spurs run westward, and Freddy was travelling north,
so that he had to cross them, spur after spur, seven or eight of them,
climbing 1,200 feet through the jungle up over them, and then dropping down through tangles of bamboo and thorn to wade across the
surging water.

He was still suffering from a high fever, but each night his guides failed to reach the planned safe house. They were caught out with no time to build a shelter whilst the light lasted, so that they lay out all night hunched in a groundsheet, chilled and wet to the bone. He kept himself going with quinine and aspirin – they had plenty of both for once – but his leg muscles gave up, and he was pulled up the last long slope to the camp, about six miles north of the Slim river. He collapsed when he reached it: 'my strength and resolution only just lasted out'.

Blackwater fever now felled him. He thought, rightly, that it was the result of chronic malaria, triggered by constant small doses of quinine. It caused massive destruction of his red blood cells, chills, fever and vomiting, and he passed black urine. The pains in the small of his back and across his pelvis were so excruciating that he felt 'as if all my bones must come apart'. He shook with rigors so violent that two men had to hold him down. 'For a whole month,' he wrote, 'I was as ill as it is possible to be without actually dying.'

Slowly, he revived, and by mid-December 1943 he could travel again. His destination was a new camp at Bidor, about eighteen miles to the north-west. The route took him over the Sungei Sungkai, fifty yards wide, a mountain stream in full spate in the monsoon rains, and he spent a freezing night under a groundsheet in pouring rain as his little party tried to find a way to cross. A young Sakai guided them over next morning. This was Sakai country, and Freddy marvelled at their beautifully made houses. They were raised high above the ground on stilts, the interiors airy and light, with fine views from their elevation at 2,000 feet, westward over the coastal plain and north and west to the high blue mountains of Perak. At this time of year, the Sakai were living on hornbills, caught with *jereme*, bird-lime sticks smeared with a sticky gum made from the sap of the jackfruit tree, their meat tender and delicious when cooked fresh. Freddy felt the same affinity for the Sakai as the Eskimo. 'I was enchanted with these shy little brown men,' he wrote, 'who were so friendly once we had won their confidence.'

They came on a wide track cut by a large Japanese force that had passed through not long before. Freddy was again struck by their lack of fieldcraft. They had bivouacked for the night at one spot. He was astonished at the amount of gear they left behind: three pairs of socks, which he took for himself, handkerchiefs, a leather belt, a torch, mosquito coils, half-eaten tins of 'M&V' – captured British Army Meat-and-Vegetable – and enough biscuits and sweets to give Freddy's little party a meal. He could still see the marks of their nailed boots on steep traverses where they had slipped in the rain.

The old camp at Bidor had been bombed by Japanese aircraft. A new one was built by the Seroi river. Old friends from the Slim river camp greeted him with a feast and concert in his honour. It was Christmas Eve. There was 'some mystery' over one of the meat dishes he ate. He found it very good – 'less rank than monkey though not as good as jungle pig' – but his hosts would not tell him what it was until he had finished it. Then, 'I was told I had been eating Jap.' He never knew whether this was true or not, but he had heard that the guerrillas sometimes ate the heart and liver of Japanese they killed in their skirmishes. 'Though I would not knowingly have become a cannibal,' he wrote, 'I was quite interested to have sampled human flesh.'

He crossed the Seroi next day and followed a pipeline to a deserted kongsi-house. He was given coffee and asked to wait while they sent for the anonymous Party bigwig who had asked him to come. He had travelled for four months for this meeting.

CHAPTER 14

A WORLD TURNED UPSIDE DOWN

'On Christmas Day 1943,' Chin Peng wrote, 'I walked into the rambling timber house to greet a pleasantly surprised Chapman . . .' The young guerrilla had soared in the Party hierarchy since they had last met, filling the shoes of dead men betrayed by Lai Te. He told Freddy that his old friends Davis and Broome from 101 STS had returned to Malaya by submarine. They were waiting for him in a new camp three hours' march away. As they walked in pouring rain, he gave Freddy the latest news on the progress of the war.

The site of the camp had been chosen by Chin Peng. It was close to the summit of a hill called Blantan, about seven miles northeast of Bidor. The El expressway now carves through the jungle to the east of the township and the old Route One but in 1943 the camp was safely hidden a hard two-hour upward climb from the nearest roadway. Any attempt by troops to encircle it could be seen by its sentries. The guerrillas enjoyed pilot's-eye views across the coastal plains to the west. When the air was clear, they could see Pulau Pangkor thirty miles away, the island silhouetted against the hazy blue of the Malacca Straits. The Perak river slithered southwards in shallow curves down the middle of the plain until it made a bold turn westward to curl past the big town of Telok Anson before debouching into the Straits.

Freddy thought the new arrivals to be 'the very antithesis' of each other, and hence a perfect team. He found Broome 'quite the laziest man I have ever come across', frail, quiet, but able to see any flaws in plans made by Davis, who was strong, vigorous and sometimes over-confident. Both spoke fluent Chinese and Malay. Davis was the ranking Force 136 officer. Freddy had to accept this. 'I think he didn't like it,' Davis said. 'He obviously can't have done.'

The two briefed Freddy on Force 136, the new organisation which absorbed 101 STS men who had escaped from Malaya. They were both old Malay hands, Richard Broome a former colonial district officer in Ipoh, and John Davis the chief of police in Kampar. After the fall of Singapore, they had made it to Padang in Sumatra, and then sailed a small junk to Ceylon, a thirty-five-day voyage with almost no food – and water only from rain squalls. Force 136 was formed under the Special Operations Executive (SOE) to disrupt the Japanese in all occupied countries. The Malaya country section had been created in July 1942, when the Japanese advance was finally held on the edges of India and Australasia. Its aim was to infiltrate agents and to supply and train the guerrillas, ready for an all-out campaign of sabotage and ambush when the Allied landings in Malaya began. The infiltrations, by submarine at this stage, were codenamed 'Gustavus'. Most of the Chinese agents were nationalists, not communists, and supported Chiang Kai-shek's Kuomintang (KMT). Davis had made his first landing, 'Gustavus I', paddling ashore from a Dutch submarine with five Chinese agents and supplies north of the large island of Pulau Pangkor, on 24 May 1943.

The agents set themselves up successfully in the coastal town of Segari – one as an under-coolie in a coffee shop, another as a fish-monger – and Davis returned to Ceylon by submarine. He was landed back on the Perak coast on 4 August 1943. Broome followed a month later. At the end of September they met Chin Peng, who outlined the combined guerrilla and civilian organisation, the Anti-Japanese Union and Forces (AJUF). He told them Freddy was still alive, and had been training guerrillas in the AJUF camps for two years. The Japanese were now too active for Davis to get through to the coast for the next submarine rendezvous, so Chin Peng went. The Force 136 agent Lim Bo Seng, an exceptional young Straits Chinese, and a fluent English speaker, was landed but plans to land another British officer were abandoned. Lim Bo Seng began a rice-trading business from a safe house at 77 Market Street in Ipoh. Another agent, Ah Ng, was a born businessman, appearing at the camp one day with products he dealt in, boxes of cheap cigars, and bottles of White Stag, ersatz Japanese whisky made from rice spirit coloured with burnt sugar.

Two B Mark II radio sets were brought ashore and hidden. It was hoped to bring them inland later. But Davis and Broome had no way of contacting Ceylon when Chin Peng's guides brought them to the Blantan camp on the forty-mile journey from Segari. Chin Peng then arranged for Freddy to come to Blantan from Pahang.

Another meeting was to be held now, in January 1944, with a very senior figure from the guerrilla headquarters. This was Lai Te, the treacherous Secretary General, but he had ordered Chin Peng not to tell the Englishmen this. Instead, he should be introduced as a member of the Central Committee with powers to conclude an alliance with the Allies. Freddy christened the mysterious plenipotentiary 'The Plen'.

With the slaughter of senior comrades, Lai Te was now running the Party virtually single-handed, trusting no one, his movements secret, his contacts limited to a few. Fortunately for Freddy, he kept the MPAJA organisation intact, and did not betray those he was sure were super-loyal to him. The Kempeitai's Major Onishi only realised how much Lai Te had kept back – Freddy's whereabouts, the sites of MPAJA camps – when British officers interrogated him at the end of the war. Lai Te was 'farsighted', the Japanese told them. 'He realised that Japan would not win the war, and therefore he did nothing to damage the real war effort as he was looking forward to his future as dictator of the MCP.' That was hindsight, of course. Onishi must also have realised that double-agents – and Lai Te was a quadruple agent, Comintern, the Sûreté, British Special Branch and the Kempeitai all enjoying his favours at one time or another – almost invariably guard some secrets as an insurance policy.

For all his brilliant spycraft, however, Lai Te drew attention to himself with his car. He drove round Malaya to meet Party subordinates, alone or with his Vietnamese mistress, in a Morris 8HP saloon, with a genuine Singapore registration plate, S4678. He used main roads and made no attempt to hide his movements from the Japanese. He drove up from Singapore to Kuala Lumpur, immaculate in white suit and dark glasses, where he stayed at the old planters' hotel, the Coliseum on the Batu road, or at a Chinese hotel in Jalan Sultan. His contact point was a Chinese store on the Klang road. His usual meeting place with his underlings from the Selangor party was a mill twelve miles north of the city on the Ipoh road.

He then motored on to Perak. Here he met Chin Peng, so loyal he was known as 'Lai Te's little boy'. He was grooming Chin Peng, who knew nothing of his treachery, as his number two. In 1943 he appointed him the head of MPAJA liaison with Force 136 officers.

The Morris car belonged to the Singapore Kempeitai, and Lai Te could drive where he pleased, of course, because he was under their protection. The few individuals in the Party who did suspect him were themselves liquidated by their more trusting comrades. No one queried the way that the women couriers who carried coded messages to him were never intercepted, though they travelled to Singapore by train, and were sometimes met at Bukit Timah station by Lai Te in person. He had more lives than a cat, where his comrades had but one, which all too often came to a brutal and squalid end in Kempeitai hands.

He created for himself a superhuman aura, of great wisdom, humanity and courage. An awestruck member of an MPAJA regiment in south Johore told of a bicycle ride that Lai Te had made from Kuala Lumpur to Singapore. He had barely set off when he saw a crippled worker hobbling at the roadside. He gave him the bicycle and finished the 200-mile journey on foot. There is a black humour to a man as utterly self-seeking as Lai Te preparing this fable, but the Party faithful drank deep of it. Freddy mentioned how the guerrillas in his camp believed that Lai Te could pass through Japanese positions with ease: he could 'pilot an aeroplane, drive a tank, speak many languages, and hoodwink the Japanese in any way he liked'.

Had he wished to, he could have destroyed Freddy in an instant. That he did not, and that he left the MPAJA very much to its own devices, was because he valued the British connection. He was hedging his bets on the outcome of the war.

Lai Te arrived from Singapore in the black Austin Ten. Chin Peng met him at their rendezvous, a communist-controlled kampong at the closest point of the road to the camp. Chin Peng had been a Party member for four years, devoted to it heart and soul, yet, he said, 'our leader had remained an enigma'. No one knew his real name. He was familiar to them only as Lai Te, his main alias, though he also went as Chang Hong, Wright, Wong Kim Gyok and Wong Show Tong. He was an ethnic Vietnamese, a rarity in an essentially Chinese movement. He was greatly feared. Any order linked to Lai Te commanded 'immediate attention, absolute respect and unquestioned obedience', Chin Peng said, and it was this that prevented any questions, even one as relevant as how he could drive his black car at will under the noses of the Kempeitai.

He looked pallid. 'I realised immediately that he was ill,' Chin Peng recollected. 'He was emaciated and continually short of breath . . .' Every thirty minutes or so, they had to stop whilst he recovered. On reaching the camp, he had to rest for a further hour, 'getting his strength and composure, before meeting the British'.

A sudden downpour had drenched the camp but now the sun came out and Chin Peng remarked on the 'familiar dank smell of rotting vegetation' that reached them as they gathered at a long table of gnarled rain-forest timber in the lecture hut. He gazed at the three British officers facing him across the table, finding their 'measured tones' a stark contrast to constant buzzing of the jungle cicadas. Freddy – 'an unconventional warfare expert whose exploits would make him a legend in his lifetime' – was opposite him. They knew each other of old, of course.

Richard Broome was a 'hunched presence . . . Wracked with pain, the captain could scarcely utter a comment as he rocked backwards and forwards, sweating, shivering struggling to follow proceedings.' Chin Peng found Davis 'physically fit and agile'. He was to become closer to Davis than to any other European and their respect for each other was intimate and friendly. As for Chin Peng himself, Davis described him at the talks that were to follow: 'round boyish face . . . courage marked and commands naturally respect of men without fuss or formality . . . quiet character with incisive brain and unusual ability . . . frank and reliable and very likeable'.

Chin Peng had not the slightest doubt that this bonhomie would not last. In the long term, the alliance was doomed once the Japanese were driven out: 'The British were bent on regaining priceless colonial territory. Our aim would be to deny them.' A parting of the ways was inevitable, he said, and both sides knew it. For the moment, though, their mutual enemy ensured that their short-term aims meshed well enough. Broome drew up an agreement on a single sheet of lined paper torn carefully from a school exercise book. The original survives in the Public Record Office in Kew, London, handwritten in Broome's scholarly script, with headings neatly underlined, filling both sides of the sheet.

It was an extraordinary scene: the most wanted man in pre-war Malaya, Lai Te, was sitting down with the very people – Davis a senior police chief, Broome a government official – who would have incarcerated him. Or so Chin Peng thought at the time. But Freddy, as Chin Peng later found out, knew much more about Lai Te than he did. 'Chapman expertly concealed the fact that he knew exactly who Chang Hong really was,' Chin Peng revealed in his memoirs many years later. 'He had been present at a meeting in a dingy second floor office in Singapore's Geylang area on 19 December 1941 to negotiate with Lai Te – now Blantan's "Chang Hong" – who had been clearly identified to him as the CPM secretary general.' What was more, the two Special Branch officers who were accompanying Lai Te had already 'briefed Chapman on the staggering circumstances surrounding the communist leader's role for British intelligence. Lai Te, Chapman had been told, had been a British agent from the moment he joined the Party in the early 1930s. He was a plant . . .'

Freddy made no mention in his book, *The Jungle is Neutral*, that he had already met Lai Te, and knew him to have been turned by Special Branch. He wrote simply that:

The Plen was a young-middle-aged Chinese of great charm, considerable intelligence, and quiet efficiency. He had a large mouth and perfect teeth, and when he became animated his eyes grew round and his eyebrows rose about an inch and a half. The conference lasted two days and was most cordial . . .

The 'round eyes' is correct – a photograph shows that, though the mouth is narrow and tight-lipped – but the rest reveals nothing. John Davis, too, was perfectly aware from his role in police intelligence that Lai Te was a British agent. He certainly knew of the December 1941 meeting – he may have attended it – but he also made no mention of it after the war. To see why, we have to go forward to 1947, when Freddy was writing *The Jungle Is Neutral.* By then, the victory over Japan achieved, the communists and the colonialists were fighting one another in the Malayan Emergency, as Chin Peng had predicted. Lai Te had recently disappeared with $1 million of Party cash and gold, and Chin Peng had replaced him as Secretary General. The Emergency was a major military undertaking. 'A total of 41 British battalions would be deployed to confront my army' – Chin Peng wrote of 'my army' of five thousand men and women with justifiable pride – 'and local police, Royal Malay Regiment forces and units from Australia, New Zealand, East Africa and Fiji . . .' With the fighting gathering pace as *The Jungle Is Neutral* was written, and Lai Te gone, SOE's successors were not willing to have Freddy expose the Secretary General's past as a British agent.

Lai Te haggled over some points at the meeting. He did not like the word 're-occupation' to describe the British return to Malaya. He thought that had overtones of permanence. He preferred 're-taking'. The translator was Lim Bo Seng – 'in every way a most attractive and outstanding character', Freddy wrote of him. Despite minor disagreements, the main points under discussion – the Allies providing money, supplies and training to their comrades in arms – were agreed and the document was signed.

The Anglo-Marxist alliance reflected the equally upside-down world outside. The new elite in Singapore and the Malay cities were 'the former scums and dregs ... notorious gentleman-crooks, swindlers and well-known failures ... puppets, pimps, informers, flatterers and nothing-to-lose adventurers'. Opium dens flourished. Lottery mania swept the peninsula and the Japanese licensed gambling farms. The biggest and noisiest was at Ipoh, visited by 30,000 gamblers a day, kept sweet by the girls who made up a third of the 2,000-strong work-force.

As for the distant war in Burma, the Chindits were suffering anew. They had returned behind Japanese lines in March 1944, with the task of pushing through northern Burma to establish an overland supply route to China. But Orde Wingate was killed in an air crash on 24 March. Critical battles at Imphal and Kohima, as the Japanese attacked furiously and sought to break into India, stripped the Chindits of the air support they needed. The result was another mauling before they withdrew in June.

The Japanese were becoming more and more active. The Blantan camp was not secure – it could be approached along a ridge from either end – and Freddy set out with Sakai guides to find a better site. He was looking for a place that was open to the west, for wireless reception, when they brought the set that had arrived by submarine up from its hiding place on the coast. It needed atap for thatching, water, tree cover to conceal the huts from prying aircraft, and an open space where they could get a view and lie in the sun to lift their spirits.

He enjoyed being with the Sakai. The women were naked to the waist, with a sarong of cloth or bark, and they had red or ochre paint on their cheeks, and he found some 'comely if not beautiful', and their children enchanting. The men tucked bright flowers into the circles of woven bark they used as hair bands, and wore amulets on their arms, and carried eight-foot blowpipes and bamboo quivers for their poisoned arrows.

They were terrified of the Japanese, however, and were afraid of reprisals if guerrillas were found camped too close to them. Freddy found a spot just above the confluence of the Ayer Busok with the Woh river. The Sakai headman here, Pa Kasut, told Freddy that the water was foul, the area was plagued with gales and rain and bitter cold, and it was bad for malaria. All these things transpired to be true, but Freddy put it down to the headman's natural nervousness. The whole party moved from the Blantan camp in the middle of February.

They were able to bring some Sten guns, rifles, pistols and ammunition up from the coast, though they still had no functioning radio. They missed a rendezvous in February with a submarine from Ceylon. It was too dangerous for an Englishman to keep the April rendezvous, but a Chinese on his own would not arouse suspicion along the coast. Ying, one of the Force 136 agents, left the camp on 6 April to make his way to the coast. He was back the same evening with Tsing, another of Davis's men, who was tongue-tied with nerves. He blurted out that he had just fled from the Kempeitai, who were unravelling the network.

Rumours of the 'Gustavus' operations had reached the Japanese. They knew that submarines were involved, and they intensified patrols and interrogations along the coast. They had arrested a village headman called Choy, who had helped Tsing set up as a fishmonger. He had talked under torture. Tsing himself was then picked up by the Kempeitai. He was taken to their headquarters, a large house in Ipoh they shared with Chinese detectives and a few girls. They treated him well, as they were hoping to turn him to work for them, but he escaped from a second-storey bathroom. A taxi driver had taken him to Bidor – when he had admitted he was on the run from the Kempeitai, the driver had shouted *'Tai ka t'ung pau'*, 'we are all one blood' – and from there he had rushed to the camp.

It was too late to save Lim Bo Seng. He had returned to Ipoh from the safety of the camp. On his last night in camp, he spoke to Davis of his ambitions after the war, to open schools and factories and hospitals. He had a 'real dream with marvellous things', Davis said, but he feared for his friend's life. He was stopped at a road block as he tried to flee Ipoh by car. The Japanese soldier asked to look at his watch – the standard prelude to helping himself to it – and noticed that it was new and British-made. It was, in fact, Force 136 issue. Lim

Bo Seng was arrested, and remained silent under torture so severe that he died in Batu Gajah prison on 29 June. Ah Ng – 'small and pale and harassed looking', Freddy said, 'but such courage and initiative' – was also taken.

CHAPTER 15

THE SEARCH FOR NOONE

'I found myself becoming increasingly restless,' Freddy wrote at the beginning of April 1944. The April submarine rendezvous had been hopelessly compromised by the arrests, there was no prospect of getting through to Ceylon on the radio, and he was tired of camp life. He needed a new adventure. He found a perfect excuse in a young ethnologist called Pat Noone, missing in the northern jungles. Frank Quayle, whom Freddy had last seen at the Slim river camp with Chrystal and Robinson, arrived and reported that, while he had stayed with the communists, Chrystal had left to go to a non-communist camp with Noone, and nothing had been heard of either of them for more than a year.

Freddy had never met Noone, but they had much in common. Each was a *beau idéal* of the Englishman in remote places among remote peoples, tough, with striking good looks, and a lust for local beauties, but with a scientific purpose underlying their boyish enthusiasms. Pat Noone had come out to Malaya in 1931, as field ethnographer for Perak, with a First in anthropology from Cambridge. His father was an amateur palaeontologist who had made his fortune trading in India, and had retired to France to study fossils and cave paintings. Young Noone inherited his father's deep interest in prehistoric peoples. He was captivated by the Sakai, the term then used for the Malay aborigines, now replaced by *orang asli*, 'original people'. His particular passion was for the Temiar and Semai, all but unknown peoples in the vast central block of mountainous jungle in the Main Range.

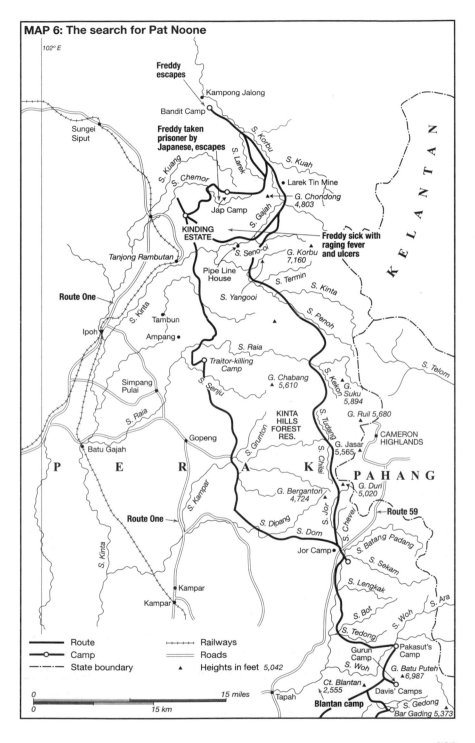

MAP 6: The search for Pat Noone

Noone set off from the Cameron Highlands to contact them, with porters carrying his kit in special tinplate boxes he had had made up for protection against the rain. 'I am steeled for a high purpose,' he wrote home. 'I carry the pistol [his father] gave me and a parang at my belt. I am taking a mandolin and a few books, including the Complete Works of Shakespeare and Arnold's *Light of Asia*. So I shall be well accompanied.' He followed the Bertam river on his first expedition. The Semai treated him with 'amazing sullen reserve'. When he camped on the opposite bank to their settlements, the women and children disappeared. The men would say no more to him than '*Ta Tahu*' and '*Entah*', 'I don't know . . . I'm not sure'. He left them gifts of tobacco. They still spurned him.

His breakthrough came when he found what he thought was the dead body of a young girl in a small hut half a mile from a Semai settlement. It was taboo for the Semai to approach a dying person. Noone found that she was still alive, though she had been abandoned without food and water. He noted her symptoms and sent a runner with a note to the medical officer at Tapah. The runner returned with the diagnosis, tertiary yaws, and medicine. Noone treated her. She was soon so much better that the taboo was lifted, and she returned to the longhouse and made a full recovery. Her father Batu, who loved her dearly, was the local Sakai headman. Headmen were known as 'Bah' – Freddy always referred to them as 'Pa' – and Bah Batu toured the high jungle with Noone, in his gratitude, introducing him to other headmen.

These included the Temiar. Noone was the first white man to contact them. He went up the Telom river, past granite gorges and waterfalls with crystal pools, and stretches where it flowed as softly as an English stream. 'Magnificent specimens,' he wrote of the Temiar, 'tall for Sakai, slim-hipped, and light fawn or pale cinnamon in colour. There was a refinement in their features I had not seen in the Sakai before, their faces being lozenge-shaped, with no marked depression at the root of the nasal bridge. The eyes were a deep brown, and the lips only of medium thickness.'

They lived in groups of between forty and a hundred in communal longhouses built of bamboo and palm and leaf thatch. Though some traded with Chinese merchants, they lived entirely from the jungle. Each year, they cut a ladang, or clearing, by felling trees and burning off the leaves and undergrowth. They planted tapioca, maize, millet, hill tobacco and hill-rice between the fallen trunks. Jungle flowers were food, too, and leaves, bamboo shoots, wild fruits, mushrooms, certain ferns and palm hearts. For pig and wild boar, they made pig fences of rattan that guided the animals to tapioca roots. As the pigs dug for the roots, the Temiar speared them. Fish were hooked, speared, netted and stupefied with a poison pounded into a milky juice from tuba fruit. Their blowpipes used darts whose tips were dipped in poison from the ipoh tree. Monkeys were their main prey, their presence in the trees betrayed by falling berries as they ate. They made cloth from the bark of the terap tree, with the texture of canvas, and decorations from fibres and grasses. Their baskets were woven from rushes, and their fishing nets from flax. Bamboo and rattan were used for spears, for their drums and pipes, for houses and rafts.

The individual owned no more than his blowpipe and quiver, his loin-cloth, and his parang. Otherwise, everything was held in common: a man could share his brother's wife, for sex had no particular significance for them. 'They have an emotional maturity that is quite phenomenal,' Noone wrote. 'As far as I have been able to ascertain, acts of violence and crime are unknown and there is no memory of inter-tribal warfare.' There is, as we shall see, a terrible irony in that statement.

They enchanted him. He based himself at Tanah Rata, the hill station in the Cameron Highlands, in the cool air at 5,000 feet and above, where the British came to escape the muggy heat of the plains in half-timbered hotels with blazing fires, with tea and cucumber sandwiches from the surrounding tea estates and market gardens. He made long expeditions, on foot, by dugout and by raft. He wrote monographs on Sakai customs, and lobbied furiously for a Reserve to be set up for them, to stop Europeans encroaching into the forests from the Highlands. The Sakai responded to him. They honoured him as 'Tata', 'grandfather', a mark of respect.

He fell in love with the niece of a Temiar headman in the summer of 1933. She was called Anjang, a girl of tender and striking beauty, a fifteen-year-old ten years his junior. Noone went on leave to England in 1934, and promised to marry her when he returned. Dreams were of great importance to the Semai and Temiar – Noone called them 'the Dream People' – and he lectured brilliantly on the dream psychology of their shamans at the joint Oxford and Cambridge anthropology faculty, and at the Musée de l'Homme in Paris. He went back to his old school, Aldenham, to talk and show films of his work in Malaya, as Freddy had given his talks on Eskimos at Sedbergh. The headmaster did not allow him to include clips of the bare-breasted girls who so captivated him, much to the regret of his younger brother Richard, who was still at the school. He was offered the chair of anthropology at Cambridge but turned it down.

Noone was briefly engaged to an English girl he met on the boat back to Malaya. Richard Noone followed him out after he left school, and found the engagement had been broken off. (The girl transferred her affections to a man called Goode, inspiring a famous one-liner from a wag at the planters' club in Ipoh, that it was a case of 'Goode after Noone'.) Anjang was the love of Noone's life. He adored her still.

He took young Richard with him into deep jungle to the north of the Cameron Highlands. They came to a Temiar longhouse, on stilts ten feet above the ground, 200 feet long, with matting walls, lit by wood fires burning in earthen hearths in the central floor. It was decorated with jungle flowers and plaited palm leaves. A dance was held in the brothers' honour. A line of girls served as an orchestra, beating a log with lengths of bamboo for rhythm, and a gaunt and wild-eyed old man sang and groaned. The air was thick with the scent of hill tobacco wrapped in nipah leaves. The men were garlanded with leaves. The women wept as they danced, a Temiar custom.

One of the girls in the orchestra glowed with beauty. Pat Noone turned to his brother and said, 'That, dear boy, is my wife.' He had paid the bride price for her, beads, sarongs, parangs, salt, copper wire and fishhooks. He became the government adviser on the Sakai, based in Taiping, and took Anjang with him on several trips to the large cities before the war. He had to keep her in the background. It was not the done thing, as his brother said, to 'flaunt an association with a native woman', and he did not tell his parents of his marriage. So many Sakai stayed at Noone's house in Taiping that his relationship with Anjang was not noticed. He deflected curiosity when travelling by always taking with him a young Temiar called Uda, his guide, friend and porter, whom he taught to read and write. When he was at a hotel or rest house, Anjang stayed in the servants' quarters with Uda. At some time in 1938, Uda became Pat Noone's blood brother. As an adopted brother, under Temiar practice, Uda was entitled to sleep with Anjang, and she with him, when Noone was away. Noone was constantly with her, and they travelled as a threesome, and this may not have been put to the test at first.

After the Japanese invaded and the front line passed him in northern Perak, he gathered men from the Argylls and the East Surreys who had been cut off, but they either gave themselves up or died. During 1942 he spent time among the Sakai, then with a KMT nationalist guerrilla band, and then with a communist one, together with Bob Chrystal. But Noone disliked the communists and returned to the Sakai. In mid-1943 Chrystal saw him at a KMT camp in Pulai, and again in October. He was suffering bad bouts of malaria: he was thin and his belly distended from a swollen spleen. He appeared restless. He said he would move over to the Sungei Siput area in Perak to see if he could get any rock salt and any war news from the Japanese papers. He talked of opening a jungle settlement of his own in the upper reaches of the Korbu river, where he knew a lush and isolated valley, and he would gather his friends and live there in peace and harmony.

Chrystal urged him to stay. But Noone was set on departure, and he said he would find some stomach powder for Chrystal, who suffered from ulcers: 'Don't worry, Bob, you shall have that stomach powder even if I have to ambush a Japanese convoy to get it.' With that he left by the path along the Telom. He was followed by Anjang, and then Uda and another young Temiar called Busu. Chrystal watched the quartet until they were gone. He felt unease. Something was amiss. It was 7 November 1943. No white man ever saw Pat Noone again.

*

'Our plan to look for Noone,' Freddy wrote. 'Very vague. All we know is that at one time he was at Jalong and at another at Temelong half-way to Grik.' He planned to go north to Jalong, a sprawling little town of coconut groves and vegetable gardens in the rolling foothills of the Main Range about fifty miles north of Blantan. From Jalong, where he hoped to replenish his stores, he would go further north towards Grik, now Gerik, if the Sakai suggested it. Chin Peng said that there were guerrillas in the southern part of the route, but warned him of Chinese bandits operating near Grik.

Freddy knew the bandits from his time in Johore, but there were more of them in the north, in Perak and Kelantan along the new border with Thailand, where they battened on to the smuggling trade. They had nominal links to the KMT, wearing a single star on their caps, where the communists had three. Robert Chrystal had left the communist camps in Perak to join a bandit group because he had had his fill of the 'monotonous round of traitor-killing, hymn singing and heart searching à la Oxford Group Movement'. He found nothing prim about the KMT men, a 'band of rough, swashbuckling bandolieros, who drank, whored and gambled hard'. Their leader, Yong Kong, was a sixty-year-old opium addict. The local communists were led by a devoted and serious young man, who imposed puritanical habits, and trained his men in the drills taught him by Freddy. Internecine war broke out between the single and triple starred guerrillas: the bandits were noto-rious for eating the heart and liver of suspected communist spies, and drinking their blood mixed with samsu liquor.

Freddy's route took him through the mountainous terrain on the high flanks of the Main Range. No Malays or Chinese penetrated the high jungle: neither had the British, apart from Noone and a few survey parties. It was a major expedition for a well-equipped team to attempt in peacetime. For a fugitive in wartime, it was a startling undertaking. The only tarmac road Freddy would come to – and dash across – ran from Tapah to the Cameron Highlands. For the rest, he was in wild Sakai country, and hoped that the headmen along the route would give him guides. He would also ask them if they knew Noone's move-ments. He went with a guerrilla, Ah Lim. 'I liked him,' he said, 'because being unable to read or write, he was much less politically minded than most of the guerrillas and he could be relied on to do what he was told.'

They left at 9 a.m. on 13 April. He was not superstitious. His pack weighed about forty-five pounds. He had blankets, spare clothes, curry, ginger, prawns, dried flatfish, salt, pepper and chilli. He expected to get rice from the Sakai guides along the way. He packed a book of essays and a Malay vocabulary. He took a .38 pistol, and Lim a .45. They had a grenade and twenty rounds each. He asked the guerrillas to give him a chit to introduce him and act as an identity card. Ah Yang, a senior cadre at the camp, refused because he had no official stamp.

For the next two weeks Freddy was guided along the western slopes of the Cameron Highlands by a succession of Sakai guides, sleeping each night in a different Sakai hut. One high point was a feast that lasted until 3 a.m. The owner of the hut provided freshly trapped rats and a pangolin, a scaly ant-eater, and Freddy lobbed in with dried fish and curried prawns. Another night Freddy curried some frogs, which he pronounced excellent.

He was away early on 20 April, guided by two bullet-headed men. They shouted all day to each other and to any Sakai they met. 'In fact, for the next few days everyone shouted all the time,' Freddy wrote in his diary. 'Very distressing to me!' He had taught himself to move silently, his ears so alert that he froze at the snapping of a twig, and his sense of fieldcraft was outraged by their chatter. He soon recognised, however, that the Sakai were so attuned to the jungle that they sensed the presence of strangers intuitively, long before they could see or hear or smell them.

A day or two later the guides seemed to know the way no further than to the next little group. They knew every pool and path in their own little district, and almost nothing outside it. They followed a maze of tracks, following ridges and crossing steep passes, well above the 3,000-foot contour. They reached another house, where a man had just caught a blue pheasant in a noose, and he gave them some pheasant stew. The full magnificence of the Cameron Highlands was on the eastern horizon. Six-thousand footers cascaded in the evening light, in graceful and distinct shapes, some so sharply fretted that they reminded him of Alpine aiguilles despite their thick cladding of jungle. He spent half an hour sketching the skyline.

The twenty-second of April was a day of wiry bracken and thorns, which scratched his knees and arms as he forced a way through. They climbed a steep ridge to 4,000 feet and then dropped a thousand feet steeply to the river. Here they found a 'wild and rather handsome woman' with three children in a hut. She was roasting some hard green jungle bananas, which seemed to be the only food she had. Her husband was away on a hunting trip. to She did not know the way north, but she led Freddy at a tremendous lick down the river and then left him for two hours whilst she looked for guides. He had eaten nothing in the morning. His appetite had gone.

From this point on, the diaries which Freddy kept have survived, and we are no longer so reliant on *The Jungle Is Neutral*, and the memoirs of others. The day turned into 'nightmare', he wrote in his diary, as he was struck by a fresh bout of fever:

> Felt ill. Temp 104! Took 2 Q [quinine]. Terrible afternoon, travelling with malaria. Followed river down & tiny paths, at last struck up a terrific hill. Here I could only just go & had to stop frequently. At last after 2 hours climbing reached the highest house I've ever seen. 30 feet off ground! Just collapsed and did not want to eat. Very few people. Eat quinine.

For the last part of the climb, his leg muscles lost their power, and he had to be towed by the Sakai at the end of a rattan lead. He rested every few yards and pulled himself up by holding onto the trees. He had to climb a staircase cut from a tree trunk to get into the house. He was so giddy he crawled on his hands and knees.

Two days on, Freddy and Lim were led to the most magnificent house Freddy had seen in the jungle. It was vast. At one stage sixty-four people had lived in it. It had a ceremonial dance floor in the middle the size of a tennis court, surrounded by a square of living rooms. Each had its own roof with big half-cylinders of bark acting as gutters. A small musicians' gallery was built out at one end of the great central room, with two Sakai drums. As with most Sakai houses, it was built over sloping ground, so that the rainwater ran off. One side was ten feet above the ground, with four well-crafted staircases leading up to it. The other was almost twenty feet up.

Everyone was friendly at first. The headman, with a pointed grey beard, was grave and courteous. He was married to a pure Malay girl, flashing with jewels in a brightly coloured bodice and sarong. Then a man came back from hunting and Freddy noted in his diary how the atmosphere became tense and violent:

> the new arrival suddenly started a tirade against us in a loud sing-song voice as if he were praying. Lim immediately took up the cudgels & argued with him flat for 1½ hrs in an equally loud voice. He said we were bad men, fugitives from the Japs & our coming could only bring trouble to them. Lim put things straight.

The man was armed with a pig spear, a stout six-foot pole with heavy flat metal spearhead, and Freddy and Lim slept that night on the dance floor with their pistols beside them.

They were away again with a new set of guides on 25 April. They went down steeply to the Sungei-oi river, and then had to climb an atap ridge. Freddy's route was the most exhausting he could follow. In moving northwards along the western flanks of the Main Range, he was traversing a wilderness of valleys and ridges. The rivers that drained the great jungled mountains ran westward to the sea, each carving out a deep rock-strewn valley in its spate, separated from the next by a high ridge that also ran westward, across Freddy's track. His progress was a switchback of numbing climbs and raw descents. He was north-east of Ipoh now, and to the east the massive face of Gunong Korbu towered to over 7,000 feet in outcrops of bare grey rock and soft green bands of jungle.

The next morning his weight was a factor, as they traversed gorges by walking along bamboos kept up by pegs stuck in crevices in the rocks. The Sakai only replaced these when they actually broke, and

Freddy was half as heavy again as they were. They crossed first, and then looked back with great interest as he made his way above the tumbling river. After the rain, the water heaved and pulsed as it raced through the gorges, flinging mists of spray that dampened the mosses on the rocky walls and made them treacherous. The Kew Herbarium was not forgotten. Once clear of the river, he was able to indulge in some flower-collecting:

> Fierce short day. Down ladang to river & across an almost Himalayan bridge with hand rails. Across the foot of an old ladang. Vile going over trees etc & all day either on sloping rocks over river or in river, or up & down steep traverses holding on by hands. Lot of primula with wrinkly leaves. Collected a lot of seeds & mauve flowers too.

The Sakai who aided Freddy did so without reward. They were terrified of the Japanese, and they knew that had the Japanese found out that they were helping a white man – and the tentacles of the Kempeitai penetrated wherever there were informers – they would have paid for it with their lives, and most probably of those of their women and children, too. Yet they guided him, fed him and sheltered him, and carefully passed him on from hand to hand, as if it were the most natural thing in the world.

· That night the headman where they stayed repeated the usual mantra on Noone: he knew of him – Noone had visited Jalong years before – but since the invasion he had heard nothing. He and his wife gave Freddy a fowl and some bananas next morning, 27 April, and took him onwards to the house of a 'gap-toothed man with a tiny nose squashed-up showing two large nostrils & a blue serge coat'. He gave them a huge meal of rice and curried mushrooms, and then led them to the house of the next headman, a young, clean-looking man called Bras, dressed in grey shorts and a drill jacket. He was the most prosperous Sakai that Freddy had met. He gave Freddy sweet coffee when he arrived, and a china bowl of water and a mirror and comb to spruce up his tangled hair and dirt-engrained face. The house was spotless and Freddy was embarrassed to cover the clean bamboo floor with blood from his leech bites. The leeches in the Korbu valley were the worst he had come across. Mats were laid and spread with dishes of rice and a huge bowl of pumpkin with chilli and spices.

After lunch, Bras said that he did not know where Noone was, but that the old headman of the Jalong Sakai might be able to help. He said that the headman's daughter, Anjang, had once been the most beautiful of all Sakai women. She had taken part in an exhibition of Sakai culture that Noone had organised at Singapore before the war. Anjang was now away from her home, Bras said, but the father might be able to help. Anjang, of course, was Noone's wife, which Bras would almost certainly have known from Sakai gossip, though Freddy may have thought she was only his mistress. The Jalong headman was Pa Bintang, and Anjang was not his daughter but his niece. Bras warned Freddy that there was no way of going further north towards Grik without passing the group of Chinese who controlled the Chinese village at Jalong. This puzzled Freddy. Chin Peng had not told him of any guerrilla patrol based at Jalong. But he thought he was still south of what Chin Peng had called the bandit country, and that the Chinese at Jalong would be reliable and help him. Bras obviously feared them. He said that it was unsafe for Freddy to go there and begged him to return. He offered to take him to the Sakai headman at Jalong, but he refused to go on to the Chinese.

They left in the early afternoon. The path soon widened and they came on fresh elephant tracks. This had been a trail before the war for the elephants that carried supplies to a Chinese-owned tin mine further into the jungle up the Larek river. The mine was no longer working, but the Sakai now used elephant to carry rice and vegetables down to sell to the Chinese merchants at Jalong. They passed warm springs. Bras said he heard a *rusa*, a deer, and pointed out tracks of *kijang*, barking deer (muntjac). The leeches were bad. They reached the Jalong headman's house by about 4 p.m. after an hour and a half. In *The Jungle Is Neutral*, Freddy wrote that: 'he said that his daughter Anjang had been away for years and that he had never seen or heard of Noone since the war'. In his diary, though, he is more detailed. Far from her being the headman's 'daughter', he says all Anjang's family were dead. He mentions a further warning about the Chinese at Jalong, referring to them as 'g', his diary abbreviation for 'guerrilla', since he still thought they were guerrillas rather than bandits:

> He says Anjang used to live near here years ago but N. [Noone] took her to Grik 4 years ago & he hasn't heard of her since. All her relations dead. Some fear our reception by g. who are only a little way down the valley now.

Ignoring that warning very nearly cost Freddy his life. Perhaps that is why he rather glossed over it in the book. But there was, as he said, 'nothing for it but to go and visit the Chinese at Jalong', however forbidding they seemed. It was that, or abandon the search for Noone. It was clear that if the young anthropologist was still alive, he must be to the north, round Grik, and the route passed Jalong. Lim agreed with him.

The headman sent two men with them who knew the Chinese. They had walked for about half an hour downriver when the valley broadened out towards Jalong, a sprawling place, only a little larger today, its houses spread out on dusty roads amid large vegetable gardens. They came across the first Chinese. Freddy noted in his diary:

> I saluted [them] smartly. A big open valley dotted, lower down with houses. All C. [Chinese] In this house 2 old men who grow tobacco & own the house. 4 g. (?) with no weapons under a typically ratty big-eared, toothy, oily leader & 4 coolies who are shortly recovering a veg. [vegetable] place higher up in the hills. While we were bathing the leader put on my pistol & told us they wanted to search all our gear as we had no *surat*. Of course I raised no objections and they went thro' everything there & kept both pistols & ammo & grenades, promising they would not leave the house. Terrific noise all night. Very hard to sleep. I suppose they are guarding us.

The cryptic '4 g. (?)' – four guerrillas and a question mark – showed that Freddy suspected from the start that he had not fallen among friends. But he could not object to the confiscation of his gun and grenade because Ah Yang had refused to give him a *surat*, a 'certificate', back at the Blantan camp. Freddy had appeared unannounced from the deep jungle, a wild-looking white man, his legs bloody with leech sores. Little wonder, he had to agree, that they had taken away his armaments.

They told him that they were under the orders of a leader who lived in a camp further down the valley. He would decide if they should help Freddy and Lim to further their search for Noone. Freddy wrote a polite letter to the leader, explaining who he was, and asking that an officer should be sent up to speak with him. Next morning, 28 April, the rat-faced man asked if he could use Freddy's .38 to go and shoot a traitor, as they were short of pistols:

> I could hardly refuse & all the weapons were taken elsewhere & never saw them again tho' he promised them back next day. Lim is furious about it all as they cannot strip a .45 & have only coconut oil. We are not at all happy about things.

There was little they could do about it. They were well fed, with excellent rice, beans, fish and pork, and as much papaya as they could eat. 'Days all the same now,' he wrote in the diary entry covering the period from 29 April to 9 May. He spent much of the time sitting in the sun, the open air restoring him after the permanent gloom of the jungle. He bought salt, onions, garlic, fish and bananas to replenish his stores. No letter came from the supposed camp leader. It was more and more likely that these were bandits, not guerrillas, and that Freddy was their prisoner. One of the old tobacco growers confirmed this. Making sure no one could see them, he warned Freddy that he was in the hands of *orang jahat*, 'bad men', and that Ratface had told him that Freddy was a friend of the Japanese. Lim was also convinced they were bandits, as they knew none of the songs and slogans from the communist camps.

About 2 or 3 May, Freddy decided he would go on to Grik on his own if the letter from the camp leader came. He wanted Lim to get back to the Blantan camp, carrying a letter Freddy wrote to John Davis, explaining his predicament. He stealthily gave Lim a share of their food, medicine, tobacco and money and Lim slipped out of the house shortly after dawn. He was spotted, though, and Ratface and the others rushed after him and barred his way. They faced each other on the elephant track for some time, until Freddy brokered a compromise. Lim would stay until a captain came from the main camp where the leader was supposed to be. No captain came, but Ratface sent a man off on a bicycle who returned to say that Lim had permission to go. Lim left at once.

Freddy bathed in the river with what he now called his 'gaoler' and felt very hot when he got out. He hoped it was the sun, but found he was running a temperature of 104 degrees. How took quinine. He was better by 8 May, but the atmosphere had become very strained:

Nothing happening at all. They are playing with us. I went to swim with the one who can speak a little Malay, leaving [Ratface] alone. The water was too shallow so I slipped quietly home and found him quite alone going through the seams of my clothes and all my papers. I watched him for 7 or 8 minutes! He said he wanted to borrow my razor and was looking for it. Bastard! Food worse, He even asked for some $ to buy veg, tho' I know he has some money. Nothing but lies, false promises, deceit . . . I sent two very rude letters up to HQ. Hope they could read them!

He enjoyed watching a large elephant that went up and down to Bras's ladang every two days or so, accompanied by a child. There had been another one, but it had destroyed crops and so Ratface's men had shot it: '18 shots, mostly TSMG [Thompson submachine-gun]' Freddy noted in disgust.

His fears became darker. 'About 50 men & women know that I am here,' he reckoned, and the chances of betrayal were getting higher. He befriended one of the coolies who was clearing land above the house. The man had worked for a British rubber planter called Robinson on a nearby estate before the invasion. He brought Freddy a few English books from the estate bungalow, Jules Verne's *Lost in the Pacific* and a couple of Western novels by Ridgwell Cullum. He warned Freddy that Ratface was playing a lone hand, that he had split with the communists, and that he had written to the nearest communist patrol, offering to hand Freddy over to them for $1,000. Worse, the friendly old tobacco grower told Freddy that he had seen Ratface talking in a shop in Jalong to a Chinese who was notorious as a Japanese agent. It seemed that Ratface was prepared to sell him to the highest bidder, communist or Japanese. On two successive mornings, twin-engined Japanese reconnaissance aircraft flew low over the valley.

CHAPTER 16

TAKEN BY THE JAPANESE

Reluctantly, Freddy decided to give up his search for Noone, to slip away as soon as possible and return to the Blantan camp. He wanted to avoid the elephant track, which his gaolers would know, and head for the old Jalong headman's house by a more direct route. He swam as far upstream as they would allow to reconnoitre the route. A gaoler was with him all the time now, even when he went out to pee during the night. He quietly packed his rucksack on the evening of 9 May:

> I got all ready & slipped out at 11.30. I intended to go by the old man's Kongsi but the fire suddenly flared up & somebody was smoking! I returned & took the elephant's route. Packed 45 lbs. Used torch with blue shade. Crossed river well above S [Sakai] house (bare feet to avoid tracking). River very high. Dropped torch in but no harm done! Followed track for 1 hour. Lost it once cross river. Only just got across – too low on far side & had bad hour over slippery rocks. Tried to cut up into jungle but could find no path. Came on a house I hadn't seen before. Heavy rain off & on. Up wet clay elephant track very leechy & bad going, had a few falls.

Here, and elsewhere, there are differences between the diaries and his book. In the diary, he says simply, 'I got all ready & slipped out at 11.30.' That is that. He's away. In *The Jungle is Neutral*, he says that two of the most alert bandits – 'Ratface and the Stooge' – were on guard duty. It was their habit to stay noisily awake drinking coffee far into

244

the night. There is no question in the book of 'slipping away'. He had to knock them out. Freddy explained in the book how he had been issued with an 'L-tablet' – L for 'lethal' – in his 101 STS role to use if he was captured and faced torture. He had long since lost his tablet, but Davis and Broome had been issued with morphia tablets by Force 136, and had given him eight of them as replacements. The passage in the book continues:

> I decided to give them [the guards] four each. That evening I joined them at coffee, and having previously crushed up the little white tablets, it was quite easy to slip them into their mugs before they stirred the sugar. I waited until they had drained their mugs and then, feeling singularly elated, I left them and climbed the ladder to my loft. They talked noisily for some time. Quite suddenly, there was silence. Whether they ever woke up or not I do not know – or care.
>
> To make doubly sure, I had already removed part of the atap wall in one corner of the hut so that I could slip straight out into the night without walking past the sentries. Shortly before midnight I tiptoed down the ladder from the left, pushed my bulky pack through this gap and crawled out after it.

No word of the morphia tablets appears in the diary. Why? Because the incident was so burnt in his memory that he needed no aide-mémoire? Hardly. The diary details other dramatic incidents in full. Was it for security, for fear that the diary might fall into the wrong hands? He later claimed – lecturing to the Royal Geographical Society, for example – that sensitive parts of it were written in Eskimo. This is not so. The surviving diaries are all in English, written in a small neat hand, and only occasionally illegible. They contain large amounts of material, names, places, details of camps and weapons and strategy, that would have been of immense value to the Kempeitai. Both Davis and Broome complained bitterly to him that his diary-keeping threatened the security of them all. He persisted because, as we shall see, he intended them to be the raw material of the book he intended to write.

The morphia incident is not in the diary almost certainly because Freddy concocted it later for the book. We shall soon come to other inconsistencies that make this clear. But we also need to see that, in the overall terms of his ordeal, this is a by-the-by. We are taken back, so to speak, to Freddy's account of his escape from the Chomolhari crevasse: as his friends said, we need to 'divide what Freddy says by two, and call it nearly'. No more than that.

We are not dealing with a myth-maker, in the style of Lawrence of Arabia. We have already noted that Field Marshal Wavell knew both men. He wrote the introduction to *The Jungle Is Neutral*. In it, he said that comparisons between Spencer Chapman and Lawrence were inevitable, but if only Lawrence became a legend, it was because Freddy 'has not T.E. [Lawrence]'s literary genius; nor his introspection. He does not reveal the innermost thoughts that came to him in the many hours he lay alone waiting for his fevers to pass. Colonel Chapman has never received the publicity and fame that were his predecessor's lot.' In *Seven Pillars of Wisdom*, Lawrence nurtured his legend by boasting of personally blowing up seventy-nine bridges. The true figure was twenty-three. Freddy could not have exaggerated his own exploits during the 'mad fortnight' on such a scale even had he wanted to. John Sartin was with him throughout. Sartin survived a Japanese prison camp to confirm Freddy's account as accurate after the war. Indeed, he said that: 'Freddy doesn't make enough of what he did.'

Lawrence made a drama of writing his book. He claimed to have lost the first draft and most of his notes on Reading railway station. This is most probably untrue. The fate of Freddy's notes, his diaries, was dramatic – but true. He lost his first diaries when Haywood was shot, and he buried them in the plantation beside the Menchis road. As we shall soon see, he was forced to burn the second set. The survivors are in the Pitt Rivers Museum in Oxford. The morphia tablets may be – perhaps we should bite the bullet, and say *are* – an invention. They matter little in the whole. The whole of the drama of *Seven Pillars*, however, and Lawrence's very soul, is affected by its most sensational incident, when he is whipped and sodomised by the Turkish governor in Deraa. He describes it in the greatest and most intimate detail – 'he began to fawn on me, saying how white and fresh I was . . . he lumbered to his feet, with a glitter in his look, and began to paw me over . . . he began to lash me madly across and with all his might . . .' and it transfixes the reader.

It is make-believe.

Freddy is the reverse. His book sells him short. In his search for Noone and its aftermath, the cumulative effect of the diaries gives a more overpowering sense of the desperate struggles of this solitary and exhausted fugitive as he staggered towards what seemed his end:

May 10. 37th birthday, very nearly 40! At 5.30 reached a stream R to L [right to left] & washed. Soon after took R track instead of L & reached a milky river at 6.30. 10 yards wide running over red laterite sand & track across & up to an S [Sakai] house & a fishing shelter by the river. Went up river. A number of walled conduits made at waterfalls, 2 or 3 big ones, went up unbelievably steep tracks. Made my usual mistake & followed a faint path up a ridge hoping to meet the river again. Heard a dog bark so came down to river again. Here the mine starts. All derelict. Secondary j [jungle] blue flowers & thick scrub full of grey ants' nests. Many rusa [deer] tracks. Found a S shelter here & decided to stay. Cooked rice & onions & prawns & fish. Pity I decided not to bring coffee. Recce'd tomorrow's track & sat in sun, bathed & had another meal as before. Asleep at dusk. Terrific rain & had to move my bed.

The reconnaissance aircraft suggested that the Japanese were on the look-out for him, and for guerrilla camps. But he did not know how much he had stirred them up and he still felt safe in mountainous jungle, where their patrols seldom penetrated. His confidence was misplaced:

11 May. Cooked up remains of supper & away 5.45. Decide to follow R tributary of stream. Found a queer track parallel to stream. Very steep traverses. Cut up hill to avoid upper part of stream.

Terrible going. My plan: to find the FR [Forest Reserve, pre-war colonial equivalent of national park] route on top & follow it along E to the summit of the Termin–Gajah watershed. Fought my way up last 500 feet – only tiny tunnelled paths thro bracken & impenetrable springy scrub. Went N & found top . . . Tried to follow the ridge for an hour but had to give it up & return. Decided to go down S [South] and look for S [Sakai]. Map shows many. Terrible going. Waterfalls. Tried to bypass them but all very steep & in one place I got down, a terrible place near the foot of a face & had to return as no way on. Pack very heavy & all the stumbling has skinned my shoulders. Found a track up R bank but it went on up & up. At last past waterfalls. Very weary. Saw the track of a heeled boot? Could not be Japs up here. Saw 2 S bathing & smoke of a camp fire. Hurray. Went cautiously close & suddenly saw a Jap in tall hat with coppery star. Tried to hide. Too late. Pandemonium. I had no weapon & could not run with pack. Completely dazed with exhaustion. About 5.30 p.m. 100 Japs 100 Bengalis and 2 or 3 S prisoners.

Dozens of Japanese surrounded him, waving their arms, and crying 'Killy-kollack, killy-kollack!' One hit him on the head with a rifle butt, but his was a skull that had shrugged off cricket bats when he was a boy at Ilkley, and it made no impression. He was in the hands of a large patrol that was specifically looking for the Englishmen who were thought to be behind all guerrilla activity. A Malay-speaking NCO interrogated him in Malay. He was asked specifically: 'Do you know an Englishman called Colonel Chapman, who is the leader of all the communists.' When Freddy had gone into the jungle so long before he had been a major, but his Corps Commander had given him the honorary – i.e. unpaid – rank of Lieutenant-Colonel, to increase his prestige with the guerrilla leadership. He was thus known as 'Colonel Chapman'. His British identity card, which the Japanese now had, still identified him as 'Major Chapman'. So he said, yes, he knew the colonel, who was in fact his elder brother. 'Have you any news of him?' he asked. 'I heard he had been killed in an ambush in Pahang.'

They took his pack and searched him for weapons. They asked why he had two pistol holsters and no pistols. He told them that Chinese robbers at Jalong had taken them. They studied his marked maps, and he made a silent vow never again to mark maps. He made a careful note of their uniforms. Even in extremis, his intelligence training was still in his mind. He noted that they had two Thompsons, shotguns and Japanese rifles, but no pistols. The English-speaking officer wore two silver stars pinned over his left breast on a bit of scarlet flannel two inches by one inch. Several wore a similar length of cloth with a yellow stripe. They had no shoulder or arm markings. Most wore heavy leather boots, nailed, with puttees with tape crisscrossed right over left, loose breeches, shirt and tunic. They had long mackintoshes with belts and hoods that came up over their high-peaked hats.

The questions continued – 'Am I alone? Where have I come from? Where am I going?' – and he told them that he was travelling alone and was looking for Noone. He realised that they would find the letter from John Davis to Noone in his pack, and he tried to limit the damage. He said he had been at camps in Bidor and Pahang, but he did not like the guerrillas as they were communists. He asked the officer if he knew the whereabouts of two Japanese whom he had known at Cambridge, the ornithologist Prince Hashisuka, and Kagami, a famous skier. It was Hashisuka, we recall, who gave the talk to the Cambridge Bird Club that had inspired Freddy to go bird-watching in Iceland. The officer could give him no news of them, but was impressed that the fellow-countrymen his prisoner knew were so well-bred:

I bathed, changed, then they gave me some rice & fish & water – with apologies! They couldn't have been nicer. The officer said 'You are an Eng [English] gentleman & officer, you must tell me the truth.' I said how glad I was to be out of the jungle & how hard it was living with the S [Sakai]. I said I was waiting for the British to return. He snorted . . . We start for Ipoh tomorrow.

The Kempeitai would be waiting for him in Ipoh, he knew, and the pleasantries would be over.

He had played the psychological aspect of his capture with a brilliance made the more dazzling by his physical exhaustion. He had, within ten minutes or so, persuaded his captors to relax. He had charmed the two who interrogated him – the NCO had congratulated him on the fluency of his Malay, and the officer was so taken with his prisoner that he apologised that 'the absence of whisky' meant they could not take a drink together – and this warmth spread to the infantrymen. He lulled them. He seemed too nice to want to escape. They fetched his rucksack for him and:

let me go through my stuff but stood round to watch. I hid my pipe then searched for it & managed to get my diary rolled up in my handkerchief inside the pack. They said I could put it in my pocket. Then I hung up my blanket to dry – they kept a roaring bamboo fire going just in front of the officers' tent – & I picked up a bamboo to light my pipe. I managed to slip the rolled up diary inside & threw it onto the fire! . . . Then we slept. The Bengalis were in 3 or 4 lean-tos down near the river & the Japs in 3 or 4 great bamboo lean-tos with banana and atap leaves & over the officers' tent a tarpaulin. I slept plumb in the middle of the tent with my feet only 5 inches from the fire & between 2 officers who slept in boots & all clothes but no blanket. An NCO or officer stood by the fire in charge, & 2 sentries with fixed bayonets, one watched me & the other wandered around. They all watched me very closely. I managed to work the tarp loose behind my head. The Japs slept like logs, touching me on either side. About 1 a.m. I persuaded them to let the fire die down a bit by going out & pretending to be sick – it *was* terribly hot. Then I put on my shoes . . . I managed to shove a lot of the officer's gear down to the foot of my sleeping bag – his despatch case, spare clothes & other bundles while I doubled myself up & watched the guard thro half-closed eyes. At 1.30 I made a dash for it. As I was half out, without much difficulty, I heard the guard exclaim or grunt. I longed to take the despatch case & a rifle which lay under my head but it was not worth the risk.

I dashed towards the river below the camp. Bamboo thickets & then a fallen tree, very well lit up by the moon. I skipped over it & was in the river – unfortunately up to my armpits. It was then I felt for my watch. I found it had broken loose in the rush. I never heard a *sound* of pursuit, not a shot, or shout, or even a broken stick. I went downriver for 100 yds, then up a steep bank on the far side. After 20 mins I found a track & came on an S [Sakai] house brilliantly lit up in the moonlight with ladang [clearing] round it & banana trees. The house was empty. I saw Aquila & the moon & soon got my bearings.

He was free, but he no longer had anything – maps, compass, watch – to navigate by. Their loss would have been fatal in jungle terrain to most fugitives. For Freddy, though, the astral navigational skills he had learnt in Greenland were a lifeline. He made a list of what he had lost in his diary:

The Japs got:
.38 holster and belt, .45 ditto, blanket, 2 khaki shirts, 1 ditto shorts, 1 pants, 2 vests, 1 gym shoes worn out, letter from me to P.N. [Pat Noone] May '43, letter from John [Davis] to P.N. 12 April '44, 5 1" map S. Siput, Korbu, Ipoh, B. Gajah, 4¼" or ½" maps, my map showing route, Adrift in the Pacific, Weavers of Webs [his books], 1 cooking pot and lid, 1 mug, 1 spoon, pocket knife, 3 tins Q [Quinine], few (9) MB [sulfadiazine], 3 acquaflavine, 1 make-up in gun oil bottle [for Tamil disguise], 1 tin ½ full salt, 1 tin prawns, 1 small tin pepper, 1 tin curry & chillies, 1 tin onions garlic ginger, ½ g rice in S [Sakai] bag, pipe, bag cut tobacco, roll of leaf tobacco, seeds of primula etc, box matches, rubber for fire [kindling], small bottle oil, small pencils, Malay vocab (& lists of words all over maps), waterproof map case, ditto bag for clothes & canvas bag, 250$, 1 field dressing, 1 pris [prismatic] compass, tooth brush, sarong, guerrilla cap (less peak and stars), parang & case.

The prismatic compass, the pocket knife and parang, and the medical kit were the most serious losses. He needed the quinine for his fortnightly malaria attacks. He also lost the sulfadiazine powder he used to prevent the leech bites and cuts on his legs turning into ulcers. The books were a real loss for him, too. As for the diaries, although everything up to 13 April was lost, he rewrote them whilst the events were still fresh in his mind. He was left with no more than he stood up in: 'I had my shoes, long trousers, blue pants, aertex vest, flannel shirt, handkerchief. Wish I could have quinine, compass & knife.' (Aertex was a cellular cotton, cool in summer, warm in the cold, worn by generations of English schoolchildren.)

He kept moving through the dark, listening for Japanese pursuers. He followed a path that ended in two very small graves. He passed through terrible hills and gullies and found a ridge track. He waited here for an hour and a half for dawn. It took him an hour to find another track, and he hoped it would lead him down to a river, since the best bet of finding Sakai was by following one. But it led nowhere, and he felt he was going back too close to the Japanese. He found a track that led him north for an hour, and he came to a cave that had been used by Sakai. Some *ubi* (tapioca) was growing there and he picked a pocketful of shoots. He then found another track that led up steeply to what he hoped would be a ridge and the watershed down to the Chemor river. It was dark when he got to the top, marking his track by bending twigs. He camped in the lee of a rock near the top. He cut banana leaves, and made a roof propped up with saplings coming down from the rock. He piled other leaves below for a bed. It rained heavily but they kept the rain out.

This was the·first real sleep he had had, under his banana leaves in the pouring dark, since waking in the bandit camp at 6 a.m. on the morning of 9 May. It was now about 8.30 p.m. on 12 May. He had been on the run, first from the bandits, now the Japanese, all that time.

He had a frustrating day on 13 May. He followed a river down a very steep valley. It was overcast until about 11 a.m. when the sun came out and he was able to see the plains below him stretching west towards the sea. He needed to go south. He went back up the valley, a very hard climb, and slept again in the same banana leaf shelter. Confirmation that he had been making a giant circle came in the late afternoon of the 14th when he came to the cave he had found on the 12th. He was much disturbed to find fresh tracks here. The tapioca leaves he was eating gave him a raging thirst and stomach pains. He ate two small unripe pineapples he found: 'not hungry, but weaker & light-headed'. He slept in the cave, protected from the heavy rain that began falling.

He was away at 5.30 a.m. on 15 May. He came across wrapping paper from Japanese biscuits on the track he took. They had not been there two days before. It worried him: the Japanese were so close. He tried to find the Sungei Chemor, but felt the Japanese might be along the river, and decided it was too risky. He returned to the empty house he had seen in the brilliant moonlight as he had fled from the Japanese camp. When he heard a cock crow below he went down a steep, rocky hollow to investigate and found a track covered in Japanese boot marks and littered with cigarette packets. He got back to the empty house at 3 p.m. as heavy rain set in. He made himself a hideout under the sleeping bench in the house, concealing it under palms and leaves. The rain was terrific. He had eaten nothing but a few rattan berries and tapioca leaves. He was sleeping in the hideout when he heard voices under the house, which was raised six feet above the ground. Whoever they were, they were sheltering from the rain. Two of them looked in through the door, but the floor was rickety, and there was no ladder, so they went no further. Freddy did not know if they were Japanese or Sakai. He was very lucky. Discarded papers he found next morning revealed that they had been Japanese. Later the same evening, three naked Sakai came running fast along the track. The Japanese were clearly killing and abducting, and the Sakai were fleeing them. He dared not call out to them.

Next day he followed the track the Japanese had made to the Chemor river. It was littered with cigarette packets and empty food bags. He found some sugar cane and nearly ripe pineapples. Eating them made his lips very sore. There was a Sakai village of six fine houses nearby, but it was deserted. On a track he found two Sakai, an old woman and a girl, distracted with fear. They gave him bananas and a very old parang.

He now had a cutting blade for the first time since his escape. The Sakai had lost all they had, looted by Japanese and Indian troops. Some had been shot as they fled into jungle, accounting for the graves Freddy had found. The old woman refused to guide him to Sungei Gajah, but she showed him the way across the Chemor river and pointed up to where she said there was a tributary of the Gajah. She said he would find a wide unmistakable track. He soon came to a waterfall and the track finished. He fought his way past it and over a ridge, climbed down steeply and came to the Gajah. It was all waterfalls at this height and there was no sign of Sakai tracks. He built himself an atap shelter, cutting saplings and pushing them into the ground in an inverted V with a ridge pole, from which he hung atap. It rained heavily overnight.

He found a track leading from the bank of the Gajah next morning, 17 May. It ran to a stream, and he followed it downstream. An old Sakai shelter was set in ground rooted up by pigs, but he had no rifle to hunt them. The track petered out amid some giant boulders. The going became impossible, and he turned back. After one-and-a-half hours he came to a wide track. He followed it for another one-and-a-half hours, dropping height all the time, and came to some newly cut jungle. Two Chinese were there. He spoke to them, saying he was trying to find guerrillas. They sent him further down the track to a small nine-inch pipeline. He felt he was moving into very risky country. He rounded a corner and saw the end of an estate motor road. Rubber was growing on the hill next to it. People in sunhats were working on tapioca bushes next to two Chinese houses.

After he had observed them very carefully, Freddy worked his way through the tapioca towards one of the houses. Six Chinese were there, astonished and delighted to see him. They were kindness itself. One kept watch on the road whilst Freddy bathed in a stream. They fed him a large meal of rice, sweet potato and dried fish. One of them gave him an old pipe and tobacco and an ancient hat. They smoked and talked. They told him that he was on the edge of the Kinding Tea Estate, and that it was very dangerous. The Japanese could come at any time. The water pipe was for the Tanjong Rambutan asylum, whose red roofs he had seen three weeks before. The town itself was only three miles away.

They said they could put him in touch with the guerrillas, but the Japanese were so active that it might take a week. In the meantime, they took him to a well-hidden small house on the edge of the jungle where they said he would be safe. It had half a dozen fugitives crammed in it, dressed in rags. An old man had a terrible fever, and a pulse 'going like a machine'. They told him that the Japanese were killing Chinese in the kampongs along 150 miles of jungle edge from Grik in the north to Kuala Kubu. They gave him rice, yams and fish. He smoked a lot. He slept under two sacks for warmth. They had a 'bamboo pee pipe for night, an excellent thing'.

Another old man appeared in the early hours of 18 May. 'They are all very afraid,' Freddy noted. He saw why. In the morning, a Japanese aircraft began circling so low that he could see the pilot's helmeted face looking down. He wondered how they could fly a twin-engined aircraft so low in the steep valleys. They were spotting for anyone who fled from the kampongs towards the jungle. The roads were sealed by troops, Japanese and Indians who had volunteered to fight with them, whilst others scoured the villages and estates, rounding up the young men and women. The men were sent to forced labour or shot. The women were taken to military brothels. Hundreds of Chinese were tommy-gunned or bayoneted. Others were driven into their atap houses and burned alive. Everything of value, money, watches, clothes, cooking pots, was taken away. Freddy could not see the kampongs but he heard the noise of firing and screaming:

> the planes fly around very low & every 25 yards along the road is a lorry full of Bengalis, etc. They are killing the people, taking the girls & robbing everything. That evening a lot of distracted females appeared & said the men must return to the kampong as 1000 mata mata [Sikhs] are searching the jungle. They all went off – including the very sick man – at dark, with all their gear on Xpoles. Only 2 old men remained. They made big meals of pork and fish but they only gave me groundnuts & leaves but excellent yam rice. They are very nervous & say I must go as they are returning to the kampong.

JUNGLE SOLDIER

At dawn, they sent him on his way with a little rice, a half cigarette tin of salt, a handful of groundnuts, an old sack and a box of home-made matches with eight inside it. He was glad to get back into the jungle. He thought the rumour of the thousand Sikh police was ridiculous, and felt sorry that the others had abandoned the safety of the jungle to 'return to the hell that was still going on in their kampongs'. He returned to the abandoned Chemor settlement. There were still no Sakai there, but he found three fresh eggs and a better parang and a sleeping mat. He went on along a track that petered out. He found a hunters' hut, full of pig, monkey and hornbill skulls. His matches would not light, so he could not cook his rice. He ate groundnuts and some sweet-potato leaves he had stuffed in his pocket in the Chinese kampong. When he lay down to sleep, with his ear close to the ground, he heard rustling everywhere. The hut had more cockroaches than he believed existed.

On 20 May, he retraced his steps past the two little graves and the moonlit empty house he had passed in the first moments of his escape. He went on to the Japanese camp, now abandoned, and searched for his watch but could not find it. He decided to make for Larek. He found a track that passed two Sakai houses, empty but with a cat still living in one of them. Another broad track led up to a ridge. It was littered with cigarette and biscuit papers and he realised that it had been cut by the Japanese. As it reached the summit ridge, he looked over and saw the country changed. It was all the red cliffs of old tin-tailings and open going with much bracken and tall mauve and white orchids. He found the cold ashes of fourteen fires where a large Japanese force had bivouacked. He slept in his old shelter. The matches remained 'NBG', no bloody good, and he had nothing to eat but half a pineapple and some bananas.

He breakfasted next day on the other half of the pineapple. He followed the Japanese track where he could over sand flats and thickets. He lost it going down the Chemor and he had some bad going bypassing water-falls, then found it again at the foot of the falls and came across another Japanese bivouac site with old bonfires and masses of scrap paper.

A track went off to the right before he got to Pa Bras's house, and he coasted along for miles up and down and over streams. It had been used by elephants for some distance, but then it got smaller and smaller. He was wearing shoes – he thought the protection they gave was worth the added risk of leaving shoe prints – but his ankles and shins were badly cut about. He reached the Korbu river, and a ladang and an empty house. He stripped and dried his clothes, spending an hour there. He found some small Sakai footmarks on the track when he went on, saw two Sakai girls but they fled from him. He crossed the river and went up a long steep track that had been used recently. At about 4 p.m. he came to a house on the right bank of the Korbu. He found the headman Pa Murdah, whom he knew. He was surprised to be greeted with bows and 'Selamat datang', the formal welcome, rather than the usual cordial 'Tabe tuan' ('greetings, sir'). He discovered that this was because Ratface and his men had spread word that he was a Japanese agent and that he was responsible for the massacres that were taking place. The two girls who had run away from him had reported that a Japanese was coming.

Freddy managed to convince them that this was not so. They told him that the Japanese had captured some Sakai and carried them off, and shot others. Houses had been burned down. All Pa Bras's rice had been taken. Bras, the young headman Freddy had much liked, had disappeared and they thought he might have been killed. They were all moving deeper into the hills next day, and they wanted Freddy to go to a house further up that night. He did not want to – he was exhausted and his feet were badly cut – and they reluctantly let him stay. Pa Murdah's father, a beaming old man with a squint and a long stiff moustache, gave him a bowl of pumpkin with curry, chillies and shoots of wild ginger, and some champada (jackfruit). His hosts killed their six roosters as they were afraid their crowing would give them away to the Japanese. The birds were very tough, but they polished them off with some rice. Freddy smoked hard all evening, then slept well.

They were all up at dawn on 22 May. Pa Murdah gave him half a box of matches and a flint and steel and some tinder. A guide took him down a steep and slippery track and over the river to house standing in a field of *jagong*, maize, left him there and went off to look for other Sakai. He ate some champada and waited, but the guide never returned. It was the only time Freddy had been let down by a guide. He made a fire, and cooked champada, nuts and rice.

He went on alone next day. He slipped on a log and fell flat on his back in the river. Water even got into his ears. On he went along a track that led uphill. He took stock of his possessions. He had a parang, a little rice, the half box of matches, a little salt in a cigarette tin, a mat, a sack and a tin plate to eat off, and a few pieces of cloth for bandages. He tied the ends of an old pair of Chinese trousers and pulled them over his feet to protect his bloodied ankles and shins. The river was very swift and brown after the rains, and passed through some dark gorges where he had to work his way round the steep walls. He followed a track going up a long hill for three hours, before it dropped to a lovely winding stream where the land was marshy. He came out onto the red scarred cliffs of Larek, ate a little cold rice, then took another path along a ridge which got fainter and fainter.

The going became fearful, very steep rattan, bracken, atap and thorns. He heard a river running below him, sometimes to the left, sometimes to the right. He came to a stream that was too precipitous to follow, and he lowered himself over rocks with a rattan. A fishing hut stood where the stream joined a brown rushing river. He thought it must be the Korbu. At 4.30 p.m. he found a track following the river down. It began to rain heavily. He was slow in making a shelter and got soaked to the skin. When the rain stopped he went on. Suddenly, he found he was on the track up the hill that he had taken at dawn. He had spent twelve hours of violent toil to come in a vast circle to a position 300 yards from his starting point. He went back to the house and lit a fire, then made a frame of bamboos and put his clothes on it to dry. The skin of his scrotum had been rubbed raw by his wet clothes. He cooked some rice and slept well.

He found himself making a perilous traverse of a rock face above some gorges early on 24 May. He had to wade across the river, waist deep, and then the going was terribly steep and thick. He hoped to find a pass over the Termin but he had to return. He followed a track for two hours but it petered out and he began to feel ill. He fell whilst crossing a small river. He found some hard pineapples in a fishing hut and took two of them. He knew he had to get back to the house in the field of maize before the fever took hold of him. As he struggled back past the gorges he felt his strength was ebbing, and the diary tells of his 'absolute determination' to get to the house. It says he got there at about 5.30 p.m., just before dark, and that he cooked himself rice and maize with pineapple. The book says: 'for the last part of the journey I had to crawl on my hands and knees, eventually arriving long after dark'.

CHAPTER 17

ON THE RUN

He knew what was coming, and prepared himself. 'Washed legs, very badly cut about,' he wrote on 25 May. 'Collected yam leaves, sugar cane. No sign of ubi [tapioca]. Realize I have fever.' Then it was on him. He was very sick with malaria, and he had twenty to thirty deep ulcers on his legs and feet from infected leech bites and scratches. He had tried to protect his legs by tying the Chinese trousers over his shoes but he was festooned with cuts. A thorn prick is enough to start an ulcer on the lower leg, the front of the ankle and the back of the foot, where the bone is immediately beneath the skin and the blood supply is less. In the acute stage, violently painful and itching swellings of the skin form into blisters that fester and burst, bringing fever and blood poisoning with them. The ulcer extends outwards and inwards, until in the acute stage it becomes necrotic and purulent, destroying tissue and filled with foul-smelling yellow-green pus. The base bleeds easily, and the edge is raised. If the fever and blood poisoning are severe, or gas gangrene sets in, ulcers can kill. If not, the ulcer heals slowly but spontaneously, although the skin is left fragile and depigmented, and the ulcer will flare up again at the least opportunity.

He did what he could. He bathed his legs as often as possible, with hot water into which he stirred the last of his salt, and covered them with leaves from the maize. Local Sakai came occasionally at odd hours of the night, but the Japanese were still searching the jungle, and they were too frightened to come by day. The desperation of his situation is vivid in his entry for the period from 25 May to 9 June, and in the rare bout of introspection that led him, feeling himself alone and dying, to sing in defiance the cheek-to-cheek love songs of distant England:

> Alone in S [Sakai] hut with raging fever. Exactly 15 days since last attack. No actual shivering. About 9 or 10 felt v cold & sat over fire then wrapped myself up and slept if I could all p.m., boiling hot and racing pulse and thirst. Early a.m. and late p.m. better & I could stagger round hut, wash my lips, collect some jagong [maize]. S came every other day or so. They got me water and brought me ubi [tapioca] and jagong. They cooked jagong by scraping it off with rotan [rattan] then cooking it in bamboo. Sweet and tasty. I cooked rice and ubi or ubi and jagong most days. Stamped out message with a nail on an old tobacco tin asking for help – but they [the Sakai] would not take it

The message read SEND SAME ROUTE MB Q $ SALT FOOD AM AT 'ROTI' HOUSE WHERE STEPS BROKE FEVER CAUGHT BY JAPS ESCAPED LOST ALL GEAR FSC.

The 'Q' he wanted to be sent was quinine for his malaria. The 'MB' was sulfadiazine for his ulcers, an early antibiotic made by May and Baker Pharmaceuticals and known by the company initials. '$' meant that he needed money. He identified his hut as the 'Roti' or 'bread' house, where flour for maize bread was made, with a broken entrance ladder because he wanted the message to go to the Blantan camp where Ah Lim would recognise the location. The Sakai were too frightened to carry the tobacco tin and its message.

> They come in at night & spend an hour drying bamboo for fishing & cooking. By means of several huge logs I kept a fire going all the time. I was comatose, but never, I think, delirious. Used to pee in a coconut shell & throw it out & shit in leaves & throw it out. They [the Sakai] are scared stiff of Japs in daylight. Say all C. [Chinese] have left Jalong [Kampong Jalong] & Japs have a big gun there. All S up in hills.

Then, on 8 August 1944, he recorded this:

> Had very strange experience. Was quite certain I was going to die
> and in horribly melodramatic way tried to analyse my feelings,
> sang old songs of Ruth & Joss & Sue's time (Oh gosh gosh, Cheek
> to Cheek, Just the Way You Look Tonight, I've Told Every Little
> Star & of course Berkeley Sq) I just roared and roared with laughter.
> Tried to pray. Said Lord's Prayer over & over but could not get
> beyond childhood's picture of bearded old man sitting on clouds
> ... Decided I had had a superb but not successful enough life.
> Then old Nansen's head appeared and he said (on religion) 'The
> thing is not to worry. They're all the same. What you've got to
> do is to help other people.' Then I decided I darn well wouldn't
> die there but next day I'd collect all the S together and say, 'Look
> here, if I die here my ghost will haunt this place ... I want 4 of
> you to carry me down to near Jalong on a litter. I'll pay you later
> if I possibly can.' Then I hoped to find some C. [Chinese] who
> would get Q for me and help me.

Ruth Ware, Joss Balfour and Sue Baker were old girlfriends, and the
songs were those he had danced to and kissed to at long-gone parties
and balls. There is something wonderful about the gossamer-fragile
words floating defiantly from the fever-hut in the jungle.

> *I dream about you, scheme about you*
> *Night time and day*
> *Mad about you, sad about you*
> *When you're away*
> *Oh gee Oh gosh Oh golly I love you ...*

And – as he said, 'of course' – he sang 'Berkeley Square', like every
soldier with bittersweet memories of London:

> *there were angels dining at the Ritz*
> *and a nightingale sang in Berkeley Square*

At times, he wanted badly to get beyond God as the bearded old man, but he never could. It was what had been dinned into him, and it stuck. He remained convinced both that thinking was dangerous – he dismisses his rare little bout of self-analysis here as 'melodramatic' – and that morality underpins life. He had 'old Nansen', the great explorer, give the essence of his belief. 'What you've got to do is help other people': he was always to stick to that.

None of this – no God, no Nansen, no Cheek to Cheek – did he vouchsafe to his readers in *The Jungle is Neutral.* In the book, he wrote that: 'I reached the jagong house on the night of 25 May and was very ill there with malaria for more than a fortnight.' He records a single incident, though it is one of high drama. He wrote of his concern that Japanese patrols were working their way closer and closer up the Korbu valley. He said that he made sure he could slip out of the hut by making a small hole in the atap wall at the far corner. He could crawl through it from his sick-bed and slither down a felled tree trunk outside the hut to get into the edge of the jungle. He screened the tree trunk with maize stalks to hide it from anyone coming into the clearing along the main track. He said that there was a dog at the house – not mentioned in the diary – which ignored him but which the Sakai told him hated the Japanese. It would bark if they came near.

On 2 June, he wrote, the dog started to growl. He heard voices and the noise of parangs slashing along the track. He smothered his fire in ashes and crawled down the tree trunk into the jungle. He watched from cover as two Japanese and 'about a dozen Sikhs' climbed into the hut. The dog barked furiously at them and a Japanese shot at it and missed twice. The patrol set the hut on fire and left. It had rained all night, and the atap was so soaked that Freddy was able to beat it out. 'The only damage,' he concluded his account of the incident, 'was a large gap in one wall.'

Why there was no mention of the Japanese in the diary – or even the dog, described in detail in the book, a 'small dun-coloured terrier bitch' – we cannot say for certain. Perhaps this narrow escape was so burnt in his memory that he found it superfluous to burden his diary with it. Perhaps. It is more likely that he is gilding the lily. He does so three times in his book – here, with the morphia tablets, and on one other occasion that we will come to later – but for all the added drama, the book is the less powerful. The pain and the fevers, the festering legs, the constant screaming need for effort, the sense of banishment to the edge of existence, is clearer in the day-in, day-out format of the diaries. God alive! we think, as we endure with him. How much more? How much longer?

And then came a little respite. On 9 June, both diary and book agree, the climax of the fever had passed. He woke feeling better. His ulcers had healed somewhat. He thought he would be ready to continue upriver next day. An old Sakai came and they shared some rice and ubi. On 10 June, he was up early. He felt better but 'most terribly thin and weak'. He cooked, and fed the old man, who told him that the house at Termin that Freddy wanted to go to had been burnt down by the Japanese. All the people had fled and he said he would not guide Freddy to them. 'At last I persuaded him,' Freddy noted in the diary. 'Away 8.' The diary catches the slogging pitilessness of it all:

> Crossed river much earlier than I did before. I went very slowly and he said we would never get there and ought now to return. I rallied a little. Leeches bad. Very tropical veg [vegetation] up this valley tall ferns and palms ... Went very slowly so weak. At last when near the ladang [clearing] we left the path and went straight up an atap ridge for an hour, very steep. I managed to keep up. No track cut at all. Found a small closed-in atap shelter with a door at each end. I lay down. He went out to look for people. 3 p.m. after a good hour he returned with the little guide we had before and two small bamboos one full of 'roti' ubi [tapioca flour] & the other a ubi variety I haven't met before. Burnt right out [the Termin house]. They have all run away, he doesn't know when. He is with women & children up in the hills. He does not know the way over [the watershed] to Gajah & cannot help me. They both disappeared about 4. Very heavy rain all p.m. Ate my ubi. Kept fire going. Slept well in spite of animal moving about I presume a rat.

11 June. Very dark a.m. Waited till 8 to see if little man would arrive. Decide to try to get to Gajah myself. Followed ridge down to track & across foot of old ladang all bridges over fallen trees and very steep ... Tried several tracks before right one (up rotten log and along traverse over river). Found a house razed to ground. Ate sugar cane & took some with me and 4 keladi [taro roots] and ubi. Followed trails. No sign of Japs, no paper no cutting of track. I don't believe Japs burnt house. All way now saw new track of a man (todays) followed winding of river past old ladangs & at last reached watershed & went down to Gajah. Followed strip up and down traverse on far side. Tired but kept going. At last went well uphill. Searched for pig fence [a pig paling on the ridge that would indicate where the house was.] Passed a small atap hut & beside it a S. [Sakai] ladder 50' [feet] up a tree for some fruit. Went on S. trail clear now & then. On for another hour up and up. No sign of pig fence. Track petered out. Returned & luckily found it again. Got back to shelter about 6. Dead beat. Ate sugar cane & ubi & keladi. Repaired hut & cut bamboo furiously. Slept well but very difficult to keep fire going. Decided to follow G. [Gajah river] down to find S. No food left.

12 June. Searched for pig fence for a.m. then found a trail taking me straight down to Gajah. Very rough. Lot of old S. ladangs on the banks. River very big. Met Seno-oi [river] coming in from L [left]. Bigger than G. [Gajah] Followed it up looking for track. No sign. Very bad going, rapids, deep pools, vertical rocks & very heavy jungle for cutting bypasses [skirting rapids]. Spread all my gear out on rocks in sun for an hour. Kept a careful aeroplane watch. Got going & found new S. tracks with sand still scattered on rocks. At last (2 or 3 p.m.) saw some S. Approached cautiously. They did not run. About 20, fishing. They have built rock and stone walls [to make a fish pool] and put in Bubu traps [fish traps made of bamboo and rattan]. They gave me some ubi which I washed through with difficulty, so dry. I know some of these S. One was at the big Sungei-oi Ho. [house]. They say they will take me to a C. kongsi [large Chinese house] by a pipeline lower down.

They only gave me 2 tiny fish and some ubi. Suddenly they all moved off & I was terrified they intended to leave me. Packed my gear & only just caught them up. A fair track up above river & then X [across] it thro' bamboo groves & more jungle. Hard work to keep up.

At last they reached the kongsi. One of the Sakai went off and returned with some Chinese. They gave him some bananas and tobacco. After he had eaten a little dry rice and fresh fish, they set off for a house in the woods where two Chinese fugitives had lived for some time. It poured with rain. They gave him a wide-brimmed rain hat but he still got soaked. The house was down by a river in an old overgrown clearing, and made of bamboo with a waterproof atap roof. He got a fire going and dried his clothes. An old man appeared at dawn next day to talk to him. He bathed in a hot spring near the house – 'Lovely!' At midday, though, he fell flat on his back in a faint. He had a bad fever – 'terribly hot & furious pulse' – for the rest of the day. He had lost his sleeping mat. The old man sent him a big replacement and a fine new sack on 14 June. He was still weak and tired, and could not sleep. At 9 p.m., he saw what he thought was a bright firefly. Then he realised it was a light approaching:

Japs? Got up. No, the leader of the Kongsi and a young very charming & efficient C [Chinese]. Ah Sang & an old intelligent looking C. Long paka-paka [pow-wow] I told him all. Not a single word of reproach. Can I travel tomorrow? I suppose I can. He will come at 8. He told me plenty of news of war in Europe & Pacific. I like him very much. God knows how I will get on tomorrow. Legs still full of holes & very malarial. Did not sleep a wink. Wanted to tell him I want to find some S. [Sakai] & go over the hills if he can give me Q [quinine] and a little $.

They came at seven next morning, not eight. Freddy had already eaten a little rice – he had no appetite – and he was ready. The old man went far ahead to spy out the land. They followed the pipe for some miles downriver, crossing over gorges on the slippery pipe with a single ramshackle handrail for balance. Freddy was slow and exhausted going uphill. Ah Sang was very patient with him. The old man left them and they turned into the jungle. They passed near a group of other Sakai and heard them talking. The Japanese had recently raided here and had killed some of them. They crossed some young rubber and followed a small stream. They could see the big rock stacks and the plains near Ipoh. The rock stacks still tower above the new expressway, unmistakable landmarks, jungle clinging in tufts to their almost vertical rock faces, with deep scars where they have been quarried. They walked through fields of ubi (tapioca). The Chinese crushed it with foot-pedalling machines, spread it out to dry and sold it for making bread and cakes. Freddy did not hide from Chinese, but they went up a steep hill covered with half-wild ubi and thorn thickets to avoid a Malay house. They had an hour of very hard cutting with their parangs before they came to a small Sakai settlement. They rested for half an hour.

Freddy's feet and ulcers hurt badly. Sand got in his shoes and his ulcers and rubbed the skin from his feet. He drank a little tea but he was too exhausted to eat the bananas he had. After another hour and a half of ladangs and ubi, they passed a group of girls, 'some young & pretty in sunhats, scarlet scarves round shoulders, black trousers, bare feet & black coloured blouses'. There was a larger settlement at the foot of the hill. It smelt vilely of pigs. Freddy was in a poor way:

I could only just stagger & was unable to stop dribbling at the mouth, never known this happen! Could not see, walked with arms out in front. At last reached a big K [kongsi-house]. Lay flat on floor. Recognised a man & sat up – the VERY Kongsi I came out to before at T Rambutan on 17 May! A month of utter hell and all for absolutely *nothing* to satisfy my pride and sense of independence. Christ what a bloody fool I am. The man here keeps his w-watch [wrist-watch] in an old medicine bottle so that the Japs won't find it. They [the Japanese] have already robbed this K. once & taken the clock, blankets, cooking utensils & any rice etc.

His beard had more than a month's growth, and he combed it and his hair to smarten himself up a little. Two young guerrillas came and they set off up a valley into the jungle. Sand got into his shoes again and he felt desperately weary. They came to a *padi* (rice field), higher up. The Japanese had been through not long before. A big kongsi was standing empty, though cats were still there, and the ripe rice was uncut. He found more houses going north that were still occupied. They stopped at one. The people were very nervous. Ah Sang gave him pen and paper to write to Itu, the military commander at Blantan:

> I wrote an account of the whole story. Apologised for the trouble but said it wasn't entirely my fault & I wanted to discuss it all in detail with him & asked him to ask Davis for MB, Q & $, and to let him know all. I only want to get home I said. 5.30 p.m. (got to ho. [house] at 4.30) we move again! Retraced our steps but before reaching watershed turned L up hill into jungle up path. Rain threatens. Passed a house full of youths cutting jungle & then path ended at a K [Kongsi-house] where I am to stay 6.30 p.m. What a day! There are Japs within 2 miles here.

He spent the next three days in this house. It had no windows. The walls were bark on atap. Piles of ubi and sacks of rice half-filled the single room, along with a table with log seats, and a bicycle. Masses of rubbish were piled outside the door. He slept in a loft of split bamboo and mats that covered half the floor, reached by a ladder. The lamp fuel was rubber-oil, a mixture of latex and oil, and it was very smoky and smelly. But the roof did not leak, and he had a puppy and two cats for company. They fought and played all day. A young Chinese was with him all the time to take him into the jungle if the Japanese came. He was not sleeping well, but he was eating splendidly, for they grew long beans, ubi, millet, sweet potatoes and aubergines in the gardens: 'I am very happy & getting fit here but nothing to read. On 18th Ah Sang appeared with a very self-possessed tough C. [Chinese] in karki [khaki].'

Little of this – no soul-searching ('God what a bloody fool I am . . .'), no bitter frustration at tracing a giant circle, no traverses of gorges, not even the pretty girls with scarlet scarves – is written up in the book. Freddy detailed the news Ah Sang gave him of the war: 'a "second front" opened in Italy, where there was heavy fighting and – which I hardly believed – British and Americans had landed in force in France . . .' Other than that, he said only that he was delighted with Ah Sang and that: 'He took me to an atap hut near Tanjong Rambutan (we passed, in fact, the hut where I had stayed a month before, on first emerging from the jungle) and handed me over to a tough, burly-looking Chinese in khaki.'

This new man was a guerrilla called Lau Ping. He came from a 'traitor-killing camp' a few miles south-east of Ipoh. As its name suggested, this housed a liquidation squad whose mission was to shoot or beat to death suspected traitors and collaborators. Lau Ping was to look after Freddy in this camp until he got permission from Chin Peng to take him back to the Blantan camp and Davis and Broome.

They were on the move all day on 19 June, a 'ghastly nightmare of a day', though he had two young Chinese to carry his gear. They followed a stream for some time and cut through jungle to a small pipeline. They spent an hour moving through some rubber and crossed a wide river before taking a tiny path for two hours that led to a ladang with sweet potatoes growing in it. A series of paths curled round the hills so that they did not lose height. The guerrillas went 'like hell' and they got close enough to Tanjong Rambutan to see its red roofs and the rock stacks only two miles off. A tarred road led on. It had chips of tapioca drying on it, and a man shouted at them. 'I was scared,' Freddy wrote. 'He ran across & away up the opposite hill. I was panting & sweating!' They took a rough cart track, stopping briefly for 'tea', which was little more than hot water. They moved on again at 2.30 p.m., through newly felled jungle, and rotten red cliffs hidden in bracken, with bits of pipe that crossed several streams, until they entered real jungle by a small Chinese house. They climbed two long steep hills, and then began:

3 hours of *absolute hell*. The path half grown over so always coming off it, bracken scraping across face & lips & pulling at clothes. Thank God I carry no gear bar a parang tied round my waist with

an old bandage & a few odds & ends in my pockets. Pipeline most of way only 1'–18". [1 foot to 18 inches] Once we crossed a gorge 30 to 50 ft up with no hand rail ... At one stage I started to stagger & thought I was going to collapse. The 2 g [guerrillas] tried to bully me – the worst possible treatment! Staggered on. Down now. Path worse & worse. Hands & knees under thickets in places. At last saw vast limestone stacks in front of us. About 5 p.m. suddenly heard a growl in sec j [secondary jungle] on left. Little guide whipped a Luger out of his belt & we all clapped our hands. Saw nothing. Leopard? Passed quite near line of stacks on R. Astonishing they are: 500' high, bare cliffs at bottom & in patches higher & bushes then trees clinging on at phenomenal angles. In one place a crazy wooden set of ladders ran up to a cave – for bat shit I suppose. Going like hell. 2 more hours! Crossed a fair river. Really beautiful country now. Sunset behind stacks. Palms at foot of stacks and padi runs steeply down from orange & red stained white limestone.

They came down to level *sawah* – wet rice fields – in a valley. It reminded Freddy of his cruise on the Courtauld yacht. 'How lovely sawah is! Shades of Bali!' They were able to walk on a big one-foot pipeline for three-quarters of a mile, whilst the glow of sunset reflected on plantations of bananas and papaya. There were Chinese about, but he noted that no Chinese ever seemed surprised to see him. He had shaved his beard off in the windowless house, and he had borrowed an old felt hat, so perhaps he looked more respectable than usual. At 6.45 p.m. they reached a big kongsi-house where tapioca flour was made. Fifteen people were there, an old shaven-headed-man, a pretty girl with a baby, two older women, some small Sakai taking refuge. Lau Ping came in later, with a Mauser in his belt. Freddy was given a bowl of groundnuts, and then a good meal of dry rice, a little duck, dried fish, and tea. He went to bed in a tiny loft at 9 p.m., but there were a lot of noisy pigs outside, and it was 2 a.m. before he got to sleep.

He had trekked for eleven hours that day. He reckoned they had covered twenty miles, and he wondered that his heart could take the strain. He got on well with Lau Ping, though he did not find him as likeable as Ah Sang. They had not far to go on 20 June. They crossed several streams and climbed a track above a stream until they came across a wonderfully hidden kongsi-house built with one corner over a stream in a steep valley so narrow that both sides had to be dug away to fit in the house. It had only been finished five days before. Lau Ping gave a shout as they neared it, and six men came out with Thompsons, rifles and shotguns.

CHAPTER 18

THE TRAITOR-KILLING CAMP

'So this,' Freddy reflected, 'is the den of the traitor-hunters.' He found it a very secure place. Even today, though the Second East–West Expressway now slices through the jungle less than a mile to the north, the site is still well hidden beyond a wilderness of old tin-tailings. The ground is despoiled by quarries and marble cutters, the mountain flanks slashed with vertical wounds of yellow and white rock. The plain stretching towards Ipoh has the little sugar loaf mountains – Freddy's 'stacks' – with more quarries on them. There was less development then, but the Japanese were still very close. Ipoh was only four miles to the west, and what Freddy called Simpan Poli, now Simpang Pulai, was even closer to the south-west. The Japanese had bombed villages they suspected of harbouring guerrillas, and had shot those who had not run away, looting and burning the houses.

Chin Peng called the groups of assassins his 'mobile squads'. He had five of them in Perak, equipped with pistols, hand-grenades and tommy-guns. The Ipoh squad with whom Freddy now lodged was the most feared. It had a 'broad variety of targets', Chin Peng said, 'and our hit lists were being constantly updated.' He drew them up himself, with input from other cadres. It was easy to implement the death warrants in the kampongs and countryside, he said: 'it was only when an elim-ination was required in a heavily populated town that careful planning was necessary'. Most victims were locals who had cooperated with the Kempeitai. Sometimes, though, they got a Kempeitai man himself. At Bidor, a Japanese intelligence officer disguised himself as a local Chinese and went to a roadside coffee stall to hear what was said. His shirt slipped, his pistol was seen, and a mobile squad was alerted to shoot him and dispose of the body.

Innocents were murdered in small numbers, or so Chin Peng said: 'perhaps from time to time errors were made in identifications'. A blind ferocity was at work, though, because Chin Peng, and others high in the Party, *knew* that a viper was loose at their level, and, unable to identify *who*, they became caught up in a welter of killings. Japanese documents revealed aliases of central committee members – 'Wong Shao-Tong' was one – that were only used in the most secret communications with the Party in China. 'In our heart, we said, perhaps among those senior cadres arrested one of them had betrayed,' China Peng said. 'And we didn't know who. At that time, nobody suspected Lai Te . . .'

Fourteen traitor-killers were based at the camp, and they were busy men, if good hosts. Their victims, in numerical order, were Chinese, Sikhs, Malays, Japanese and Tamils. They did away with them – Freddy's diary says they had killed 'literally hundreds', the book 'well over a thousand' – with grenades, tommy-guns, their bare hands or with *changkols*. These were the heavy hoes the Chinese used in place of spades, brutally effective at beating out brains. Freddy sketched one in his diary. They operated in little groups of two or three. In the kampongs, they marched in openly with tommy-guns to impress the villagers, and made a spectacle of executing collaborators. They were more circumspect in dealing with sleeker victims in Ipoh and the towns. They carried pistols hidden under their shirts. A favourite modus operandi was to shoot the target in the head at a coffee shop in the town centre. They escaped in the panic and tumult that followed the sound of the gunshot.

Freddy was still sick. 'Very ill, terrible pain behind eyes unless I lie down. Weak as old woman,' he recorded in the entry for 21–30 June. 'Dizzy if I do anything. Pulse 80–90. No appetite. Sleep badly.' But he found his new comrades a 'very good lot of men'. They got on with their job, grim though it was, and wasted no time making speeches. They usually told the truth, he found, and they did not bore him with endless propaganda on life in Soviet Russia. They were very young. The oldest was thirty-three, and the others called him *Dato*, 'Sir' or 'grandfather'. Discipline was very lax. They kept guard on a high point from 4 a.m. until dawn at about 5.30 a.m. That was the only time they felt vulnerable to the Japanese. No guard was kept during the day. It was assumed that the villages towards Ipoh would warn them of any patrols.

They treated him well. They brought him 'some Jap papers' published on 17, 18 and 19 June with news of the war. 'Things are really happening – God I want to get back,' he wrote in his diary. 'The Italy show going well & under Eisen-Hower [sic] we have landed in F [France] & are doing pretty well. Russia's done marvellously. Hitler has a new weapon – a manless plane load of explosive – which seems to be shaking London.'

Best of all, they got him seven books. They were a random selection, clearly looted from the bookcase in some planter's abandoned bungalow. He had a Western by Zane Grey, Scott's *Ivanhoe* – 'much abridged with copious notes & bad illustrations', he grumbled – and an Arnold Bennett. Sexton Blake's *The Murdered Mahout* gave him a thriller, and he had Rupert Hughes's racy American stories, *The Patent Leather Kid*. Any self-respecting Marxist and the ideologues at the Blantan camp would have bridled at the other two books. But the gunmen had no English, and no idea that the author of *The Bronze Eagle*, Baroness Orczy, had created one of fiction's great anti-revolutionaries, the Scarlet Pimpernel. Worse still, the hero of *The Last Command*, the novelisation of an Emil Jannings film, was a Tsarist general caught up in the 1917 Russian revolution. Freddy was free all day to devour these reactionary tales in a camp devoted to the liquidation of enemies of the people. 'Have read all twice,' he noted. 'They do not seem to be able to get me any more, *blast* it.'

They did their best to attend to his creature comforts. He found shaving a terrible ordeal, with a very blunt cut-throat razor, but one of the killers cut his hair for him. There was plenty of food. Freddy was impressed by a fat guerrilla who carried up a load of more than seventy pounds of rice on his shoulder, with a sack of vegetables in his hand. They sometimes came back from their sorties with pigs they had shot. Freddy had to be careful not to eat too much. His stomach was still very fragile, and wild boar upset it if he ate in their style, without vegetables. He cooked the midday meal himself, making rissoles out of leftover fish and rice from breakfast. They made very strong Chinese tea for him all day. He used it to wash the ulcers on his legs three times a day.

One evening they brought him a bottle of samsu. After he had drunk some of it they told him it was made from tapioca and not rice. 'I got the worst squitters I have ever had,' he recorded. 'One night I had the worst pain in upper stomach. I groaned & groaned & got them to light the lamp . . . It passed in air. By God it was awful.' On 28 June, a party returned late at night with another pig. 'Over-ate again in spite of care. So tummy worse, 10 times day, 8 times night. I am as weak & depressed as hell. God knows when I can travel.'

For a few days, he stayed in a little thatched hut the guerrillas built for him twenty feet off the ground on a huge tree stump. It was on the edge of an old tapioca plantation and had a wooden bench that he slept on. A guerrilla on his way to kill a traitor brought him his food in lengths of bamboo early each morning. Freddy used the hut as a hide. He saw rusa, large dark deer with big horns, and kijang, barking deer, smaller and brightly coloured. He caught sight of a serigala, the wild dog of the jungle, only a glimpse, though he heard them often enough. He spotted crab-eating and pig-tailed monkeys, and the charming spectacled leaf monkey, its eyes surrounded by thick white rings, a graceful gibbon, swinging long-armed through the forest with its loud whooping call, land porcupine and squirrel.

One night he was woken by three elephants, a bull, a mother and a young one only the size of a cart-horse. The mother thrashed the young-ster with an uprooted sapling for fooling around, whilst the bull pulled up tapioca stalks with his trunk and stuffed them in his mouth. He came over to the tree stump to use it as a scratching post. As he rubbed himself, he found the ladder. It made him angry, and he smashed it, snorting and belching. Freddy feared he would get on his hind legs and tear the hut to shreds, but he moved off into the jungle. Next day, the whole look of the clearing had changed, with trampled plants and uprooted shrubs.

He had his first news from the Blantan HQ on 4 July. Lau Ping arrived late at night with a message to say that it would be two weeks before guides came to escort him back. 'Just as well seeing how sick I am!' he noted. They also sent him $200, a .38 pistol with 19 rounds, a .45 pistol with 22 rounds, and, to his great joy, a bottle of sugar-coated quinine tablets. He promptly ate fifteen of them, 'just to clear out any fever'. He was also taking some Chinese medicine sent by a herbal doctor for his stomach. He did not know what was in the pills – only that they 'looked home-made' and cost $1.50 each – but the 'squitter cure' worked. On 8 July he had his first night of undisturbed sleep.

The next day, the fat fellow accidentally shot a young lad at a range of three feet as he fitted a new hammer to his 12-bore shotgun. Two bird shot as big as large peas went into the victim's knee, with the others going under Freddy's bed. They put on a poultice of banana flowers, crushed-up snails and the tiny red fruit of a rambutan tree. The guerrillas had a friendly doctor in Ipoh, but the Japanese were too much on the alert for him to come. Freddy heard explosions to the west on 10 July, and heard later that five aircraft had been bombing supposed guerrilla targets in the jungle, and that one had crashed on landing, killing seven Japanese. Freddy was able to move to the other side of the house that day. It was more peaceful and the bed was made with bamboo rather than planks, so it was springier, and further away from the stream and the cold breeze that blew along it. He put new compresses on his legs and they were very painful for an hour. They were still bad in three or four places and his feet were swollen. The lad who had the gunshot wound was more cheerful. Chinese medicines had got through for him. Freddy was fascinated by them – 'one looks like a bunch of claret coloured grapes only they are prickly . . . another is like crushed raisins' – but their ingredients were kept secret by the herbalists.

Only seven slept at the camp on the night of 10 July. The others were away at work. A group came back with a sack full of girl's clothes and cheap jewellery. Freddy noted their provenance in his diary. They came from:

a noted spy girl who has tried to catch several of the men here. They beat her on the head with a changkol. They went to a samsu and whore shop & called her out to a lonely place. The other girls were all good ones. They have killed many this way, also pulling rope to strangle, knife etc.

The violence was mutual. Freddy noted what one of the killers, a young lad from Selangor, had himself suffered when the Japanese had caught him. His stomach all round his navel was burnt by cigarettes. A two-inch pole had been put across his shins as he lay in his cell, and two men had stood on it and rolled it up and down. He had also been filled with water until it had begun to pour from his orifices. He had escaped before they killed him. 'Words cannot convey the pain,' the Kempeitai victim Sybil Kathigasu said. 'They ran needles into my finger tips below the nail ... they heated iron bars in a charcoal brazier and applied them to my legs and back ... they thrust the rough ragged ends of canes into the hollows of my knees and twisted them until I screamed ...'

Freddy became 'rather bored' – 'oh! for some new books' – but a butterfly made his spirits rise most mornings:

A Rajah B. butterfly comes floating down the stream nearly every day. Once he flew thro the house. He never settles, only pounces like a hawk. He has a rapid bird-like wing beats & then floats, he has bright red eyes, blue-green on the wings and the rest black.

This was a Rajah Brooke birdwing butterfly, named for the old white rajah of Borneo, an exquisitely elegant butterfly almost the size of a swallow. But he found the fauna here disappointing. Dawn was 'devoid of music & noise. The robin & the magpie start to sing & that is all. Few insects, frogs, etc.' A 'terrific gale' came in from the south. 'Good thing no big trees here,' he noted. He passed the time cooking ubi in many guises, skate-like boneless fish, beans, maize, curry, chillies, and noting the cost of food. He reckoned it at $100 per guerrilla per month. It was a useful figure to pass on to Force 136 as they planned British backing for guerrilla camps.

On 12 July, two runners appeared from the Blantan HQ. They said it had only taken them five days, but Freddy realised it would take him much longer. Fortunately they did not want to start out right away, and one of them went 'out on a job'. Freddy had arrived in the camp with only the clothes he stood up in. Lau Ping gave him a grey forage cap with green buttons – 'most pansy', Freddy sniffed, but he added a heartfelt 'they're *darn* good to me' – and a .38 holster. A slender man called Ah Far was the busiest of the assassins. He was out most nights and much of the day with a tommy-gun or a 12-gauge shotgun, and spent the few hours he was in camp sleeping. He brought in a sackful of gear from his victims on 13 July, including some smart silk bajus, the traditional Malay tight tops and long skirts. He gave Freddy a small blanket, a sarong, a clock and some shirts. Freddy had been copying the words of songs into an exercise book, with sketches on the cover, and he gave it to Ah Far as a thank-you.

They gave him a farewell party on 15 July. He did some yodelling for them. They loved it, and made him sing every Chinese song he knew, about twenty of them by now. He was up at five on 16 July, eating two bowls of sweet potato, rice and fish to get his strength up. He shook hands with them all, and felt sad to leave. Then he added, in a revealing little phrase, that 'I am longing to get home and hear the latest news.' It is revealing that he thought of the camp in the Blantan jungle as 'home'. For the orphan boy, with no roots in England, that is what it had become. They set off up the Senju river at 6.45 a.m., over miles of red sands from tin-tailing, so flat and level that Freddy noted it might even be possible to land an aircraft as well as use the open as a drop zone for parachutists. There were plenty of derelict pipelines from old tin mining. After a while, they went into the jungle heading south-east. Freddy found it hard going up a long ridge, though he was rewarded at the top with a fine view towards Gopeng and Route One.

Some time after 1 p.m. they reached the house of a Chinese married to a Sakai. 'Very happy, going home. Legs OK. Bath. Washed under-c. [underclothes] Sat in sun. Learnt songs ... We have got one labu [pumpkin], hurray! Lots of birds here. One moans like a cow.' A charming Sakai came who spoke Chinese and Malay. He chatted to Freddy: 'Good stories of seladang and bears – he says bears *can* climb down trees!'

They made no progress the next day. A rumour went round that some Malays were coming to check on the rice crop for the Japanese. Freddy hid in a Sakai house built thirty feet up a tree, reached by a rickety bamboo ladder. When the scare passed, he cooked up and ate some greasy rissoles of tapioca, millet flour and fish. 'I really am a BF [bloody fool],' he confided in his diary, though not in his book. He was ill all afternoon and evening, but 'slept well & long' despite noisy frogs.

They hung around next day until 4 p.m. for fear of being seen by Malays if they left any earlier, then made rapid progress following a monster pipeline, five feet in diameter, the largest in Malaya. They reached big corrugated-iron coolie lines for the Chinese who worked on the pipeline. Freddy did not bother to hide from them – he well knew what would happen to anyone who betrayed him – and he found they were 'very glad to see me'. He went on through clearings farmed by Chinese who had fled from the towns, with millet, groundnuts, acres of sweet potato, ginger, and tapioca. He stayed that night with two Chinese couples in a house on the edge of deep jungle. They were very happy to help him – the Japanese had been there some time ago, and had shot two of the children – and they gave him a big meal, tobacco for his pipe, and a mosquito net.

It was cloudy and dark on 19 July. Freddy was out of sorts. 'These C [Chinese] are BFs [bloody fools],' he railed. 'I *told* them to buy fish & I would pay, but no, they have bought salt only.' For two hours, he slithered over cut bamboo, the poles treacherously slippery in the rain. A two-hour climb up a 'colossal' ridge followed, and a steep ninety-minute descent. The holster for his .38 was 'NBG', no bloody good, and he had to mend it. He was exhausted by 3 p.m. when they found a small house to lie up in. There was a girl there who had been in Menchis. She had 'heard tell of me and knew Ah Yang', and Freddy sent her off with one of the guides to buy fish and pork. When they came back, they said that they had seen Japanese 'just where we had been' an hour before. They had hidden the food for fear the Japanese would interrogate them. When they went to collect it next morning, wild pigs had eaten the fish, but they had not touched the pork. They climbed a deep valley with clearings where the Sakai had come to get further away from the Japanese. Freddy scraped his ankle badly, but was compensated by finding some delicious ripe durian.

He was up at 4.30 a.m. on 2 July with a fresh guide. 'Terrible day,' he noted.

> River – followed it up, mostly in it, for 2 hrs. Purgatorial. Weak & ill today ... The new bloke left the track & went away up into the hills & into a terrible thicket looking for S. [Sakai] NBG so followed stream down, fearful going. A big paper making K [kongsi where paper was being made from bamboo for the Japanese] so we made a long detour up a vast hill & round miles by tracks & then down to road.

This was the road from Tapah to Jor and the Cameron Highlands that he had dashed across on 16 April. They could hear Japanese lorries on it. 'We crossed the road near Jor, I think, bad 15 mins to river, followed it down for 1½ hrs. I fell once & hurt my arm.' He felt an attack of fever coming on and took 40 grains of quinine over the day.

> I had to stop & lie down. He [the new guide] went on up the hill & sent an S [Sakai] back to me. Slight rain. Colossal hill again for a mile. Absolutely done in, can only just move. A big new house here. Split b [bamboo] walls, no shutters, one end open to light. 3 c [Chinese guerrillas] here, one knew me at Ulu Slim. Traitor hunters. Coffee. They cooked 2 fowls & lot of wood mushrooms & rice. I recovered (3 Q at 1.30) & ate quite well & smoked. Bed in loft after 3 more Q.

There was a strange incident next day, 22 July, that appears only in the diary. Two of the Chinese went off at dawn to track down a traitor. Freddy was eating with the third guerrilla when a young Sakai called him outside:

> He gave me a letter written today by a Tamil missionary among S [Sakai] enclosing a pkt [packet] of cigs [cigarettes] & 10$ & a

New T. [New Testament] Also a copy of a letter from Gov [the Japanese Governor] of Perak asking Noone to come out of the j [jungle] & talk with him!! Very dangerous.

It was indeed so – a go-between for the Japanese could hardly be trusted, even if he was a missionary and had sent a Bible with his letter – and Freddy blamed himself for having let too many people see him. 'I answered,' he said, 'asking for books, & I may get them this evening.' No books were forthcoming, but, fortunately for Freddy, nor were Japanese troops. He told the two traitor-hunters when he met up with them again: 'The 2 C [Chinese] very het up, naturally.' None of this appears in the book, perhaps because it showed a slip in Freddy's usually impeccable fieldcraft: 'I ought to have been more circumspect,' he admits in the diary.

His old Sakai host Sempatan came with his wife and daughters – 'small faces smeared with red stripes from a small berry'. That evening the Sakai had an entertainment which reminded him of an Eskimo witch doctor's séance, but more light-hearted. 'They all sang, most beautiful harmony, I thought, some kept deep organ-like notes going. Wah! 3 days – home! Yam rice, fish, lovely rice. They danced in p.m. to bamboo drums. 2 hours. Many different steps. Extremely energetic.'

He had a good day on 23 July. The fever had gone, and so had his 'quinineitis', the muzziness he suffered when dosing himself with large amounts. He descended a deep valley down to the Sungei Lenko, past a little group of women carrying sugar cane with their hair wreathed in yellow flowers. Then they climbed five hundred feet to a long low house. They ate boiled tapioca and he bought four eggs. They went on, over streams and bamboo thickets to find Pa Blanken, the headman he had stayed with at the start of the journey. The houses where Freddy had rested on the way out to find Noone had been burnt. The Japanese had been on the trail. He met up with Pa Blanken again.

He tells me the Japs beat our place up a month ago [Blantan] & we lost all heavy gear & moved up hill. Hell. Lot of fuss over the Tamil [missionary] . . . Gosh the meal was good . . . The people down in the houses across the river singing for hours into the night. We talked late. Tummy OK! Smoked too much. Yodelled to them!

They were across the Sungei Woh the next afternoon, close to Blantan HQ. They reached a Chinese house where Freddy cleaned his pistols, smoked, ate bananas and drank coffee. The men of the house returned in the early evening – 'tall whimsical man, man bitten by snake, youth, fat-jawed man' – with a lot of fish they had caught by stunning them with explosives. Freddy cooked one inside a bamboo with chopped-up sweet potato: 'Quite excellent.'

He was up at dawn on 25 July, and away at 6 a.m. He met Ah Chew, the guerrilla who liaised with the Sakai. He did not recognise Freddy, so thin and ill did he look. He was almost at the end of his strength during a final two-and-a-half hours on a terrible switchback track. At last he was close. 'I yodelled as I got near & they are so unaccustomed to the noise they thought it might be Japs & some turned out with Stens.'

So, after 103 days of travail, he was home.

CHAPTER 19

HOLLOW DAYS

Pat Noone, the cause of the journey, was gone, blowpiped to death by his blood brother in a crime passionel over Anjang. It was what Bob Chrystal had suspected. On 17 November 1943, ten days after he had last seen him alive, Chrystal had found Noone's boon companion, Uda, in a ladang. He told Chrystal that he had taken Noone to a ladang below the Blue Valley Tea Estate, which is north of the Cameron Highlands. Uda said that Noone had then sent him back to look after Anjang. It seemed very odd to Chrystal.

Two weeks later, still with no news of Noone, Chrystal and J.K. Creer went up to the ladang by the tea estate to see what they could find out. Uda was there with Anjang. He seemed very ill at ease. That evening he took part in a gensak, a spirit dance, and during it went into a violent trance. He approached Chrystal and Creer on the platform and rattled his leaf whisks in their faces. 'Tuan Noone? You seek Tuan Noone?' he asked, sneering. 'Ugh!' he said and wrinkled his nose. The headman led him away. Next day, Chrystal and Creer went on up the Telom river. Each Temiar settlement they came to had been deserted so recently that the hearths were still warm. It seemed the Temiar wanted to avoid them and their questions. The headmen who told Freddy that they had no knowledge of Noone were lying. A taboo had been pronounced on the ethnologist and his death. Richard Noone, his brother, confirmed this after the war, in 1947.

Uda, the constant companion, had fallen for Anjang. He had used his status as a blood brother to have sex with her when Noone was away. When he returned from one of his journeys and found that Uda had been sleeping with Anjang, Noone had spoken sharply to him. Uda was resentful and continued to be attentive to Anjang. They were travelling on the River Wi with Uda's cousin called Busu. Busu told a Sakai called Akob what had happened a few days later, and it was Akob who would later tell Richard Noone of his brother's fate. Uda and Busu had started cutting staves for themselves from rokap wood, hard and thorny. Noone had asked what they were doing. 'Uda approached him with a strange look on his face,' Akob said.

> Tata [Sakai always called Noone 'Tata', grandfather, as a mark of respect] drew out his revolver and held him at bay, but Busu knocked it out of his hand. Uda took a dart from his quiver and ran after Tata. One of Uda's darts struck him in the eye. Two other darts were in his right thigh, and he was vomiting. He knew he was dying, for he cried out that his people would avenge what they had done. Uda then killed him with a stroke of his parang.

A special poison was needed for this. For the normal brew, the Semai slash an ipoh tree, much like a rubber tapper, with diagonal cuts from a machete, catching the latex in a bamboo cup as it trickles out. The tree weeps as much as a pint and a half of the poison before the latex darkens and congeals. The latex is left to stand for three days. The Semai lights a fire and dips a bamboo spatula into the poison. He holds the bamboo over the fire. As the liquid blackens and dries in the fire, he dips the spatula in the poison again until he builds up a thick coating. He dips the tips of the darts in water, and rubs them on the spatula so a film of poison settles on them. The poison is strong enough to paralyse small game and monkeys, which fall from the trees. The meat immediately round the dart is cut out and left, but the rest can be eaten safely. Snake venom and the pulp of poisonous fruits are added to make a poison so toxic it will kill a man before he can take more than three steps.

The murder was declared taboo, for fear of what the British would do if they returned. Uda cited a dream – Noone had called the Temiar the 'dream people' – in justification. He had dreamed, he said, that the Japanese would kill all the Temiar because of Noone, and then he repeated the communist propaganda line, that the white men were finished and the Chinese would be masters after the war.

In the months he had been away, Freddy expected that radio contact would have been made with Ceylon, and that a submarine rendezvous had been kept. None of that had happened. The batteries and hand generators had been lost during a Japanese attack on the camp, and their dynamo was faulty. The Mark II radio sets were still hidden and silent on the coast. Two KMT agents had been landed from Ceylon, but Davis and Broome had been unable to get any message through to the submarine, so Force 136 had no clue whether they were alive or dead. After much toil, and at great risk, the radio sets were eventually brought up from the coast and set up in a special hideout near the camp. Chin Peng sent them the dynamo after it had been rewound. It still would not charge and they had to send it back. They brought a bicycle in. Frank Quayle, ever the practical engineer, rigged up a pedal generator from its bits and pieces. It worked well enough, but the batteries the guerrillas had found would not retain a charge. They stayed stubbornly flat, for all the effort put into pedalling.

Life was wearisome, fractious, ill-tempered, empty of adventure. Freddy did not take well to monotony. It began to rot him. This was the real reason he had made the trek to find Noone: there was no great purpose to it other than getting out of camp. Having company did not help. One or other of them was always ill. They were hungry and the food so poor it upset their stomachs. The gloom and the rain were trying to their nerves: it was always twilight on the jungle floor. The lack of progress heightened the tensions of living crammed next to one another and the Chinese. Freddy would have been better off alone.

He began to find Davis 'rude and dogmatic'. Broome was worse: 'I was delighted with his wit and scholarship, but his indolence drove me to distraction.' He suspected that he himself was not too easy to live with – 'I have always been horribly energetic and must have driven the others to distraction with my restlessness' – and he was right. 'One must face the fact that neither John Davis nor I got on terribly well with Freddy,' Broome was to tell Ralph Barker. 'We admired his tremendous guts . . . but he grated on us after a while, and no doubt we did on him. Superficially, we were always on fairly good terms, but we had a different outlook on things. Freddy was a great man for adventure, and on the whole we felt he was enjoying himself, whereas to us it was a job of work, a job we didn't much care for.' Broome resented Freddy taking notes and writing up his diaries. He thought it a security risk if the Japanese got them – as they had so nearly done already – and he suspected that Freddy was almost doing things in order to be able to write them up later.

Davis echoed this. 'His stamina enabled him to do things far beyond the ability of his fellows, and this probably made him into a loner,' he told Barker. 'He was completely self-centred. But the most striking thing was his tremendous drive towards adventure and danger, and his insistence on its being recorded.' For Freddy, he thought, adventure always came first. If he seemed sometimes to exaggerate, Davis said, it was because of his 'keen sensitivity to experience. If Broome or I went out for a walk, we would get some exercise. If Freddy went out, he would have an adventure. He always managed to stumble on to something.'

These were hollow days:

Tuesday 5 Sept. Terrible day: rain started about 10 & continued all day. The others made a hell of a row giggling all day: they drive one quite mad. Steamed vegetables & groundnuts at midday. I spent all day mending my clothes. R[ichard Broome] made a pump. J[ohn Davis] played patience. We played ABC game playing very obscure subjects – emotions, things you take on a house party, non-firearm weapons, murdered men, etc. Tried liar dice. No enthusiasm shown.

They moved on to mahjong – 'first time since Flookburgh days' – and he thought of the future:

Secretary of the RGS [Royal Geographical Society] probably out of the question. Director of Scott Polar Research seems ideal bar small salary ... And always the chance of a headmastership at home or abroad. Anyway I can live for a year or two without worry and find a wife (!) and *write* and get back to former fitness ... Whatever happens to me when I get out of the jungle I shall not be able to settle down to steady work.

Davis made a dart board from a strip of bark, after experimenting with straw and atap. It was a great success with the Chinese, though Freddy held the record, scoring 103 round the clock. They had history quizzes as a variant from ABC. He had run out of books, and was reduced to reading a dictionary. His diary entries in October 1944 showed that a future obsession over his health and particularly his stomach problems was already present:

Sun 1 Oct Terrible headache. Temp 100. Tummy ... Mon 2 Oct Still pretty lousy, my temp 103 so retired to bed ... Tues 3 Oct Temp down but headache very bad & general low feeling ... Wed 4 Oct In bed most of day Thurs 5 Oct Bad night. Tummy wrong & big tooth coming loose & sore gums ... Fri 6 Oct Jaw swollen up more ... Sat 7 Oct Swelling down a little, but still v uncomfortable ... Sun Oct 8 Rather seedy with aching bones.

He went off hunting for days at a time when he could bear being cooped up no longer. He was feeling much fitter by 10 October – 'almost like old times' – and he set off with Lim. They spent the night in Sakai huts, and the days hunting pig, but more often catching rats. One Sakai was the most accurate shot with a spear Freddy had ever seen. He got six rats in a few moments, 'big grey-brown rats all white below with long tails'. They cooked them with onion and ginger, and Freddy found them excellent, 'like rabbit or cat'. They were plagued with rats at night in the huts, and with cockroaches, too, but Freddy enjoyed himself: 'I love these trips!' Now that he moved so softly in the jungle, with fewer vibrations to warn of his approach, he began to see more snakes. He noted the beauty of one of them: 'scarlet head & tail & belly, bright blue down flanks & navy blue back'. Another was five feet long, its head 'as red as sealing wax', its body black edged with white. He waited for it to slide over a log as it made a dignified retreat.

Lai Te held a secret meeting in October of senior Party cadres in the jungle near Serendah, a few miles north of Kuala Lumpur. Chin Peng was there. Lai Te said that the guerrilla forces would be split into an 'open army' that would cooperate fully with the British, and a 'secret army', Mi Mi Tui, that would seize as much territory as possible the moment the British invasion force landed. Freddy had no idea of this, of course, and the guerrillas remained helpful. They brought a motor-car battery to the camp on 22 October. They had carried it upside down, however, and all the acid had run out. A second battery was said to be on its way, with an old car dynamo. On the morning of 5 November, Freddy and John Davis heard aircraft manoeuvring and machine-gun fire high above them. The sky was hidden by trees, but guerrillas who had been in a clearing were breathless with excitement. They had seen giant four-engined bombers being pursued by Japanese fighters. In the afternoon, the battery and dynamo arrived. They connected the radio, and to their joy picked up the evening news on All India Radio in Delhi. They heard that the Allies had taken Antwerp and Budapest – and then that thirty Superfortresses had bombed Singapore, and that all had returned safely to their bases. The aircraft that they had heard in the morning were among them.

He was in a routine by 7 November: 'Played MJ [mahjong] 2–4. I can never get tired of it. Spent 6–8 trying to get news again. Lord Moine [Moyne] assassinated in Egypt. This new bitter coffee is excellent.' From now, he made regular comments on mahjong – 'I was dealt a hand . . . 10 out of 14 cards!' – war news – 'Roosevelt on again, Japs being cleared out of Burma (in matter of fact voice!)' – food – 'all this pork tends to get on ones stomach' – books – 'got a new book, *Crescendo*, no normality, just sex, sex, sex' – health – 'smoked too much, headache' – and sleep – 'slept badly'. Lim wrenched and cut his knee so badly that Freddy had to dose him with morphia. The diary for Armistice Day, 11 November, was cryptic: 'Lim still screaming all night. Lots of squirrels round camp now, also hornbills.' No sympathy there. Freddy set off to cut a new hunting track but met a Chinese he had not seen before and followed him back to the sentry post to be sure he was not an informer. He spent the afternoon putting slats in a garden seat he was making.

He started making notes for books, and fretted about the competition, and how he could make his stand out against 'the inevitable spate' of postwar books. 'Definitely one on jungle & Sakai & hunting, probably woven round a boys' story,' he said, with another on guerrilla warfare illustrated by his own experiences.

The dynamo that had been brought turned out not to work. They had distilled water acid for the batteries now, but no way of charging them. Once one went flat, it had to be carried out of the jungle to be recharged. They had only one pair of headphones, and one of them dictated what he was hearing, and another scribbled it down. Even if they could not transmit – and Chin Peng missed the November rendezvous with a submarine because of bad weather, so Colombo still did not know if they were alive or dead – the news of Allied advances cheered them.

At Christmas, he put all his enthusiasm into the day. He had a dig at Davis – 'unfortunately John very gloomy all day so our efforts to make merry somewhat frustrated' – but his pleasure showed through:

> I cooked all the a.m. making mince meat. Chopped up red beans & groundnuts or rather crushed them in the pan with sugar, salt, chopped pork, very sweet and smooth. Then a *super* meal. Roast chicken stuffed with same as mince pies but more pork also bean & a little garlic & pepper. I had to cut it up small but not splintering the bones. We had sweet prawns & the chicken giblets chopped in milled flour batter. The mince pies had a sauce of Klim [condensed milk] (gone rather cheesy) & 2 eggs & sugar with sweet coffee. At 6 got the news. Offensive seems to be stopping. Finished the samsu and sang songs til 10.30. Carols first, then shanties, old foxtrots, & finally Frankie & Johnnie. The samsu not so good after a blow-out meal. We were all quite sober when we went to bed.

R [Broome] is a very good man to have at a party. We all took aspirin.

That, no doubt, was why he recorded after Boxing Day: 'No hangovers for any of us. I did my PT. Cooked up all the remainders in rissoles.' The batteries, however, were tired. The sound faded half-way through the news. On 31 December, the British reoccupied Akyab island in Arakan, after two earlier attempts had been flung back. The Japanese were weakening as the British advanced in western Burma, but their propagandists in Singapore conceded nothing.

The *Syonan Shimbun* greeted 1945 as the 'year in which Enemy will be Driven Out of Entire East Asia Area'. The New Year editions spoke of the Allies 'trapped in Manila'. 'Body Crashing Pilots', kamikaze, from Japan's Special Attack Force were carrying out a 'bleeding strategy' that was certain to lead to victory because every Japanese death caused 'tens or even hundreds of Allied deaths' and when the target was a battle-ship or an aircraft carrier, 'thousands' of them.

Camp life was dullness, monotony. Happiness was being with the Sakai. It was the preserve of the 'so-called uncivilised', as he called them. 'So long as they are not so primitive as to be obsessed by fear', it was they who 'really seem to be enjoying life'. He listed 'them' as the Greenland Eskimo, the herdsmen of Tibet, and the Sakai. He ascribed their happiness to three things. They spent their time in the open. They depended on the exercise of a craft to stay alive, hunting seals from a kayak, or tending yak, or hunting monkeys with blowpipes and poison darts. And they came in conflict with the forces of nature, being 'forced by circumstances to face hazards and even to live dangerously'. This sense of satisfaction had four sources: 'a simplification of the objects of life . . . a degree of companionship . . . beautiful surroundings . . . *and* the element of danger'.

All of these conditions had been perfectly fulfilled for him twice. In Greenland, life was 'wonderfully simplified'. They were all young – he had been just twenty-three – and all working together for the same end, exercising a craft as surveyors filling in a large blank on the map, and having to learn to drive a dog team and handle a kayak to do it. The least thing seemed to have significance. 'If you happened to shoot a seagull, well, it might be the first record for the country – a new fact for science,' and even if it wasn't, 'you could always cook it up for supper'. There was beauty in Greenland, too, in the summer daylight that lingered so long that sunset merged into sunrise, and 'the scarlet and orange of the sky is reflected in the intense blues and greens of the ice-floes'. And to all this was added the zest of living dangerously. He had never known when his sledge 'might go through the sea-ice or down a crevasse on the ice cap', and Gino Watkins had lost his life in his kayak.

These same conditions returned to him in the jungle. 'Once more life was strangely simplified,' he said, 'but this time we were blowing up Japs instead of pioneering air routes, and shooting monkeys for food instead of seals.' There was a sense of companionship and dependence on one another, at least, he added, 'until the rest of the party were killed or taken prisoner'. He made an important distinction there, recognising only his original team as comrades, and excluding Davis and the Chinese. The life skill now was fieldcraft: 'we *had* to be aware of the Jap before he was aware of us'. He wrote of catching the pungent smell of tobacco at great distance, and of judging the phase and direction of the moon as it travelled the sky, so that it would not shine on him as he 'crept along a railway line or a jungle path'.

He found a beauty in Malaya, in the 'green crepuscular gloom' of the jungle, so different to the clear cold gun-metal colours of the Arctic. And there was always the element of danger, of course, the tigers and elephants, snakes, scorpions and poisonous centipedes, the 'revolting tropical fevers' and the 'ever-present hazard of being shot at by the Japs'. This danger 'must be essential' to bring contentment, he said. It was no use to live dangerously just for the sake of it. It had to have a purpose. Otherwise, he said, 'you might just as well play the stupid child's game of "last across the road" in front of a car, or fly a faulty aircraft, or swim in shark-infested seas. You *must* be able to justify to yourself the reason for running into danger.'

Every precaution must be taken to minimise the risk of injury and death. 'You must,' he concluded, 'live dangerously as carefully as possible, so to speak.' At sea, one had to know the effects of wind and tide, and in the mountains to read a map and compass. There was an absolute rule: 'You must always hold the initiative and keep *fear* at bay ... I like danger but I hate being frightened – and I am very easily frightened. On a rock face, if it is an off day or the weather suddenly changes or you are being stupid enough to tackle a climb beyond your capabilities, the exhilaration of danger can so easily change to cold fear. Here knowledge can come to the rescue and vanquish fear.'

He found a deep satisfaction in knowing how much men had endured in the past, and 'then trying to do the same, or just a little more'. Whilst wandering without food after his escape from the Japanese, he had thought of the Troubles and the hunger strikes in Ireland in the 1920s. 'I remembered that the Lord Mayor of Cork had fasted for – how many days was it? Seventy I think – and he managed to survive. And so I was certain I could last as much as a fortnight without any food. That certainty, that piece of knowledge, helped me to keep going.' [In fact, Terence MacSwiney, the Sinn Féin Mayor, died 74 days after going on hunger strike to protest against his imprisonment for sedition in 1920.] Without it, he said, 'I have seen men die. I met in the jungle six NCOs and men who had been cut off. A month later they were all dead. Yet there was nothing wrong with them. They were just not able to believe that they could live in the jungle, on rice and tapioca, like the Chinese, amid a thousand known and imagined horrors. And they died.'

His felt that his own life had prepared him for his ordeal. He had been hunted as a boy – lying in the icy water of the River Lune as the beck-watcher and his dog searched for the young poacher – and that helped him when the Japanese came looking for him. He knew from his ice cap and mountain journeys the excitement he now found in war. There were things he could never forget – 'the companions shot down beside me, every detail of whose inner life I knew ... the screams of defenceless Chinese women and children bayoneted to death by the Japanese' – but of his own inner life and horrors he said little.

In essence, he believed that anyone who preserves self-control can survive extreme peril. 'A man masters himself,' he said, 'by mastering hazards from which there is no escape.' He then need only be 'reasonably fit' and have the skill necessary to his predicament. There was no need to be a countryman: he noted later that the Chindits, the British force operating behind the lines in Burma, were mainly from Liverpool. Field Marshal Slim and other commanders at the time believed that men must not be exposed to fear for too long, otherwise their stock of courage may be all used up and disappear. Freddy disagreed. He was sure that a man can develop and increase his courage by experiencing fear, and learning how to overcome it, 'just as an athlete trains his muscles and builds up his stamina before a race'.

Fear was most acute, he said, in anticipation – before making a speech, before a parachute jump – and when there is no freedom of choice and nothing active to be done. He described his night on the sea ice off Greenland, where the floe had split beneath the tent, as an example of the latter. 'The worst of it was that we just could not do anything about it. We just had to wait and wait, getting more and more frightened.' It was then that thoughts had to be diverted to something else. In 'normal' infantry warfare, the soldier is 'sustained by regimental tradition and upheld by the presence of his companions'. Alone, as Freddy was, he found comfort in thinking of the hardships he had already encountered and survived. He had lost all his finger- and toenails in Greenland, and lived for a week on margarine and pemmican. In Malaya, he was wounded, he was unconscious for seventeen days with malaria, and for months existed on 'tapioca with a little rat or snake or cooked leaves – anything that would add a little flavour'. He had lived.

Illness was not finished with him yet. He fell sick again, on 21 January 1945, he thought with tick typhus. It is caused by a tick bite, with an ulcer – a *tache noire* – at the bite site, a red rash, and a litany of other symptoms, high fever, vomiting, diarrhoea, headaches and swollen lymph nodes. Davis diagnosed leptospirosis – 'from getting rat piss in the blood' – and didn't think he would recover. 'Personally I ceased to care very much either way,' Freddy wrote. His temperature the first day reached 105 degrees, and for days it varied between 102 degrees in the morning and 103 or 104 degrees in the evenings. He would fall asleep at midnight, only to wake again at two or three in the morning, with tremendous pains in the small of his back and behind his eyes, which made it impossible for him to get back to sleep. 'Acute discomfort from aching pelvis,' he wrote. 'Hard to shit too.' The news that the Japanese had withdrawn to behind the Irrawaddy river in Burma on 27 January failed to stir him. He could eat nothing but a little powdered milk, sometimes with an egg beaten into it. Only in mid-February did his temperature return to normal. His diary was blank between 24 January and 13 February.

CHAPTER 20

DELIVERANCE

The great breakthrough happened during this bout of illness. A second dynamo was brought into camp. It was in a poor state, but Quayle succeeded in making one good dynamo from the two duds. He also discovered that by giving the generator two bicycle pedals, with a man turning each furiously by hand, there was just enough of a charge to get the battery plates to bubble. He then put the generator on wooden supports so that it was possible to pedal it by foot. To begin with, it took two or three hours pedalling to get fifteen minutes reception on the radio, but Quayle refined it until by late January the pedaller was generating enough power to transmit. Five days after the first transmission they had a reply from Colombo on 1 February 1945. They were in contact with the world again.

At first, Colombo was naturally suspicious that they should have come through after months of silence. They had no answers for some coded questions. 'We sent back giving various interesting facts they will know,' Freddy said, such as their next of kin, and Colombo was then satisfied. One of the first messages told them that Freddy – and Davis – had been awarded the DSO. They were also able to send a shopping list for the next air drop: 'We ask for 1 Eng[lish] and 1 C[hinese] radio operator also new charging motor & a few things for ourselves – clothes, combs, toothbrushes, good books etc. All terrifically exciting.' The war was going well. 'Landing on Ewajuma,' he wrote on 19 February, misspelling Iwo Jima because, like 'Eisen-Hower', it was a word he had only heard on radio and never seen in print. 'Russians darned near Berlin. Made a goat pie.' He fretted, though, about the possibility of

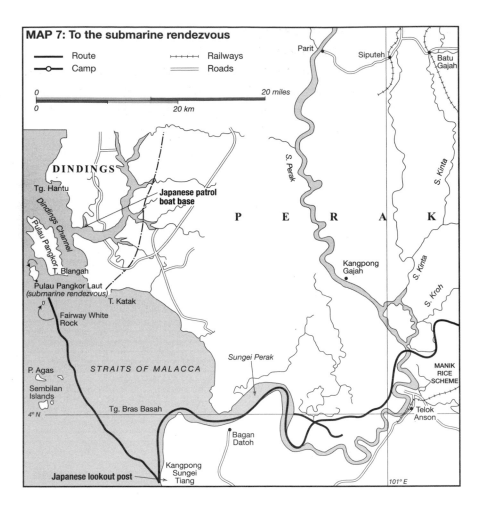

MAP 7: To the submarine rendezvous

missing the invasion of Malaya if he was taken out by submarine to Ceylon: 'The balloon should go up soon. If I go out I must stay at least 4 months to get fit & may miss the boat . . .'

Then there was an air drop. If the aircraft arrived at first light, enemy fighters would be able to attack it freely until it got out of range. At last light, the aircraft would have to cross the dangerous coastal belt while it was still light, and would have difficulty in finding the drop zone (DZ) in the gathering darkness if it was slightly delayed by head-winds. Moonlight was best – four days either side of the full moon – and a drop from two aircraft was arranged for 25 February. A DZ was found in old tin-tailing ground to the east of Route One between Tapah and Bidor. It was level and sandy and well clear of the mountains, so that altitude was not a concern for the pilot.

By now, the charging motor for the radio was so overworked that it needed to be nursed continually. They feared it would give up the ghost before Ceylon had confirmed the recognition letter they had to flash to the pilot from the ground. The date was put back to the night of 26/27 February. They needed a hundred men to deal with the shower of two-hundredweight containers from the two aircraft. They had to be broken down into individual loads and be carried deep into the jungle well before dawn. They prepared a T-shape with piles of dry atap to light the drop zone.

The Liberators were overloaded with fuel and supplies, and were operating at the extreme limit of their range on the eleven-hour flights. The pilots' arms quivered as they lifted the sluggish bombers off the runway, their senses pounded by the desynchronised roar of engines at full throttle. By late February, the weather was improving and it was a magical flight when there was only a light scattering of cumulus over the prodigious expanse of ocean. The pilots dropped to fifty feet and marine life swirled below them, the flash of leaping swordfish visible, and the bat-shaped shadows of manta rays, with flying fish skipping over the surface. Every now and then the vivid blue surface was 'mottled in a thousand pastel shades by huge colonies of jelly fish'. As they closed in on Malaya, and the sun slipped below the horizon astern, a 'wondrous purple shade' deepened and spread 'in the profound blue of the moonlit sea'.

The aircraft were over two hours late. Freddy had almost given up hope when he heard a faint hum at 2.20 a.m. At last a Liberator came, following the Perak river, with a brilliant moon lighting high clouds. The atap pyres flared in the night as the huge aircraft circled, and four small dots jumped from it, followed by a rush of containers. The parachutes opened, and another Liberator flew in and loosed a new swarm of containers. Everything had to be cleared before first light when Japanese reconnaissance aircraft began their searches.

The new arrivals were Majors Hannah and Harrison, and two radio operators, Corporal Hempleman and a Chinese, Chuen. Freddy wrote in his diary:

> I daresay the happiest day in my life. John & I are colonels. God how good that is ... How did I ever think of going out? Also medals arrived. A guard of honour at camp & slogans on trees. Welcome, etc. We had a bottle – 2 actually of whisky. It went to my legs. Had a concert. New men not great performers. But very excellent concert. I yodelled. Bed 11. Mind in absolute whirl.

He was thrilled with the medical supplies that arrived, particularly a new anti-malarial drug, mepacrine. He and the others were incapacitated between a third and a half of the time by bouts of malaria. With mepacrine, none of them had a single attack. The food, too, was splendid: bacon, cheese, chocolate, new concentrated rations, rum, Australian whisky. There was just one cruelty, the orphan's sadness: 'No letters for me.' The others all had them.

He was fit enough on 2 March to do PT exercises for the first time in six weeks. He worked hard all day on stores. The supplies coming in on the Liberator drops included personal kit. Freddy now sported a wool hat, thick green jungle boots and even had a 'green battledress for special occ[asions]'. Two days later, a Sunday, they had a bottle of rum before supper, and he blessed the 'supreme luck' that had brought him on 'this show'. The Liberators were so efficient that he had asked for his Seaforth regimental badges and shoulder flashes to be dropped. He was even hoping for news from home. 'All my friends, U Sam, Joss, Sue, Ruth cabled I am OK,' he wrote, 'so should get letters or cables this drop.' He was impressed to learn that a friend with Force 136 had been dropped in Burma and brought out by submarine. 'God what fun all this is,' he wrote. 'Wish I could take a parachute course.'

A little later, though, he complained of feeling 'so grey – from toothache, stomach & bloodpoisoned leg!' The weather was foul, with much rain and mist. 'These are dog days, nothing happens,' he wrote on 20 March. 'I eat, read and sleep.' He had plenty of books now, sometimes racing through two in a day, including the 1943 bestseller, *The Song of Bernadette*, about the miracles at Lourdes. He devoured *Reader's Digest* too. They had regular conferences with Chin Peng. Freddy was concerned that Ceylon was keeping them in the dark about 'other parties that have been & are to be dropped in Malaya. *They* [the communist leaders] know all about Johore and other parties; *we* know nothing, nothing, and we must know.'

On 16 April, 'the Plen' returned for a conference. Once again, Freddy makes no mention in either his book or diary that he knew Lai Te's real identity. The meeting was so important that all the British party went, including Hempleman, with his radio set, so that they could be in direct touch with South-East Asia Command (SEAC) in Colombo during the talks. Freddy and the others were ready to set off by 7 a.m., but they were kept waiting by their escort of six guerrillas. They were sewing red stars on their caps in honour of 'the Plen'. It was a seven-hour march to the rendezvous at a specially prepared camp not far from Route One and dangerously close to Blantan and Japanese patrols. Chin Peng chose it because Lai Te was incapable of walking any distance from his car. He was himself suffering from a bad bout of malaria, but when he saw the British arrive he thought Richard Broome was worse off. 'He was emaciated with a variety of illnesses,' Chin Peng said, 'and used a cane and had to be supported by Davis and Chapman.'

In fact, he was drunk. It was a gruelling trek, across the swollen Telom river and steep hillsides and close jungle with bamboo thickets and streams. Broome had collapsed a mile from the hut, and Freddy revived him with rum. He had only an eggcupful, but he was so exhausted it went to his head, and they had to hold him up. To Freddy's horror there was a guard of honour drawn up. He had to put Broome's head into a stream to sober him up enough to take the salute. He noted two girl guerrillas smartly turned out in shorts and shirts and short hair.

The conference was held next day, from 10 a.m. to 10 p.m., with breaks for lunch and coffee and biscuits. Lai Te and Chin Peng were with the influential commander of the 5th Regiment, Commander Itu, whose real name was Liao Wei Chung. With their honour guard, and smart starred caps, the communists put on a good show. 'They had built kongsi-houses in the jungle,' Broome recalled. 'And they got a number of the Young Communist girls to be waitresses and maids inside the house, looking after us, and the food was terrific.'

Despite their illnesses – Itu's fevered head was massaged by one of the girls throughout the proceedings – Chin Peng found that both sides shared an 'optimism and cheer bordering on elation'. Freddy noted in his diary: 'Plen quite a different man: agrees with everything so business concluded rapidly . . . I wrote out an agenda of decisions for them to take away.' Operation Zipper, the plan for the seaborne British invasion of Malaya, was well advanced. Force 136 air drops of men and supplies were accelerating. Plans were made for the guerrillas to begin attacks on roads and railways as the British came ashore and the Japanese moved men and supplies north into Malaya from their base in Singapore. In return for weapons, arms and £3,000 a month, Lai Te accepted all the British proposals, including the attachment to each guerrilla patrol of a British liaison officer with a platoon of Gurkhas. Freddy's years of work with the guerrillas were reaching fruition.

But there were no illusions. 'You must realise,' Chin Peng told Broome, 'that our ultimate aims are very different from yours.' It was as well that an old hand like Freddy was there. Hannah, the Force 136 officer who had arrived on the Liberator drop, had none of Freddy's insights and affection for the guerrillas. He wrote that his opposite number, Colonel Itu, 'is a complete moron and nothing more than a political agitator of low cunning but without the brains of a louse'. Hannah had been a businessman in Malaya before the war. Itu, with his 5th Independent Regiment, had raised and maintained a force of 700 fighting men and women. He was also organising Mi Mi Tui, the clandestine army.

Freddy spent much of 18 April coding messages to transmit to SEAC. He was getting good at this – 'I am quite fast. 10 groups in 4 minutes' – and the Japanese planes that were overhead added to the sense of urgency. A Liberator flew over at dusk, on its way to drop liaison officers and supplies to another patrol.

Colombo wanted a British officer to be extracted by submarine to work on detailed plans. It was agreed that Broome and Freddy should go. A rendezvous was made for the pick-up after dark on 13 May – another 13 – off a sandy inlet on the small island of Pangkor Laut, close to the south-west corner of the larger Pangkor island. Chin Peng was to provide guides to get them there, through the heavily patrolled coastal zone, with a river journey followed by a long final leg at sea from the mouth of the Perak river to the island. The Japanese had flying boats and high-speed patrol boats based close to Pangkor.

He was busy packing on 26 April, though he found time for a last hunt. He thought he was going to miss his Chinese communist friends more than his compatriots. 'Rather sad to leave MCP but darn happy to get rid of J! and Frank too tho he is a good-hearted man.' It rained all night. He was up at six on 27 April, a Saturday. He listed his gear in his diary:

> I take small rucksack, groundsheet, cream blanket tied up, sweater. J[ohn]'s black C[hinese] coat, Ching's pants, k[haki] shorts, 2 green vests, gym shorts, small pants, 2 Bata boots, rubber sandals, mug, spoon, glasses, compass, parang. Torch each and 2 sp[are] bats, bulbs & red filter. .32 [pistol] and 14 [rounds], Sten. Q[uinine], mepacrine, tonic, benzedrine, aspirin, M & B tabs and pr scissors, aquaflavine, morphine tabs, para[chute] cord. Malay vocab book. Tactics & Demo books [the training manuals he had written], guerrilla newssheets, 3 maps in w-p [waterproof] case.

Not since the long-ago days of the Ford V8 had he enjoyed such abundance. The medicines were the greatest of the luxuries that had come down from the Liberators. Davis and Chin Peng and a small escort of guerrillas went with them to the edge of the jungle, close to the drop zone for the next Liberator flight. Ah Yang was to take them as far as their final boat trip out to Pangkor Laut.

Freddy found his new Bata shoes were very slippery, sliding on the laterite clay tracks. The Telom river was swollen after the night's downpour. They moved on to low-lying ground, along fallen trees over swamps. They came on an old sawmill, ruined and covered in climbing plants, and then moved on past the camp where they had met the Plen. Davis left to go back to prepare for the drop the next night. At times, the two of them had argued themselves speechless, Freddy admitted, but they were held together by having lived and worked alongside each other for so long. It was a 'bond which is certainly never expressed' – not between men trained from boyhood to contain their emotions – but Freddy confessed to 'quite a lump in my throat' as he looked back at Davis standing alone in the bracken and rhododendrons. It was a rare admission of feeling.

They left the great jungle, and moved through recently felled timber where Chinese huts and vegetable gardens were interspersed with stumps and fragments of fallen trees. Freddy and Broome were wearing Chinese clothes, grenades and pistols crammed in their jacket pockets, with old felt hats pulled down over faces they had stained with potassium permanganate. The rubber they came to had not been cleared since the invasion, and the elephant grass was high enough to swallow them. After so long in the camp, Freddy revelled in the kampongs, the cries of children and the noise of dogs and pigs. He felt a sudden and powerful excitement, his mind racing forward to the submarine to Ceylon, to India and on to England. He realised now that, at times, 'I had sometimes been very, very homesick.' That in itself was a change. Before, 'home' had always meant a camp.

They came close to Route One at about 9.30 p.m. They heard a lorry chugging past – it sounded like a British Jowett or Trojan – burning the synthetic petrol the Japanese were making from rubber. They could hear a train whistling on the railway a little further west. They dashed across the road and followed narrow trails through old tin-mining ground cut by streams. They passed under three big power lines carrying electricity down from a dam to the tin mines. Towards midnight, they stopped at a little shelter in an old ladang. Their guides brought them coffee, rice and vegetables from a house nearby. Freddy and Broome sat out, smoking and chatting and drinking coffee, still elated at being on the move and homeward bound. They heard mournful whistles from trains towards Tapah Road.

On Sunday morning two or three Japanese planes went over heading south as they breakfasted, luxuriously, on coffee, rice, fried fish and prawns with a few bits of pork. Chin Peng went off on business. Freddy spent a pleasant two hours birdwatching and ruminating. 'My present plan: to come in with Gurkhas,' he wrote. 'Germans almost finished.' The Japanese were not. Three more aircraft roared over at 9.30 a.m. He kept a log of what he saw as he wandered around in the sun. He found orchids, pink and purple with a faint fragrance, and a big five-star marrow and clumps of Straits rhododendrons in the bracken. A fine crested warbler flew by, with a yellow belly and blue head, and he saw buzzards and jungle fowl. They ate again at 5 p.m. – 'rice, fish & prawns, chicken, coffee'. Freddy noted every meal he ate, compulsively.

At 7.45 p.m., safely after dark, Freddy said goodbye to Chin Peng. He was sad to leave him; he had been his first English-speaking contact among the guerrillas back in March 1942. To Richard Broome, too, Chin Peng was 'more than any of the other Chinese, a real friend'. The warmth was on both sides. 'As I shook hands with the two Europeans I had been so closely associated with for over two years,' the young guerrilla leader wrote later, 'I had no doubt about their expressions of gratitude. It was an emotional moment ... They were both fine and brave men and I truly hoped neither would be sent back to defend British interests in Malaya after the defeat of the Japanese.'

Freddy and Broome had a new guide, Ah Tong, who claimed to be a traitor-killer with eighty-seven victims. They went fast along lanes and through vegetable gardens, until barking dogs became 'the very devil', and they took to the rubber. Tong was soon hopelessly lost. Freddy took out his compass to show that they were going round in circles, but Tong would not believe it until they heard a train behind them instead of in front. They reached the line. Freddy and Broome lay in the undergrowth whilst the guides tried to find a tiny path on the other side of the tracks. Three trains went past, heavily laden and unlit, showering sparks. They felt more vulnerable than ever on this last journey to the submarine.

The next air drop – by four aircraft this time, as the pace picked up – was due after midnight. They heard the first drone of engines approaching from the sea a few minutes before that. A Liberator flew almost directly over them at only a thousand feet. Three others came singly over the next two hours, visible through the slight overcast on their approach, but too high to see when they returned after dropping their loads.

The drop was certain to stir up the Japanese. The guides failed to find the path, so they walked southwards along the track. Freddy took notes on the railway line, for future sabotage operations, counting the number of sleepers and bolts to a length of rail. He had been told that the Japanese had dug a single foxhole within sniping range of each bridge, to shoot at British sappers when they came to repair them. It seemed rather far-fetched. As they passed some coolie lines, a Tamil came out and spotted them before Ah Tong could hide his tommy-gun. They feared he would telephone up the line to the Japanese garrison. The guides at last found the path they were looking for.

It led them into an expanse of slime and mud in which they slid and fell. At 2.30 a.m. they crossed the old branch line that ran from Tapah Road to Telok Anson, now Teluk Intan. The Japanese had taken up the rails to melt down for the steel. They slipped across the suspension bridge over the broad Batang Padang river. It had no sentries. By 4.30 a.m., Malays and Tamils were already cycling and walking to work, and the dangers of being seen were acute. Freddy and Broome lay up in some undergrowth whilst Ah Tong went off to find out exactly where they were. It started to rain and the mosquitoes attacked. The guide came back and said they had to take special care, as the police from Telok Anson came here to hunt pig.

They moved on, hiding when they came across people gathering firewood. They came to a dense patch of rubber seedlings, and hid there for the rest of the day, whilst Ah Yang and the guides went off to look for food. In the middle of the afternoon, Yang sent back a warning. They were not to smoke or talk – they could hear the firewood collectors all around them – because a party of police were carrying out house-to-house searches. It seemed that the Tamil coolie had betrayed them. The Japanese, too, had been very close to them the day before, they were told. The soldiers had taken some men away to ransom them, and shot dead one who tried to run away. They took clothes, watches, jewellery, anything they found, and beat anyone they thought might give them information on the guerrillas and the white men. But Yang had good news, too: he had found a place where they could safely lie up for a week whilst waiting for a sampan for the next leg. Ah Tong suffered malaria all day – they hoped no one was close enough to hear his groans – but was ready as darkness fell to carry his load and tommy-gun.

They crossed a swamp on half-submerged trees. A little before midnight on Monday 29 April, they came to a patch of jungle, and a tiny atap hut where they were to stay for over a week. They could only stand upright in the middle, and half of it was a sleeping bench covered in a pile of soft atap. Rain dripped through the roof and the mosquitoes were ferocious. But there was a muddy stream for water, and the visibility through the dense foliage was less than five yards. They could look out from the edge and watch the Chinese working in their gardens and chopping wood, and hear children's voices and dogs barking, without being seen themselves.

Yoh An Soon, one of their guides, was off at 7 a.m. on Tuesday to get food. He was back two hours later with coffee, two packets of cheroots with a hundred in each, a big bag of sugar, biscuits, and a bottle of samsu, and the fattest fowl Freddy had ever seen. They ate well that day. The weather was clear, and Freddy spotted a white-eyed warbler, a fork-tailed black flycatcher, buzzards, bulbul, and a big woodpecker. From then, two trusted local men brought them an earthenware pot of white rice each morning and evening, with a bowl of chicken or salt fish, and cucumber or cabbage.

He found it 'a very delightful existence and an idle one'. He was up at 6.30 on Wednesday to do his exercises. Breakfast of coffee and biscuits was followed by 'superb' chicken and rice. He could hear voices all round, and the sound of trees being felled close by. He watched Japanese aircraft flying over. His only gripes were mosquitoes – 'we have a mozzy net but NBG' – and shortage of paper for his diary. He wrote intelligence reports and manuals on jungle fighting, and made notes on Chinese types for SOE to use in recruiting:

The majority Hokkien, Amoy. Trade, shops, easy to get on with, reasonable.
Swatow, v jungly, fishing, woodcutting, v pleasant, not v int[eresting].

Cantonese, here as merchants, mining coolies, rubber tappers.
Kwong Si, very jungly, mining (lot in Pahang) tend to panic.
Hakka originals, gipsy people. Very bright & determined.

'Jungly', of course, was a compliment in guerrilla terms.

A thunderstorm came with squalls so violent that scores of trees and branches were flung to the ground. They feared one of the dead trees near the hut would be blown onto them. When the gale had passed, Freddy heard a 'dry scratching noise' on the atap beside his head. Broome switched on his torch, and was able to brush away a huge black scorpion that was crawling towards Freddy's face. Other wildlife abounded. He noted sixty-seven species of birds, several of them new to him, and six kinds of monkey. He also heard the calls of tiger and kijang, barking deer. At night, he listened to the Chinese banging tins to frighten wild pig away from their vegetable gardens, and watched the stars, revelling in seeing the Great Bear and the Southern Cross at the same time.

They had two bottles of samsu on Friday night, with mild hangovers next morning. Ah Yang went off on Saturday to find the man who was supplying a sampan for them. He came back with a huge tin of creamed biscuits and the news that Hitler had 'surrendered'. The sampan would be ready in four days. Ah Yang said that they would have to travel at night. Japanese river patrols were very active, searching boats even on smaller streams and creeks, looking for smugglers and the British officers they knew were infiltrating by submarine and air drop.

The weather became overcast with bouts of heavy rain. 'Hitler shot at Berlin, Musso taken, Germany finished,' Freddy wrote on Tuesday 7 May. 'Pity we are missing details of this great news. Lot of hornbill here.' A seaplane flew over them on Wednesday very slowly, flying north-west towards Pangkor, its sound reminding him of an old Vauxhall car engine. At dusk they had a last meal. A new guide arrived, a boatman from the Perak river who worked for the guerrillas carrying messages, and they set off once it was dark. The land was flat and eerie with dead trees and patches of jungle. They passed a platform with an atap roof with four Chinese sitting gambling and drinking by the light of a brilliant lamp. The Chinese called out to them, and Broome replied to them in Malay. A new guide came, a Hokkien in a straw hat and a patched blue coat. He took them at speed along a raised yellow clay bank. From far off they heard the strange sound of women and children singing a tuneless song, though it was well after midnight. The sampan was lying in a dyke.

It was twenty feet long, pointed at each end. The oars were three feet above the gunwale, and the rower stood with them in front of him. They cleared the dyke and were swept down the Sungei Kroh, now the Keroh. The banks streamed past and they nursed their tommy-guns in case they encountered patrols. They heard the noise of Malay drums beating in the distance. The Kroh flowed into the broader Kinta. Then they were swept into the Perak river – the same river he had drifted down past Japanese lines three and a half years before – so wide it seemed like the ocean, its banks invisible. The rowlocks kept breaking. Mending them, the boatman turned north in the darkness for some way. Freddy was checking their course by the stars, and had him turn south. Japanese motor boats patrolled the river from their base in the river port at Telok Anson a few miles further downstream. Well before dawn, they turned off the river up a creek. The Perak makes a great half-loop to Telok Anson here, and they were to walk overland to pick up another boat to avoid the town and its police and Japanese garrison. They walked for two miles on a path between vegetable gardens and fields of groundnuts to the head of another creek. Here a larger boat was waiting for them.

This backwater was overgrown and tangled, and they needed torches of flaming rubber to find their way past fallen trees and creepers. The air was heavy and close after the fresh breezes of the open river. They were startled by splashes as frogs darted into the water from the branches, and a violent smashing of water in front of them gave notice of the many crocodiles in the stagnant pools. The mosquitoes were 'simply enormous' and they saw the wriggling coils of a water-snake on the calm surface of the creek. Hanging greenery brushed them as they passed, and the intricate patterns of creepers harboured other snakes. Then they were hurtling back down the river. Before dawn, they turned into another creek and left the boat to lie up for the day. The tough little Hokkien took them for two miles along a slippery clay track to a large hut. It had an earth floor, but there was a photograph of a Swatow family on the wall, done up in their finery, the old man in a collar and tie, doubtless lent to him by the photographer. They heard the splashes of crocodiles. They were close to the Sungei Buaya, the Crocodile River.

They went on after dusk, well downstream from Telok Anson now, past dykes with small boats pulled up on the banks. They moored well before dawn and hid under a boat. It was now Thursday 9 May. They had four days to go before the rendezvous with the submarine. The Hokkien went off and came back with a man who said the house where they were to have stayed during the day was not safe. Two strangers had appeared there the evening before, and they were thought to be Japanese spies. He took them instead to a hut in a rubber estate. After a few hours sleep, they woke in mid-morning to find a small boy cooking rice and fish for their breakfast. Two shots suddenly rang out. Freddy and Broome seized their weapons and got ready to fight. They thought the Japanese had them surrounded. The boy said that perhaps someone was shooting an informer. 'It doesn't matter,' he shrugged, and got on with his cooking. In *The Jungle is Neutral*, Freddy said that they never discovered who had fired the shots. In his diary, though, he wrote that it turned out to be boys amusing themselves by making pistol noises by letting one plank spring back against another.

A memorable feast was served at dusk. They had rice, sea-slugs with garlic, salt pork, squares of soya-bean paste that tasted like Camembert cheese, and fresh mud-fish cooked with ginger. Just before dark, two Liberators flew over them low, gleaming silver in the last of the evening light. They were off again an hour after dark, along banks above banana trees and huts where they heard laughter and the sound of an accordion. An hour's walk brought them to a tiny creek where a sampan lay, eighteen feet long, with a five-foot beam and pointed ends, and 'very wobbly'. It was provisioned with fresh water and two live fowls. They poled along the creek which widened out into a huge swamp, with clumps of nipah palm growing out of the water like gigantic ferns with fronds a foot thick and thirty or forty feet high. They wound through a cleared channel. A few fishing boats were out with fires burning on the foredeck for smoke to keep off mosquitoes.

Swarms of fireflies hung over the trees with the same brilliance and colour as the brightest stars. Jupiter was overhead. Freddy looked up at Vega, Aquila, Andromeda – 'good to see old North country friends again' – and a coppery moon. They came out onto the Perak river and moored to wait for the tide. At dawn they saw the hills on Pangkor island to the north and Batu Puteh and the rounded tops of the Main Range back to the east. Groves of coconuts lay along the bank with Malay villages in the clearings. A tiger prowled along the sand at the river's edge, hunting for pig or deer as they came down to the water to drink. His chin and throat gleamed white and he gave them a brief and lordly glance as he stepped delicately to avoid getting his paws wet.

Fine trees here reminded him of the paintings of Corot, their trunks rusty red and the leaves emerald. Crabs with aquamarine shells abounded, and he sketched a pop-eyed mud-fish in his diary. He got four hours sleep before a group of crab-eating monkeys gathered in the tree above the sampan and howled at them. They were stranded on the mud with the tide out, powerless to move had the monkeys caught the eye of the crew of a patrol boat. As the tide turned, a boat came up to them. Freddy and Broome hid beneath a *kajang*, a canopy of thatched palm, and fingered their weapons. It was only a Tamil begging a match.

They were under way again in the vivid bruised glow of a stormy sunset, the clouds over the Main Range purple behind them, and the hills lining the Dindings Channel looming to the north. They kept to the right bank of the river to avoid the port at Bagan Datoh, now Datuk. Freddy picked out scores of moored boats through his field glasses. The river became wider and wider and then they were in the open waters of the Malacca Straits. As they were swept by the tide towards the light at Tanjong Bras Basah, he heard a fearsome loud roaring noise. He made out a row of stakes in the dusk, vibrating furiously in the tide, with huts built on stilts next to them. This was a long tidal fish trap, the noise coming from the stakes driving the fish into a funnel-shaped trap where they were stranded at low water and taken by the fishermen from the huts. White water foamed between the stakes and a capsize was imminent. The boatman rowed furiously and they scraped past the end stake. A few junks with lights were out at sea but they did not pick out patrol boats or engine noise.

It was still two days before the submarine was due. They planned to go south of the river mouth on the ebb tide and enter a creek by a Chinese village to lie up for a day. About half a mile offshore, though, they ran aground on a sandbank. It was too shallow for a patrol boat to get close to them. It was hot and the faint breeze was heavy with the scent of palms and shrubs and damp earth, 'like some great dragon's breath'. As the tide refloated them, they coasted slowly south, until they saw a junk lying at the mouth of a river, riding lights showing, with Chinese crewmen talking quietly on deck. Across the water, a platform thirty feet high stood next to a large building. It was clearly a coast-watching post, though they could see no one on it. Freddy felt 'more than a little anxious' – whoever manned the post clearly had to answer to the Japanese – and it was only later that he was told that the Malay coastguard had agreed to take no notice of them. The Japanese sometimes manned the station themselves, arriving without warning. Had they done so that night, a small boat would have been moored offshore to warn Freddy and his companions of their presence.

They rowed on through a fishing village, Sungei Tiang. The junks and sampans moored by the houses were already blazing with naphtha flares although it was only 4 a.m. on Friday 10 May, Freddy's thirty-eighth birthday. Men were getting nets ready and gutting fish. In his diary, he wrote of a 'foul smell of pig shit', while in *The Jungle is Neutral* it was a more genteel 'powerful smell of pigs and bad fish'. They tied up for an hour whilst Yang went ashore. Freddy and Broome lay hidden under the kajang, listening to the Chinese 'palaver' going on about them. A boat moored alongside them and the fishermen clambered over the sampan to get ashore. Yang came back, and led them over rotten slimy boards across swamp holes to a pig-sty. From there a local guide took them for ninety minutes of 'ghastly going' through mangrove swamp and knee-deep slime. Despite the risk of snakes, he went bare-foot – for security, as shod footprints might betray him, and his instinct not to fall captive blazed the more furiously for being so close to the submarine.

The guide made them stop whilst he went ahead to disconnect a lethal booby trap. Freddy sketched it next day, adding it to his reports on guerrilla fighting as an example of local ingenuity. A trip wire was connected to a 16-pounder shell that had been fired by a British submarine at a Japanese-manned junk. It had embedded itself without exploding in the mud of the foreshore. The hut they were making for was a few yards further on, in the heart of the swamp. It had been built specially for them by locals, so many of whom, like their guide, were risking their lives for them. The walls and roof were made of leathery pandanus palm and a floor of planks was raised a little above the swamp. Freddy could hear surf and the voices of fishermen as they put out to sea. The guide had doubled back parallel to the river, and the hut was close to its mouth and the coastguard station.

It was a restless place. Dogs barked, and pigs and cocks added to the cacophony. Dawn, on Saturday 11 May, was 'all grey-blue mud & mangrove'. Yang went off to get new guides. A fearsome bellowing broke out. Freddy could not place it, but the local man told him it came from a large black-faced monkey. The tide came up in the afternoon, to within a few inches of the floor. They saw numbers of sea snakes swimming past the door. Freddy said 'some' were very poisonous, but all twenty-two types of front-fanged sea snakes in Malaya are venomous. The most common, the beaked sea snake, is also the most aggressive, a dull olive green with dark crossbands and a cream belly, with a nostril at the front that gives it its beak-like look.

Yang returned with two young Hainanese who were to take them on the last leg. Freddy and Broome blackened their faces. They left the hut at dusk. Freddy was wearing shoes this time. He was leaving for good. The return to the sampan through the swamp was easier in the faint light. 'Farewell to Yang,' Freddy wrote as the guerrilla left them before they boarded the sampan. 'Gave him my watch.' It can seem patronising today – a tip from the *tuan* – but it was a gift of real gratitude for the way Yang had arranged their journey and shared its dangers. The tide was ebbing and they were soon past the coastguard tower. As they gained the open sea, one of the Hainanese rested on his oars. '*Mana mau pigi, Tuan*?' he asked. 'Where do you want to go?' Yang had impressed on them that they were to obey orders. But they had no idea of where they were to go. The Hainanese could not understand Broome's Cantonese, nor he their dialect, and they had only a few words of Malay.

When they understood that the Englishmen wanted to go to Pangkor, they said they must be mad. They explained that the main island was not what it was when the British had gone weekending there before the invasion. The rest houses and hotels were now full of Japanese, and there were patrol boats and seaplanes based on the mainland at Lumut, just across the Dindings Channel. Freddy and Broome almost burst out laughing. They assured the young boatmen that they did not want to go to the main island, but to the little island of Pangkor Laut to the south-west.

It was overcast. They decided to keep well out to sea and make direct for Pangkor Laut, rather than sticking to the coast and lying up during the day. They passed the fishing stakes. There was no roar this time but the huts had men in them. From midnight to 5 a.m. they anchored during the flood tide. They were glad to see other junks and sampans at sea, as they made them less conspicuous. At dawn, they were abeam of rocky Pulau Agas, the most northerly of the Sembilan Islands. They took comfort from their sten guns and grenades. They could probably deal with police in a junk, though they were dead meat if they met a Japanese patrol boat from Lumut.

Just after sunrise, several seaplanes appeared from Pangkor flying very low and scouring the sea north from the Sembilans. They were looking for submarines, and somewhere out there was Freddy's. They picked up the observation post on Pangkor island, and watched it go out of sight as it was hidden by Pangkor Laut. Terns flew close and they disturbed some big vulture-like birds. As they closed on the little island, Freddy half-expected a patrol boat to come charging out from the Dindings Channel.

The shoreline here is rocky on the parts open to the sea and sandy in the sheltered coves. On the approach at low tide, granite rocks are exposed. Above them the flanks of the hills have thick jungle cover and high outcrops of granite. A horseshoe-shaped bay with a beach of silver sand has big outcrops of rock at its extremities. It gives onto the thick jungle that covered the island. A startled crab-eating monkey, scurrying from the rocks for the safety of the forest, was the only movement. They landed in the centre of the bay. Rows of big trees stood at the water's edge with a big fig and another laden with lovely white flowers. Freddy found a 'soft hidden place' ten yards beyond the high-water mark. They stowed their gear. They had a large pot of rice, Australian emergency rations, four gallons of coffee and twenty of water, a tin of biscuits, two hundred bananas and a pound of tobacco, 'enough for a week' though Freddy and Broome were getting through twenty cheroots a day between them.

They swam, and walked to the southerly point of the bay. The rocks were too steep for the submarine's boat to land, and they gave directly onto a fearful tangle of atap, fallen trees and thorns. Freddy decided they would have to be picked up from the beach. The water shelves quite gently for the first forty or fifty yards off the beach. A hundred yards out, it drops sharply and there is plenty of depth for a submarine. More rocks and islets lie to the north of Pangkor Laut, sheer-sided with dramatic granite shapes. They gave protection against large Japanese ships, which had no room for manoeuvre, but patrol and torpedo boats could operate freely.

The little island is a place of beauty. Sea almond, *Terminalia catappa*, with almond-shaped edible fruits, and sea lettuce flourish. The puff-ball flowers of the sea putat, *Barringtonia asiatica*, bloom at night and drop in the morning. An abundance of beach morning glory, goat's foot, lies by the palms. The island was once the site of a leper colony – a most luxurious hotel-resort nestles on it now – but it was abandoned before the war and only a trace or two survived. Freddy made sure the signals for the submarine were safe:

Hid torch & red f. [red filter] & white cloth in tree ... A two man proa far out to sea, sailing NE. Could not get the Hainanese to go! They want to stop & see the fun! Ate rice, fish, bananas. Bathed.

Prepared to sleep out on bed of banana leaves. 2 seaplanes over SE very low & fast at 5. Later 3 going N out to sea. 5.40 pm as I was in sea a Lib [Liberator] very low from NW. I went out and waved! Back 6.30 further S[outh]. Bed 7.30 pm.

The submarine crew were to look for a white sheet during daylight, with a code letter flashed in red after dark. The sheet was a length of parachute silk from the air drop.

They slept well. After dawn, Freddy rigged a mast to carry the white sheet. He kept a look-out on a high rock at the entrance to the bay, showing off the sheet seawards. At 7.10 a.m., Broome saw two bright flashes like reflected sunlight to the south-west out to sea. No boats were in sight. There was a distant sound of aircraft. They opened ration packs – each with two compressed prunes, two chocolate bars, eight caramels, four sugar lumps, tea, salt – but they were not hungry. The day was dragging, and then:

about 2 I saw a periscope so rushed out & put up our sheet. It comes up & down 6–8' [ft] out of water. Then further out. Back again an hour later. One proa far out to sea. Lovely warm day. Sunbathed swimming. Packed up all our gear & hid it. All set by 6. No sign of ship since 3. Flashed 7–8.30. Get very tired of it. Each ¼hr at first, then each 5 minutes on & off. Walked up & down. New moon up but soon set. About 9.10 saw a shadow. 5 secs after heard a hail Ahoy! Saw appearing 2 men in a boat. Collected gear & ran to edge. 'How are your feet?' 'We are thirsty.' [The agreed reply for identification.] All OK. Then: 'You'll have to swim, we have got no boat.' I could not believe it. I made them repeat it! Swam out with gear on back. Phosphorescence. Easy: only 50 yds. Saw c. tower [conning tower] & 3" gun. Climbed up slippery side by line & over rail. Found a group of very tall, very young, darkly bearded men wearing sarongs. 6 men. Went to wardroom . . .

Freddy Spencer Chapman was back from the dead.

CHAPTER 21

THE LION IN WINTER

He was six days in the submarine, sleeping on a camp bed under the wardroom table, the crew tripping over his feet as they repeatedly rushed to crash dive when enemy aircraft were picked up on radar. A Japanese cruiser had been sunk off Penang by British destroyers, and these aircraft were out looking for them.

They entered the Royal Navy base at Trincomalee on Ceylon's east coast and moored next to the submarine mother ship on 19 May. Innes Tremlett, whom Freddy had last seen at the meeting with Lai Te in Singapore in 1941, was waiting on the dockside to greet him. The Special Branch man was now head of the Malayan Country Section of Force 136. Freddy was taken to a Force 136 camp, where he bathed, shaved, sent his ragged clothes to be burnt, and drank 'large quantities of pink gin'. Then he was flown to Colombo.

He discovered how ruthlessly the world had written him off. His car had been sold to pay off his debts. Most of his belongings, books, records, photographs, had gone. He was staying with Tremlett, and noticed a book called *Memoirs of a Mountaineer* on his bookshelf. He picked it up idly to see who the author was, and was astonished to find that it was himself. His publishers, three years after he was first officially reported 'missing believed killed', had reissued two of his climbing books under a single title almost as an obituary volume.

He had money, for once, three and a half years back pay from the army, and royalties from his publishers. Although he was not awarded the Victoria Cross that Admiral Mountbatten, the Supreme Allied

Commander in South-East Asia, felt was his due, a bar was added to his Distinguished Service Order. Yet he found himself emotionally 'in a flat spin and still spinning'. Members of SOE in Colombo realised that he was vulnerable, likely to fall for the first woman he came across, and they formed a Freddy Protection Society to ward off women who wanted a trophy affair.

After he had finished his report on conditions in Malaya, he was flown to England for three weeks' leave. For some days, he woke screaming in the night. He had never done that in the jungle, he noted, and he had certainly never burst into tears, as he now did when he saw anything emotional at the theatre. On 6 August 1945, the atomic bomb was dropped on Hiroshima. Freddy had been back in Colombo for a fortnight. Three days later, another was dropped on Nagasaki. Emperor Hirohito ordered Japanese forces to surrender. But those in Malaya were entirely intact. Indeed, the Japanese commander in Singapore went on radio threatening to fight on.

No invasion of Malaya was now necessary, and Freddy sensed this was a serious blow to the return of British rule. 'Only by kicking the Jap good and hard could we restore our prestige there,' he said. He feared that the communists would use their guerrillas to take control before British troops were landed. The MPAJA with its Force 136 liaison officers was the only organised force in the country. The situation was particularly acute in Pahang on the eastern side of the Main Range. Chin Peng had not given John Davis any details of the camps there, and the British liaison officer who was sent to Pahang was dropped blind. He had difficulty contacting them – though he had been a game warden before the war, and knew the country well – and when he did he found them hostile. Freddy volunteered to parachute into Pahang to relieve the tensions with the guerrillas, many of whom he knew from his time in the Pahang camps.

The drop zone was on the Sungei Lipis ten miles north-west of Batu Talam. He was scheduled to go with a Liberator crew on their first flight to Malaya at the end of August 1945. The WAAF officer who liaised with Force 136 was horrified. She told him no flight was available that day, and switched him to an aircraft flown by a very experienced crew.

They took off at dawn from Ceylon – now Sri Lanka, then a British colony – and crossed the Malayan coast at the mouth of the Perak river ten hours later. Freddy made out his old ambush sites on Route One and the railway, and the S-bends on the Gap road. He confessed he was 'scared stiff'. He had never parachuted before – it was clearly so unpleasant to drop out of a moving aircraft, he said, that he saw no point in trying it beforehand 'just for practice' – and he felt like 'a trussed chicken'.

He hit the ground hard. The WAAF officer read in the pilot's report: 'Body appeared to land on head, but got up and waved.' Freddy saw several 'dark little men' running towards him. He thought they were Japanese for a moment, and fumbled for his pistol, but realised they were Malays. He was the first British officer into Raub on 3 September, and into Kuala Lipis, the capital of Pahang, two days later. The Japanese were loath to surrender to 'a handful of scruffy British officers emerging from the jungle'. When he drove over the Gap road in a small car he had commandeered – no Ford V8 this time – he followed a Japanese armoured car. Its turret gunner kept his gun trained on Freddy the whole time. On 30 September, though, eighteen days after the Japanese ceded in Singapore, Freddy took their surrender in Kuantan on the east coast.

A naval officer aboard a ship where Freddy gave the crew a long talk on his Malay experiences noted that, though he held them enthralled when he spoke, in private he seemed to have a sense of failure. He seemed 'curiously unsure of himself, as if he had to justify not having fought an orthodox war in the last years'.

He was very conscious that the only direct damage he had done the enemy was in the 'mad fortnight' early in 1942. For the rest, he had simply survived. Mountbatten told him that Operation Zipper, the Allied invasion plan, would have forced the Japanese to transfer thousands of troops from northern Malaya southwards along Route One and the railway. The guerrillas Freddy had trained would have ambushed them continuously, and would have inflicted heavy casualties. But the dropping of the atom bombs meant that Malaya did not have to be invaded. There was no need for Freddy's guerrillas: indeed, before long, as Chin Peng had predicted, they were fighting the British in the Malayan

Emergency, and Chin Peng himself was no longer a friend, but hunted as the arch 'CT', Communist Terrorist.

So Freddy never gave himself the credit he deserved. For, in a less obvious and non-military way, he had continued to stand for the qualities of honour and decency that the Japanese invasion seemed to have swept away. When he returned to Pahang, the people, particularly the Chinese, 'literally wept with joy to see Englishmen again'. He had, in his own person, the traits which brought such relief and happiness.

The Chinese writer Low Ngiong Ing wrote, in his memoir *When Singapore was Syonan-To*, of how they had seemed engulfed in the 'unseemly stampeding' by the British from Penang in December 1941. Low recalled the 'chagrin and disgust' he felt at finding no Asians in the 'wilderness of Europeans' when the refugees arrived in Singapore. Then the Japanese had come.

Low remembered the Englishman who had warned him as a boy against sycophancy and grovelling when he 'sirred' him too assiduously. He remembered as a teacher taking his pupils to a prize-giving when a white in a rickshaw insisted that they gave way to him, and two other whites intervened to stop him. 'It was an expression of the Englishman's love of fair-play.' By such little things, Low said, 'we realised that the Pax Japonica was far inferior to the Pax Britannica we had known'. Like Freddy, Low was an orphan. Both his parents had died of cholera when he was seven, and an Englishman had paid for his schooling. For people like himself, Low said, England was a 'kindly foster-mother, whom, if they owed their physical existence to China or India, yet owed all their mental and spiritual development to England . . . For that high courtesy they could never be sufficiently thankful.' During the occupation, the 'cry of anguish of every heart was "How much longer? Why are the British so slow?"' When Allied bombs began to fall on Singapore, people did not seek cover. They climbed trees, in 'exhilaration and exultation'. For days after the British troops at last landed, Low said, Chinese boys tumbled over themselves to touch them, referring to them among themselves as 'Red-haired Devils', but 'in affection, as it were pronouncing a pet-name caressingly . . .'

He thought he caught the essence of this Englishness at the formal surrender of Singapore on 12 September. The crowds greeted Admiral Mountbatten with 'abandoned joy' as he drove up. After the signing, cars were brought up almost to the steps of the Municipal Building to take away the Japanese generals. Low knew why. It was done to save the vanquished being humiliated by the crowds massed at the periphery. 'We felt disappointed,' Low said, 'but could not help approving of the generous instinct that prompted the gesture . . .'

Freddy owed his life to this affection – now largely forgotten or mocked – for the Englishness he embodied. It was the reason he was never betrayed. It was also why he fulfilled Chin Peng's hope that they would not fight each other. Chin Peng was awarded an OBE and campaign medals by the British after the war. Lai Te – Freddy's 'the Plen' – was again being run by British intelligence, and he ensured that the MCP at first acquiesced in the restoration of colonial rule. In 1947, though, he was about to be unmasked as a British and Japanese agent, and traitor to the Party. He disappeared from Singapore, together with the MCP's reserves of a million dollars in cash and gold. He was never seen again, but he is believed to have been killed by MCP executioners in Thailand. Chin Peng replaced him as Secretary General.

In 1948 three British rubber planters were murdered by communist guerrillas at Sungei Siput, in northern Perak not far from where Freddy had escaped from the bandit camp, beginning the Malayan Emergency. Freddy had no wish, however, to take up arms against old friends. He turned down suggestions that he return to Malaya.

On leave in New Delhi, at the end of January 1946, Freddy married Faith Townson, the WAAF liaison officer who had wangled the experienced Liberator crew for him. They sailed back for England the next month. He was thirty-nine. He thought of returning to teach at Gordonstoun, but Faith disliked the 'frozen North'. Instead, he worked for Outward Bound, schools set up under the aegis of Gordonstoun's founder, Kurt Hahn, to give one-month courses in sea and mountain adventure to fifteen-to-eighteen-year-olds. The purpose was to use adventure to teach 'something of the deeper values of life', as Freddy had seen with young Tibetan herdsmen, and Eskimo and Sakai boys.

We are spoon-fed with television 'survivors' now – often ludicrously so, with some career 'adventurer' crossing a glacier made safe by the absence of snow, or 'living off' the jungle, 'alone' but for television crews and helicopters – and yet we lack examples of real fortitude. It is easy to mock Freddy's affection for scouts and guides and youth hostellers as dated and naive. But what he said was true. At sea and in the mountains, the young in peacetime could escape their background and limitations, and nourish the same qualities that were awakened in war: 'enterprise, skill, persistence and above all service . . .'

After Outward Bound, he became headmaster of a new school for the children of British servicemen at Plön in Germany. He named the houses for men he admired. There was not a military hero among them. He chose the explorer Nansen, for his sense of justice and the humanity of his relief work in post-Revolution Russia; Churchill – 'in spite of his Conservatism', for Freddy was a natural liberal – as a parliamentarian; Roosevelt, for his campaign against the excesses of capitalism; and Archbishop William Temple as the champion of the underdog, and crusader against slums. He had to think of a school motto, too, and he chose a line from the new film of Terence Rattigan's *The Winslow Boy*, 'Let Right Be Done', because, he told the school, it echoed 'the cry for freedom and justice which lies like a gold thread through the tangled skein of our national history'.

The school had no chapel or chaplain, and little prospect of getting them. Freddy was determined to have both. He had, as we know, his fill of prayers and sermons as a boy. He gave a talk, 'In Search of a Moral Code', on the BBC in 1948. He said that, throughout his jungle years, 'I could not pray . . . I could not with a clear conscience ask for divine help as if God was a sort of celestial insurance company that one only applied to in extremity.' In the guerrilla camps, though, he had been impressed – 'and frightened' – by the 'burning sense of vocation and sacrificial enthusiasm' of the young Chinese. Marxism, he realised, was 'nothing less than a religion' but one that brought 'physical and spiritual enslavement'.

This taught him to appreciate more than ever, he told his BBC listeners, the 'fundamental rightness' of the way of life in which he had been brought up. 'I am driven – yes, I use the word deliberately – to admit that the most satisfactory code I know is that taught by the carpenter of Nazareth two thousand years ago.' It did not mean that he was a born-again Christian. Far from it. He simply acknowledged that his English upbringing meant that the core values 'exemplified in the life of Christ' were in the blood. Clergy families were a distinct breed during his vicarage childhood. They were, the writer A. N. Wilson observes, 'often impoverished' but grew up with 'a certain set of shared values which could loosely be defined as decency ... notably more bookish, more self-reliant than other families who had more servants ...' That, of course, is Freddy, decent and self-reliant and, natural historian that he was, bookish too. It was one of his great regrets that he brought no seeds back from Malaya for Kew.

The Jungle Is Neutral was published in January 1949. It was a great success. *The Sunday Times* gave its annual literary prize that year to Winston Churchill, for the first two volumes of his war memoirs. The newspaper awarded two other prizes, to Alan Paton for his *Cry, The Beloved Country*, and to Freddy.

It was to Paton's Africa that Freddy went in 1952. He and Faith had three small boys by now, and he sensed he had time for a last adventure before he was tied down by school terms and school fees. He drove the family in a camper van round southern, central and east Africa, through what were still British, Portuguese and Belgian colonies. He fussed over the children – the orphan boy made a fine father, singing them to sleep with the Red Flag in Chinese – and encouraged their sense of adventure. In Kenya, during the Mau Mau uprising, he heard drumming and chanting as they stayed in an isolated spot in Kikuyu tribal territory. He thought it might be an oath-taking ceremony: 'I went round twice with torch and rifle. I love emergencies!' He hunted with pygmies in the Ituri forest in central Africa. It reminded him of happy days in Malaya, 'the beauty of the great forest, the joy of hunting and above all, the wonderful companionship'. Each night in the forest, though, he had bad nightmares, and all the old terrors he had forgotten flooded back. He listed, too, his ailments: eye strain, stomach pains, bilious attacks. He climbed Kilimanjaro, suffering from a sore throat and severe headaches.

The bishop of Coventry, who had been a chaplain at Sedbergh in Freddy's day, helped him to be appointed headmaster of St Andrew's College at Grahamstown, a leading South African public school. The bishop said he found it difficult to reconcile Freddy the soldier and man of action with the 'attractive quiet person with many of the instincts of the poet'.

Freddy was too generous and open-hearted to survive in South Africa as apartheid tightened its grip. He urged his boys to learn a native language, and to get to know Africans, not only the servants and farm labourers their parents employed, but the better-educated as well. 'What do we know of their life, their aspirations and fears?' he asked. He arranged meetings and exchanges between Afrikaans and African boys' clubs. At Speech Day in 1958, he warned boys to resist political pressures, to think for themselves and retain their individuality in the face of apartheid. He quoted Edmund Burke to them: 'For evil to triumph, it is only necessary for good men to keep silent.'

When South Africa declared itself a Republic outside the Commonwealth on 1 June 1961, he resigned. It was a brave step. He was fifty-four, with three children, and he had no job to go to. He said that his years as a headmaster in Germany had given him insights into how Nazism had developed before the war – muzzling radio and press, taking control of education – and he warned that South Africa was developing along similar lines. He was prescient.

He came back to England, to an unhappy period as warden of the Pestalozzi Village, an international home for deprived and refugee children, at Sedlescombe in Sussex. The idea was 'magnificent', he said, but that was all. The children were 'aimless, stateless, maladjusted'. They stole, swore, vandalised, and threatened staff who were too inhibited to discipline them. 'I remember a houseparent being badly beaten up by a boy,' his son Christopher recalls. 'He aged during his time at Sedlescombe. He didn't have time for the things he loved, bird watching, wild places. I remember going shooting with him one lovely evening, but that was all.'

He appeared on *This Is Your Life*, one of the most popular BBC shows, in which the subject was inveigled into the television studio by subterfuge, and confronted with people from his past. The presenter,

Eamonn Andrews, said that Freddy's story had to be spread over two shows, since 'we cannot condense this epic story into the half hour allotted to us'. It was a last hurrah.

A friend from SOE days suggested that he became warden of Wantage Hall, the oldest residential hall at Reading University. He did so. He found the students difficult – 'they are hell these days', he wrote, 'they search for issues and go out of their way to make trouble' – but it was his health and declining strength that most depressed him. 'In his fifties he'd still been incredibly fit,' Christopher says. 'He'd carry us up mountains in a rucksack. Now he was plagued by stomach upsets, he wasn't well. As brothers, we never said anything to our mother, but we felt she should have led his lifestyle more. He was constrained and office-bound, and in Reading, not the most sympathetic town.'

In the summer of 1970, he fell ill on holiday in Italy. 'Tummy not right . . . Tummy worse . . . Want to pee all night. Can't. Bladder rush at 12 and 12.30. PAIN. Can't pee all p.m. Stoppage. To Levanto hospital 5 pm – Catheter.' Waiting for an aircraft back to England, he went to the airport lavatory. The hospital had told him to open a clip on the catheter if he wanted to urinate. He did so, and 'about a quart of blood splashed all over the lovely green loo and the floor and walls'. He spent the next quarter of an hour cleaning it up with a box of tissues. The plane was late and was delayed further by strikes by French air traffic controllers. 'I suffered more pain than in the rest of my life,' he told Quintin Riley, his old Greenland friend.

For the next year, he suffered depressions. As he had years before at Cambridge – 'I really shall shoot myself soon' – he associated these fits of melancholy with bilious attacks. He could not sleep and he could not eat. He lost his interest in birds, and sold his bird books to a dealer for £200. He was told on 15 July 1971 that he would not be granted the extension he had sought as warden. Retirement loomed. 'Dull pain at top, sometimes bottom, of stomach,' he wrote on 6 August. 'Sleepy. Loss of appetite. Wake up 4, worry, sweat. Bowels – once normal, then like time bomb. Not only rich food & drink. Often no cause.'

On 8 August, he helped Faith to hang up some curtains in the hall porter's flat in the morning. 'Oh, God, I can't do this any more,' he said. A little after midday, before leaving the house, he picked up a copy of *The Times*. It was still a large-format broadsheet – as it had been when he wrote in it of Gino Watkins' death, and of his own triumph on Chomolhari – and it was large enough to hide the double-barrelled shotgun he wrapped in it. He went to his office, and wrote a brief note to Faith: 'I don't want you to have to nurse an invalid for the rest of my life. Thank you for being the most wonderful wife and for 25 years of very great happiness together.'

He clasped the stock between his knees and pointed the barrels upwards below his chin. In an instant, he was gone.

'What does one leave of oneself?' he said once to his son Christopher. 'One's children, one's books, the memory people have of one. It's all that lives on, for a limited time.' Less limited, we may hope, than he suspected. For his life is surely that of a very English man, of a type we should not lightly forget.

GLOSSARY

Climbing terms

aiguille	sharp needle or peak of rock
arête	sharp ridge dividing glacial valleys
belay	anchor for climbing rope to protect climber
bergschrund	crevasse separating head of glacier from mountain
couloir	gully
moraine	rock debris from glacier
piton	metal spike driven into rock or ice as a belay
sérac	pinnacle of ice on glacier

Malay words

atap	leaves for thatching, roof
babi	pig
beras	rice
bukit	hill
champada	jackfruit
gunung, gunong	mountain
kampong	village
jagong	maize
jalan	road

JUNGLE SOLDIER

labu	pumpkin
ladang	clearing
orang asli	aborigine
orang jepun	Japanese
padi	rice field
parang	stout sharp knife
proa	canoe-like boat
pulau	island
roti	bread, flour
rusa	deer
Sakai	aborigine
sampan	boat
samsu	rice spirit
sungei	river
tuan	master, sir
ubi, ubi kayu	tapioca
ubi keledik	sweet potato
ulu	jungle

ACKNOWLEDGEMENTS AND BIBLIOGRAPHY

I am particularly grateful to Christopher and Nicholas Spencer Chapman, to the Royal Geographical Society in London, and to the Pitt Rivers Museum in Oxford.

Ralph Barker's biography of Freddy, *One Man's Jungle*, was published in 1975. Chin Peng's *My Side of History* was published in 2003, in Singapore, where N.I. Low wrote *When Singapore was Syonan-To* in 1973. Richard Noone wrote of his brother and the Temiar in *The Rape of the Dream People* in 1972. Pat Noone's fate was the subject of *Noone of the Ulu* by Dennis Holman in 1959: he also wrote of Bob Chrystal's experiences in *The Green Torture* in 1962.

For fine recent accounts: of Gino Watkins, see *Dancing on Ice*, by Jeremy Scott; of the Malayan campaign, see *Singapore Burning* by Colin Smith (2005); and for the impact of the war with Japan on Britain's Asian Empire, see *Forgotten Armies* (2004), by Christopher Bayly and Tim Harper.

Freddy Spencer Chapman's own books are: *Northern Lights* (1932), *Watkins' Last Expedition* (1934), *Lhasa: The Holy City* (1938), *Helvellyn to Himalaya* (1940), *Memoirs of a Mountaineer* (1945), *The Jungle is Neutral* (1949), *Living Dangerously* (1953), and *Lightest Africa* (1955). Freddy's wartime diaries are in the Pitt Rivers Museum, Oxford.

Picture acknowledgments

FIRST SECTION
p.1 Sedbergh School (upper right and middle), the author (lower); *p.2* Pitt Rivers Museum, Oxford; *p.3* Pitt Rivers Museum, Oxford (upper); *p.4* Pitt Rivers Museum, Oxford (upper and lower); *p.6* British Museum (upper right), Pitt Rivers Museum, Oxford (lower); *p.7* Pitt Rivers Museum, Oxford; *p.8* Pitt Rivers Museum, Oxford (upper)

SECOND SECTION
p.1 Getty Images (lower); *p.3* the author; *p.5* Pitt Rivers Museum, Oxford (upper); *p.8* Mrs Fullalove

INDEX

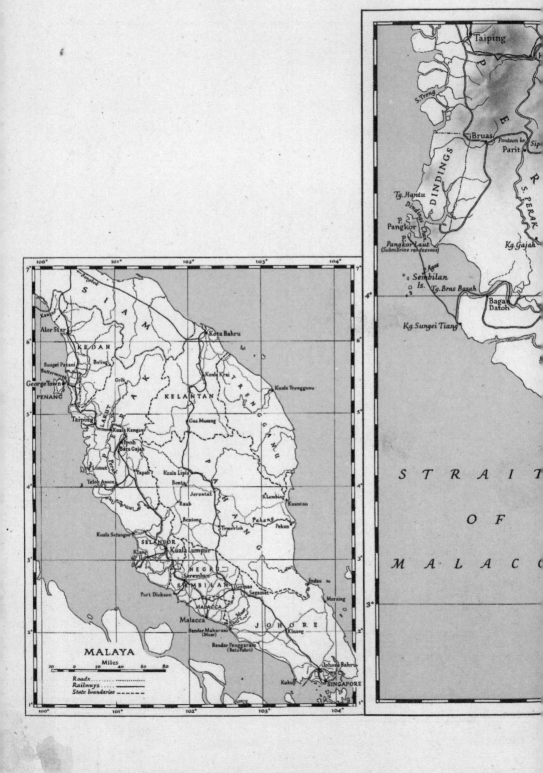

MALAYA

Miles

20   0   20   40   60   80

Roads ....
Railways ....
State boundaries ------